ALSO BY JANE M. HEALY, Ph.D.

*Failure to Connect: How Computers Affect Our Children's Minds
—and What We Can Do About It*

*Endangered Minds: Why Children Don't Think
—and What We Can Do About It*

*Your Child's Growing Mind: Brain Development and Learning
From Birth to Adolescence*

How to Have Intelligent and Creative Conversations with Your Kids

Different Learners

Identifying, Preventing, and
Treating Your Child's
Learning Problems

Jane M. Healy, Ph.D.

SIMON & SCHUSTER

NEW YORK LONDON TORONTO SYDNEY

Simon & Schuster
1230 Avenue of the Americas
New York, NY 10020

First Simon & Schuster hardcover edition April 2010

SIMON & SCHUSTER and colophon are registered trademarks of Simon & Schuster, Inc.

For information about special discounts for bulk purchases, please contact Simon & Schuster Special Sales at 1-866-506-1949 or business@simonandschuster.com.

The Simon & Schuster Speakers Bureau can bring authors to your live event. For more information or to book an event contact the Simon & Schuster Speakers Bureau at 1-866-248-3049 or visit our website at www.simonspeakers.com.

Designed by Diane Hobbing

Manufactured in the United States of America

10   9   8   7   6   5   4   3

Library of Congress Cataloging-in-Publication Data

Healy, Jane M.
   Different learners: identifying, preventing, and helping your children's learning problems / Jane Healy.
      p. cm.
   Includes bibliographical references and index.
   1. Learning disabled children—Education. 2. Attention-deficit-disordered children—Education. 3. Dyslexic children—Education. 4. Learning—Social aspects. 5. Learning—Physiological aspects. 6. Parents of children with disabilities. I. Title.
   LC4704.H43 2009
   371.9—dc22   2009027287

ISBN 978-1-4165-5641-1
ISBN 978-1-4391-7020-5 (ebook)

To Tom:

With love and gratitude.

CONTENTS

Foreword and Acknowledgments   ix

PART ONE
Brain Crisis: Problems and Possibilities 1

1. Too Many Dyssed Kids   3

2. What's the Problem? Diagnostic Dilemmas   30

3. What Should We Call This? Understanding Learning Disorders   57

PART TWO
Your Unique Child 93

4. Brain Differences and Learning Differences   95

5. Rewiring Children's Brains: How the Brain Builds Itself
    and How We Can Help   124

6. How Your Child's Brain Works: "Brain Juice," Emotion, Motivation,
    Attention, and Medicating Children's Minds   150

7. Genes, Learning, and the Environment:
    Biology Isn't Always Destiny   177

8. Who's Intelligent?: Learning Styles and One-of-a-Kind Brains   207

PART THREE
Childhood in the Twenty-first Century:
Pathway to Problems or Gateway to Success?   239

9. Stress: The Great *Dys*-abler   241

10. Brain-Cleaning 101: Banish Brain Disruptors   271

11. Brain-Cleaning 102: Tackling Lifestyle Factors   291

12. Successful Environments for Successful Children   316

Appendix A: Terms of Dysfunction: Learning Problems,
Seen and Unseen   349
Appendix B: A Few Thoughts About When to Worry   353
Appendix C: A Primer on Getting Professional Help for Your Child   355
Appendix D: Reference List   359
Notes   361
Bibliography   383
Index   391

FOREWORD AND ACKNOWLEDGMENTS

In the course of an alarmingly long career as an educational psychologist, I have never found myself eye-to-eye with a student without puzzling about two questions:

- What is going on with this particular child's brain?

- How much of this child's learning ability—or problem—came from genes and how much from lifetime experiences?

Searching for answers has impelled and energized years of gratifying study and work. The first question has turned out to be easier to address because so much effort has been poured into brain research, although many questions remain. The nature-nurture problem has also begun to yield some tentative but vitally important information. Integrating this information for practical use has been an engrossing challenge.

In this book I have tried to view scientific findings through the lens of my own experience in teaching, testing, observing, raising, and granny-ing children and teens. I have written this book to help parents, professionals, and the kids themselves. However, nothing in this book is meant to replace professional advice from a physician.

People often ask, "How long does it take you to write a book?" For this question there are two answers: "Three years"—or "A lifetime." In either case, many people have helped out. I am most grateful to my own parents, teachers, and mentors. I also thank the innumerable professionals who have offered time, advice, wisdom, and research findings as well as the families who have candidly shared their experiences.

No book would have appeared without the assistants who keep

my life together: Natalie, Valerie, and the eminently resourceful Emily. I also thank the staff at the Vail Public Library for cheerfully setting new records on interlibrary loan.

As always, I appreciate the professional expertise and sales talents of my agent, Angela Miller, as well as the unfailingly practical advice, encouragement, responsiveness, and superduper editorial skills of Bob Bender, Johanna Li, and the rest of the staff at Simon & Schuster.

Friends and family are the main means of keeping an author's psyche intact during the course of writing a book. My dear friends have not only been supportive and suitably forbearing, but many have made helpful suggestions and shared stories from their own experience. I hope that I will get to spend more time with them now.

This book contains many stories about children and their families. Although each is based on a real situation, all names and identifying details have been changed.

It is impossible to capture on this page how much the unfailing support of my family means to me. Not only have my sons and daughters-in-law fed, entertained, and counseled me, but they have candidly kept me in touch with the ever-perplexing world of modern-day parenting—an art in which, I am happy to say, they are all experts. I can confidently state that Nick, Kate, Andrew, Nat, Emma, and Sarah Jane are the world's most wonderful young people. They lift my spirits, make me laugh, regularly help me make a fool of myself, challenge me with interesting questions, and reassure me that, somehow or other, all's right with the world.

And, as always, thanks beyond measure to my wonderful husband. Tom, you're the best!

Vail, Colorado

Back in the twelfth century, a poet and philosopher named Hildegard of Bingen came up with a metaphor that remains relevant today. At birth, each child comes equipped with a golden tent of creative potential all folded up inside. It is the task of the individual, throughout life, to unfold that tent—and to the adults in each child's life to assist that process.

Nine centuries later, I seriously wonder, how well are we doing?

A great deal has been written about Hildegard of Bingen,
now regarded as a visionary who was far ahead of her time.
For her own writings, please see Hildegard of Bingen:
Scivias *(Mahwah, NJ: Paulist Press, 1990)*

PART ONE

Brain
Crisis

Problems and Possibilities

CHAPTER 1

Too Many Dyssed Kids

"I'm just wondering if there's anything I can do. . . ."

M y first educational therapy session with Edward took place before he was born. Actually, the meeting was with his mother, but Edward was very much in evidence as Susan, eight months pregnant, shifted uneasily on my office couch. We were both aware that Edward's activity level was vigorous, to say the least.

"I need some advice," Susan began. "I don't mean to be all freaked out about this, but you worked with my girls on their reading and attention problems, and this is going to be a boy, and I know that dyslexia and attention disorders run in families and problems are usually worse in boys, and I'm just wondering if there's anything I can do, now or later. . . ."

The answer to Susan's question is an emphatic "Yes!" Parents have a powerful role in shaping a child's learning abilities. Along with teachers, they create the environments that help determine how talents, skills . . . and problems develop. Positive environments at home and at school can prevent, ameliorate, and maybe even extinguish many types of learning and behavior difficulties. They can even improve the outcome for genetic learning disorders.

Nonetheless, we are experiencing an unprecedented number of "dyssed" kids—youngsters labeled with some sort of learning problem. This new "epidemic" affects children in every part of the socio-economic spectrum and includes disorders of academic, social, and personal learning skills. Learning problems upset families, discourage teachers, impair educational quality, and make children miserable. They are all too real, but many could have been prevented and most can be significantly helped.

Unfortunately, today's lifestyles are a big part of the problem. Even in affluent communities, the most basic needs of a youngster's developing brain are violated on a daily basis. How are parents, teachers, or children to succeed in a culture that does not respect its most important asset—the developing mind?

The purpose of this book is to help you understand and improve every aspect of your child's or student's learning. We will be exploring the latest research on many categories of learning difficulties to understand the nature of these problems, where they come from, and how parents and teachers can help prevent them as well as deal with them once they surface. We will focus especially on the all-important interaction of nature (in the form of genetics) and nurture (home and school environments) in determining a child's ultimate success.

Crisis in Childhood

Watching a child struggle unsuccessfully in school—with learning, with social relationships, or with skills such as motivation or paying attention—is a devastating experience for everyone involved. To make matters worse, there is often no obvious reason for the difficulty. Learning abilities are an incredibly complex interweaving of genes, environment, and brain development, with each of us possessing a very special, one-of-a-kind combination.

> Just because a learning difficulty is "in the genes" does not make it inevitable. Nor do genes alone determine its severity.

In the following chapters you will learn about new research showing the significant effects of positive environments on the complex interaction of genes and brains. You will also learn why children are being diagnosed with disorders that might have been prevented and can still be remedied if only the adults involved had the right information. If you have a child or a student who might fall into the "problem" category, please take heart. The more information you have, the better you can help! This book provides what you need to help children learn, succeed, and feel confident about themselves in the process.

Quick Take: What This Book Is About

1. Learning differences, which are the cause of many school and personal problems, are variations in the way the brain processes information. They include academic, personal (as in attention or motivation problems), and social skills.

2. These patterns are caused both by genes ("nature") and the environment ("nurture"). Both can be influenced by a child's experiences before and after birth. Just because something is genetic, or inherited, does not mean that it is either inevitable or unchangeable. Nor does it mean that when problems arise, medications are the only solution.

3. Medications may be helpful in some cases, but probably should not be the first or only approach used. Many proven therapies are available, and many of them start right in your own home or classroom.

4. Emotional development, which is one important aspect of learning, is tightly intertwined in the brain with academic and social learning. Stress is a significant and often underestimated contributor to children's learning problems, and love is a powerful remedy.

5. Every child—and every child's problem—is part of a much larger system of home, school, community, and culture. It is short-sighted simply to label and treat the child without examining how the larger system may be contributing to the problem.

6. Today's lifestyle habits can cause problems and make existing ones worse. Fortunately, many of these negative outcomes can be prevented or reversed.

7. Learning "disabilities" and special talents often come in the same package. It is important to nurture the abilities at the same time we help with the difficulties.

8. "Late bloomers" are easily misidentified as "learning disabled." Often the children with more leisurely developmental timetables turn out to be the smartest of all. Parents and schools that push too hard cause problems.

9. In our efforts to make kids "smarter," we must not forget that brain development is closely tied to the development of the body. Neglecting play and perceptual and motor skill development may endanger foundations for other types of learning.

10. The human brain is wonderfully "plastic" and can be altered by experience. The more we understand about the way it works, the better we can help each child unfold his or her own tent of potential talents.

11. There may be positive reasons for certain types of learning differences. Unique thinkers could have important future roles.

12. Never give up. The brain retains its ability to change throughout a lifetime.

Sick Culture, "Sick" Kids

Most youngsters' problems do not develop simply because the child has a genetic "flaw" or the parents somehow "messed up."

I have never met a parent who did not truly want to do a good job, but our stressed-out world does not make parenting easy. Parents feel under incredible pressure to produce a "successful" child, yet find they must constantly battle against the many factors in everyday life that interfere with development of solid brain systems for intellectual and emotional skills. Likewise, overwhelmed schools and time-pressured physicians wonder how to cope with a seeming avalanche of learning and behavioral disorders in a culture that does more to cause them than to cure them.

The childhood and teen years are critical for optimal brain development. Environments can shape brains into more efficient learning patterns, *but* remember—and this is important—they can also make an existing tendency worse or even create a problem. At all levels of the economic spectrum, children's daily lives allow and even promote habits that can severely disrupt both the developing networks in the brain and the chemistry that makes them work. Why are such record numbers of children being labeled as educationally, socially, and emotionally "sick"?

> Our culture is sick and our children are getting the diagnosis.

Each child is a complex, growing, learning system who develops as part of a much larger system including home, school, neighborhood, the supports available (or not), and the habits and expectations of the surrounding society. Consider:

- frantic, stressed-out lifestyles
- brain-hazardous types of media use
- physically toxic everyday environments—at home and at school
- unrecognized brain disruptors in daily habits, such as food choices, sleep habits, and uses of playtime
- one-size-fits-all expectations for how children should act and what they should achieve
- some professionals who are overly eager to pin a label—and maybe even a medication—on normal developmental differences
- a medicalization of problems that should be treated educationally

> We live in a culture that is both clueless and careless about what kids' brains really need. No wonder there is trouble in the schoolroom!

Learning Disabilities or Disabled Expectations?

Not long ago I presented an evening workshop about young children's brain development to a group of parents in a section of an East Coast city noted for its competitive school admissions culture. During the question and answer period, a concerned-looking mom was the first to speak.

"A group of us here have four-year-old sons whose teacher has told us she thinks our boys may have problems with auditory discrimination [difficulty listening effectively to the sounds in words]. She wants us to have them evaluated for a learning disability. Do you agree? And, we are wondering"—she looked around, clearly embarrassed—"do you think it could be something we've done wrong?"

Of course, without meeting her son, talking to the teacher, getting a family history, or finding out if the school's expectations were unrealistic for four-year-old boys (it happens), I wasn't able to come up with a very helpful response. But this incident got me thinking. I was troubled by the guilt trip laid on this concerned mother. I was even more troubled that no one had taken the time to help her understand the many factors that might be contributing to her son's problem or how he could be helped.

> *"It seems odd that parents have been driven to seek a diagnosis that something is wrong with their children. In the past, such a diagnosis was probably the last thing most parents would have wanted. . . ."*
>
> —Robert Sternberg in *Our Labeled Children*[1]

For example, do these little boys—at a critical period for development of language circuits in the brain—have caregivers who do not speak clearly or who do not speak much at all? How much time do they spend watching screens as opposed to listening carefully to stories? Do adults have the time and patience to carry on conversations with them to build language and comprehension skills? Are they under brain-damaging stress because they don't have enough free time or unprogrammed play? What, if anything, do they eat for breakfast? Is the school expecting rambunctious little kids to sit quietly at desks and complete worksheets for which their brains aren't ready? These are the questions that should first be addressed. As critical as it is to heed early signs of a language problem, we must also admit that the "problem" may lie as much in the child's environment as it does in the child himself.

Nicole Kroupa, a preschool teacher and graduate student at Gonzaga University, recently sent me an unsolicited e-mail emphasizing this point. "I have seen such a change over the years in the speech/language development of kids that it is VERY disturbing. And I am NOT talking about special ed kids either. Children from educated/straight-A adults whose four- to six-year-old children have retarded language skills. ["Me do." "Me no want." No past tense verbs, etc.] Really bright children. It's scary."

What's Broken—the Child or the System?

I am thrilled that things have changed dramatically since I first started teaching, when there were very few services and little understanding for students who couldn't keep up or were somehow different. These unfortunate kids were ignored, blamed, sometimes emotionally destroyed, or turned into antisocial horrors by an ignorant and uncaring educational system. Yet progress sometimes goes too far. Now we need to be concerned about categorizing too many youngsters who fall outside rigid expectations as "disordered" and in need of "fixing" rather than as "different" and in need of patient, effective teaching within an understanding and flexible system.

> My challenge here is to help you walk the critical line between celebrating each child's uniqueness and taking positive steps to avoid the enduring pain that can accompany too much "difference."

Many children who are tortured by learning differences are bright and talented, with the potential to reach high goals if they receive the proper support. A recent study by Julie Logan of London's Cass Business School found that almost half of a group of successful entrepreneurs in the United States met the criteria for dyslexia, a learning difference that affects reading and written language.[2] Adults with Asperger's disorder communicate online about their unique talents, which they attribute to not being "neurotypical." Many creative, high-energy adults are also sure they would have been diagnosed with attention deficit disorder had the current diagnostic criteria been applied. It seems that what looks like a flaw in school sometimes looks like a talent later on!

Yet if such youngsters are part of a system lacking the understanding, patience, or expertise to deal with individual differences, they may find themselves in the growing pile labeled "broken." Tragically, they may never realize their inborn potential.

Grown Up and Turned Off. On a recent vacation with a tour group, I happened to be seated one evening at dinner across from a couple who, when they discovered my profession, began to tell me about their twenty-four-year-old son.

"Well, he's still sort of finding himself," Mom acknowledged in anxious tones. "He just dropped out of community college again—he never did like school very much, and he's not motivated."

> ". . . his teachers have always said he's smart enough and just needs to apply himself."

Every time I hear this story, which comes up with amazing frequency, I immediately suspect an undiagnosed learning problem.

"Did he ever have an evaluation?" I inquired.

"Oh, yes, but they said he didn't have a learning disability. His teachers always called him an 'underachiever.' "

As these parents described their son's history, it became apparent that this boy had clear symptoms of a specific language disability that had never been identified or treated. He was smart enough to bluff his way through for a while, but his reading and writing were painfully slow and laborious, he couldn't concentrate on teacher's lectures, and he eventually just turned off and gave up. As our dinner ended, tears welled in Mom's eyes.

"Is it too late," she asked. "Can he still be helped?"

Fortunately, it's never too late, so we may hope that this story ends happily. But stories like this make me want to scream—or write a book that may help other children who end up feeling "broken" and don't know why.

No Easy Answers. Parents often feel they are helpless, at the mercy of a societal system that passes judgment, accurate or not, on their child. What they don't realize is how fuzzy our definitions really are and how much power they themselves have to get a child on track. Often a parent's work involves making changes in the child's environment or daily activities to eliminate contributing factors, as well as working with the school to make sure expectations are realistic and supported by the right kind of teaching. This book is meant to serve as a guide for developing a systematic, effective, and multipronged plan.

In today's technological world, we are conditioned to want quick results. If a problem shows up, we want it fixed. But children are not machines. They are complex and precious individuals who learn and flourish, or fail to, as part of a much wider system of home, school, community, and popular culture. Children with learning problems need help, but the system also needs a remedy.

The Reality of Learning Differences

Learning differences, whatever their cause, are not a figment of anyone's imagination. Many youngsters come into the world with inborn propensities that set them up for problems. Often these problems are related to innate brain patterns that help determine whether various types of learning will be easy or difficult. Some children seem preprogrammed to be poor spellers, readers, or writers, math challenged, personally disorganized, clumsy at athletics, inattentive, or socially clueless.

> The more inflexible the system, the more kids will find themselves with a label.

The term *learning disabilities* usually refers to specific problems with school subjects such as reading, writing, spelling, or math. These problems have nothing to do with overall intellectual capability. Many learning disabled individuals are very smart or even gifted. If your brain easily accommodates tasks such as keeping your attention focused on an oral lecture, writing a neat page, reading a text, spelling nonphonetic words like "said," or instinctively understanding what another person's facial expression or gesture means, it may seem peculiar to you that such routine skills can be so difficult for some people, especially if they seem bright.

> A brain with a specific learning disability may need to exert many times as much mental effort as that of a typical student to do a seemingly "simple" task.

In this book I will be using the general term *learning problems* to include both specific learning disability and a range of other "learning disorders," such as attention deficit disorders, sensory processing problems, and disabilities in social learning such as autism or Asperger's syndrome. Here are some of the reasons I prefer this term:

- Learning disorders rarely occur as tidy diagnostic packages. They tend to overlap and are often *comorbid* (a nasty-sounding term meaning "occurring together") with behavioral or emotional issues. For example, reading problems are often comorbid with attention disorders.

- As we learn more about the brain, we recognize that it is impossible to separate its *cognitive* (thinking) and *affective* (emotional) capacities.

- A problem at one level often creates other problems elsewhere.

- One of the primary purposes of this book is to urge that we view each child as a whole person, rather than as a diagnosis. Your child's math disability (*dyscalculia*), for example, may have several contributing factors, such as a fundamental problem in visual-spatial reasoning, a poor "gut-level" understanding of quantity (Is 9 bigger than 7?), a language disorder (what, exactly, does *equals* mean?), the quality of the teaching she has received, her willingness to take intellectual risks, or her physical and emotional health. Perhaps she has lacked adequate experience with quantities of real things, such as children get from playing with unit blocks or moving a counter on a board game. Each factor should be considered when we plan a treatment program for her.

TIP: Your child's math disability may be helped (or even prevented) by playing board or card games with her.

Learning Problems: A Broader View

Academic skills are really only the tip of the learning iceberg, since successful students must master many other learning tasks during the childhood and teen years. As they do so, they exercise and improve important brain connections. Particularly critical are the brain systems associated with

- self -control
- directing and controlling one's own attention
- getting oneself motivated, even when things look hard
- interacting effectively with others and in groups
- managing emotions
- harnessing the creative forces of one's brain

All these qualities profoundly affect school progress and later success in life. New research tells us that genes are often involved in how easily children master these personal skills, so it is very good news that they, like cognitive skills, can be significantly improved by parents and teachers who employ the right strategies.

Currently, however, our children's lives contain many influences that can derail these skills—especially in a brain that is genetically more vulnerable. Moreover, it often appears easier to treat this type of learning problem as a medical condition, especially if a pill is available that seems to do the job.

Does He Have to Take Pills?

Before I presented a recent workshop for California teachers, one of the conference organizers urgently drew me aside.

"Are you going to talk about ADHD?" (attention deficit hyperactivity disorder) she asked. "My fifteen-year-old son was just diagnosed and the doctor and the school are pressuring us to put him on medication, and we're just so confused. We don't want to medicate him, but they told us it's a brain problem, that it's genetic, and all we can do is give him the pills."

"Did they ask anything about his activities, his sleep habits, his diet, his school environment, his media use [all of which have been linked to attention problems] or recommend any other changes?" I inquired.

"No, the doctor was pretty rushed."

At lunchtime, after I had showed slides illustrating how both the biochemistry and the physical connections of the brain can be changed by appropriate intervention (which doesn't always start with drugs, by the way), my anxious questioner approached me again.

"Thank you for giving me the ammunition I needed! Now I understand at least where I can begin."

In my experience, most parents do not like the idea of putting their child on medication. I hope later chapters will also give you the information you need to make wise decisions about everything that goes into your child's brain.

A Lot of *Dys*sed Children

In Appendix A you will find a list of accepted terms (and, trust me, there are dozens of others) used to describe conditions that affect children's academic, social, and behavioral learning. Many of them begin with the prefix *dys* (or *dis*), meaning things aren't working exactly as they're supposed to. The prefix *a* means inability, such as in the medical condition *alexia* (inability to read) or *apraxia* (inability to carry out purposeful movements). A *syndrome* is a collection of symptoms that are often found together. For example, *autism*, or *autistic spectrum disorder* (ASD), is a syndrome characterized by difficulties in social communication usually accompanied by certain specific symptoms. Many syndromes, like autism, are *spectrum* disorders, meaning that different individuals have different degrees of severity.

So-called emotional or mood disorders, (e.g., bipolar illness and childhood depression) are outside the scope of this book. Nonetheless, they often co-occur with specific learning disorders, and it can be hard to sort out what is responsible for what. Their alarming recent growth is one more clear indication that something is drastically wrong in the world of childhood today.

Improved diagnosis accounts for some of the rising numbers of children's problems. Yet experts agree that other factors—some as yet unidentified—are involved. Adding up current estimates of learning, behavioral, and emotional disorders suggests that a child born in the United States now has up to a 30 percent chance of being diagnosed with some type of problem that affects learning.[3]

Difference or Disability?

Most learning problems are *variations in normal development* and are better viewed in terms of *difference rather than outright disability*. Whatever it is may not be working "right" as is currently expected, but let's think seriously about who is defining "right." Consider a five-year-old boy who cannot sit patiently at a desk, coordinate his fingers around a pencil, or use advanced visual tracking skills to copy sentences neatly and accurately. Both common sense and brain research support the fact that he is having a problem because these expectations are out of line with his level of development. Moreover, his individual style of learning may require a more effective style of teaching. In later sections you will find other examples of youngsters deemed "disordered" who in another time and place might have seemed just fine.

Academic Failure: Who's Disabled and Who Will Pay?

> *"If things keep going the way they are, we'll have more kids in special ed than in regular ed."*
>
> —Midwest school superintendent

Special Education was designed for students with problems that can't be addressed in the regular classroom without special help. Yet "special" education threatens to become the tail wagging the educational dog. Unfortunately, it is also a morass of confusion. With more than seven million students and a spiraling budget in the United States, Special Education receives federal funding, but every state (and often school district) operates under its own set of rules that dictate who gets services according to how much money is available. Exactly what constitutes "learning disability" or "special needs" and the type of help available varies enormously from state to state. Other disorders that affect learning (such as autism, Asperger's, and sometimes attention problems) usually receive funding from different sources. Are you confused? So are the parents who brave this labyrinth. Enough educators are also confused that they are redesigning the current system, so stay tuned for plenty of changes.

It has been estimated that 80 to 90 percent of those in Special Ed are there primarily because of reading failure, but most of these students also have other areas of academic weakness, such as writing, spelling, or math.[4] Many also have emotional and/or behavioral problems. According to Robert Pasternack, formerly of the U.S. Department of Education, these numbers are a vast underestimate since *only about one-fifth of students needing specialized services to help them learn are receiving them.* Yet the kids who truly need help and don't get it are at severe risk, especially if they come from a home unable to provide needed support. Some estimates suggest that up to 85 percent of current inmates in U.S. prisons have some sort of a diagnosable learning disorder and 75 percent of school dropouts report difficulty learning to read.[5]

Learning problems are found at all levels of the socioeconomic spectrum, but they come disproportionately from neighborhoods without the financial clout to fund adequate services for families and kids. It's not surprising that many kids never make it through the daunting (and often expensive) obstacle course of getting an evaluation and a diagnosis. School psychologists can't keep up with their referrals, even while teachers are crying out for help with too many troubled students. These kids can continue to struggle miserably without anyone taking any action to alleviate the problem. Needless to say, they are at high risk for dropping out.

> Learning problems are fundamentally about a mismatch be-
> tween the child and the learning environment.

Disordered Children: A Red Flag for Trouble

One clear index of trouble is a disturbing cascade of emotional and conduct disorders even in our youngest children and even in financially secure families. In 2006 a report from the Yale Child Study Center found that unprecedented numbers of children were being expelled from preschool for serious behavior problems.[6] Dr. Judy Ripke, director of early childhood education at Concordia University in Nebraska, commented on the reality of this new trend.[7] "We are seeing so many preschool children who are out of control," she told me. "They're aggressive to the teacher and to other children—hitting, throwing things, and they can't choose an activity and follow through with it. What is going on? We're actually having to expel more and more!"

Further evidence of serious disorder—and an area in which the United States is unique—involves increasing numbers of youngsters at all ages who take powerful psychotropic (mind/brain-affecting) drugs for learning, behavior, and emotional disorders. U.S. children place far at the top of international charts. About 2.5 million children in the United States take stimulant drugs (e.g., Ritalin, Adderall) or attention and hyperactivity problems.[8] Such statistics are not surprising, according to Leonard Sax, in his pointed book *Boys Adrift*, since "For white boys in affluent suburbs, the odds of being diagnosed with ADHD at some point in childhood may be as high as one in three,"[9] and drug treatment is a common sequel to diagnosis.

Many physicians are also skeptical about overlabeling and overtreating children and teens. Growing numbers (up to two million) take at least two psychiatric drugs in combination.[10] Highly controversial diagnoses such as "bipolar disorder" are increasingly accompanied by prescriptions for drug cocktails of multiple prescriptions, some of which have been insufficiently tested for safety with children. Peg L. Smith, CEO of the American Camp Association, whose members serve three million campers, says about a quarter of the children at its camps line up for pills each day for attention deficit disorder, psychiatric problems, or mood disorders (e.g., depression or bipolar disorder).[11] "This is the American standard, now," states one camp owner. "It's not limited by education level, race, socioeconomics, geography, gender, or any of those filters."

The use of potent new antipsychotic drugs that were designed for seriously sick adults "amounts to a huge experiment with the lives of American kids," maintains psychiatrist John March of Duke University. When children are taking three or four different drugs, "How do you even know who the kid is anymore?" asks pharmacologist Julie Zito at the University of Maryland.[12]

> Could this trend toward multiple medications for children
> be evidence more of problems in the systems surrounding
> the child than of problems within the child's brain itself?

While such psychiatric diagnoses as mood and conduct disorders are outside the focus of this book, they (as well as the medications involved) clearly affect children's learning abilities. Or perhaps it is the other way around. "If the learning problems were addressed, we wouldn't have so many behavioral and emotional problems," I was informed by Glenda Thorne, a psychologist who treats developmental and learning problems. "I expected to be a psychologist, not to deal with learning disabilities, but I found this was impossible—learning problems and emotional problems are a two-way street."[13]

Autism: A New "Epidemic"?

Autism is a serious disorder, once thought of as rare. The *autistic spectrum*, which includes *Asperger's syndrome*, often has genetic origins and affects language and social and personal learning skills. Current data now put the chance of an autistic spectrum disorder at a staggering rate of 1 child out of 150 and rising.[14] This increase is partially, but far from fully, explained by improved awareness and diagnosis. Many experts believe that environmental influences are implicated in an unprecedented recent rise in cases.

"This has been an almost 2,000 percent increase in autistic spectrum disorders since 1987! There are clearly some sort of environmental triggers operating here," Dr. Ricki Robinson told me.[15] As a noted autism specialist in California, she is overwhelmed by the number of new cases that come to her attention, although she points out that the earlier the diagnosis, the better the child can be helped.

Martha Herbert, a pediatric neurologist at Massachusetts General and McLean Hospitals and an expert on brain structure abnormalities in developmental disorders, has specialized in looking for causes of autism. She describes alarming recent changes in the type and severity of problems she and her colleagues are seeing. Herbert is not shy about delivering a searing indictment of the role played by our culture: "Overall, more children are presenting with diffuse difficulties—not discrete learning disabilities where everything else is more or less intact, but difficulties spread over multiple cognitive, sensorimotor, social, and emotional domains. And the scale of this is enormous. . . . I think we are dealing with the impact of the disintegration of family and community bonds and a profound environmental insult on our very neurological wiring."[16]

No matter what statistics you use, the fact is that far too many children are in educational and personal trouble. As the saying goes, however, "Statistics are really people with the tears wiped away." Many teachers would like to weep, as well, as they find themselves unable to meet the complex needs and demands of this generation of students and are forced to spend far too much time on problems they feel ill qualified to address.

The Power of Environments

One thing that brain research tells us—loud and clear—is that the way we raise and teach our children not only helps shape their brains, but can also influence or even alter the way genes play out their roles. This promising news also means, however, that we have a serious obligation to attend to factors over which we have some control—namely, most things that happen to children at home and at school throughout their growing-up years.

The prestigious *Journal of the American Medical Association* recently published a series of articles pinpointing recent changes in children's daily environments that are causing, according to the authors, these "new epidemics" of problems—both physical and mental from all walks of life. The *JAMA* authors acknowledge the importance of genes, but they insist:

"Nonetheless, gene pool changes cannot explain the recent dramatic growth of these conditions. Changes in families and communities over the past few decades have greatly affected the social environment and life experiences of children and adolescents; for example, parents with less time and energy available to nurture children, many parents working away from the home, increased stress on parents, decreased social and family support for parenting, increased television watching and other media use, decreased physical activity opportunities, increased indoor time, increased consumption of fast foods, and unsafe neighborhoods."[17]

Barry Brazelton and Stanley Greenspan are two eminent physicians who have spoken out about the extreme pressures on today's parents and children. In their book *The Irreducible Needs of Children,* they point out that overstressed parents, too, need help. Instead, the trend is to diagnose even preschoolers with brain disorders and apply "alarming" numbers of drugs—sometimes up to three or four—which may or may not even be approved for use with children, all without offering the family any counseling or support to learn better coping strategies. Such unhealthy mental and emotional environments for families, they insist, are a recipe for societal disaster.

What Counts

In 2007, when UNICEF conducted a study of children's well-being in twenty-one industrialized nations, the United States and the United Kingdom came out near the bottom. The Netherlands, Sweden, Denmark, Finland, and Spain were at the top. In all these relatively rich countries, a child's position on the economic scale wasn't nearly as important as factors such as physical health, feeling safe, adequate free playtime, and nurturing relationships.

> When children all over the world were asked about the most important ingredient for their well-being, they overwhelmingly named their families.

Parents and educators are in a double bind. Advertisers and popular opinion exhort them to produce brainy children who are "ahead of the curve" for success in a competitive, product-oriented world. Yet child-rearing and teaching have become uphill battles in a culture that is physically, intellectually, and emotionally damaging to growing brains.

> Many extremely able children naturally learn "outside the curve." They are at the greatest risk.

This book will offer both the understanding and the tools to help you structure a brain-positive environment for your children or students. Even with the most supportive environments, however, we need to acknowledge the reality of some types of learning problems. Let me close this chapter by telling you about a few of my students with real problems that were either helped or worsened by their environments.

The Reality of Learning Differences

Some children just seem to come with some sort of glitch in the learning system. Take Mollie, for example. I learned a lot from her, both about the power of love and determination and about the reality of what we call a learning disability.

A Glitch in Learning. I first encountered this earnest little girl early in the 1970s when she was in the third grade at a school where I had just taken a job as a reading specialist. In those days the term *learning disabilities* had only just been invented, and kids who didn't learn in the standard ways were mostly viewed as lacking in intelligence. Although I am now horrified to think of how little I—the "specialist"—knew at that point, even with my shiny new graduate degree, my job was to "fix" the kids who didn't fit in. I was assigned to work in a former storeroom, which could best be described as cozy. (Like many specialists who have worked in hallways and unused corners of gymnasiums as well as a beautifully equipped "learning lab," I was happy to have any space of my own.)

Mollie appeared at the classroom door my first day on the job, part of a group of third-graders referred by their teacher for special help. With long skinny limbs askew, a confusion of blond curls asserting their individuality, shoelaces flapping (Velcro hadn't yet been invented), and shirt untucked, she always struck me as a child who had been hastily assembled by nature. When I assigned a simple written exercise, Mollie attacked it earnestly, her fingers white-knuckled as they clutched her pencil and her tongue gyrating as she struggled to form the letter shapes. (I learned only later that this "overflow movement" of the tongue or other body parts, normal in a four-year-old, is a sign of neurological immaturity at age eight.) Even with all this effort, Mollie's output could, frankly, only be called a mess. Her letter formation and spelling would have embarrassed a first-grader, and they took up so much mental energy that her sentence structure completely fell apart. When I asked her to read out loud, the results were equally disastrous. As I got to know her better, I realized that Mollie had difficulty not only with reading and writing, but also with expressing her ideas clearly in grammatically appropriate sentences. She had experienced good, standard teaching, but it just hadn't worked for her.

Here is an original summary of the story "Beauty and the Beast" that Mollie wrote when she was in third grade.

In case you are not a learning specialist accustomed to deciphering such text, it says:

"Buty(Beauty) was sherd(scared) at fast(first) and stad(stayed) in the plais(palace) for the and the fell in love and mered(married) the best(beast)."

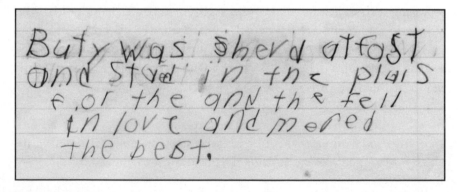

1. Mollie's story of "Beauty and the Beast" (3rd grade): "Beauty was scared at first and stayed in the palace for the and the fell in love and married the beast."

Mollie came from a family riddled with subtle language problems that showed up especially in reading, writing, and spelling. We know now that her difficulties fit a pattern of "dyslexia," which research has shown to have a genetic base. As you will see in later chapters, dyslexics' brains tend to be structured and to work somewhat differently from those of nondyslexics. Yet this family had not only attained a considerable degree of material success through work in creative fields but they were delightful people, with a wonderfully loving and supportive family life. I give them credit for the fact that, for all the years I have known Mollie, she never failed to be cheerful, hardworking, and exceptionally thoughtful. They showed me it is possible to hold high standards for effort while simultaneously providing that unconditional emotional support so badly needed by any child.

Many talented teachers and specialists contributed to the rest of Mollie's story. She gradually began to capitalize on her many attributes while working on her weaknesses. The day Mollie strode confidently to the platform at college graduation to deliver a motivational speech—which she had written herself—I wasn't the only teacher in the audience with very moist eyes.

One reason for Mollie's triumph is that the type of teaching she received changed her brain—quite literally—to enable it to accommodate verbal tasks more easily. Fortunately, those changes did not remove this child's charming and insightful character and her quirky originality.

You may be intrigued, as I was, to hear what a fellow teacher observed when Mollie was in the sixth grade. "You may not believe this," he told me, "but that child has been beating all of the middle-school faculty in chess!" Moral: Don't judge a child only by her symptoms, and don't assume that child with a "disability" is necessarily a disabled child!

"Weird but Wonderful." Marko also taught me a great deal when I encountered him while still in graduate school. The principal of his small middle school phoned me one day.

> "Do you know anything about a learning disorder that sounds like 'asparagus'?" he asked. "One of our students

has just gotten this diagnosis from a hospital clinic and we
don't have any idea what it is or how to treat it."

At that time I was conducting research for my doctoral disserta-
tion on hyperlexia (an unusual sort of reading problem that I will
discuss in a later chapter), which often accompanies Asperger's syndrome or autism, and I was indeed aware of this diagnosis. Asperger's syndrome is now in the news as a high-end variant of autism,
but at the time not many people—even professionals—had heard
the term.

When I met Marko in an unoccupied classroom at his school soon
afterward, I understood the reason for the diagnosis. This handsome
seventh grader had difficulty looking me in the face, much less the
eyes, when I attempted to shake his hand. Instead of responding to
my efforts to strike up a conversation, he launched into a lecture,
delivered in a near monotone, about the intricacies of the layout and
technical workings of the school's heating system, which he finally
concluded by jabbing his finger toward the floor at my feet,

"And your chair is sitting on one of the pipes, *right there!*" This
last phrase was delivered at such an inappropriately loud volume
that several students passing in the hall peered in the door. Seeing
it was Marko, they exchanged knowing looks and went on.

Like Mollie, Marko was lucky to have a very supportive family.
Among other things, his mother's brother had many of the same
characteristics and really related to Marko's unique personality.
Marko's mother once described them both as "weird but wonderful." His middle school, too, was an unusually small and nurturing
one, which prided itself on human as well as academic values. And
Marko had a champion: a classmate who was not only popular as a
leader but also quite formidable physically. All the kids knew that
it wasn't in anyone's best interest to be mean to Marko. These factors reduced the biggest difficulty that youngsters like Marko usually face—social ostracism, teasing, and a sickening sense of social
isolation that they really don't understand.

Although Asperger-type youngsters are often very bright, they
have difficulty reading the normal social cues—gesture, facial expression, the appropriate use of social language—that the rest of us
recognize and use instinctively. These youngsters can be challenging for others. Nonetheless, like Marko, they often possess excep-

tional talents, along with needs like any other child. I am glad to report that Marko completed high school and at my last contact, his story was playing out happily with a promising job in a plumbing company that installs and services heating systems. This success is due in no small part to the fact that other people have accepted and worked with Marko's abilities and his disabilities, and that special programs and wise choices have helped him along the way.

Until we return to the topics of Asperger's syndrome and autism in Chapter 3, I thought you might begin to understand Marko's world better by looking at a picture he drew when he was in eighth grade. The fact that the people are portrayed without facial features is neither an accident nor Marko's attempt at a new sort of surrealism. It is simply the way he perceives the world. Research has shown that the brain activity of individuals on the autistic spectrum differs from other people's when they look at human faces. Their brains react to faces as if they were looking at inanimate objects. What a puzzling world that must be!

2. Marko's Picture: Marko, who was diagnosed with Asperger's syndrome, drew this picture when he was in the 8th grade. Note that his people lack facial features, which is probably the way Marko sees the world.

Clearly, learning problems are not only—or even primarily—caused by neglectful homes or bad schools. Genes are powerful determinants of who we are and how our individual patterns of learning are set up. But genes definitely aren't everything.

An Environment That Spells TROUBLE. A few years ago I met a little boy who worried me a lot. His mother had called for advice in dealing with the school and the problems her child was having there. We had agreed to meet in a nearby restaurant during her brief lunch hour, but when I arrived, to my surprise, I encountered not only Mom but also Joshua, aged five.

> Joshua had just been sent home from kindergarten—for the third time that month—in the middle of the school day.

While Mom and I tried to talk, Joshua roared around the restaurant, unrestrained, testing every rule that anyone—including our frazzled waitress—attempted to impose on him.

At the school's recommendation, Joshua had recently received an evaluation from a pediatrician who, after a twenty-minute meeting, had diagnosed attention deficit/hyperactivity disorder (ADHD) and prescribed a psychotropic medication (Adderall). When the pills did not seem to have the desired effect, the doctor suggested by phone that the dose be doubled. (If this mother's account is accurate, it is a particularly bad example of superficial diagnosis and prescribing by a physician. Such treatment would be deplored by most pediatricians, although with doctors' hurried schedules, it seems to be more common than it should be.)

"I gave him a double dose, and he chattered nonstop until midnight—he wasn't even making sense," Mom reported. "I just couldn't get him settled down, so we went back to a regular dose. But it doesn't seem to be doing much good. Today he tried to choke a little girl in his class, and that's why they called me to get him—again!"

Joshua had been in trouble of one sort or another since he had been in day care, and as I learned more about this case, I became increasingly annoyed about the questions that had not been asked along the way. The school had arranged for a limited amount of diagnostic testing, which suggested that Joshua might have some treatable problems with his language development (which can sometimes show up as attention and behavior problems), but not much had been done about it. Josh had a lot of trouble with expressive language, and was inclined to strike out physically instead of expressing his ideas or feelings in words. What's more, this child's life to date had been disorganized, to say the least. His developmental history contained innumerable red flags: emotional and physical upheavals; erratic and inappropriate early child care arrangements that probably contributed to language delay; multiple ear infections with temporary hearing loss; a steady diet of TV and, now, semiviolent video games, which he played when he visited his father on the weekends. In addition, his fractured home environment was compounded by inconsistent expectations and inappropriate exposure to adult problems of all sorts.

> "I think most of my family has ADHD," Josh's mom told me with a shrug, "so there's not much we can do about it—right?"

Josh certainly had difficulty paying attention, but there were plenty of other possible contributors to his outrageous behavior than an organic attention deficit alone. Until some of these other issues were addressed, I seriously questioned any hasty decision to put him on a powerful, brain-altering medication without a thorough evaluation and ongoing supervision. Medications may help, but they may also mask critical and treatable issues—either organic or environmental—that should be attended to sooner rather than later.

Joshua is a very lovable little boy despite his exasperating behavior, so it was possible to get lots of adults to help. We were able to work with his school district to get him a more thorough evaluation and some specialized teaching in a small, therapeutic classroom. Mom has agreed to meet regularly with a counselor to try to put her own life and Josh's home environment on a more positive track. In addition, Josh's grandmother has stepped in to invite Josh for frequent visits and to spend the summers with her. When he returns from her home, he seems calm and happy.

So Many Stories...There are so many stories—and behind each one is a real, live, feeling kid. I think, for example, of sad-faced little

Juana, whose "reading disability" was probably caused, frankly, by poor early teaching in a shockingly overcrowded and ill-equipped classroom. And Harrison, a very smart little boy, the youngest in his class, whose parents had insisted that he be accelerated in kindergarten. They relentlessly pressured both school and child, despite the fact that his perceptual-motor and social development were lagging far behind his intellect. Harrison ended up with a "learning disability" that he might not have suffered from had he only been in the right class at the right time. And Zack, who came from a home where reading was not a regular activity, and where his overstressed caregivers didn't have the time to talk to him. Unfortunately, when Zack got to kindergarten, he was expected to start dealing with the alphabet and words he didn't understand. It didn't take long before his lack of background experience translated from bafflement to frustration to serious discipline problems, to a label of "learning disability, attention deficit/hyperactivity with a tendency toward conduct disorder." Zack came into the world with a potentially keen mind, but he now has a high probability of dropping out and even tangling with the law.

The Ecology of Failure—and the Strategies for Success

Unsuccessful learners are costly for many reasons, but the most important is the human price paid in lost potential, family stress, societal disruptions, and personal anguish, which can last a lifetime. I hope the following chapters will set a positive course through the maze of genetic, neurological, and environmental factors that we must understand to address this growing "sickness" among our young.

It bears repeating, also, that the very notion of "disability" implies a value judgment. While academic skills are vitally important, there are other things in life that count, too. I often reflect on the many children I have treated who struggled academically but were simply fantastic human beings—kind, thoughtful, insightful, original, morally responsible. I have been in this business long enough to see many of my students grow up to become terrific adults. The fact that some of these kids turned out much better and are happier people than some of those who were much faster out of the scholastic gate strikes me as worth contemplating. After all, in terms of a human life and what you want for your children, what is "success," anyhow?

Seeking Answers

Education consultant and reformer Andy Hargreaves tells a story about a gentleman who is taking a stroll by a riverbank when he comes upon a man who is frantically jumping in and out of the water to pull out drowning people. No sooner does he rescue one than another struggling person floats by, and then another, and another.

"What's the cause of all these people drowning?" the observer asks.

"I don't know," gasps the rescuer. "I'm too busy jumping in and out to go upstream and find out who's pushing them in."

In the following chapters we will go upstream to seek both causes and remedies for our children's learning problems. We will consider different categories of learning disorders or differences and review research on effective treatments. In Part Two, "Your Unique Child," we will turn to the fascinating story of how and why children learn, how genetics interact with brain development, why "difference" does not always mean "disability," and how environments quite literally reshape brains and learning skills. Part Three, "Childhood in the Twenty-first Century," will identify specific factors that are harming children's development today and recommend steps for creating successful learning environments at home and school.

CHAPTER 2

What's the Problem?

Diagnostic Dilemmas

"Please tell me, what caused this?
Does it have a name? Did I do something wrong?
Is it in his genes? And what do we do now?"

All brains—and all children—are unique, but some are just a little more unique than others. These are the youngsters who develop and learn on a nonstandard schedule or in nonstandard ways. They are the ones most likely to receive a diagnosis, and they are the ones who keep teachers and parents awake and worrying in the middle of the night. Parents are often the first to suspect a problem, although it is not uncommon for an astute teacher to spot a specific learning difficulty.

In this chapter we will introduce a few basics of diagnosis, important signs and symptoms of trouble, and how to start pinning down a problem and finding help. Then in Chapter 3, "What Should We Call This?," we will go into a little more detail about the most common categories of disorders affecting children's learning. Here are points to know:

Quick Take: Confronting Learning Problems

1. Most organic learning disorders show up early in life.

2. Certain warning signs should prompt further evaluation.

3. A misfit between child and school can cause problems or exacerbate existing ones.

4. Diagnosis is useful only if it leads to effective treatment.

5. Overlabeling wastes time, money, and children's potential.

6. "Differential diagnosis" is a useful starting point.

For the purposes of this book, we are considering a "learning problem" to be any innate or acquired characteristic that consistently interferes with one or more aspects of learning. In its purest form, a learning disorder involves some variation in the wiring of the brain—often, but not always, inherited—that makes it harder than "normal" for an individual to master one or more of the following:

- *traditional academic learning* such as language, reading, spelling, writing, math (these are termed *learning disabilities*)

- *social skills*, such as understanding and relating to others

- *language development*

- *perceptual-motor and sensory skills*, such as balance, athletic ability, eye-tracking, using markers and pencils, copying geometric figures, keyboarding, coping with sudden sensory changes such as unexpected touch or flickering visual stimuli

- *executive or personal skills*, such as paying attention appropriately, managing one's behavior, organization, planning ahead, motivation

Whether or not a developmental problem becomes a serious disability depends on

- its severity

- our expectations for the child at any given age

- how important teachers, parents, and society think this skill is
- how much help we can enlist

Most true learning disorders are *neurodevelopmental* in origin, meaning that they involve the brain and nervous system and that they "came with the package"—i.e., that whatever is causing the problem is an intrinsic part of the child's nature and has been present, although perhaps hidden, from birth. A smaller number of children have "acquired" difficulties caused by accidents, illnesses, or other types of brain "insults" that occurred after birth.

I say *true* learning disorder because, in the troubled world of childhood today, it is becoming increasingly difficult to decide which so-called learning disorders stem from supposed flaws inside the child and which ones are due more to flaws in the culture. When children live in environments that ignore the needs of the developing brain, learning casualties are a natural result.

We are fortunate to have access to a great deal of information about learning and its problems. Remember, however, that we are a long way from knowing everything. Sometimes a parent's instinct trumps even the best available science.

Each child presents a unique situation and a very special package of abilities that is not easily stuffed into one diagnostic category. Pasting labels on children as if they were cans of soup on an assembly line risks both overdiagnosis and superficial treatment that misses core aspects of the problem. Instead, let's broaden our view to consider all the factors—neurological, genetic, and environmental—that characterize each child.

Recognizing Problem Signs

Acknowledging that one's child may have a learning problem is very upsetting for any parent. When you suspect trouble that has *lasted for at least six months*, try to stand back, take a deep breath, and follow some logical steps toward an effective solution. Here are four sensible steps for starters:

1. Read this chapter and the next to inform yourself about the basic facts and symptoms of learning problems. Appendix B:

A Few Thoughts About When to Worry suggests specific questions to ask and steps to take if you have concerns.

2. Analyze and identify all possible sources of trouble for your child or student, including factors in home or school environments described in Part Three.

3. Be as objective as possible in observing your child with agemates. Children are, by definition, immature and sometimes adults expect too much too soon. Familiarize yourself with the general principles of child development as laid out in my book *Your Child's Growing Mind*. Get an objective point of view from your child's pediatrician and teacher or day care provider. Ask for a specific description if any aspects of your child's development are notably delayed.

4. Observe and analyze where specific breakdowns in learning are occurring. Your careful observations will add a valuable perspective when talking with professionals.

> Inform yourself. You do not need to be a helpless consumer of other people's judgment or advice about your child.

Parents and teachers in general are much more astute than they usually get credit for, and wise professionals take a parent's concerns seriously. For some children, the word *problem* is practically engraved on their foreheads from birth. For others, the symptoms of trouble may be much more subtle. Here are some examples to give you an idea of important things to watch for:

Case #1: Jared's "Cloud of Disruption"

> *Jared was a beautiful baby, but his mother admitted that her son had been difficult even since infancy. While his twin sister slept, ate, played, and learned mostly in the expected ways, Jared cascaded unpredictably through each day, leaving behind a trail of frazzled adults.*
>
> *"This sounds terrible," confided Pam, his mother, "but my son reminds me of those cartoons of 'Pigpen' in Charlie*

*Brown. Except it's not only dirt around him, it's this major
cloud of disruption. We just love him so much, but we never
have known what to expect. When he was little he'd throw
a fit about the smallest things—like a label in a shirt that
'hurt his neck' or some food he didn't like. We do our best
to set limits, but he is just an exhausting child."*

*Jared barged through a low-key preschool without too
much difficulty, but by the time he entered kindergarten,
red flags were flying high. Despite his good oral language
abilities, he was baffled by letter sounds and numerals. He
had trouble sitting in a circle, joining a discussion, or following other classroom routines. Fortunately, his teacher
appreciated his affectionate nature and somewhat off-beat
personality; she told Pam and Roy, his dad, that she was
sure Jared was motivated to learn, but he didn't seem to
know how to go about it.*

*"Sometimes he seems to learn it, but the next day he
can't remember," she lamented. "Poor kid! I know he is getting self-conscious about not being able to keep up and
that's just making it worse."*

Jared showed many classic symptoms of a neurodevelopmental
problem. His teacher suggested that he might have an attention
deficit disorder. After consulting with her pediatrician and the
school psychologist, Pam took Jared to a clinic specializing in developmental learning problems. (Appendix C: A Primer on Getting
Professional Help for Your Child lists practical steps for obtaining
an evaluation.) While her son did a series of learning activities with
a friendly psychologist, she was interviewed about his development.
Here are a few of the warning signs:

Warning Signs: Risk Factors for Learning Problems

- *Male gender:* Boys are at much greater risk for almost all
  types of developmental problems, including learning disorders, for reasons that are still being debated. Girls' problems
  appear to be less frequent, but they may be overlooked be-

cause they are less severe, or because girls tend, overall, to cause less trouble in class than do boys.

- *Prenatal or perinatal (at birth) complications:* Birth complications may be associated with a later diagnosis of learning difficulty. Other than difficulties commonly associated with carrying twins, however, Pam had suffered no complications.

- *Preterm birth and low birth weight:* Both factors applied in Jared's case and both are associated with a higher risk of later learning and attention problems. Exceedingly small infants, who now survive thanks to advanced technologies, are at very high risk. (Jared and his sister were lucky, being only slightly premature and close to normal birthweight.)

- *Family history of any type of learning or developmental disability:* None were reported. In Chapter 7, "Genes, Learning, and the Environment," we will explore the connection between genetics and various types of learning differences and learn why "none were reported" does not necessarily mean they didn't exist.

- *Allergies:* Both twins suffered from eczema and tested allergic to pollens, molds, cats, and horses. Jared had also been colicky, which some experts link to food sensitivities. He also suffered from several ear infections while in preschool. Early ear infections with partial hearing loss may interfere with prereading abilities if they block accurate perception of the sounds in words at a critical period for language development.

- *Delay in major developmental milestones for gestational age* (i.e., from when he would have been born in a full-term pregnancy): Language development was on the late end of normal limits. Jared had been on schedule in large-motor development (walking), but his fine-motor skills were delayed, as were his abilities to self-regulate and calm himself. He had more difficulty with transitions than most children his age. He was an erratic sleeper and required a long winding-down period at bedtime with a quiet story and often a reassuring backrub. His parents did not approve of television or videos in their children's bedrooms, preferring close and loving human interaction to "electronic pacification," in Pam's words.

- *Tactile defensiveness:* Jared was unusually sensitive to textures against his skin (e.g., a shirt label) or in his mouth, which might help account for his food tantrums. Although he loved being firmly hugged and calmly held, he didn't like being surprised by any sudden or unfamiliar touch. When at school, he often kept his sweatshirt on with the hood pulled up, almost as if he was trying to screen out an overwhelming classroom world.

- *Problems remembering letter names and sounds* that are inconsistent with the child's age and level of previous teaching. Everyone agreed (and psychological testing later confirmed) that Jared had adequate intellectual ability even though he was struggling with prereading tasks that most of his classmates had already mastered. Fortunately, his school district had initiated an early prevention program, so Jared was one of a small group receiving intensive reading help from a trained specialist who came into his classroom.

- *Difficulty with sequences of small, fine-motor movements* inconsistent with age: Jared resisted cutting with scissors, doing jigsaw puzzles, or building models because he found these activities difficult and frustrating. In kindergarten he produced "messy" work when writing with a pencil or trying to crayon within the lines.

- *Signs of crumbling self-confidence and the onset of emotional problems secondary to the learning difficulty.* Noticeable mood changes or negative physical symptoms related to school are a warning flag that should be investigated.

- *Duration of symptoms for more than six months:* All children experience ups and downs in developmental progress, and some need extra time to latch on to "age-appropriate" behavior or learning. Nonetheless, significant organic disorders generally show up early in life. Problems that don't appear until after the child starts school may signal specific learning disabilities (e.g., dyslexia) and/or a school program that is inadequate or out of step with developmental needs.

- *Generalized problems:* Jared's problems did not fit readily into one single diagnostic category. Many if not most learning disorders come with overlapping diagnoses, and it is often difficult to affix one accurate label or a single treatment to the child's difficulties. For example, reading and attention disorders often overlap. The best evaluations come with a descriptive analysis of your child's relative strengths and weaknesses. They avoid one-size-fits-all recommendations.

"This is impossible!" wailed one graduate student after a seminar on diagnosis of learning disorders. "Everything overlaps with everything else!"

Jared was diagnosed with an attention deficit/hyperactivity disorder (ADHD), a specific learning disability (dyslexia) and a sensory processing disorder. (Chapter 3, "What Should We Call This?," explains the major diagnostic categories and how they are determined.)

The report recommended continued in-school support for early reading and writing skills as well as sensory integration therapy (also to be discussed later). Jared's pediatrician had already recommended monitoring his daily environment and diet for potential allergens. She advised limiting and supervising "screen time" (TV, computer, and video), which, fortunately, was not a problem in this household because the children's media use was already carefully monitored.

Jared's parents and teachers also received instructions for setting up a behavior plan. Pam and Roy were adamantly opposed to giving Jared medications to manage his behavior. Instead, they decided to consult with a psychologist who could help them and Jared structure a program for behavior self-management. The purpose of such programs is to support the child as he learns to take better control of his own actions and reactions. This type of cognitive behavioral therapy is an important adjunct to treatment for attention problems whether or not medications are used. It may even improve brain function, as we will discuss in later chapters.

The psychologist, who admitted he had been charmed by Jared's energy and puckish sense of humor, advised Pam to make a special effort to regulate Jared's environment, minimize excessive stimulation, and keep regular mealtimes and a regular bedtime. "Children like Jared need a lot of structure and predictability," he added, "and lack of sleep significantly worsens attention problems. You're absolutely right to keep the TV and computer games out of his bedroom." He also prescribed increased amounts of free outdoor playtime after school and on weekends. "I'm not talking about structured sports with a bunch of rules and adults telling him what to do. Let him run around and develop his own games. And take him to the park. We find that interacting with nature has a calming effect on kids—it seems to get them in better touch with themselves," he added. "Keep an eye on him to be sure he's safe, but let him work off as much of that energy as possible."

Sounds like a large prescription for Mom and Dad, but for a child like Jared, extraduty parenting can make all the difference. When brain maturation is assisted by appropriate interventions with caring adults, children show a remarkable ability to overcome problems.

Case #2: Why Is Sierra Resisting School?

Sierra, age four, has announced that she wishes to drop out of preschool, and she definitely means it. Her grandmother is understandably concerned, as she explains after adroitly cornering me at a dinner party.

"What four-year-old doesn't like preschool, for heaven's sake? She's started having these major temper fits when it's time to leave in the morning. This is a kid who was always so happy—never any separation problems in day care—and now, suddenly... I don't want to meddle, but my daughter is frantic. She's a single mom with a time-consuming job. I'm really sorry to catch you at a social event, but are we right to be worried?"

Yes. (And don't worry, Grandma, people in my profession are quite accustomed to being asked for advice at social events.) There are many, many reasons for "school refusal," but if they continue for any length of time, such situations always warrant attention and good detective work to look for possible sources of the problem. Frequently it turns out that the child feels threatened, inadequate, or embarrassed by something that is happening at school, something that the youngster herself may not understand or be able to explain. When I hear a story like this—an otherwise well-adjusted child of any age in a stable home setting who suddenly begins to resist school or show related signs of anxiety, I have to suspect an underlying learning problem.

In fact, Grandma had already given me an important clue in the question with which she had started our conversation.

"Is it normal not to be able to understand a thing a child says by the time they're four? Sierra is so smart, she's musical and really creative, but when we talk on the phone, I don't have any idea what she's saying."

Curiously, as I chat with Sierra's grandmother, I note that her own speech contains a very subtle articulation defect, a trace of a confusion between the sounds of l and r, which would probably not even be noticeable to an untrained ear. Because problems with language development are heritable, I am not surprised, in a later conference with Sierra's mother, to learn that Sierra shows several symptoms of language delay. She has difficulty not only with pronouncing words clearly, but also getting her ideas and even her needs into appropriate sentences. I suggest a thorough evaluation by a speech / language therapist, arranged through Sierra's preschool.

"Do you think it's possible that she is embarrassed or frustrated in school because of her speech delay?" I ask Sierra's mom. "Maybe the other kids make fun of her, or she can't tell the teacher what she needs, as in, 'I don't want graham crackers, I want the pretzels.' 'I want to finger paint with Maria today.' If she can't get those words out quickly and understandably enough, it could be really

> *frustrating for her. And if they're introducing letter sounds, she may not be getting them."*
>
> *"Well, I never thought of that," she muses, "but you may be onto something. Do these things run in families? I always felt like I might have had some sort of learning disability—they labeled me an 'underachiever,' and I was really shy with other kids. I don't want Sierra to have to go through all that! I'll see that she gets an evaluation and some therapy if she needs it. I'm relieved, and I know Sierra's grandmother will be, too."*

Language development is at the heart of almost every aspect of school learning (even math, believe it or not), and any disorder or delay in this critical apparatus for success should be investigated and treated. A huge percentage of diagnosed learning problems involve some aspect of language learning, because language skills are needed for most schoolwork.

Language Skills: A Foundation of Learning

Reading
- *Word reading.* Sounding out words (decoding) requires accurate processing of the sounds (phonemes) of oral language. This essential skill for good reading comes from plenty of experience with accurate intake of the sounds in the first place. It's best learned from face-to-face language interaction with real people.

- *Comprehending and remembering* written text, which again starts with oral language and story reading. This is one reason why reading to children gives such a powerful boost to later reading scores.

- *Fluency.* Ease and speed of reading requires having an automatic grasp of words and sentences. Children who cannot speak fluently tend to be slow, inaccurate readers.

Listening Intelligently

- *Understanding what the teacher says.*

- *Paying attention* in class. Students who lack good listening skills often appear to be inattentive, which may be mistaken for an attention disorder.

- *Following oral directions* also requires good listening, understanding, and verbal memory.

- *Understanding the language of math.* Terms such as *plus, greater than, divide,* and *equal* are learned from oral language combined with real-life experience with quantities of things.

- *Understanding written text* requires "listening" to an author's voice when reading silently. When something is really hard to understand, even skilled readers tend to mumble the words to themselves.

- *Spelling.* One strategy of good spellers is to listen in one's mind to the sounds in order when spelling a long word.

- *Writing:* "listening" to your own thoughts when trying to compose a sentence or paragraph.

Speaking

- Speaking (*articulating*) understandably.

- *Answering questions* appropriately.

- *Asking the right question* when you need help or don't understand.

- Getting ideas arranged and spoken (*formulating*) in grammatically appropriate sentences.

Using Language Strategically

- *Knowing what is appropriate* to say to a teacher or classmates.

- *Getting others* (including the teacher and classmates) *to understand and appreciate your ideas.*

- *Negotiating* problems without resorting to hitting. (A problem here may also be mistaken for symptoms of attention disorder.)

- *Using positive self-talk* ("Now, I should wait and think before I jump into this." "This looks hard, but I'm going to try my best.") to control *attention, behavior, and motivation.*

- *Using language as a memory aid: Repeating* "three times four equals twelve," "three times four equals twelve," etc., is one strategic method of memorizing the multiplication tables, your phone number, or many other things. *Retelling* or summarizing a story or concept in your own words can fix it into memory. Children with weak verbal memories don't use this technique effectively.

Linking language to "mind movies" to improve memory and understanding

- *"Seeing" the story or the math problem* ("Sue had ten apples in a basket. Seven fell out. How many does she have now?"). Children who can't create their own mental pictures are likely to add 7 + 10 because they can't imaginatively represent what happened.

- Picturing the action in a history text, or visualizing the steps in a science experiment are effective methods of *understanding and remembering content* in high school subjects, which are often taught through either textbooks or lectures with no pictures attached.

This is only a sample of the many functions that language serves in the school curriculum—not to mention in later life success. In my book *Endangered Minds,* I explain why intelligent speaking and listening are such powerful brain-builders, not only for academic skills but also for the attention and self-management that are such problems in today's classrooms. Language has to be actively used and practiced to build the needed brain connections. Yet students today spend too much time watching screens and too little using language in active social play and family conversations around the dinner table.

Even though language abilities and disabilities run in families, they also depend heavily on a child's environment. When we totaled up Sierra's screen time, her mother was shocked to realize that it occupied at least five hours of the little girl's day. Even Sierra's early day care center had frequently used children's videos to keep the kids quiet. Her Brazilian babysitter spoke only minimal English but kept background TV on most of the time. Sierra's mom easily understood how this overpowering amount of visual stimulus was crowding out time for language development and depriving her daughter's maturing brain connections of critical practice.

In Chapter 11, "Brain-Cleaning 102," we will look at some surprising research showing why background TV may be particularly hazardous for preschool brains. We will also deal with how media can be used constructively rather than as a learning disabler.

Sierra's mother has followed up with a speech-language evaluation for the little girl and is in the process of attacking this problem with appropriate therapy, firm new guidelines for the babysitter, and a major revision in the balance of screen time and conversation, story reading, story hours at the library, and quiet playtime so that Sierra's "inner voice" can begin to be heard.

Language Development: Red Flags

- *Family history* of language delay, reading, or other language problems

- *Failure to reach appropriate milestones* in language development. (My book *Your Child's Growing Mind* lists ages for developmental language milestones.)

- *Lack of interest* in communicating, avoidance of *eye contact*, repetitive (*echolalic*) *speech* that mimics isolated phrases inappropriately and without understanding of what they mean. (These symptoms can be early warning signs of autism and should be promptly reported to your pediatrician.)

- *Unclear, "slushy" speech* inconsistent with age

- *Resistance to listening to stories.* (But make sure the stories are short and interesting to the child.)

- *Delayed ability to remember and follow age-appropriate oral directions.* ("Please go to your room and bring down the blue sweater.")

- *Teacher concerns.* Early childhood professionals have an informed and objective view of all aspects of your child's development. If you are concerned, ask for the teacher's advice.

- Repeated difficulty in coming up with familiar words. (*"The uh, uh, you know, uh, the thingy."*) This is called a *word-finding* or word retrieval problem. One quick test for children who have already learned to recognize colors by name is to take a box of crayons or markers and ask your child to quickly name them.

Case #3: Curtis. Whose Problem Is This?

Curtis is a winsome, slightly built eight-year-old who lives with both parents in a lavishly appointed apartment in a wealthy urban enclave of a midwest city. For a child with every apparent advantage, however, this little boy's life is far from enviable. Of an artistic and "dreamy" temperament himself, he struggles to survive in a world where achievement *is the word of the day—every day.*

I met Curtis and his family as part of a research project on a rapidly expanding problem category called executive function disorder. As you will learn in later chapters, the brain's so-called executive system, commanded by the frontal lobes behind the forehead, is responsible for organizing, planning, sequencing, controlling, and managing actions, behavior, and thinking.[1] *If you know any children who have been diagnosed with attention problems, you may understand why they are often included in this category.*

Since birth, Curtis has been a child who preferred to march to his own restless and erratic drumbeat. He showed some early signs of developmental problems: poor sleep habits, irritability, anxiety, expressive language delay, and a fleeting attention span. Now he can become intensely involved in creative artwork projects, drama, noncontact sports, block-building, video games, and reading books of his choice. Curtis is a good reader and speller. It's a different story, however, when it comes to other aspects of formal learning such as memorizing math facts, sequences—days of the week, months of the year—or retelling the events of a story concisely in order.

Between his homework load and an organized sports league, Curtis does not have much time for free play. Apartment living limits his playtime outdoors. When you stop to think about it, Curtis spends most of his time being directed, observed, and judged by performance-oriented adults.

When he was five Curtis entered a large, highly rated private school noted for its "fast-track" curriculum and its record for getting students into top colleges. Overwhelmed by the first day of school, he ran away and hid, an apt beginning for a rocky academic career. He "graduated" from speech-language therapy, now sees a tutor twice a week at his parents' expense, and dutifully completes a homework load that is unusually heavy for a third-grader. Nonetheless, Curtis remains in all the bottom groups in his classroom. (For the uninitiated, this means that his academic skills are below the level of many of his classmates—and in this school all the other children know it and so does Curtis.)

"Curtis needs more self-confidence," stated his last report from school. A few days later the teacher handed out extra work to only the bottom groups—in front of the whole class.

"It's a type A school, and if your kid doesn't fit it, they're not going to help," comments Curtis's father.

Curtis is a sweet and obedient little boy who doesn't cause much trouble—except perhaps within himself. When upset, he usually shuts down, calming himself by a simple activity such as bouncing a ball.

When I asked about his media use, his mother answered, "We've cut way back on his video games. He can play for hours and gets totally zoned by them. We just didn't like what we were seeing."

A previous unsuccessful trial of a medication for attention deficit disorder was discontinued, but after one terrifying "rampage" in which Curtis threw himself around and trashed his room, his doctor feared he might have bipolar illness and prescribed a psychiatric drug that is still controversial, although approved, for use with children.

According to Curtis's father, approximately one-third of the students at the school are taking some sort of medication for psychiatric problems, including attention disorders.

Highly complicated situations like this one are not as uncommon as we might hope. It was not my role in this case to evaluate or make recommendations, or even to comment on the somewhat obscure rationale for the diagnoses that had been attached to this little boy. I could not help speculating, however, that Curtis is trapped in a daily setting—albeit one in which some children might thrive—which is out of step not only with his particular needs but also with the normal developmental needs of many children. Unrealistic pressure—however well meaning—and an intensely fast-track curriculum can defeat even bright children and may create their own set of problems. Many developmental learning problems improve with maturation and appropriate targeted support, but only if the child has retained enough self-confidence to help make it happen.

Curtis would very likely do better and even thrive in a more "hands-on" project-oriented curriculum, with less reliance on abstract verbal content, less overt achievement pressure, and more creative, varied approaches to building skills without sacrificing quality. For example, since Curtis has had trouble mastering calendar sequences (days, months), a different approach using color, artwork, and Curtis's own personal experience might be helpful. Unfortunately, his particular school culture encourages a teaching style based on lecture, little hands-on learning, and high levels of competition. This combination can be especially unhealthy for children in early grades, and even more so if they are "different" or "late-blooming" learners.

A quality school can be suitably challenging without being "fast-track." Some brains simply do not take well to "decontextualized" learning—that is, memorizing names, facts, rules without anything tangible (to touch, feel, build, take apart, manipulate) associated with them. "Multisensory" experience is almost essential if younger children are going to engage in meaningful learning, but older students may also need to understand in a context that is personal and relevant to them. Trying to rush through a curriculum can result in superficially memorized answers, and for many children it is a recipe for failure.

As I left the interview, Curtis's father confided that change is forthcoming. Curtis will be moving to a different state and a school where standards are high, but where art, music, and drama are intrinsic parts of the curriculum, with less pressure and more in-school support for differing learning needs. I could only agree that this was probably a fortunate move. Unfortunately, the reason for the change is that Curtis's parents are separating.

"We've all been under a lot of stress lately," said Mom, sighing.

According to neurologist Martha Denckla, who was instrumental in first describing "executive function disorder," there are at least two conditions that can mimic the symptoms of this disorder and create what she terms "pseudo-ADHD" and "pseudo-dysexecutive" conditions. They are (1) a language-based learning disability, such as expressive language disorder or dyslexia, and (2) "a kind of overload/exhaustion phenomenon," which she attributes to "performance anxiety" that reduces the child's ability to tolerate stress. Such anxiety is exacerbated, she finds, by increases in "high-stakes testing and overzealous homework assignments."[2]

Identifying Problems in the System

Children are our canaries in the coal mine—the first to succumb when the environment becomes toxic, a warning signal that something is seriously wrong somewhere along the line.

> When analyzing what is going wrong with a child's learning, it is a mistake to look for a problem only within the child. There may also be a problem at some level of the system or environment in which the youngster is expected to function.

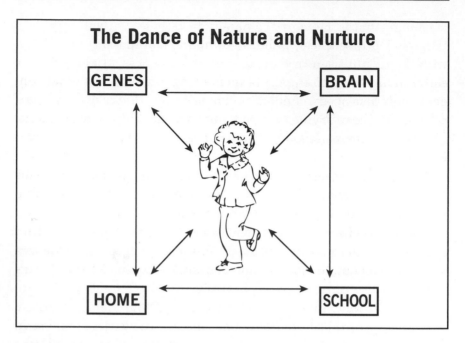

3. The Dance of Nature and Nurture: A child's development is a complex interaction in which each factor both affects and is affected by the others. We should treat the child as part of this dynamic system, not simply as a collection of problems or symptoms.

Children today learn—or fail to—within a frazzled culture of busy parents, marital stress, environmental assaults on the brain, escalating expectations, time-pressured professionals, and overwhelmed teachers. We may attach a label, a treatment, or a pill, but these measures are usually inadequate if we fail to take the time—and do the detective work—to address every potential area of trouble. One useful resource is Amy Egan's book *Is It a Big Problem or a Little Problem?* Figure 3 displays a diagram of the most significant influences that affect children's development and learning. In the remainder of this book we will explore how these formative influences may be affecting specific aspects of your child or student's learning.

Are We "Overlabeling" Children?

Any child in the United States who is diagnosed with a "handicapping condition" is entitled to receive specialized services, but parents usually have to take an active role in making sure this happens. Different states, counties, and even school districts have their own ideas about what constitutes normal development and what constitutes a learning disorder—and what, if anything, should be done for those with a problem. These decisions depend heavily on available funding and vary dramatically from community to community.

Working cooperatively with the school is always a first step, and many problems can be dealt with at this level, especially if teachers and specialists understand how to accommodate different children's learning styles. If such cooperation is not possible, you will need to arm yourself with information about laws in your particular area. (See Appendix D for organizations and Web sites that can help you. Appendix C contains suggestions for considering treatment options.)

Because waiting lists are long and services can be scanty, many families seek outside diagnosis and/or treatment. In order to receive reimbursement for evaluation or therapy for a learning disorder, health insurance companies and school service providers usually require a specific diagnosis that is recognized as a handicapping condition. The standard reference for these terms is called the DSM (*Diagnostic and Statistical Manual of Mental Disorders*).[3] Experts argue furiously about (1) the validity of these particular diagnostic categories, (2) their definitions, (3) the fundamental concept of using "labels" to characterize complex developmental problems, and (4) the resulting medicalization of variations in development. Some object to the fact that a psychiatric diagnosis encourages the use of psychiatric drug therapies (e.g., Ritalin, Adderall) as a first-line or sole treatment rather than more time-intensive therapies (e.g., home or classroom management techniques, educational or behavior therapy). Authorities such as Peter S. Jensen of Columbia University insist that DSM categories encourage far too superficial an approach to diagnosing children's disorders, which require a much deeper look at personal, environmental, and cultural factors.[4]

Parents and school personnel in the United States may push for a specific diagnosis so that treatment will be covered by state or federal funding. In some communities, physicians and psychologists dish out DSM diagnoses about as readily as a short-order cook dishes out burgers.

I was recently asked to consult on a case in which a boy had been tested, at his teacher's insistence, by a Ph.D. psychologist who diagnosed the problem as nonverbal learning disorder. When his parents and his teacher read the psychologist's report and checked out the definition and manifestations of NVLD, they were puzzled.

> "This report reads as if it had been written about a different child than my son," commented his mother.

When questioned about his diagnosis, the psychologist readily acknowledged that it was certainly not a clear-cut case, but that the boy's profile "sort of fell between the cracks and I thought you wanted a label."

Child First, Disorder Second

As important as it is to get an accurate picture of what may be wrong and how to remedy it, we should keep our priorities straight. No matter what the problem is, your child is always your child, not a disorder or a collection of symptoms. Any steps you take to solve a learning problem will be much more effective if they are enclosed in an envelope of love, support, and overt recognition of your child's many abilities.

Generally speaking, parents are relieved to learn that their child has "something that has a name." Yes, it is reassuring to identify the nature and scope of the problem. However, the unfortunate fact is that, unlike medical problems, educational ones do not show up in such definite categories. Nor does a diagnosis always lead to a generally accepted solution. Clear-cut diagnostic labels such as *appendicitis*, *strep*, *fractured femur* are few and far between, as are "evidence-based" treatments. I just received a 161-page dossier of evaluations for a little boy I have not yet met. Sean has been through so many diagnoses (hyperlexia, autism, Asperger's syndrome, sensory integration disorder, low-average IQ, abnormal auditory perception, speech disorder, and mixed receptive/expressive language disorder), that I wonder when anyone has ever had time to work on helping him. Going through this massive listing of scores, charts, symptom checklists, labels, and clinical observations, I kept wondering who this child really is, what his interests are, how he feels about learning, or how his parents might restructure his environment to help him. They are obviously concerned about their son, but, sadly, they will not find a magic bullet solution through yet another testing session.

Sean's file contained an unusually large number of "recipe" reports, which have become prevalent since the advent of computerized test scoring programs. In this unfortunate practice, the "diagnostician" administers tests of ability (e.g., IQ) or skills (e.g., reading accuracy) and enters the scores into a computer program, which then proceeds to spit out both a diagnosis and a standard set of recommendations. This method removes a great deal of clinical judgment or accountability from the psychologist and saves him the trouble of writing individual reports, but it smacks of treating children like automobiles in a repair shop.

> *"What does concern me . . . is how many of our children are being treated* only *on a symptomatic level and thus are being lost to their labels. When this happens, the true source of the upset often remains unidentified and unaddressed."*
>
> —Scott M. Shannon, MD[5]

For Sean, the only personal glimpse came at the end of the report from his first-grade teacher. She wrote, "I think someday Sean will discover the cure for cancer." What? This kid, a 161-page litany of problems, actually has some potential? You could have fooled me (and maybe the computer, too)!

"Labeling our children often cripples them instead of liberating them," claims Dr. Shannon.[6] He objects to the *reductionist* practice of reducing a living, breathing, feeling child to a bunch of numbers, especially since numbers alone are highly inaccurate predictors of what a child's potential really is or how to help realize it.

Don't let anyone reduce your child to a label or a list of numbers. Always remember, whatever the problem, there's still a child in there!

A Good Start for Pinning Down a Problem: Where's the Breakdown?

One helpful way to start looking at a learning problem is to take the time to try to analyze exactly what is going wrong. This process, called differential diagnosis, means becoming a careful observer and asking the right questions to uncover the real roots of the difficulty. By applying some detective work and learning to ask the right questions, we may find clues not only to what is going wrong but also where to start helping. Let's consider some common examples:

"Ashley has a memory problem."

- Ashley, a second-grader, has no trouble remembering lots of things, such as:
  - how to set up and play Mousetrap
  - when to leave the house for her schoolbus
  - how to get her dad back into a good mood when he's had a difficult day
  - time and days of her favorite TV programs

- What is it, exactly, that Ashley can't remember?
  - how to spell the simplest words when she writes a composition, even ones that she just spelled correctly on the Friday test
  - how many "bumps" are on the cursive capitals M and N
  - How to pronounce "tion" at the end of a word
  - The sum of 6 + 9

Now we can see that this isn't exactly a "memory problem," but a specific language-learning problem which shows up only with printed symbols. In the next chapter you will learn that these symptoms are warning signs of developmental dyslexia, which should be identified and treated with specialized teaching methods. Now we have definite clues where to start seeking help.

"Doreen has a motivation problem. She just won't do her homework now that she's in the fourth grade."

- Doreen enjoys playing the piano, hardly has to be reminded to practice, and has made extremely rapid progress since she started taking lessons last year. Yesterday she told her mother that she thought she might also like to learn to play the saxophone. Doreen also loves to cook. Doreen is not "unmotivated." Her lack of motivation is restricted to one type of situation—doing her homework.

- This difficulty has only cropped up in fourth grade. Doreen has previously been a good student, so we should look for what may be happening now that is different from previous years. Sometimes difficulties that come on suddenly suggest a mismatch between student and teacher, but Doreen genuinely likes her teacher—except that "she gives too much homework."

- Perhaps Doreen, a preteen, is newly concerned with her social life and is spending too much time either texting her friends or on some other nonhomework activity. But Doreen does her homework at a desk in the family room where her parents have started keeping an eye out for how she uses her time.

- Doreen is not a well-organized student. She forgets homework assignments and has trouble planning her study time or completing long-term assignments.

- Fourth grade is often a year of more written assignments and reports, content-area reading, such as a social studies textbook instead of a novel, and extra need for organization (managing several different binders, making outlines, planning and carrying out long-term assignments). The brain's "executive system" has a role in all these tasks, but it is not fully developed when a child is nine or ten. Many children who have eased through primary grades suddenly confront a wall when they hit fourth grade. Schools should—but don't always—teach students these more complicated *processes of learning* and guide them through each step in, say, how to organize their assignments or follow specific timetables in preparing a long-term project. Very often parents end up having to pick up the pieces.

Doreen's "motivation" problem begins to look like a problem with organization and study skills. Her parents should schedule a conference with the teacher and school learning specialist, if there is one, to determine if she needs extra support and explicit lessons in how to make her learning more efficient. This step is a logical beginning in determining whether Doreen's problem calls for a more intensive evaluation.

"Calvin can't pay attention."

By now you may be able to come up with the first questions we should ask: "What is it, specifically, that Calvin, an eighth-grader, can't pay attention to? Can he pay attention to anything?"

- Calvin's attention problems are mostly confined to school subjects that he finds "boring," especially Algebra 1. This problem started two or three years ago, but it seems to be getting worse, and Calvin's grades are dropping. His teachers want him to be tested for an attention problem, as they are frustrated by his seeming inattention and "spaciness" in class.

- Calvin has no problem paying attention on the sports field, especially in anything having to do with soccer, at which he stars and demonstrates leadership skills. He is also a whiz in the computer lab, troubleshooting problems for other students and even for teachers. His most intense attention, however, is reserved for online video gaming, which he plays in his room with the door shut.

- When asked, "How much time does Calvin spend online?" his father shrugs. "I don't even want to know, but I do notice that his light is often still on when my wife and I go to bed. His mother thinks we should try to limit it, but I think those games are just as educational as schoolwork in this modern age—aren't they?"

Media use is one of the thorniest issues in the lives of today's students, particularly for adolescent boys involved in online gaming. In later chapters you will learn about what it may be doing to their brain chemistry, the many ways in which it can affect other types of learning and attention, why it is so addictive for some kids, and why young teenage brains in particular need reasonable limits. Suffice it to say here that having a game demand and hold your attention is very different from what is needed in learning algebra—to gain command of one's own brain and consciously direct and maintain its focus.

We need to suspect some relatively new influence, probably environmental, because Calvin's attention problem is relatively recent, and because organic attention disorders generally show up before age seven. Moreover, it is showing up mainly in one situation, algebra class. We can also identify some relevant environmental concerns:

- *Recent increase in online gaming:* The potentially addictive distraction of online gaming can easily draw a fourteen-year-old brain away from "boring" homework that demands more mental effort.

- *New and more difficult math concepts in seventh grade combined with lack of adequate homework preparation:* Calvin has fallen behind and doesn't understand what is being discussed in algebra class.

- *Tiredness mimicking symptoms of attention disorder:* Lack of sleep as Calvin plays long into the night causes symptoms of attention disorder.

Calvin and his parents should ask to schedule an appointment with his teacher and the school learning specialist, if there is one, to arrange for some special help. His parents also need to make sure he is doing his homework where there are no distractions. In addition, they should begin some serious conversations about priorities. Firm rules are needed at home so that Calvin's talent with electronic media can be used to enhance rather than impair his development. We will return to this very timely issue in Part Three of this book.

Understanding Difference

Many of history's most creative, smart, talented, and successful people had learning patterns that didn't quite fit the usual mold. There is a fine line, however, between accepting (or even celebrating) a child's uniqueness and ignoring a significant and treatable problem. On the other hand, I have known families who became so overinvolved with the problem and a "sickness" model of learning that they lost sight of their whole child. Maintaining perspective while slogging one's way through this emotional and technical swamp is not an easy task.

It takes a lot of time and effort to recognize, identify, and deal with any youngster's needs, especially in a culture in a rush for "success." But the fact that some children's individual tent of talents seems especially hard to unroll doesn't change the importance— or the ultimate rewards—of this job.

In the next chapter we will consider the most common diagnostic categories of children's learning difficulties: what they are, where they come from, and what we can do about them.

What Should We Call This?

Understanding Learning Disorders

I used to think my brain was broken," recalled an acquaintance who is now a thriving professional photographer but who went through childhood with a constellation of symptoms—attention problems, disorganization, poor reading and writing skills, acute test anxiety—and a laundry list of diagnoses to match.

In an ideal world, of course, we could treat each child individually, "enabling without labeling" as Dr. Mel Levine puts it.[1] In practice, however, given the daunting task of pinning down multiple problems and what to do about them, professionals usually assign symptoms to a particular category, or syndrome. Validated research helps us understand them more effectively. Assigning a child to a diagnostic category does have its problems, however. Oftentimes it is hard to know where some extreme version of "normal" stops and a clear-cut disability begins. Does Clark have Asperger's syndrome or is he simply a smart, shy, and slightly odd child? Should we treat Janice's math difficulties as a learning disability or an extreme fear of taking a risk and making mistakes? Another complication is the fact that there are so many terms for most kinds of problems that there is little agreement among different professionals, even in the same community. Pity the poor parent who can take her child up and down the block and get three or four different diagnoses, depending on which office they enter.

> Ideally, we can walk the fine line between ignoring real
> problems and overreacting to normal variations in develop-
> ment. But ideals are sometimes hard to reach.

Different states and school districts also differ in their criteria for diagnosis and treatment. At a national conference on dyslexia, I conversed during the break with a speech/language therapist from a school district in a midwestern state. "I constantly see children with this problem who need help," she fumed. "But our state doesn't even accept the term 'dyslexia!' "

Even the validity of the terms sometimes comes into question. Although *attention deficit disorder* is an accepted term, many experts are now sure that the problem is not a deficit of attention at all, but rather a difficulty deploying it appropriately.

Remember that children's problems don't usually fall into easily treated categories. Much as we welcome clear-cut diagnoses and validated remedies, they are few and far between, so be wary of anyone who tries to sell you a "cure." Generally speaking, successful treatment involves a labor-intensive and multipronged approach that includes home, school, and all other aspects of the child's life.

If reputable research studies have validated the usefulness of a certain therapy, it is called an *evidence-based* treatment. For example, specific teaching programs have proven effective in treating certain types of reading disorders, including dyslexia. For most problems, however, evidence-based treatments don't yet exist. This chapter introduces the major learning disorder syndromes and possible treatments. New research is constantly coming out, however, so you will need to keep current with the recommended authors in the Bibliography and online sources in Appendix D.

Appendix A contains a quick checklist of some of the terms currently in use. In Appendix B you will find some commonsense steps to take if you suspect a problem. As a starting point for your own research, here is a *very abbreviated* rundown on the most common types of problems that directly affect children's learning.

Problems with Speech and Language Development: Developmental Language Disorder, "Specific Language Disability" (SLD)

What Is It? Language disorder comprises a significant delay in normal acquisition of skills in *receptive* (listening, understanding) or *expressive* (speaking) language. This category includes difficulty with pronunciation/articulation (phonology); syntax, or acquisition of grammatical forms ("He wented"); vocabulary development and comprehension; and appropriate social usage, including understanding people's gestures or facial expressions. These conditions often overlap with auditory processing difficulties such as *central auditory processing disorder* (CAPD), in which the child's hearing is adequate but the sounds and meaning are not being accurately processed once they get to the brain.[2]

> *"Some mothers don't realize how lucky they are just to be able to read a book to their child or enjoy a movie together. Of course, we could do neither, because David avoided situations that required him to listen."*
>
> —mother of a child with a language comprehension
> disorder (diagnosed as auditory processing disorder)

Where Does It Come From? Language abilities are heritable (i.e., run in families), but depend heavily on the type of usage promoted (or not) in the home, school, and day care settings. The brain has critical periods for different aspects of language acquisition, and these circuits must be stimulated during a child's early years if they are to develop fully.

What Do We Do? Developmental language problems may cause or be related to reading, math, attention, behavior, or other problems, so early intervention is recommended. A reputable speech/language therapist can evaluate a child's development and determine which therapy, if any, is needed. Schools often have screening for all students.

Reading Problems:
Dyslexia, Hyperlexia, "Garden-Variety" Reading Disorders

Dyslexia

What Is It? Dyslexia, the most common reading disorder, may be present in up to 20 percent of children but often goes undiagnosed. Dyslexia is defined as otherwise unexplained failure to acquire age-appropriate reading skills not due to inadequate intelligence or poor teaching. It involves a fundamental difficulty in "phonological processing": the accurate perception of the order of sounds in words. Children with dyslexia have trouble mastering sound-symbol correspondence, which means the ability to quickly and automatically look at a letter combination (*sh, ing, car*) and pronounce it, or the ability to sound out a word ("r-a-n: ran"). This is called decoding. Dyslexic readers tend to read slowly and inaccurately, and may also have difficulty in word retrieval. This lack of fluency causes comprehension difficulties, although dyslexic readers may have very good comprehension of oral language. Dyslexia often overlaps with other language problems, writing and spelling difficulties, problems memorizing math facts (e.g., multiplication tables), and mastering a foreign language. As Tom West explains in his book *In the Mind's Eye*, Dyslexia is also associated with certain talents in creative, artistic, and visual-spatial ability. In fact, I have met many surgeons, engineers, and artists who claim to have dyslexia. Dyslexia often co-occurs with or is mistaken for attention disorder.

Some bright children, especially those from enriched language environments, may have a dyslexic condition that passes "under the radar." These youngsters learn to read, although usually not up to their expected level. Their problem shows up with the mechanics of written language (spelling, writing speed), fluent oral reading, and later when they inexplicably struggle to learn a new language such as French. Often they have trouble memorizing math facts (e.g., multiplication tables.) Because the child's problem has never been identified, he is usually blamed for not trying hard enough, and school life becomes a misery for everyone involved. With appropriate help, these students quickly catch up.

Any student who shows symptoms of dyslexia or is having unexplained difficulty should be evaluated by a knowledgeable professional (check the reference list for the International Dyslexia Association's wealth of helpful information and referral sources in your area).

One ongoing controversy concerns whether or not there is also a "visual dyslexia" caused mainly by deficits in how the brain handles what comes in through the eyes. Less research support has been assembled for this possibility. Also controversial are claims that visual or motor training programs or devices will directly improve academic performance. Such programs are not currently accepted as evidence-based, although there are anecdotal reports of good results. Because there may be more than one neural pathway to a single end result (reading difficulties in this case), and because children—and children's problems—are each a special case, it is important to determine whether factors other than linguistic ones do, in fact, enter into this complex picture and, if so, how best to treat them.

Specific problems with visual imagery, which is the ability to create mental movies when reading, have also been linked to poor achievement. Specialized programs that combine verbal and visual training have shown promise in improving both comprehension and reasoning skills.[3] Nanci Bell, author of programs that have shown good results, is not surprised that these problems are multiplying in an environment where children encounter most of their images ready-made and where video images replace visual imagination.[4]

In his helpful book *Dyslexia: A Complete Guide for Parents*, Gavin Reid of the University of Edinburgh reviews a range of alternative theories as well as treatments. "Parents will always be at the vulnerable end of a new product or treatment," he reminds us, and should be wary of expensive programs that promise quick results. Under any circumstances, however, identifying core deficits in phonological and other language skills is an important first step."[5]

Where Does It Come From? Dyslexia is a heritable brain difference that may involve ten or more different genes and affects specific neural areas involved in processing written language. Perhaps because it affects so many bright and successful people, this "disorder" (or "talent" according to some) has received significant research funding. Multiple studies of dyslexic readers have shown a special pattern or "signature" in brain organization, in which areas responsible for reading are not functioning as robustly as those of good readers, while other areas are unusually active. Additional research has confirmed that the method by which children are taught to read makes a major difference in how—or even whether—dyslexia shows up. Sally Shaywitz at Yale is one of many researchers working in this field, and her book *Overcoming Dyslexia* is a landmark account of why things go wrong and how brain function for reading may be improved by appropriate instruction. In Chapter 5, "Rewiring Children's Brains," we will look at some of this important research.

Even though reading disabilities are heritable, multiple studies show that home environments are also crucial. For example, in one study that looked at the reading abilities of 262 adopted children, the adoptive parents were interviewed about the degree to which their home environment encouraged reading skills and interest in reading. When the children were tested on their reading abilities, they performed similarly to their adoptive parents, even though there was no genetic relationship between them.[6]

What Do We Do? If your child is at risk for dyslexia, the best known prevention and treatment involve the following steps:

- Ensure that the young child has a rich language environment from birth. Lots of experience with books, stories, and careful listening experiences with the individual sounds (phonemes) in words are critical. This "phonemic (or phonological) awareness" is a strong predictor of reading ability.

- Check out the amount and quality of language experience before choosing caregivers, a day care center, or a nursery school program.

- Identify and treat any language problems as early as is reasonable. Decoding is only the tip of the reading iceberg and sounding out words isn't of much value if the reader can't understand what she is reading. As with any language skill, the best methods of problem prevention start in the preschool years, with plenty of high-quality language experience in a loving, verbally sensitive environment.

- Insist that your child's school use a proven approach to prevent reading problems.[7] Fortunately, like other language skills, phonemic awareness can be taught through validated methods and should be established before beginning formal reading instruction. School-wide programs where teachers were trained in specific techniques not only improved reading scores but also reduced the number of students who developed reading problems.[8]

- If your beginning reader shows signs of difficulty, insist on evaluation sooner rather than later. Reading problems are often easier to remedy than emotional ones created by repeated failure.

- Be aware that bright children with dyslexia can slip through the cracks. If your child has academic problems at any age, dyslexia should not be ruled out. A youngster with high overall ability who is reading "at grade level" may be seriously underachieving.

> **TIP:** Expose your child to rhyming words. Inability to think of rhyming words at ages four or five is a sign of phonological problems that predict reading difficulties. The ability to match and blend rhyming sounds comes partially from children's experience with rhyming words. Yet teachers tell us that today's kids are unfamiliar with poetry, nursery rhymes, or rhyming word play—inexpensive, fun, and a proven means of building reading readiness. The rhythm of poetry may also help reading fluency.

- Check out the Web site of the IDA (interdys.org) for a wealth of resources.

Hyperlexia

What Is It? *Hyperlexia*, which literally means "too much reading," seems like the opposite side of the coin from dyslexia and is often grouped with disorders on the autistic spectrum. Children with hyperlexia begin to read words at unusually early ages, even as early as age two, but they have delayed language, social, and personal skills characteristic of autism. A significant gap exists between their ability to "call out" words and their much more limited comprehension of what they read. An obsessional focus on print rather than on meaning is a "splinter skill," often developing in the place of imaginative play and interpersonal interaction.

> Did you know that unusually early word reading can be a sign of serious trouble?

Where Does It Come From? Hyperlexia is a rare condition, usually appearing in families with a history of language-related disorders. As with most other problems, however, environmental effects are undoubtedly influential.

What Do We Do? If you suspect hyperlexia, seek a speech/language evaluation with someone familiar with the condition. Because it is not clear that hyperlexia is actually a separate disorder from autism or Asperger's syndrome, therapies effective for autism are often recommended. A skilled therapist can also work with the child's reading talent to start making sense of language (for example, giving the child a motivating written note such as "Look under the desk to find a present").

It is tempting to convince yourself that this advanced skill means that your child does not have a problem, but this is a mistake. Intensive early intervention can make a big difference. In one case on which I consulted, a three-year-old boy named Charles was recognizing words, but his mother was concerned because his development had been distinctly abnormal. Charles had no spontaneous speech, did not want to play with toys, and was totally obsessed with any type of printed material: newspapers, circulars, books, words that appeared on the TV screen, and the letters being presented on *Sesame Street.* His mother, a former kindergarten teacher, devised a daily routine in which she removed the reading material, turned off the TV, got down on the floor with her son, and gently involved him in more appropriate play and interaction. She focused especially on symbolic play (for example, pretending that toy cars are going somewhere instead of repetitively lining them up). After several months she began to notice changes in his behavior, which also showed up at his preschool. "Whatever you're doing, keep it up," the teacher said.

Charles is now in college, having graduated from special education in elementary school and eventually a gifted program at his high school. I assume he is grateful to his wise mother, who created—without knowing it—a program similar to Floor Time, which was developed by Stanley Greenspan, discussed later in this chapter, and is now used for children diagnosed with autistic spectrum disorders.

"Garden-Variety" Reading Disorders

Believe it or not, this term is used by researchers to describe reading difficulties that don't fit into any recognizable syndrome. Perhaps the most common reason for these problems is, I'm sorry to say, a lackadaisical approach to reading instruction that leaves students high and dry when they need to read quickly and accurately and to apply reading skills to serious content.

It is estimated that 10 to 20 percent of children are naturally gifted readers who will learn to read and comprehend if they are given adequate exposure to books. Another 20 percent are at high risk for a disability unless they receive specialized, targeted instruction by well-trained teachers. The remaining 60 percent or so are not at special risk, but may develop reading problems unless they receive an adequate language environment at home and good instruction at school.

"We have learned that for 90 percent to 95 percent of poor readers, prevention and early intervention programs that combine instruction in phoneme awareness, phonics, fluency development, and reading comprehension strategies, provided by well-trained teachers, can increase reading skills to average reading levels," asserts Reid Lyon, chair of the National Reading Panel.[9] At the New York City Department of Education, Linda Wernikoff, executive director of the Office of Special Education Initiatives, is making this plan work—even in schools serving disadvantaged at-risk children. Dr. Wernikoff positively glowed—even at the end of a long workday—as she told me about the success of a pilot program using research-based techniques that help identify and prevent problems before they materialize.[10]

Home Environments + Effective Schools = The Magic Combo. With our growing understanding of how children learn to read and what they need in the way of teaching, we should be able to teach almost anyone to decode words. Unfortunately, both comprehension and enjoyment of reading are not so easy to convey, especially to a generation with declining language skills and little training either in thinking deeply or managing their own attention. Reading that goes beyond simple word-calling requires language and thinking skills as well as the mental persistence to dig out the meaning from the text. Without these skills children tumble off the "third-grade cliff"—having learned to read words but not being able to understand more complex, written language.

U.S. parents invariably list reading as one of the most important things children need to learn, but many forget that skilled reading starts at home. TV and electronic amusements have a way of gobbling up family time and encroaching on conversation and sustained thought—even in households where parents fully expect their children to be successful at a good college. If a child is language-deficient, he is almost sure to be reading-deficient unless he receives special help.

> Parents and policy makers, please take note: literacy skills start at home. Don't expect the school always to patch up the products of literacy-poor environments.

Pervasive Developmental Disorder (PDD) (The Autistic Spectrum): Autism, Asperger's Syndrome

Autism

What Is It? Autism is a brain-based disorder involving abnormalities in social interaction and communication, sensory regulation and behavioral interests. This means that autistic children show

- delays in understanding and use of language

- unusual sensitivity to sensory stimuli (e.g., vacuum cleaner, cell phone ring, textures and tastes)

- resistance to change and insistence on routines

- intense focus on a limited range of interests and activities

- difficulties with typical social interactions, including "joint attention" (e.g., looking at a book or toy along with a parent)

Autism usually shows up before age three, and symptoms may be noticed by twelve to eighteen months of age. Boys are up to four times as likely to be affected as girls. Early identification is critical, as intensive treatment by a multidisciplinary team of professionals greatly improves children's outcomes. If you have any concerns about your child, insist on a thorough evaluation by your pediatrician, who should have access to a questionnaire about specific symptoms, such as the Checklist for Autism in Toddlers (CHAT; some versions are also available online). Books such as *Could It Be Autism?: A Parent's Guide to the First Signs and Next Steps* by Nancy Wiseman, and the Web sites listed in Appendix D are also useful.

One specific human talent that is notably deficient in autistic syndrome disorders (ASD) is called *theory of mind* or *intersubjectivity*. It involves being able (a) to understand that other people have minds and feelings, and (b) to be able to empathize or relate to the other person's point of view. I never really understood what this meant until one day when I was asked to help on a reading assignment with a seventh-grader who had been diagnosed with high-functioning autism. We were seated across from each other at a library table, with only one book to share between us.

"I've never seen your textbook before, so we'll both need to read these questions," I suggested, "and then we'll discuss them."

"Okay," replied Mike, picking up the book and beginning to read to himself. He seemed unaware that the way he was holding the book meant I could not see the page. I decided to wait and see what would happen next.

Mike finished reading and looked up expectantly. "Now we discuss," he said.

"Mike, do you think I read that page, too?" I asked.

"Yes," he replied, obviously puzzled.

Researchers, too, have been puzzled and intrigued about this enigmatic condition, which can confer exceptional talent as well as

disability. Dr. Temple Grandin is both autistic and a highly successful university professor and author noted for her original work in
designing humane environments for livestock. Her books, such as
The Way I See It: A Personal Look at Autism and Asperger's, document her own experience of learning to cope effectively in a "neurotypical" world.

Where Does It Come From? Autism has a strong genetic component,
although experts agree that environmental factors are also involved, possibly in the degree to which the underlying condition
expresses itself. One of my students with Asperger's syndrome had
a relative who was described by his neighbors as "the stone guest"
because of his inability to relate to others socially. Although this
gentleman never received a diagnosis and was a successful accountant, we could speculate that he was also "on the spectrum." You
will read more about the genetics of autism in Chapter 7, "Genes,
Learning, and the Environment." You will also learn that several
different genes are probably involved, and the degree to which genes
become active, or express themselves, has a lot to do with environmental factors.

"Expression of these genes [for autism] seems to be dependent
on early experience, which may account for the appearance of autistic symptoms toward the end of the first year of life. These symptoms in social communication are critically dependent on social
experiences during this period of development," explains Brown
University researcher Helen Tager-Flusberg.[11]

The autistic spectrum is broad and getting broader as more
children who previously would have been considered simply "difficult" are reclassified as having some type of pervasive developmental disorder. Naturally, expanding a diagnostic category results in
a rising incidence of cases, but the recent "epidemic" of cases may
also involve any number of variables that influence the growing
brain after birth. You can stay in touch with current information through books and Web sites, including the Autism Society of
America.

Autism overlaps with numerous other conditions, including problems of attention, language, coordination, and various syndromes,
including Tourette's, which is a developmental disability usually
characterized by involuntary "tics" (physical or verbal spasms). A

skilled diagnostic evaluation is essential for ferreting out the whole picture.

What Do We Do? A comprehensive 2008 report on the efficacy of treatments for autism concluded that several approaches are promising, although not enough evidence has been collected to prove positive effects.[12] As mentioned above, early identification and a multidisciplinary approach are critical. In a recent conference presentation, Temple Grandin recalled her own experience as a young child with her devoted nanny, who spent hours a day of "face time" with the little girl, expertly encouraging her to play simple interactive games (e.g., hiding objects, patty cake, peekaboo), and working up to board games and card games.[13] Meanwhile, she focused on teaching language and social skills, which Dr. Grandin believes have been especially important to her success. "I was lucky to be a child in the fifties," she comments dryly. "The adults insisted on good manners in structured social situations. Lack of structure is bad for people like me."

Dr. Grandin acknowledges the difficulty of living in a world set up for people whose brains process information differently from hers. Excessive sensitivity to sensory stimulation, for example, causes big problems in a noisy, unpredictable setting overloaded with input that an autistic individual is unable to screen out. Even the flicker of fluorescent lights is troubling. "Ask a parent what happens when you go to Walmart," she suggests. "The child with autism has a screaming fit. Or maybe he sees a cell phone and has a fit because he doesn't know when it's going to ring. Surprises are scary."

Dr. Grandin attended a special school where she received expert help. "I can't emphasize enough the importance of a good teacher," she states. Clearly, this eminent scholar has capitalized on an unusually supportive early environment not only in learning to deal with her own unique learning abilities but also in becoming a powerful spokesperson for "different" brains.

Two major therapeutic methods, based on divergent underlying philosophies, are promising approaches to treatment for autistic spectrum disorders. They are Applied Behavior Analysis (ABA) and Floor Time, developed by Stanley Greenspan, a child psychiatrist.

ABA is a method based on stimulus-response conditioning. There are many specific programs under a variety of names that use the principles of ABA. I just happened to have a conversation this week with a mother whose daughter had experienced a recent success in one of them.

First, the therapist identified a specific problem area: *Cassie is unresponsive when her mother enters the room,* then analyzed what behaviors were needed and selected a specific behavioral goal: *Cassie will say "Hi, Mom" when her mother enters.*

The therapist then modeled the behavior, rewarded Cassie when she responded appropriately, and Cassie practiced the behavior until it became automatic. Eventually, she will also learn to generalize to other people's names when appropriate.

You can probably understand why this mom had tears in her eyes after her five-year-old daughter greeted her by name for the first time, as well as why these parents are big fans of ABA training. Many parents are grateful for the progress their children have made with ABA, and research has demonstrated effectiveness with some children.[14]

Greenspan's work looks at a bigger picture, focusing more on emotional relatedness, which he views as the foundation of all learning. "Normal" emotional closeness or understanding the feelings of another person are major problems for individuals with autism, so parents and therapists are taught specific techniques to unblock those channels. In this "floor time" adults learn how to engage children in interactive play and entice them into relating interpersonally. Gradually, these techniques enable development of more complex skills—including more advanced intellectual ones.

I was privileged to meet with Dr. Greenspan while he was preparing his book about floor time, *Engaging Autism*. He told me he believes many types of learning problems may be helped by increasing the emotional connectedness in children's lives. He is deeply concerned about the depersonalized quality of even "good" early child care settings. Add in lifestyle habits that crowd out warm human interaction and a mechanized, tech-oriented approach to child development and education that excludes the "human touch," and you have a contemporary recipe for problems, he insists.[15]

A Startling Question About Rising Rates of Autism

What gets lost when we allow electronic appliances to rear our children?[16] Are infants habituated to electronic voices instead of personally responsive human ones more at risk for autism? Could dormant genetic tendencies be activated by a shortage of "face time" with caregivers who fail to respond directly to the child's signals?

As in reading problems, there can be many different routes in the brain that lead to one group of symptoms, such as those of autism. In addition to the many potential "triggers" currently under investigation, here is one possibility over which parents definitely have some control.

Brain areas for social/emotional competence begin to form their lifelong connections as soon as a baby is born, and *contingent response* is the most critical factor in their successful development. What this phrase means is that caregivers need to pay attention to children's "signals" and respond quickly, appropriately ("contingently") and affectionately to their needs (i.e., *"I'm wet and uncomfortable," "I wonder what your nose will feel like if I grab it," "I feel like cooing and crowing and I would love to have you coo and crow back to me"*). Yet even "advantaged" children don't always get sufficient amounts of contingent response if caregivers—parents or otherwise—are overstressed, unskilled, or undermotivated.

Research suggests why contingent response is so important to the developing brain. The right *orbitofrontal cortex*, an area behind the forehead, links brain areas responsible for emotion to centers for reasoning and is a key player in normal interpersonal responding. This group of brain connections also enables us to be flexible and to adapt our behavior to the demands of changing situations. In his comprehensive book *The Developing Mind*, Daniel Siegel summarizes research that suggests how important early environments are for full development of the orbitofrontal cortex. Most critical are appropriate interpersonal interactions at young ages. He is particularly concerned about "insecure attachment in which the parent does not focus on the mental states of the child and in which parental states are intrusive or disorganizing."[17] Gentle, reassuring touch and love are the ideal.

There is absolutely no way that any electronic gadget—no matter how advanced—can provide this incredibly valuable stimulus for normal brain development. Yet the modern-day nursery is loaded with new technologies that co-opt young children's time and attention: infant videos; electronic music soothing babies to sleep; beeping, flashing toys that "capture" the child's brain but screen out human language. These technologies also substitute for the work of patient caregivers who hold, rock, cuddle, sing, soothe, dandle, play interactively, and respond instinctively to a child's immediate needs. *No manufactured item can substitute for human warmth.* Despite advertising claims, electronics are not truly "interactive" and, obviously, possess no "theory of mind" or ability to empathize. Could this unbalanced experience distort genetically vulnerable brain circuits that mediate lifelong personal relationships and social understanding? No answers are available to this question.

As you will see in Chapter 5, "Rewiring Children's Brains," extreme emotional deprivation, such as occurred in some Romanian orphanages, can retard brain development to the point where an acquired form of autism develops. But what about much milder forms of deprivation that masquerade as "enrichment"—such as can be found in a very high-tech, low-touch environment?[18]

If a child is already at genetic risk for autism spectrum disorder, can being "raised by appliances" push him over the edge? As he spends formative hours relating to screen images that cannot relate back to him, will he miss out on developing that all-important sense of self that leads to intersubjectivity?

> A very high-tech, low-touch nursery is a deprived environment masquerading as "enrichment." What are its consequences?

No one is going to claim that either inept parenting or media use by itself will make children autistic. The long-dead theory that emotionally cold "refrigerator mothers" are the cause of autism is both preposterous and cruel. Most parents create nursery environments with loving care and the best of intentions. They need solid, unbiased research—not advertising claims—to help them determine what will be good for their children's minds. Meanwhile, you might pull the plug on the electronic companions and concentrate on providing your child with real human (and humanizing) environments instead.

Asperger's Syndrome

I'm not really sure which child was my first Asperger-type student. Was it Doreen, in my very first year of teaching, who never looked up or spoke a word from her habitual seat, avoiding eye contact as she slouched in the back row of seventh-grade English? I worried about her all year, but in those days I knew essentially nothing and had nowhere to go for help. Or maybe it was many years later as David, who dazzled everyone with his advanced verbal skills, set our prekindergarten endlessly on edge with his tantrums, obsession with the computer, and exceptional clumsiness with scissors or crayons. Or Elissa, the beautiful, "weird" little girl who tantalized us with her brilliance and the vocabulary development of a Ph.D. while exasperating us with her unpredictable classroom behavior and apparent absence of concern for other children's feelings. And then there was Grant, who could barely hold a pencil and was not completely potty-trained when he was six but was solving complex algebraic equations before he was ten.

Fascinating, puzzling, and talented kids! Important research, even within the last few years, has clarified not only why these children may seem "weird," but also how to reach in and tap their unique potential.

What Is It? Asperger's syndrome is notable for its contradictions— which may include extreme brilliance in some areas of development along with significant deficits in others. It is generally defined as a "high-end" variant of the autistic spectrum, although some experts believe it is a separate syndrome. The most prominent symptom is difficulty with social relationships. You may remember Marko's picture from Chapter 1—the drawing of people completely lacking either facial expression or any suggestion of body movement. Like Marko, individuals with Asperger's have difficulty "reading" facial expressions or gestures, which are aspects of communication that most of us take for granted. Their social perceptions are limited, so they are apt to blurt out the "wrong" thing or drone on about one of their own obsessions (e.g., names of dinosaurs, the *Titanic*) without noticing the other person's discomfort.

Where Does It Come From? Like other ASD conditions, Asperger's has a genetic component, which may have shown up in the extended family as social withdrawal, "oddness," or extreme shyness. Environmental factors impact its severity and outcomes. Asperger's is generally not recognized as early as is autism because language development may be average or even superior. Children with this syndrome can be very challenging, but effective intervention improves outcomes.

What Do We Do? Treatment programs for Asperger symptoms are proliferating. Most include social skills training, in which children are taught to relate and respond appropriately to others. Such programs are now available in many schools. An occupational or physical therapist may help with clumsiness or lack of coordination. A psychologist can also help the Asperger child deal with the most painful aspect of this disorder: an increasing sense of social isolation.

As with any child, no matter what their learning style, the most important element in a successful outcome is respect and acceptance for the youngster's basic nature. I recently had a poignant conversation with a mother, a psychotherapist whose son was diagnosed early with symptoms of Asperger's. She has stood staunchly by him through multiple challenges, an assortment of therapies, and, finally, a successful college career. He now has a few like-minded new friends and realistic aspirations for a Ph.D. in mathematics. His mother described to me some of her feelings about this long journey.

> "You have to ask, 'What's happening inside this kid's world that's causing him to act like this?' You have to accept that you're not going to 'cure' the kid, you're not going to make him into someone else, you are going to take the edge off his struggles. What you forget is he's coping with so much— if you can just take the edge off, it helps a lot."

> —mother of an Asperger's "success story"

As our conversation ended, this stalwart lady's lip quivered as she related a recent conversation with her son: "Thank goodness for you, Mom," he said. "You always knew I was in here."

Like every other syndrome described in this chapter, Asperger's is a complex and multifaceted condition that deserves a much fuller discussion. If you have concerns that a child in your life may be showing behaviors that fall into this diagnostic category, please check out the several useful and informative books on Asperger's syndrome in the Bibliography. The earlier you identify and get to work on these issues, the more you can help.

Sensory Processing Disorder (SPD)

What Is It? Also referred to as Clumsy Child Syndrome, Minimal Brain Dysfunction, Sensory Integration Disorder, and Developmental Dyspraxia, SPD is defined as substantial delay or deficiencies in everyday motor abilities, either fine motor (small movements) or gross motor (large movements). It may also involve either under- or overresponsiveness to sensory stimuli—vision, hearing, touch, smell, taste—as well as difficulty integrating responses to various sensory stimuli (for example, looking and listening at the same time). SPD is a controversial diagnosis, although a research initiative is attempting to clarify and document its scientific basis.[19] Numerous parents and teachers are convinced they see children afflicted with such problems who are helped by physical, occupational, or sensory integration therapies.

We need more definitive studies showing (a) that it is a syndrome separate from others, such as attention deficit disorder or autistic spectrum disorders, and (b) that therapies commonly recommended by occupational and physical therapists actually help.

Two authors who have written and lectured about SPD are Carol Kranowitz and Lucy Jane Miller. If you believe that your child is lagging in either small- or large-motor development, and/or shows abnormal response to sensory stimuli, jumpiness or attention problems related to the ability to calm oneself, you should consult their books, which are listed in the Bibliography. (As this book goes to press, new research is forthcoming, so I suggest you check out Carol's Web site: www.out-of-sync-child.com.) Children who suffer from these symptoms must exert an enormous amount of effort simply to manage their bodies, sit at a desk, and complete school assignments.

Visual problems may also be involved in some sensory processing problems, although research on visual training as a therapy for learning disabilities has thus far been unconvincing. *Behavioral optometrists* believe that visual problems lie at the heart of some learning problems. These professionals have postgraduate training in identifying and treating difficulties in eye tracking, convergence, binocular vision, or accurate form perception, deficits that are not always picked up in routine vision screening.

Where Does It Come From? The brain's widespread motor and sensory systems, like attention systems, are uniquely vulnerable to even subtle "insult" or damage before, during, or after birth. As to possible genetic causes, only one study is available, and it suggests that genetic factors may be involved.[20]

In addition, there is almost unanimous agreement among professionals in this field that children's environments today are a serious offense to the developing nervous system and its vulnerable motor components. When we return to this point in Part Three, "Childhood in the Twenty-first Century," you will see that children's sensory needs must be taken seriously if we expect children to develop healthy, well-organized, and skillful minds as well as bodies.

What Do We Do? A large number of therapies are offered by occupational and physical therapists, and absent satisfactory research on most of them, parents should be careful consumers. Most programs focus either on "process" training or on specific skill training. *Process training* tries to remediate core issues such as balance or visual efficiency. *Skill training* might include structured handwriting practice. This particular skill may seem unnecessary in an age of keyboarding, but the *multisensory* activity of guided handwriting practice makes letter shapes more automatic in the brain, firming up neural connections for spelling and reading.[21] It also gives practice in *motor planning*, one component of attention. ("Where will I start my pencil, which direction should I go, and when will I make a turn?" More about this in Chapter 12, "Successful Environments for Successful Children.")

This sort of *multisensory* experience, involving body movement and all the senses, is the child's natural means of learning. It is an important component of instructional programs for all children, but it is sorely lacking in the lives of kids today. ("Mouse skills" don't fill the bill!) Word processing can be exceptionally useful for any child, especially in the later grades, but that does not mean that it is either appropriate or necessary for young children who are still trying to become "automatic" on reading and spelling skills.

> *"I have a lot of students who simply don't know how to use their bodies! Eight-year-olds with their physical skills retarded to the level of a four-year-old. Does that cause problems? You bet!"*
>
> —occupational therapist in a suburban school district

Schools may have to adapt classroom routines to accommodate sensory problems such as fidgetiness or resistance to vigorous—and threatening—group games for a child who is physically insecure. For children with handwriting problems, reduction of the absolute amount of written work, especially homework, makes a great deal of sense, and assistive technologies such as word processing are often very helpful once reading and spelling skills are well under way.

In a unique application of the theory that sensory training helps both learning and attention, fourth-grade teacher Tifany Miller in Fort Collins, Colorado, replaced her students' chairs with balance balls.[22] After the initial excitement subsided, both she and her students were enthusiastic.

"It helps me learn," said one child. Others spoke of "being able to wiggle" when they needed to.

"I have noticed a change. I think if you asked the kids, they'll tell you they've noticed a change. . . . They enjoy sitting in their seats now," Miller said. "I don't know if it would work for other teachers, but it works for me."

Mathematics Disability:
Developmental Dyscalculia

It is unfortunate that we know much less about math disability than we do about reading, given the importance of "numeracy" in the twenty-first century and the substantial number of children (and adults) affected by such problems.

What Is It? Dyscalculia is a learning disability that usually shows up as either or both of the following: (1) problems with *calculation*, for example, mistakes in addition, long division, or other numerical operations; and/or (2) problems with understanding the *concepts* of mathematics, such as story problems, algebra, estimation.

> Some students are whiz-bang calculators, but don't "get" story problems, while others have an instinctive under-standing of math but mess up with "careless" calculation.

I have had students who were able to induce an answer as if by osmosis but couldn't write out the equation. Often they had unique methods of figuring out the problem in their heads, a pattern that may co-occur, oddly enough, both with dyslexia and with later achievement in math or science-related professions in adulthood. One eminent physicist confided to me that he met this description and was thought to be retarded in his early school years in the 1940s.

The small quantity of research available on math disability pin-points problems in *numerosity* ("number sense"). This means that the child does not have a "gut-level" understanding of the number line.

> Is 6 bigger or smaller than 8? How much difference between them?

> Quickly, tell me if each of the following numbers is larger or smaller than 65: 82, 34, 52, 99.

> Estimate: Could 1 + 3 = 8? Could 210 - 36 = 74?

Knowing how to count (recite numerals) does not mean that the child understands what numbers actually stand for, which is the abstract concept of number. This number sense is partially instinctive and partially learned, starting early in life from manipulating objects in the three-dimensional world (e.g., blocks), rolling dice and moving a counter a certain number of spaces, card games (spit, war, rummy), or real-life tasks ("We have two extra guests for dinner tonight; please put six spoons on the table"). Touching, feeling, and manipulating objects is probably the best way to internalize these abstract concepts.

> Could recent changes in children's play habits that reduce hands-on experience with quantities of objects cause problems with number sense? No definitive answers are available for this important question.

Where Does It Come From? Dyscalculia appears to be at least partially genetic, although once again environmental factors play a substantial role. Different types of math deficiencies are doubtless related to brain differences—inherited or otherwise—in various neural areas in right and left sides (hemispheres). Math calculation may depend more on left-hemisphere analytic systems, whereas math concepts, geometry, and the abstract understanding of higher math are thought to depend more on right-hemisphere spatial skills. This difference may explain why many students do well in arithmetic in early grades but "hit the wall" when they get to algebra. Mathematics learning is highly dependent on teaching; if a child has missed out on appropriate instruction, she may not truly have dyscalculia.

Math disability overlaps with reading disability, executive function disorders, including ADHD, and is one symptom of nonverbal learning disability (see p. 80). Children with dyslexia often have a generalized difficulty with all printed symbols, including numerals. They may also have trouble reading story problems accurately or setting up equations in the proper order on a written assignment. On the other hand, many dyslexics have excellent math capabilities, especially in the area of concept understanding.

Math achievement also requires a can-do approach to problem solving and a willingness to make "good" mistakes for learning. A child who is too concerned about being perfect may panic if new lessons are initially confusing.

What Do We Do? Agreement on evidence-based remediation for math disability lags far behind that for reading, and professionals even disagree about how best to teach math in the first place.[23] For young children, hands-on experiences with counting and numerical relationships are important. For older ones, a systematic teaching program that incorporates both calculation and understanding of concepts is essential.[24] Also for older students, software programs are useful for drill and practice of math "facts" and concepts. Some researchers have suggested that specialized video games (such as Tetris) could train spatial skills, but thus far there has been no evidence of carryover from video gaming to math achievement.

To establish a can-do attitude toward problem solving, avoid overly attentive parenting (i.e., not allowing the child to make mistakes) and make sure she takes responsibility for her mistakes and for solving her own problems. In later sections of this book we will return to these points with some practical suggestions.

> **TIP:** Encouraging a "can-do" attitude toward problem-solving in real-life situations can boost math achievement.

Problems with Spatial and Social Cognition: Nonverbal Learning Disability (NVLD or NLD); Social-Emotional Learning Impairment/Disorder (SELI/SELD)

What Is It? Perhaps you can tell from the variety of terms listed above that the syndrome in question can be both confused and confusing. In fact, questions have been raised as to whether it actually is a separate syndrome, since the symptoms overlap with so many other types of problems. Nonetheless, a substantial amount of research has been published, and clinicians see and treat such children, so here is a brief summary.

NVLD was first described by Byron Rourke as a "right-hemisphere" disorder, meaning that, unlike dyslexia, it is not centered in the primary language areas of the brain (thus it is a nonverbal problem—very confusing, indeed), but rather in brain areas responsible for visual and spatial perception.[25] The major symptoms include difficulties with math concepts, social skills, perceptual-motor development (e.g., delayed ability to copy geometric figures or alphabet letters) and a tendency to focus on details instead of extracting meaning from a situation. The confusing terminology in the NVLD label has resulted in some clinicians renaming it as a primarily "social-emotional" learning impairment (SELI).

These symptoms are similar to and often confused with those of Asperger's syndrome, and questions still exist as to whether they are separate conditions. I questioned Meryl Lipton, who treats children with SELI, the term she prefers, at the Rush Neurobehavioral Center in Skokie, Illinois, about the distinction. "SELI kids have trouble with understanding three things: spaces, faces, and places," she explained. Dr. Lipton was referring to spatial confusion, missing or misinterpreting facial expressions, and problems with directions. Generally speaking these students are competent "technicians"—decoding words and completing rote-level math computation effectively. But they have trouble integrating these isolated skills into a framework of meaning.

To help you understand this puzzling condition, take a look at Figure 4 on p. 82, which is a "map" of an island where the events of a story take place. My student, Shelly, then in fourth grade, had read and discussed the story with her class, after which they were asked to imagine a map of the island and draw its features to show the travels of the characters in the story. All the other children outlined the island's shape and proceeded to draw the river, town, mountains, etc., in some type of logical relationship (that is, the town in the story was on the bank of the river with the mountains behind it). Shelly, however, apparently didn't "see" these relationships; she got the details, but couldn't connect them. I still look at this picture and wonder what it must be like to live inside a mind that perceives the world in this manner.

You may have guessed that Shelly was also socially maladept ("Gee, Mrs. Healy, that new dress really makes you look fat"), but she couldn't understand why people reacted as they did.

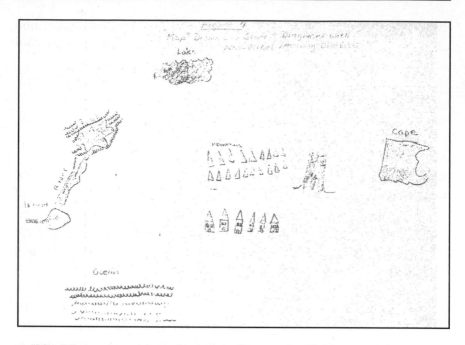

4. *"Map" drawn by a 4th-grade student diagnosed with Nonverbal Learning Disability: Although technical details are precise, this imaginary island lacks an overall outline and its features are unrelated to each other (e.g., in the story, the village is located on the river, which runs into the ocean). This student had difficulty understanding the "big picture" in reading comprehension and social relationships.*

Where Does It Come From? No definitive research is available on either hereditary or environmental factors in this syndrome. It may be one of the few disorders that has a larger prevalence in females. I have seen at least two cases in which it appeared that the acorn (daughter) had not fallen far from the tree (mother). But anecdotes don't make science and lots more research is needed.

What Do We Do? As with any pervasive difficulty, it does not matter so much what we call it as what we do about it, since effective help at home and remediation at school can change even inborn brain tendencies. Social skills training should be a first order of remediation. I strongly recommend the work of Richard Lavoie, who has been a headmaster of a school for learning disordered students. His book *It's So Much Work to Be Your Friend* is a practical guide to social skills and how to improve them. In addition, a specially trained teacher or tutor should be able to help improve math skills and reading comprehension.

Executive Function Disorder, Attention Problems (ADD, ADHD), and Organization Problems

Executive function is a term that has only recently moved outside neuroscience and into education. It describes a constellation of problems involving self-control and self-monitoring, the most well known of which are attention disorders. We will cover the development and of the "executive" systems of the brain as well as how to improve their functioning in later chapters.

What Is It? Most executive function difficulties are diagnosed as *Attention deficit disorder*, now generally referred to as ADD or, more often, ADHD (attention deficit disorder with or without hyperactivity). It is controversial, and experts disagree about whether ADD and ADHD are even the same disorder. (To simplify this description, I am using the term *ADHD* here to refer to this whole spectrum of diagnosis.) No scientific or medical tests are approved to diagnose attention deficit disorder, and thus far no specific genetic or neurological cause has been agreed on. (Even if we find brain differences, that does not prove they caused the problem, since different types of experience might be responsible for both the child's behavior and the related brain differences.) Extreme environmental "insults" (e.g., lead or other toxic exposure, prenatal alcohol, smoking or drug use) can create the condition, but many children display symptoms with no discernible cause. In Chapter 7, "Genes, Learning, and the Environment," you will learn about research implicating specific genes that may be involved, although early environments have a great deal to do with how—or even whether—these particular genes play their roles.

The most common treatment for problems diagnosed as attention disorders is psychoactive drugs, meaning they act directly to change brain chemistry. Chapter 6, "How Your Child's Brain Works," explains how these drugs work and why they are so controversial.

Mountains of research have examined what is really wrong and how best to treat children who

- "can't" pay attention

- act "hyper"

- have trouble following rules or anticipating consequences

- are just plain difficult to raise and teach

One theory asserts that ADHD is not actually an attention *deficit*, but rather a problem in *controlling attention*, caused by an underaroused brain. In this theory the brain can't focus to direct brainpower appropriately, which may be why stimulant drugs alleviate symptoms. For many children, the main problem is impulsivity—difficulty with stopping and thinking before acting. The three major diagnostic categories are *inattentive*, *impulsive*, or *combined* (inattentive plus impulsive).

Diagnosis is done on the basis of questionnaires about a child's behavior at home and at school. Symptoms—most of which are characteristic of all children at some time in their lives—should show up before age seven, must have been present for at least two years, and must occur in more than one situation (i.e., home and school). Because of the growing prevalence of this diagnosis, hundreds of books, articles, and Web sites describe both symptoms and a variety of treatments. As always, caution and careful research are advised. Much of the available research has been financed by the pharmaceutical industry, which naturally has an interest in promoting both the disorder and its medications.

There is no question that this type of youngster can be challenging. Nonetheless, questions have been raised about (1) whether some ADHD kids are actually extraenergetic, spontaneous, creative, multitasking, often very bright, and possibly underdisciplined normal children; (2) how much this condition is caused or worsened by environmental factors such as parenting style or classroom demands that are out of line with children's natural abilities and needs; and (3) whether common treatment methods involving psychoactive drugs are the most appropriate or desirable therapy. These medications are *cognitive enhancers* that would sharpen almost anyone's learning abilities. On the other hand, focused approaches and therapies that do not involve medication also show promise, although they have received far less research funding. We will return to these possibilities throughout this book.

Edward M. Hallowell, noted author of *Superparenting for ADD*, is a wise physician-expert who believes that he and one of his sons both fall into the attention deficit category. Dr. Hallowell advocates a commonsense and balanced approach: he prescribes medication when he feels it is needed, and he also champions the importance of lifestyle management. Most important of all, however, is uncompromised love. When I e-mailed to ask about his view on how important common environmental factors are in the disorder, he replied at once:

"These kids have enormous gifts. They can be hard to unwrap, but that's why they need parents and teachers and coaches. Yes, exercise, nutrition, sleep matter a lot. They need a lot of positive human connection and not too much electronic connection."[26]

Executive function disorder is a more general term, which incorporates problems in planning, organization, study skills, self-control, and self-monitoring/self-checking skills. It obviously overlaps with or is a feature of many other types of learning problems and is a useful diagnosis only if specific recommendations for treatment are part of the package. Specific skills that may be helped by treatment are planning, adapting to new situations, time management, and maintaining and controlling attention.

As just one example of how important these executive self-management skills are, one study found that a five-minute test of them predicted kindergarteners' math gains for the year. The children played a game, "Head-Toes-Knees-Shoulders," in which a leader calls out a direction, such as "Touch your head" and the children respond with the *opposite* movement (i.e., they touch their toes). The children who were best at the game also ended the year with the highest math scores.

How could this game predict math achievement? It requires the child to inhibit a dominant impulse (touching the body part named) and use mental management skills to plan and control his movements—examples of the workings of executive brain centers that also help with math learning. Other games such as "Red light, green light" or "Simon says" call on similar combinations of motor planning and mental management skills. Unfortunately, many children today don't get much chance to practice these critical control functions—which some might term "mental discipline"—either at home or at school. We will return to this topic frequently throughout the book.

> Note to teachers of young children: Do your students' executive systems a favor by making sure this sort of brain-strengthening "play" is part of the curriculum. The brain's executive systems are close next-door neighbors to areas that organize and manage complex physical movements. But be patient. These networks take a long time to mature fully!

Where Does It Come From? Some people come into the world with a genetic profile that puts them at extra risk for attention and other self-management problems. This is not a simple case of one gene causing a certain behavior, however, because multiple combinations of genes are doubtless involved, complicated by their interactions among themselves and with multiple variables in the environment (Chapter 7, "Genes, Learning, and the Environment," provides a more thorough explanation of this interaction). As just one example of an environmental variable, the American Medical Association reports that there is a "dose-related effect of early television viewing on risk for ADHD," meaning that the more the child watches, the more likely he is to be diagnosed with ADHD later.[27]

Neuroscientist Adele Diamond has studied the development of executive function in children's brains, and she is sold on the power of the environment to either teach or erode these important skills of self-restraint and self-management. "I think a lot of kids get diagnosed with ADHD now, not all but many just because they never learned how to exercise self-control, self-regulation, the executive functions early," she remarked in a National Public Radio report.[28] Curiously enough, one reason may be a decline in another type of children's play: the unstructured, imaginative kind in which they have to rely on themselves for planning and executing their improvisations. This kind of play naturally provides good exercise for developing brains—especially systems for controlling emotions, resisting impulses, and exerting self-discipline. Dr. Diamond believes that even older children can benefit from creative play. "You need games that require children to stop and think," she says, "and I have not seen any [video games] like that."

In addition, there's a "whopping interaction" between parenting style and children's development of self-control, Michael Posner recently told a large audience of neuropsychologists.[29] Dr. Posner is developing training programs that help children learn to manage their attention; he and others are also finding that parents can learn techniques for developing their children's executive skills. You will learn more about these programs throughout this book.

While no one would reasonably insist that any one factor *causes* most attention disorders, today's children suffer multiple environmental brain assaults—inadequate sleep, excess stress, toxins, too much media, inadequate exercise, and a disorganized or emotionally stressful home life, not to mention schools structured to accommodate only calm, well-behaved, and extraordinarily advanced children who can sit all day at a desk and maintain adult-level learning habits. Inept and unresponsive parenting or caregiving is simply one of many factors.

Clearly, many risk factors—including genetic ones—are involved in executive function disorders. Impulsivity, or "stimulus-bound" behavior—the tendency to respond to every available stimulus (grab, touch, get distracted by sights or sounds, and so on) is characteristic of very young children, but most youngsters outgrow and learn to manage it, usually with patient and firm guidance from adults.

> Self-control is a learned skill, and it is more easily learned by some brains than by others.

In a society where adults don't have enough time to teach or model self-management and control, where media use trains brains to be impulsive, and where schools push subject matter but neglect these important mental habits, increasing diagnoses of ADHD should not be surprising.

What Do We Do? This topic is so complex, so muddied by political/financial concerns, and so important that your first step should be to consult one or more of the books in the Bibliography, all of which are well researched, objective, and untainted by ties to pharmaceutical interests. Choosing an effective treatment depends on multiple factors, which differ in each case. Effective treatment is not a piecemeal approach of simply administering a pill; it must also involve the child's entire environment.

Present — but Absent

Rarely in my clinical practice have I come across a child whose learning problems are associated with "brainstorms," which are, unfortunately, very different from those that spark sudden bursts of creativity. Instead, these children suffer from a subtle form of epilepsy called petit mal or absence (pronounced ab-*sahns*) seizure disorder, in which recurrent mini–electrical storms in the brain short-circuit thinking and even conscious awareness. The child himself is not aware of seizures, and because he never loses consciousness or displays any of the dramatic symptoms associated with full-blown epileptic seizures, the problem is all too often missed— not only by parents, but also by teachers and even school psychologists. In most cases, the child's intermittent attention is blamed either on laziness or on an attention deficit disorder.

My first such diagnosis was with an eleven-year-old boy who had completely baffled his teachers, his parents, and his coaches with his inconsistent and "flaky" behavior. No one doubted that Liam was smart, but no matter what was tried—punishment, tutoring, promised rewards, goal-setting, memory exercises, you name it— and despite Liam's earnest pleas that he really was trying his best, nothing seemed to work. Over the years, Liam had been labeled with

- an attention problem
- a memory problem
- a motivation problem
- "spaciness"
- carelessness
- allergies

Once, after Liam had been playing with his older sister, she told their mother, "Mom, there's something wrong. Liam just spaces out so much!"

Like most parents, however, Liam's mother had no idea that such a problem could represent a serious brain disorder and put aside the comment. Thus, no formal diagnostic work was done.

When I finally saw Liam for a psychoeducational evaluation at age eleven, his fine thinking and reasoning skills were immediately obvious, along with his winning boyish personality. Liam seemed to be doing his best on all the tasks I gave him, but he was, indeed, strangely inconsistent. Several times he seemed to "leave" me mentally, snapping back with a slight start and just a hint of bewilderment. In a one-on-one testing situation, the psychologist is very closely involved with a child's every reaction, and there was definitely something strange about Liam's responses.

As it was my first case of this sort, I must admit to having serious jitters as I later presented the testing results to Liam's parents, along with a recommendation that they have him evaluated by a pediatric neurologist.

"So you think something is wrong with the wiring of my son's brain?" gulped Dad. "This sounds really serious!"

I explained that Liam obviously had a very good brain, but if he did have petit mal, the culprit was the brain's electrical system briefly and periodically short-circuiting and disconnecting Liam from awareness of what was going on around him. Such episodes, lasting perhaps three to four seconds, might be occurring as often as several hundred times a day without anyone being aware of it because Liam would still be sitting up with his eyes open. Even Liam himself would not be aware of the gaps in his experience. Meanwhile, of course, he would be missing a lot of what was going on, and would naturally appear inattentive. Moreover, these brief but repeated lapses could cause Liam to respond inappropriately because he had missed important instructions and social cues, like gestures or facial expressions.

Liam's parents immediately called their pediatrician and got a referral to a pediatric neurologist, who tested his brain responses with an EEG (electroencephalogram). This painless procedure involves placing a fitted cap on the child's head; the cap contains connection nodes that record patterns of brain electrical activity over different parts of the skull. Indeed, Liam's brain was experiencing periodic storms, and he was diagnosed with petit mal epilepsy. Fortunately, many medications are available to normalize such conditions, and, with the right prescription and a tutor's help, Liam set about catching up with a great deal of missed experience. Several years later, the doctor suggested it might be time to stop taking the medication, which he did, and he successfully finished school on schedule. Some children seem to outgrow the condition; others do not, for no clear reason.

Liam is now a successful businessman with a wife and two daughters—neither of whom has shown any similar problems, although their parents are naturally watchful. Yet Liam's mother is still haunted by the stress of those years before they understood Liam's problem.

"It was just awful," she told me recently. "He was always being scolded. He had this one horrible teacher who kept making huge red X's all over his paper. Poor kid! If only we had known."

According to neurologists who see many such problems, this form of epilepsy is very often not identified and is frequently mistaken for ADHD.[30] Before any child is diagnosed and medicated for an attention or behavior problem, epilepsy of any sort should be ruled out. More obvious seizure disorders may begin earlier or later, but petit mal generally develops after age four, and not after age eight. As in Liam's case, however, it may not be diagnosed until later. Here are some warning signs:

- hyperactivity or attention problems
- unexplained language problems or regression after developing language skills
- learning and memory difficulties
- child stopping what he is doing, spaces out, comes back with a start
- repetitive physical behaviors (e.g., walking in circles) or frequent inappropriate behavior (e.g., giggling uncontrollably without any reason)
- frequent and unexplained confusion; acting bewildered
- often asking repetitive questions

Please remember, this is not a common condition: all forms of epilepsy combined affect only about 1 percent of children. If your child shows some of these symptoms, there is no need to panic, but you should definitely consult your pediatrician. Even bad news is good news if it helps a child overcome a serious and frustrating condition.

In the following section we will investigate why and how learning problems arise. We will look at how a child's brain develops, how brain differences relate to learning difference, and how a child's genes contribute to intelligence, learning styles, and learning problems. Above all, you will see how important and powerful your help can be. First, we'll turn to the source of all learning: your child's developing brain.

PART TWO

Your

Unique

Child

CHAPTER 4

Brain Differences
and Learning Differences

*"If I had known when I was seven that my brain
was okay, it would have changed my life."*
—adult with dyslexia

When studying the brain became all the rage back in the nineteenth century, scientists performing autopsies on human brains were astonished and confused by the variety of sizes and shapes they found. Another surprise was that "bigger" didn't always equal "better."

Scientists today realize that brain differences among individuals present the most interesting—and potentially useful—research challenges. Their studies are helping explain why some people learn some things more easily or differently from others.

In this chapter we will consider *structural differences*: how brain parts are arranged and how different types of cells carry out the many tasks involved in thinking and remembering. The differences between the right and left sides of the brain have gotten a lot of attention, but you probably haven't heard as much about equally important developments including newly discovered varieties of neurons, a better understanding of how brain cells communicate, and data on what makes brains "intelligent." And finally there's the big question about the "other difference" between boys and girls—their brains.

Quick Take: Building Brains for Learning

1. Helping your child build a strong brain starts even before conception. Wise parents inform themselves and take sensible steps to prepare for and guard their child's brain before birth.

2. During prenatal life, brain cells become arranged into areas with specialized jobs. This is only a "rough draft" of the brain, however, as experience immediately begins to connect these areas into a massive system of networks throughout the brain.

3. The three-dimensional architecture of the brain can be viewed and described from several different perspectives, which relate to learning differences. For example, side-to-side differences between the right and left hemispheres are important in determining a child's best methods of learning.

4. The top front of the brain behind the forehead is called the *frontal lobe*; it includes the *prefrontal cortex*. These areas are key control centers for learning and behavior and have been implicated in attention and "executive" problems.

5. Intelligence and academic achievement depend on "connectivity"—how well developing brain circuits have strengthened through being used. Certain types of cells, called *white matter*, are especially important for connectivity. They may be responsive to environmental stimulation.

6. The quality of connectivity holds the key to many learning disorders as well as to creative accomplishment. Parents and teachers can help children achieve strong connectivity.

7. New findings about "mirror neurons" may hold clues to autism and other learning disorders. *Magno* and *parvo* cells may determine how quickly or slowly we process information.

8. Overall, the brains of boys and girls develop in different ways and on a different schedule. Boys may be at a disadvantage and may have unnecessary problems in primary classrooms. Girls' higher-level learning skills may be compromised by too many gender-specific toys and expectations.

Brain Architecture: Imagine 100 Trillion Connections!

Even children with multiple advantages can be relatively disadvantaged in the basics of healthy brain development. Let's consider some necessities for assembling a strong learning brain.

A newborn's brain is equipped with massive learning potential, but most circuits aren't yet wired up. The human brain contains something on the order of 100 billion cells, which can connect and reconnect in trillions of ways and at speeds that dazzle the imagination. Genetics provide the initial outline, but even before birth the child's experiences start rearranging the brain's circuits for thinking.

In Training for Brain-Building

It's exciting to fix up and equip a space for your baby's nursery, but far more important is the prenatal space in which your baby will develop the foundations for a life of healthy learning. The fetal brain starts as a tiny tube from which cells are produced, multiply, and migrate out to form the brain's basic structure. This amazingly complex process follows a genetic program, but even in the first days of pregnancy the brain is vulnerable to environmental forces.

> Savvy parents get "in training" by making needed lifestyle changes and getting help for their treatable problems before considering pregnancy.[1]

Nutrition, drug use, or general physical condition of parents may impact the egg or sperm and thus the growth of your infant's brain, not to mention your own comfort for the foreseeable future. Smart women seek out the best current information, such as Lise Eliot's comprehensive book *What's Going on in There?*.[2] A prepregnancy checkup can reveal certain deficiencies, such as in *folic acid*, which can be easily remedied, but is likely to cause birth defects if not treated. Mom's *thyroid levels* should also be checked prepregnancy, as a deficiency here may predispose your child to certain types of learning disabilities.[3] It is, of course, also important to seek treatment for any damaging habits such as substance abuse, smoking, or eating disorders.

Obesity multiplies risk factors. An expectant mother with a tendency toward diabetes must consult seriously with her doctor about keeping her blood sugar under control. New research indicates that *high levels of maternal blood sugar* may translate into an iron deficiency in the developing infant, creating later memory problems and other types of learning disabilities.[4] Your doctor or midwife are your best resources for updated information about current research as well as advice about other dietary and lifestyle measures to take.

Toxins (reviewed in Chapter 10, "Brain-Cleaning 101"), infectious agents, alcohol consumption, and some medications can be hazardous. The type of problem depends on the dosage and timing of the exposure. *Lead or other heavy metal* exposure at any point in pregnancy has been linked to learning and attention disorders. One significant but often preventable cause of later learning disabilities is *prematurity*, with women who carry multiples or lack adequate prenatal care at special risk.

"Why Was I So Stupid?" Sometimes in my job I feel that I'm in over my head. Such was the case when the mother of a child named April bared her soul to me one afternoon.

April was one of those puzzling students who definitely fell into the "difficult" category. Inconsistent, fidgety, and with an explosive temper, she was bright but had real trouble concentrating and remembering what she had learned. Worst of all, this little girl seemed really unhappy with herself. As her teachers and I puzzled over how to help her, April's mother requested a private conference. With my office door closed, she tearfully told me she thought I should know that she had been "careless" during her pregnancy with both alcohol and drugs.

"I want you to know this because it might help you work with April," she said. "I blame myself so much. When April was real little, I used to sit downstairs at night and listen to her rocking and banging in her crib—I couldn't comfort her and she just went on and on until she had big bruises on her forehead, and she wore all the skin off her little knees . . . and I'd think, why was I so stupid? That poor kid is paying for my mistakes. Is there any way to help her?"

Research suggests that intensive remedial efforts after birth in a nurturing, stimulating, and well-regulated environment may mitigate but not reverse some of the damage done by prenatal substance abuse. This situation is one where "Better safe than sorry" applies big time.

> "I know that too much stress can harm my baby's brain, but reading about all this stuff is stressing me out!"

The Fine Line. There's a fine line between being too casual and too uptight about pregnancy. With so many alarming possibilities, it's easy to feel overwhelmed and guilty about even small details. Fortunately your baby's brain is remarkably resilient, containing extra cells to buffer it against many types of injury. Once you have taken reasonable precautions, it's sensible to keep your own stress and anxiety levels under control. As one of the more jumpy types myself, I realize that it is easy to tell someone to "calm down" but very hard to do it if you're the one who is stressed out. Fortunately, a wealth of nonpharmaceutical remedies can be effective. Relaxation, gentle body and breath exercises, walking, listening to relaxing music, meditation, or prayer should probably be prescribed for every expectant mother. For the highly anxious, a psychologist may be helpful for changing negative underlying thought patterns. Such steps are important, as the fallout from your anxiety may affect your child. Studies have shown that the fetus of a highly stressed or depressed mother reacts to her stress levels with such changes as increased heart rate and alterations of brain chemicals, which can predispose the child to both physical and mental disorders.[5] A stressed infant is also *at greater risk of developing learning and behavior problems—most notably, attention deficits.* On the other hand, calm, nurturing maternal care after birth may buffer an infant's inborn tendencies to be jumpy and anxious by keeping "bad genes" from being activated. (We will return to this important topic in Chapter 7.)

One brain-affecting hormone that automatically improves your nurturing skills after your baby is born is *oxytocin*, which is responsible for regulating labor and the secretion of breast milk as well as motivating appropriate care of the newborn infant. Oxytocin secretion appears to be influenced both by genetics and by environmental factors such as stress, so this is another reason to work on keeping stress levels within healthy limits. In a recent study, new rat mothers lacking a gene for the secretion of oxytocin related abnormally to their offspring, even to the point of ignoring or neglecting them. The authors considered this finding particularly interesting because of a suspected relationship in humans between maternal oxytocin deficiency and the child's risk for autism.[6] While it is impossible to draw any conclusions from such a study, we have here one more hint about the importance of good prenatal care and counseling.

"Prenatal care is an optimal time to do mental health screening, but we don't," explains Catherine Monk of the Columbia University psychiatry department. "We could be intervening earlier," she believes.[7] Clearly, it is a good idea to try to get your own act together before bringing in any more main characters.

One calming note on this subject: like almost every mother, I harbor my own share of guilt about the things I didn't know and the mistakes I made when I was pregnant. Brain research is reassuring in its clear message that what you do after your baby is born can patch up a great many errors. It's much better to focus on doing things as well as you can with a positive outlook (and professional help, if needed) than to add your own stress and anxiety to your child's brain load.

Mommy Brains Get Smarter

As the hardware for your baby's intelligence develops in the womb, there's a good chance your brain cells are also improving. In studies thus far conducted mostly on mother rats, the combination of hormones that bathe the brain as a function of pregnancy and labor seem to "remap" the cortex and equip it to deal more efficiently with the challenges of raising a child. The stereotype of "Jell-O-brain" in new mothers probably comes more from fatigue and nerves than from loss of thinking skills, researchers assert.[8] Women who feel confident in their changing roles are most likely to show benefits—and perhaps even list *motherhood* on their résumé as part of their intellectual enrichment.

It wouldn't be surprising if the cognitive skills of fathers involved in child rearing also benefit from the complexity of solving a variety of new and unpredictable challenges.

Mapping the Brain

Scientists use directional signals to describe the different angles from which we can view this three-dimensional organ.

Down to Up: Older and Newer

Brain areas can be thought of in roughly three groups, which go from more "primitive" functions to the most advanced forms of human thought:

1. the *brainstem* and associated regions: basic **biological functions** such as blood pressure, breathing, digestion, drives, and reflexes that keep us safe in a rapidly changing physical environment

2. the *limbic system*: **emotional response**, basic memory and motivation, rich connections to both lower and higher areas

3. the *cerebral cortex*: **thinking**, making sense of information from the senses, language, conscious behavior, complex memory, judgment, and reasoning

The brainstem and limbic areas are generally referred to as *subcortical* areas, since they lie under the cortex, which wraps and folds like a blanket over the rest of the brain. The dividing lines between these areas are not clear cut, however, because cortical and subcortical

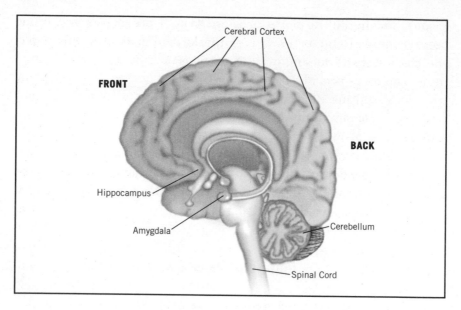

5. Mapping the Brain: Older and Newer

structures are tightly interconnected in a series of up-and-down transmission loops that can either activate or suppress brain cells' firing.

> You can't separate a child's intellectual brain from the neural areas that handle emotional and physical needs.

The more "primitive" centers in the lower brain both send and receive activation to and from the "thinking" brain. If your physical safety is threatened, your higher thinking powers may become temporarily disabled—after all, who needs to be reflecting on Proust when being chased by a tiger? On the other hand, new "cognitive" therapies, which you will read about later, help put the more rational upper regions in control of lower centers to treat attention problems or depression.

Panic Alert: Stop Thinking! In an all-too-common example of the lower centers taking control, consider a child who has trouble with math and is asked to go to the chalkboard and solve a difficult problem in front of the whole class. She knows for certain she will be teased later and perhaps even embarrassed by the teacher if she makes errors. Her overpowering anxiety is likely to mobilize those primitive brain centers to produce enough stress hormones and other danger signals to blunt her higher thinking centers. Now she can't even use what she does know, and a vicious cycle is strengthened.

> **S.O.S.!** Panic or acute embarrassment can sabotage memory and thinking.

I once observed a seventh-grade pre-algebra class in a school with a high academic rating, but whose administrators were nervous about rumors in the community that their teachers showed favoritism for boys over girls. The teacher in this particular class, a gentleman with a reputation for being "tough," obviously knew his math, but I did begin to wonder how much he knew—or cared—about seventh-grade girls, since he called mainly on a few boys who were obviously his "stars." At one point a girl tentatively raised her hand and was recognized.

"I think . . . ," she shyly began.

"I don't want 'think'!" bellowed the teacher. "Tell me what you *know!*"—at which point the child sank even farther into her chair and was not heard from again.

Plenty of books have been written about the differences between how boys and girls learn and the best ways to teach them, but the point here is that several experiences like this might readily program any student's brain to avoid math whenever possible. Ironically, the aggressive "stars" of the class probably flourished intellectually, if not personally, in such an environment—which of course is what makes being a teacher (or an administrator) such an interesting daily challenge.

We will return to the dramatic power of brain chemistry in the next chapter. For now, consider a timeworn analogy, likening the lower centers of the brain to the brains of reptiles and mammals. Indeed, their functions are roughly similar: fight, flight, survival, and basic emotional instincts. When these "primitive" brain centers are discontented, they can keep kids from paying attention, thinking, and learning.

> Unfortunately, there is plenty in today's culture to keep a child's reptilian and mammalian brains in a chronic state of upset.

The Cerebellum: Connection Central? The *cerebellum* is a large, versatile, and relatively unexplored organ at the base of the brain and the top of the spine that acts as an autopilot for timing for coordination and balance, skilled movement, language, attention, social behaviors, and higher thinking abilities. It is associated with both cortical and subcortical networks throughout the brain as well as with the *vestibular system* of the inner ear, which helps us orient our bodies in space. The vestibular system has been implicated in sensory integration and sensory processing dysfunctions. If you want to check out the working of these systems, try patting your head with one hand while you balance on one leg.

Development differences in the cerebellum may be involved in conditions as varied as autism, dyslexia, social problems, and attention disorders. We still have a lot to learn about this rather mysterious center, which has one of the longest-lasting growth curves of any part of the brain and is still maturing late into adolescence.

You may hear about *basal ganglia*, an important group of internal brain structures associated with the cerebellum. They manage voluntary movement and help put the brakes on involuntary actions. Adult Parkinson's disease, with its uncontrollable movements, is a disease of the basal ganglia.

One type of childhood strep infection, if left untreated, may cause trouble for the basal ganglia. A condition called PANDAS (pediatric autoimmune neuropsychiatric disorder) creates antibodies that attack these critical brain centers and may result in a disorder of voluntary movement (tics). Since strep infections are quite readily treated with antibiotics, pediatricians and parents should obviously be on the alert to identify and treat them promptly.

The basal ganglia are also sometimes implicated in attention deficit/hyperactivity disorders. Scientists admit that, like many brain areas, they aren't yet fully understood.

If you are getting the idea that all these areas and systems seem to overlap, you can begin to understand why it is so difficult to pin down any one part of the brain as the *cause* of a specific problem. Moreover, if the cerebellum, for example, shows up as different in several cases of autism or reading disability, how do we know whether it actually causes the problem or if its development has been affected by some other factor associated with the autism or reading problem? Nor has it been established that exercises to improve balance, for example, will directly improve a child's reading, or that auditory training with music could boost verbal listening skills.

Figuring out how to use this confusing array of information is difficult even for professionals, to say nothing of a parent trying to make sense of conflicting information and claims by therapists hawking "cures" based on inconclusive brain research. The most important priority for parents and teachers should be to identify exactly what kind of problems a child is experiencing and to implement interventions with a proven track record. The Bibliography contains multiple reliable sources to help you become an informed consumer.

The Cerebral Cortex: Many Ways of Thinking

The seven outside cell layers of our brains handle processing, understanding, and managing the data that comes in from our senses, as well as providing us with higher-level thinking skills, such as abstract reasoning, judgment, and problem solving. Let's first look at the cortex from side to side, and then review its back-to-front workings.

Half-Brained?: Two Halves, Two Ways of Thinking. You have probably heard about people being "right-brained" or "left-brained." This idea started when scientists discovered that the brain is divided into right and left halves. Each hemisphere contains the same basic structures, but they go about thinking in quite different ways.

Generally speaking, the right hemisphere prefers a visual and wholistic style, seeing systems and patterns rather than details, sizing up emotional and social situations, getting the "gist" of a conversation or story, estimating the answer to a math problem. It is referred to as a "global" processor, which I sometimes term *the lumper.* Interestingly enough, the right hemisphere has stronger connections to the emotional limbic centers than does the left.

The left hemisphere is a "local" processor, "the splitter." It grabs onto small sequential pieces of information such as sounding out or spelling a word with phonics; getting the numerals and the operations signs in the right order on an arithmetic worksheet; and analyzing the steps in a procedure, the points in an oral set of directions, an accountant's calculations, or a lawyer's argument.

The way we each balance the work of these two hemispheres (our *hemisphericity*) has a great deal to do with how we learn. For example, reading researcher Guinevere Eden describes an area in the right rear cortex called the *fusiform face area* that is specialized to recognize faces.[9] The same area in the left hemisphere becomes specialized for recognizing words.

> **TIP:** It is important to help children develop a broad repertoire of thinking skills from both sides of the brain. To simply blame a child's problems on being a "right-brainer" is overly simplistic and not very useful.

The right half of your brain controls the left half of your body and vice versa. This fact has led some to believe that left-handers (actually the category is called non–right-handers because it includes ambidexterity) tend to use a more wholistic, creative style of thinking. Researchers have yet to agree on this issue.

> Non–right-handers may be more likely either to be especially gifted in some fields (e.g., higher mathematics, arts) or to have learning disabilities—or both.

It is impossible to use only half your brain unless the other half has been surgically removed. Everything we do requires the integrated functioning of both sides, and the better they learn to work together, the better the outcome. Kids aren't half-brained, and it is important to help them develop a broad repertoire of thinking skills and flexible approaches to problem-solving.

This information has been "common knowledge" for a long time, yet new research on large and small cell types (see p. 111) might also account for some of these "learning style" differences.

One of the most interesting findings about the two hemispheres is that they have quite different emotional lives. The left hemisphere is more active when we are enthusiastically approaching something new; the right tends to be more active when we want to avoid something. Mothers who are suffering postpartum depression are heavily into their right hemispheres, and studies have shown that this can influence their infant's brain activation patterns as well.[10]

Whether people who have a more artistic, intuitive, and "global" approach to learning tend to be easily put off by negative feelings because they are more emotional than more analytic people is one interesting question that I have never seen satisfactorily answered. The corollary to that would be that more precise, detail-focused minds (such as possibly those with Asperger's syndrome) might have more difficulty getting their brains in touch with emotional intuitions. The implications of all these possibilities await further research.

Back to Front: "Smart" vs. "Wise"

Another important distinction in the brain's architecture is the difference between the back (posterior) and the front (anterior). If you have ever known someone with executive function disorder, someone who seems to be highly intelligent but completely lacking in judgment or the ability to actualize her good ideas, you will understand the difference between the posterior (back) and anterior (front) cortex. The back of the brain accumulates the information to make us smart, but only the front can make us self-controlled and wise. If you have teenagers, you can probably guess that parts of the frontal lobe are very late to mature, possibly not until age thirty!

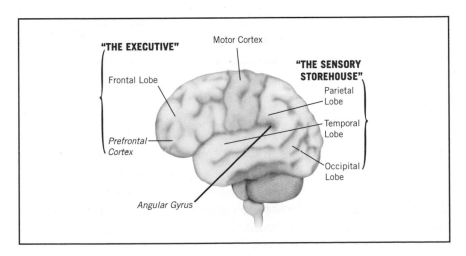

6. Front to Back: Mapping the "Thinking Brain"

The Posterior Brain: Sensory Storehouse. The back (posterior) of the cortex is like a *sensory storehouse*, where messages from the senses are received, rapidly processed into meaning ("Oops, it's hot, remove hand!"), sometimes put into words ("Ouch, Mommy, it's hot!"). Gradually, sensory stimuli become integrated with information from other senses ("My eyes and my hands remain on this chemistry experiment while I listen to what the teacher is saying"). The posterior part of the brain includes three sensory lobes, which process three kinds of information:

> *occipital:* vision

> *temporal:* auditory

> *parietal:* kinesthetic (body movement), position in space (spatial), tactile (touch)

Association Areas: Key to Good Learning. As the young child learns to use her senses, she also practices coordinating them, such as in looking at, reaching for, and grabbing a toy. These connections are especially important for higher-level learning. One especially important area where the three lobes come together is called the *angular gyrus*. Here we integrate different types of sensory information. A common example takes place when reading, as we combine the sounds (listening) in words with their visual forms (looking and "feeling" the letter shapes) for understanding. Such *association areas* are critical for higher-level thinking and learning, and naturally take both time and experience to develop. Another important association area is the *corpus callosum*, a thick band of fibers that integrates the workings of the two hemispheres. We will return shortly to how these connections develop.

Many types of learning disability involve weak association areas. Being able to recite the alphabet isn't much good if you can't associate the letter names to their sounds, what they look like on paper, or what they mean when they're in a word. Trying to memorize the U.S. presidents is meaningless and difficult if you can't link any historical stories to those abstract names.

Who Knew that Child's Play
Was So Important for the Brain?

One natural means of strengthening these all-important neural intersections is old-fashioned children's play. Object play and "pretend" play call on many different systems that have to work together. Examples are linking the sight and the "feel" of geometric blocks and figuring out how they fit together; manipulating dolls as a child pretends the dolls are conversing while making breakfast in a doll house ("First I'll do this, then you do that . . ."); coordinating whole-body movement with planning to climb a tree or walk a curb; listening to music and moving in rhythm; following sequential steps in an art or construction project; exercising visual-spatial skills and forward planning in a chess game. An atmosphere of relaxed fun also creates healthy brain chemistry to firm up new connections.

A helpful method of strengthening these sensory association areas is called multisensory teaching, which we will discuss in Chapter 8, "Who's Intelligent?" This type of remedial stimulation is especially important in a time when spontaneous child's play is being supplanted by externally guided electronic toys—probably one factor in the current increase in learning problems.

Smelling Your Way to an A*?* The sense of smell, interestingly enough, is more connected with the limbic system, or emotional brain, than with the cortex. Perhaps you know how easily a familiar smell can evoke emotionally charged memories that you can't quite put into words? Incidentally, smell may also turn out to be an aid to learning, which is just one of many possibilities that ought to be explored as we realize the importance of integrating the emotional and intellectual lives of the brain.

The scent of chocolate in a study session may help students recall the material.

The Frontal Brain: Control and Wisdom Central. The *front (anterior)* part of the cortex is the *frontal lobe,* the brain's executive command center. It is separated into the *motor cortex*, which organizes, controls, and manages our conscious movements (learning to manage a spoon, kick a ball, or master the sequence of strokes to write alphabet letters) and the *prefrontal cortex*, the "boss" of the brain, which organizes, controls, and manages our thinking, planning, self-control, moral behavior, motivation, and attention, to name a few functions. The prefrontal cortex of the brain has been implicated in just about every possible learning disorder. It has rich networks of connections throughout the rest of the brain, especially to the emotional limbic system. It also shares chemical neurotransmitters, such as dopamine (see Chapter 6, "How Your Child's Brain Works"), with areas such as the basal ganglia. These transmission loops are involved in managing one's attention.

Executive function disorder, described in Chapter 3, is associated with dysfunction in this prefrontal executive system. The prefrontal cortex has a very long trajectory of growth, starting at birth, with heavy growth spurts that occur periodically and extend into adolescence. Many parents and teachers observe that a child sometimes seems to make dramatic leaps in understanding, self-awareness, and general maturity in a relatively short period of time, and these waves of developmental change may be associated with such brain growth spurts. (Be prepared, though, for your child to regress now and then as she climbs this developmental spiral.)

Because early adolescence is one of the most important periods for rapid growth of prefrontal connectivity, we should pay special attention to the quality of the stimulation coming in to a youngster's brain during that time. *One important caution concerns substance abuse in early adolescence, which is especially hazardous to the brain's motivation/management systems.* Marijuana and/or alcohol abuse, which have been the most studied, have long-term effects on a number of different mental abilities associated with the prefrontal cortex.[11] Whether or not other addictive habits, such as video gaming, have similar effects is a worrisome possibility.

You can score very well on a standard IQ test, which mainly calls on previously stored information and skills such as vocabulary knowledge, but still suffer from executive problems—which probably explains why IQ alone is a rather poor predictor of life success. It is also true that schools, in general, tend to focus on pushing information and skills into the back of the brain and seriously neglect development of the management systems up front.

Will our culture be long on information and short on wisdom?

Different Cells, Different Problems?

Fast and Slow Cells: Dorsal and Ventral

If you look at the brain from the side, you can imagine drawing a line from the back that curves up over the top of the head to the front. This is the *dorsal* axis. The *ventral* axis runs along the bottom of the brain. Researchers have recently pinned down important differences between cell types in dorsal and ventral areas that offer very promising clues about learning differences.

The fast-acting *magnocellular* system (more dorsal) contains larger neurons that help us quickly locate *where* a sensory stimulus is coming from (temporal-spatial processing). This system may be involved in emotional processing, including face processing in the early months of life. In oversimplified terms, deficiency in these fast-acting "magno" cells may create a slower thinking speed and may be one cause of reading and other learning problems.

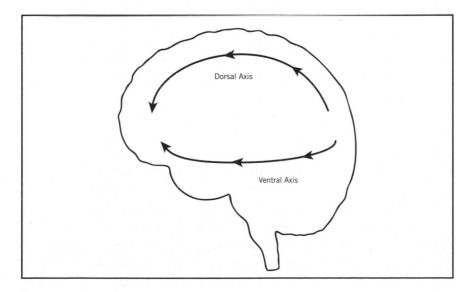

7. Dorsal and Ventral: Faster and Slower

In contrast the smaller, slower-acting *parvocellular* cells (more ventral) are more involved in *what* the stimulus means, i.e., what we are seeing, hearing, or touching.

Magno and parvo systems are important within each sensory modality—which means that each are active in vision, hearing, and spatial understanding. Perhaps they can offer a clue as to why some learning disorders seem to affect such a wide variety of skills. For example, many children with dyslexia have trouble quickly sorting out the direction of the written letters on the page (visual) as well as quickly processing the order of sounds in a spoken word (auditory), and perhaps even the steps in learning to tie a bowknot or write an alphabet letter (kinesthetic/spatial).

Some perfectly smart children just seem to be slower thinkers than others; they prefer to mull over a problem before coming up with an answer. Could this learning style relate to mango- and parvocellular differences? All these questions need a lot of research. In a recent lecture with the intriguing title of "Wobbles, Warbles, and Fish," John Stein of Oxford University shed a little light on the mystery. According to Stein, magnocellular deficiency causes, among other things, visual "wobbles," as if the eyes were slipping around the page—obviously quite a deterrent to reading.[12] A magno deficiency might also contribute to some children's coordination problems because the magnocellular system also projects, or sends messages, to the cerebellum.

> Do we need to rethink some ideas about causes of reading problems?

Given genetic variation at the cellular level, individual factors in each child's development will bring out different groups of symptoms in how the brain performs. *The brain's plasticity also means that appropriate treatments can make a big difference in these symptoms, no matter what the genetic base.* Unfortunately, even if this theory proves out, no accepted therapies are yet available.

Lacking adequate research on this intriguing theory, Stein does suggest one remedy that is inexpensive, readily available, generally safe, and may even improve your child's health. Remember cod liver oil? A small daily dose (now available in lemon-flavored or other child-friendly forms) supplies essential fatty acids that are deficient today in the diets of even well-fed children. These particular fatty acids, according to Stein, are a powerful fuel for the brain's magnocellular system, perhaps opening cell channels to help them signal faster. (You would naturally want to check with your child's physician before adding dietary supplements, as well as making sure you use only fish oil guaranteed free of mercury and other toxic substances.)

Cod liver oil might rev up brain functioning.

What Makes Us Intelligent? Gray Matter and White Matter

Scientists, educators, and the popular press have focused intently on the brain's neurons—its "gray matter." Yet neurons could not do their job without the action of another massive population of cells which, until recently, have received little attention.

Have you exercised your white matter today?

"White matter" comprises as much as 90 percent of brain cells. It is made up of different types of cells called glia, which have technical names such as *astrocytes*, *oligodendrocytes*, and *microglia*. They are "white" because they are composed of a fatty white substance called *myelin*, which develops as a child matures. Myelin growth also seems to depend to some degree on how actively a child uses his brain. The glia nourish the neurons, clean up after them, and speed messages along the fiber tracts that link separate brain areas. New research indicates that white matter cells may be far more "intelligent" than anyone believed, and may even have a communication system of their own. They have much to do with learning—and with learning problems. Research in this area is still in its early stages.[13]

The Key to an Efficient Brain: "Functional Connectivity." An immature brain has lots of neurons, but they aren't very efficient at sending messages. As nerve fibers in sensory and association areas mature, become myelinated, and are used, they can transmit messages at speeds up to ten times faster than unmyelinated fibers. The important buzz phrase here is "functional connectivity," meaning how the brain connects its widely separated neural networks so cells can communicate back and forth. For example, when your five-year-old has trouble coordinating two hands in his piano lesson or your nine-year-old complains that she can't copy fast enough from the chalkboard, immature functional connectivity may be to blame. The brain needs to form a smoothly working network connecting perhaps ten or more different locations just to perform such a "simple" task. Without adequate development of thick white matter cables, this job is difficult, frustrating, and probably exhausting.

The brains of autistic learners may lack appropriate functional connectivity, particularly between the front and the back, suggests Carnegie Mellon researcher Marcel Just.[14] Lacking effective long-distance communication systems between the visual cortex in the back and the frontal cortex isolates visual thinking from speech and other aspects of reasoning. If local networks (e.g., specific visual skills) are overconnected and long-distance ones (e.g., back to front) are underconnected, that might produce the autistic person's characteristic overfocus on small details at the expense of general understanding, according to Dr. Just.

> How can we improve these long-distance connections and where does this vital white matter come from? The answer seems to be in a combination of maturation and experience.

Myelin is found wherever neurons make connections. During so-called critical or sensitive periods, production may peak in certain areas and then ease off as the child learns to exercise and use the newly streamlined connections. We have good reason to believe that white matter also grows as a function of the proper kind of stimulation of specific networks. Any athlete understands how coordination of different actions becomes smoother, faster, and more effortless with practice—one obvious example of building connectivity. You also read in the last chapter about programs for autistic children, like Greenspan's Floor Time, which probably increase the strength of long-distance connections by simultaneously stimulating emotional, sensory (back), and executive (front) systems. Again, multisensory instruction for reading problems also gets results because it builds that all-important connectivity in association areas. In later chapters you will find many specific suggestions for increasing brain health and thinking power.

Working Together

One white-matter area that myelinates throughout childhood and teen years is the *corpus callosum*, which consists of long cables of nerve fibers that connect the right and left hemispheres. Many types of learning disabilities and attention problems have been blamed on deficiencies in the corpus callosum, as have some of the differences between males and females, although research hasn't yet produced any conclusions.

> The fact that the teen brain often seems to lack perspective and control may have something to do with late-maturing circuits in the "bridge" between right and left sides.

Nonetheless, the remarkable versatility of the brain is shown in people born without a corpus callosum. Some of these "acollossal" individuals learn to function quite normally and sometimes do not even know they have this problem until their brains are scanned for some other reason.

Functional connectivity throughout the brain holds a major key to learning of all types. You need to know about it because there may be ways to help a child's or student's brain develop connectivity. Here are some facts:

- Several current studies have linked amount of white matter to scores on intelligence tests, musical ability, and other skills.

- The invention of the scanning technique diffusion tensor imaging (DTI), which now makes it possible to observe white matter, should yield important information in the near future.

- Myelin develops *both because of brain maturation and because of the active use of thinking circuits*. For example, pianists who practice frequently have thicker connections than other players in areas that link hand movement with cognitive brain areas activated by playing.[15]

- Good remedial techniques exercise those circuits to establish better connectivity. Any time you help a child "see" how two things go together, talk about a story you have read or a video you have seen, practice writing about a picture, draw an image of a story, dance out a historical event, write and say the multiplication tables to memorize them, or practice a skilled action like handwriting, you are probably boosting connectivity.

- Using one's imagination may power brain connectivity.

- Research suggests that myelin production is facilitated by proper nutrition, especially protein and long-chain essential fatty acids (see Chapter 10, "Brain-Cleaning 101").

- Repeated practice of any skill builds stronger connectivity for it. Let your child explore and experiment with many types of skills. Some children require lots more practice than others to achieve effortless skill use ("automaticity").

A number of years ago I fielded a question from a concerned father of three daughters—lovely, cooperative students, but definitely on the "late bloomer" side. In those days we didn't know much about myelin, except that it was associated with maturation and the development of more advanced learning skills. After hearing this explanation at an evening lecture, he hesitantly raised his hand.

"Is there any place I can buy some myelin?" he wanted to know. Ah, if only it were that simple!

> There's still time! The brain is not functionally mature until at least age thirty and can grow new connections even into ald age.

Einstein's Real Brain

Through a bizarre set of circumstances described in Walter Isaacson's biography of Albert Einstein, sections of his brain became available for study. Provocative findings emerged when scientists examined cells from his cortex. This creative genius did, indeed, have a somewhat different brain from the average of a group of adults.[16] Specifically, he had *more glial cells per neuron* than did a comparison group of mature adult brains, even though at his death he was about ten years older than those in the comparison group and his brain had shrunk a bit with age. Essentially he had better connectivity in areas that link the different senses.

Structural differences in Einstein's brain were particularly significant in two areas of the parietal lobe that are key to mathematical and spatial thinking. Dr. Sandra Wittleson, who examined this part of the brain, believes this finding may mean Einstein had richer and more integrated circuits in this area. Another scientist, Marian Diamond, studied the area around the angular gyrus, the spot about halfway back in the parietal lobe that acts as a major hub for connecting incoming messages from the different sensory lobes—where visual, auditory/verbal, spatial, and body awareness connect for understanding. Diamond speculated that the unusually large ratio of glial cells to neurons suggested that this area used and needed more energy.

No doubt Einstein came into the world with a unique brain structure and a great deal of genetic potential, but this research raises an additional possibility. Was the creative, imaginative thinking that led to his breakthrough concepts in physics partially a function of above-average use of these brain areas? Throughout his lifetime, Einstein was motivated by intense curiosity and a desire to pursue complex problems. If you have a child who insists on "doing it his own way," you might find comfort in the fact that Einstein refused to conform to established beliefs—a major factor in making breakthrough discoveries.

We have no way of knowing when his unusual brain connectivity developed, but chances are it was partially constructed in childhood. Curiously, Einstein was also somewhat language delayed and thought by some to be "slow" as a young child. He preferred to think in images, "thought experiments," rather than words, and was so uncooperative in basic mathematics that his teachers despaired of him. I

have certainly met plenty of brilliant physicists and mathe-
maticians who describe their own symptoms of such "learning disabilities."

Little Albert spent a lot of time in hands-on, solitary play,
building elaborate houses out of cards and listening to or
playing music. He was particularly fascinated by manipulating and puzzling over his favorite toy, a compass. As a young
teen, he began to ponder intensely the question "What
would it be like to travel at the speed of light?" By age
twenty-one, he had played with this question enough to develop a theory that altered both scientific thinking and world
history.

Did Einstein's brain grow extra power because of the
energetic way he used it? Physical manipulation of three-
dimensional objects lies at the root of many types of mathematical and scientific reasoning.

Rundown: The Well-connected Brain

- The active, curious brain seems to grow the strongest connections.

- Brilliant and innovative adult brains retain the ability to
  play—with objects, creations, ideas—throughout a lifetime.

- Physical manipulation of three-dimensional objects lays foundations for mathematical and scientific reasoning.

- Quiet play and reflection in childhood give the brain a chance
  to connect and strengthen widespread networks.

- Einstein's mental images were self-generated; he created and
  moved them around in his own imagination. This is very different from the experience of many children today, as they
  respond to a screen crowded with visual images that have
  been created and activated by someone else.

- To build intelligence, we should promote connections between
  different types of information. True intelligence does not

come primarily from the number of facts and isolated "bits" of knowledge we push into kids' minds.

- Like many great thinkers, Einstein was a rebel.

Einstein summed it up in this famous quote: "Imagination is more important than knowledge." Neuroscience confirms that a child's imagination builds far more than castles in the sky—it builds functional connectivity to make his brain more powerful.

> A parent who buys an electronic product because the name of a genius is attached to it may find it limits rather than enlarges his or her child's real genius.

Mirror Neurons: A New View of Learning?

Neurons come in many different varieties, but one very special kind, identified only in 1990, enables us to imitate, or "mirror," what others are doing or feeling. Termed "mirror neurons," they hold promise for a much better understanding of how the brain learns everything from athletic skills to the social learning that is impaired in autism spectrum disorders and nonverbal learning disabilities.

Mirror neurons are found in widely distributed clusters throughout the brain. According to Robert Sylwester, a well-respected authority on applying brain research to teaching and learning, this discovery has the power to "transform" our understanding both of how children acquire skills and how best to teach them.[17]

Why Does an Infant Stick Out Her Tongue When You Do? As you might guess, "mirror" neurons enable us to observe and copy actions and expressions of others. "See, feel, fire" describes the way they instantly respond to another person's actions or emotions. Imitating others is the original foundation of all learning and comes pre-programmed into most infants. I treasure a photo of myself holding my newborn first granddaughter: I am sticking out my tongue, and—magically—Kate is doing the same. As she got older, I continued to be charmed by how she would automatically reflect my facial expressions. Little children do this naturally, as, for example, when playmates are looking sad. Many girls tend to be more attuned to others' emotions than many boys. Is this because they have more or different mirror neurons? Researchers are only beginning to look at such questions.

This special family of neurons makes it possible for us to mimic skills as diverse as when to smile, how to make eye contact, gesture, eat with utensils, hit a softball, perform a biology experiment, or react appropriately to a friend's happiness or distress. If you ever wondered why you can't keep from yawning when someone else does or smiling at some stranger grinning at you from the TV, you can blame your mirror neurons.

> *"If you have 'broken mirrors' . . . you likely have social problems."*
>
> —Marco Iacoboni, UCLA neuroscientist[18]

A recent study showed a reduction in mirror neurons in ten high-functioning children with autism. It was encouraging, however, that targeted therapies enabled these children to learn to imitate facial emotional expressions just as well as a comparison group of non-ASD youngsters, which suggests a certain degree of plasticity in this system.[19]

Danger! Mirror Neurons and Media Violence. One powerful study has found that if you simply watch someone else go through an unhappy or an unpleasant experience, *your brain will react biochemically as if you were actually involved*—probably thanks to your mirror neurons. For example, if you see someone get hurt, your brain activates areas associated with fear and pain. Likewise, merely watching on-screen violence creates a cascade of stress hormones that mobilize both body and brain for a fight-or-flight response. Repeated experiences of this type may create lasting patterns of a physical stress response that will very likely impair academic learning and even emotional health.

I believe this finding has enormous implications for the brain health of children who are often exposed to visual input that may seem benign to adults but is actually very upsetting and overly arousing for tenderer minds. Because we will talk about stress later, let me just add that some youngsters around the globe are forced to witness—and thus respond neurologically—to ghastly events in real life. Why in the world would we want to bring such exposure into our homes in the form of family viewing or a "game"?

Don't let your child's bedroom become a war zone!

Because this research is so recent, its full implications have yet to be explored. There may be critical periods when mirror neurons must be stimulated in any child in order to develop fully. Here are just a few possibilities for applying these findings:

Rundown: Helping Mirror Neurons Do Their Job

- All children need close, *face-to-face* interaction with loving and responsive caregivers, *especially in early months and years*. Such experience may help stimulate neurons needed for appropriate emotional and social response.

- DVDs and TV don't deliver the needed stimulation. They cannot respond directly to the child's own facial expressions and gestures.

- Interactive, face-to-face games like patty-cake or peekaboo are tried-and-true means of involving young children. They probably build up mirror neurons' power.

- The urge to "mirror" others is so ingrained that you should suspect a problem if a child seems consistently unable or reluctant to do so.

- Take firm control over children's exposure to violent or frightening material—in real life or in any form of media. A temporary "thrill" for an adult brain may have damaging physical consequences in the brain of a child.

- Educators should inform parents of the importance of family standards for inappropriate material.

- Mirror neurons may also explain why active teaching and learning, letting the child watch you and then try it himself, is so much more effective than just "telling" him how it should be done.

- Many sports coaches already understand and use the power of visually imaging excellent performance.

Male and Female Brains

If Dick and Jane are exactly the same age and enter a typical kindergarten in the United States on the same day, Jane stands a much better chance of enjoying a successful experience. Dick, on the other hand, will be lucky if he doesn't finish the year labeled with some sort of problem and possibly even on medication.

> Far more males than females are diagnosed with almost every learning disorder ever identified.

The reason is twofold: (1) Young males seem to be constitutionally more vulnerable to developmental disorders, particularly those that are language-related. Far more males than females are diagnosed with almost every learning disability ever identified (one exception being Turner's syndrome, which affects only girls with an unusual arrangement of sex chromosomes). (2) Some schools have become drastically inappropriate environments for the young male of our species.

Brain differences overall between males and females are real, but they have never been adequately addressed in most schools. Although there are enormous differences among all girls, as well as among all boys, the average little boy tends to think somewhat differently, show interest in different activities, and develop mental skills on a different cycle than does the average little girl. Female brains on average adapt more easily to reading and writing exercises in early grades. Girls tend to want to please the teacher and are usually better at it than their male counterparts. Girls may be better at remembering the details of personal experiences, which helps them negotiate relationships with other people. They may also have an advantage in remembering verbal information. Moreover, a girl on average, seems to have a faster timetable of brain maturation than does the average boy. Young teen girls tend to be about two years earlier than boys in the brain's spurt of maturation in control systems. All of these factors provide a tremendous advantage in the typical classroom.

Boys generally catch up and may even score better than girls on problem-solving and abstract reasoning by the time they are in high school—that is, if they haven't lost their steam either from inappropriate classroom demands or inappropriate administration of medications to "settle them down." Meanwhile, girls' potential may be dampened by gender-specific expectations. Since the major message of this book is about the power of environments, you can imagine how horrified I am to walk into a toy store and note that it seems today's little girls are being groomed solely to be some man's arm candy, while the boys are encouraged to spend their time in violent combat.

Concerned educators are trying to revise teachers' expectations and teaching methods to address the needs of both sexes, especially those of boys in the lower grades. In the meantime, parents should be aware of this potential problem and work actively with schools for more constructive and developmentally appropriate curriculum and teaching. All children thrive on robust activity. They also thrive on challenge, but it must be appropriate for their stage of development and learning style. Parents should question schools that fail to provide appropriate environments for *any* child. Check the Notes for some excellent recommended reading that will bring you up to date on this important topic.[20]

The architecture of the brain is only the beginning. Even more interesting is the way it grows, develops, and crafts the network of connections that will power thinking and learning for a lifetime. Parents, teachers, coaches, and the child himself are the major players in how this process turns out. That's what the next chapter is about.

CHAPTER 5

Rewiring Children's Brains

How the Brain Builds Itself and How We Can Help

An interesting plea for help came by e-mail from a special education consultant in a rural school district in the Midwest, requesting advice about one of her most puzzling cases. A second-grade boy who had suffered brain damage as a result of a stroke during birth (a rare event) was becoming increasingly difficult to teach. He was receiving support services from several special education teachers, but trouble continued to brew in both his learning and his behavior. He had recently been seen by a neurologist, who came up with a challenging prescription.

"The doctor says our job is to 'rewire' his brain," explained my obviously distraught correspondent. "But this is a new concept to me, and I am wondering how we should go about doing it."

"And I don't suppose he gave you any magic formulas," I remarked in our later phone conversation.

"No," she sighed. "That's why we really need some help."

"Your job is to rewire his brain," said the neurologist.

Changing Brain Circuits—For Better or Worse

Can parents and teachers actually "rewire" a child's brain? Yes! But with environmental "surgery" instead of the operating room variety.

The doctor's prescription was woefully incomplete, but he was fundamentally right. The way children are raised and taught, plus the skills they practice and their emotionally arousing experiences can all alter brain connections. Scientists like the term *modifying brain circuitry* for this intense interaction.

Here are some of the major points to be covered in this chapter as we explore these provocative findings:

Quick Take: Your Child's "Plastic" Brain

1. Anything a child does changes her brain, and things that she does frequently make lasting changes in the way its cells connect (*connectivity*).

2. The brain is so "plastic" that it can completely rearrange itself in the face of a major challenge such as being born deaf or learning to read. In fact, each child builds a unique, "custom-tailored" brain as genetics interact with lifetime experiences.

3. Genes create the outline of brain structure, but the environment fills it in.

4. Each brain comes equipped with a built-in developmental timetable for mastery of different types of skills. Brains mature in cycles that begin before birth and last until around age twenty-five or even later. Trying to force or accelerate mental development risks creating learning problems.

5. Whether a child is faster or slower to mature is influenced by genetics and has very little to do with overall potential. Sensitive adults try to take their cues from the child's interests and abilities as well as what needs to be learned at each stage.

6. The brain remains responsive to experience throughout its lifetime. Even old people can build new brain circuits if they remain curious and continue to learn.

7. Specialized teaching techniques can improve the efficiency of learning circuits in a child's brain. This fact holds great promise for children with learning difficulties.

8. New scanning techniques are opening our understanding of how to help kids learn, but it is important to remember that there is a whole child—and not just a brain—in the scanner.

9. The brain is incredibly complex! We still have so much to learn that you should be skeptical of "guaranteed" remedies or treatments.

Custom-Tailored Brains and Neuroplasticity

The brain's ability to respond, change, and either build or lose circuitry is called *neuroplasticity*. Brain plasticity is easy to understand if you liken brain circuits to muscles, which become larger and stronger after training and use. On the other hand, muscles can become weak and even atrophy if they don't get any exercise—and so can brain networks for unexercised skills. Thus, "brain power" depends in large part on the environment.

> If important brain circuits are not used at the proper age, they may be lost. Fortunately, these developmental windows are quite long for human brains.

A common example of weakened—or even lost—abilities is found when an adult tries to learn to speak a foreign language. Most adults—who have used at least one language all their lives—retain the necessary circuits for mastering vocabulary and grammar rules. Acquiring a perfect accent, however, is a lot more difficult. On a visit to Japan, I thought I had really mastered my Japanese language tapes, but no one could understand me! The reason is that I hadn't used the potential neural connections for processing those particular sounds when my brain was ready to learn them early in life. Thus they were a lot harder—and perhaps impossible—to activate later.

Fortunately, very few learning skills have such narrow developmental windows, which researchers call critical or sensitive periods. In this book I hope to help you (1) help your child's brain do it right when the time is right and (2) get busy building—and rebuilding—any important missing circuits.

Although new circuits can develop even into old age, the brain is especially plastic from birth until the midtwenties. Researchers constantly seek better ways to identify and treat learning problems when they first show up. Even some cases of autism, long one of the most challenging diagnoses, are starting to yield to very early remediation.

Most of these treatments are "behavioral"—that is, they go about changing the brain by teaching or reteaching the child how to perform a certain skill.[1] Eventually, with repeated practice of the improved skill, the actual structure of the associated brain areas may also change. Examples of behavioral treatments you will read about in this book include

- targeted, *multisensory teaching techniques* for reading, spelling, writing, or math

- *"cognitive behavioral therapies"* (described later in this chapter) to improve motivation, attention, or depression (also used for test anxiety)

- high-intensity *"applied behavior analysis"* (ABA) for autism

- *specialized computer software* to improve speed and accuracy of language processing, spelling, or math "basics"

- *classroom modifications* (different seating arrangements; more outdoor play or flexibility in moving around; adjusted homework demands for the needs of the child)

- *physical exercises* to boost brain functioning and alertness

- *stress reduction* to free up thinking and memory abilities

- *environmental therapies at home*, "brain-cleaning" (see Part Three)

Behavioral treatments contrast markedly with medical approaches, which depend mainly on medications that affect the brain. Medications can be very effective, but usually their effects last only for as long as they are taken. Successful behavioral treatments may have longer-lasting or even permanent effects. We will return to this important point of discussion throughout the book.

Brains That Read Are Different. The brain's ability to change according to how it is used is illustrated by the significant difference between brains of literate as opposed to nonliterate adults. Because the human brain is not genetically hardwired to learn to read, those who learn this skill develop extra systems of connections in language areas, but they also enlarge systems that control other kinds of thinking.

The environment has such powerful effects on the reading brain that the actual biology of the brain differs when people have been exposed to different languages and different writing systems. For example, Chinese readers, who have been exposed to a nonphonetic language that uses logographs instead of alphabet letters, show different patterns of brain activation than readers who learned in English. Dyslexic Chinese readers even have different neural aberrations than do dyslexics in English-speaking countries.[2]

Adults in cultures where reading has not been taught may have equally powerful brains, but they activate them differently on abstract problem-solving and logic tasks.[3] Likewise, people develop brain structures related to their occupations: Typists have more connections in the motor cortex related to finger movements. Trained musicians tend to employ more analytic (left-hemisphere) areas of the brain when listening to music than do nonmusicians. And studies have shown that cabdrivers grow unusually robust circuitry in areas related to planning and navigation in physical space—almost as if they have city maps implanted in their heads![4]

> Plasticity enables the human brain to adapt to a remarkable variety of possible environments, and in this sense each child develops a "custom-tailored" brain depending on how that brain spends its time.

Tidying Up an Efficient Brain. How does plasticity come about? Starting at conception, both genetic and environmental influences, such as the mother's health, arrange brain cells into a general pattern, like a "rough draft." That's when the fun really starts!

At birth, the cortex is overcrowded with immature cells with lots of potential connections (*synapses*). Every time a particular circuit is reinforced by the child's emotional, mental, or physical activity, it gets stronger. Once the brain has made a connection, that same connection is more likely to happen again. Technically, this process is called *long-term potentiation*. Meanwhile, the brain becomes more efficient through a process known as neural *pruning*, as extra, unused synapses are lost. Gradually, throughout the first two or three decades of life, the entire brain becomes connected into a strong and efficient operating system.

Help! My Child Is Losing Brain Cells! Some parents—and some advertisers—have taken the news about plasticity to mean that we must rush to cram in information and school-type skills. Hold on, please! There are many good reasons to be extremely cautious about trying to interfere with a child's natural developmental timetable. I have worked with children with "learning disabilities" that may have been caused by too much early pressure to learn the wrong things. Check out my book *Your Child's Growing Mind* for the complete picture of what to do and when to do it. You will learn in a later chapter that inappropriate stress is poison to good learning.

In fact, some tidying up is critical to a well-functioning brain. Insufficient pruning may be a factor in mental retardation, as the brain fails to function quickly and efficiently because it is cluttered with too many cells.

We can gently assist nature by providing an interesting and suitably challenging variety of activities and experiences. Problems start when we overwhelm the child with "stimulation" or force learning too soon. Unfortunately, even "advantaged" children now live in frenetic, multitasking households where the "endangered species" list includes brain connections strengthened by reading, intelligent conversation, unscheduled time, and relaxed family activities.

> Trying to "engineer" young children's intelligence may backfire. In early years the brain needs activities that seem "simple" to adults—real-life, hands-on, face-to-face experience to build critical connections for higher-level learning. Many of today's learning problems involve systems (e.g., whole-body coordination, imagination, object experimentation, social interactions) that should not be short-changed in early years.

Nobel laureate and neuroscientist Gerald Edelman discovered an interesting fact about a competition taking place inside a child's brain. Brain synapses must compete with other synapses to survive and grow.[5] This startling idea has important implications for, say, the brain of a child spending too much time looking at pictures on screens and not enough listening or responding intelligently to language. His brain will probably get short-changed on the synapses he will need to listen and pay attention to a teacher, or distinguish the letter sounds that he needs to become a good reader.

Children without experience in careful listening may also have trouble "listening" to an author's words intelligently enough for reading comprehension. Language development is now the source of the largest category of learning disability diagnoses and is also implicated in attention deficit disorders and other behavioral problems. Fortunately, language skills turn out to be very responsive to positive environmental influences, especially before the teen years. There is a lot you can do to ensure their development.

Overall, language abilities are influenced by heredity. Nonetheless, Edelman himself believes it is "simply silly" to blame everything on genetics because the environment has such tremendous power in determining how each brain becomes connected.[6]

> If language synapses are crowded out by too much TV and video gaming, reading and writing problems may follow.

Detour! Damage Ahead. What happens when a child's brain is physically injured, as in the case of the little stroke victim at the beginning of this chapter? Early damage can set up "roadblocks" that interfere with the normal routing of messages, even disrupting areas far removed from the original site of injury. Sometimes these deficits don't become apparent until later-developing areas are scheduled to come on line. Attention problems are a common aftereffect.[7]

Effective therapies take advantage of the brain's plasticity to create new connections that bypass injury. In addition, the brain is so flexible early in life that different areas can be partially hijacked to take over for missing ones. A classic example involves children who underwent surgery to remove an entire half of the brain (hemisphere) in order to stop intractable seizures. As these children developed, they used cell networks originally intended for other functions to fill in many of the learning gaps. Other examples come from children who have suffered various sorts of traumatic brain injury (*TBI*.) Their outlook may be surprisingly positive, depending on the quality of the home environment.

TBI may result from car accidents, sports injuries, or falls, although it is horrifying to learn that the largest source is from child abuse. The "shaken baby" syndrome, in which the infant's brain is compressed against the front of the skull, can result in serious learning, attention, memory, social problems, and even death.

Linda Ewing-Cobbs, a pediatrician on the faculty at the University of Texas, has studied children who sustained TBI early in life. She credits brain plasticity for the fact that young patients who receive prompt and appropriate therapies often make excellent progress even to the point where disability is no longer evident. While recovery obviously depends on the degree of severity and the areas of the brain affected, the young brain is capable of a remarkable reorganizing job. A critical variable, however, turns out to be the home environment, especially family cohesion and support.[8]

> Home environments make a major difference in how well children overcome brain injuries.

Emotional Damage Is Hardest to Mend. In his compelling book *The Boy Who Was Raised as a Dog*, child psychiatrist Bruce Perry relates case studies of children who have been severely traumatized by events such as witnessing their parents' murders or undergoing long-term neglect or abuse.[9] Although such stressful experiences early in a child's life may seriously disrupt brain development, Perry has developed remedial techniques at his Houston clinic that reprogram the brain through intensive nurturance and stimulation. Although plasticity has its limits and some aspects of development—particularly those centered in the brain's basic emotional systems—can never be "fixed," Perry claims considerable success in what we might call brain-mending.[10]

Perry is a popular lecturer who does not mince words. He draws loud applause from teachers as he describes the "relational impoverishment" of children today in all walks of life, as our fractured, time- and achievement-obsessed lives deprive them of nurturing relational networks in family, neighborhood, or school community. "We live in a child-illiterate society," he maintains, where even "healthy" families may spend only minutes a day with their children and allow them to view something like 200,000 acts of violence before they are eighteen years old. Perry accuses adults who are too busy to take the necessary time for relaxed interaction and consistent early caregiving. He believes school environments may likewise be emotionally "toxic," multiplying the sources of stress in youngsters' lives. Small wonder that today's children suffer more than their share of disorders in every possible aspect of learning.

> *"This culture is really stupid about children."*
>
> —Dr. Bruce Perry

Severe Maltreatment = Brain Havoc. An extreme example of brain-retarding maltreatment occurred in Romanian orphanages where children were confined to cribs, sometimes for years, and deprived of the most basic nurture and mental exercise. The longer they missed out on the normal stages of experience, the more likely they were to show seriously disordered brain development—and behavior to match. These children had deficits in language, memory, self-control, and motor functioning along with serious attention and social problems. Some developed autisticlike symptoms, even when there was no reason to believe they were at risk for autism to start with. (I must note here that it takes a *drastically abnormal* situation to create autistic behaviors where there were none, although it is certainly possible that for a child genetically at risk for autism, certain less extreme environmental experiences might act as a "trigger.")

Harry Chugani, a developmental neurologist who was able to scan the brains of ten of the orphans, found their brains stunted in growth with numerous abnormalities related to the early deprivation. He located the worst damage in areas involved in the brain's stress response. Chugani concluded that intense early emotional stressors—such as inadequate or nonnurturing caregiving—may block not only emotional and social development but also higher-level cognitive skills.[11]

Nathan Fox, a professor of human development at the University of Maryland, is one of several scientists trying to close these gaps by placing some of the orphans in caring foster homes.[12] He has found that these children often show "marked" improvement in brain functioning and in IQ. The earlier the intervention, the better the children's outcomes, although brain areas for emotional and social development seem to be hardest of all to restore. Other studies confirm that interventions for these severely compromised brains should be started by age two; even then it is impossible to bring most children completely up to the levels of a comparison group of children who had been raised by their own families.[13]

In my experience, most parents who earnestly cope with a challenging child can best be described as "heroic." A few years ago I met a special brand of heroism when I was privileged to speak at a conference for adoptive parents of Romanian orphans. It is hard to express how moved I was by meeting these generous, concerned folks and their delightful children. Many parents had not only undertaken the taxing effort involved in picking up the children abroad and then trying to help them adjust to their first healthy home environment, but they had also obtained multiple therapies for sensory integration, language development, and emotional adjustment plus academic and social skills. With major doses of TLC, many youngsters were thriving. Yet, in a closed-door session, parents acknowledged that the neglected emotional bonding and related personal skills were very difficult to recover.

Your Special Brain, Flaws and All

Although most human brains start with a standard architectural prototype, individuals differ dramatically in the size, power, and geography of various neural areas. First of all, the prenatal process by which the cells initially arrange themselves is astonishingly complex (and not even fully understood), and each of us has enough construction errors to eliminate any idea of a "perfect" brain. Actually none of us has even a totally "normal" one, thanks to the fact that brain size and shape (*morphology*) differs as much as people's facial features. Thanks to plasticity, however, most of us manage to adapt to our own idiosyncrasies.

Some network "errors" (or talents, depending on the way you look at it) seem to run in families. For example, left-hemisphere "anomalies" (differences) are often found in families with a history of language and reading disorders. Such brains may be endowed with unusual power in other brain areas because many dyslexics show unusual talents in artistic or creative fields.

Liability or Talent?

In my office I keep a yellowed and tattered poster crayoned onto manila paper. It contains five cleverly drawn illustrations that help my students remember the short vowel sounds (a/apple, e/elephant, i/Indian, o/octopus, u/umbrella). It was crafted many years ago by a third-grader named Paul, an usually advanced artist.

> Paul had an awful time pronouncing, remembering, and reading words with the short vowel sounds, but he certainly could draw!

Paul eventually learned to read and spell by multisensory methods appropriate for his style of learning, but he always preferred visual arts to literary ones and eventually excelled as a freelance artist. I cherish his poster because it continually reminds me that the same brain can have a major problem mastering some skills while exhibiting brilliant talent in others.

Rundown: All Sorts of Brains

- The fact that someone's brain is unusually formed in one or more areas does not automatically predict a problem.

- Human brains come in such a peculiar array of sizes and shapes that it is very hard to pin down a complex learning problem to one particular area.

- Parents' and teachers' most important job is to help each child, not to fuss over which brain parts are working better than others.

- The human brain is capable of compensating for or bypassing many kinds of injuries (*insults*) and inborn differences. Many perfectly normal-seeming people are walking around with significant flaws—and even large holes—in their brains!

- Any type of damage, when it occurs, tends to affect the areas that are fastest-developing at that particular time.

- The most difficult injuries to overcome are those in earlier-developing parts of the system. Cerebral palsy, for instance, strikes lower areas such as basic motor systems, which have little or no plasticity. Since these lower systems also feed impulses up to the cortex, connections throughout the brain may be disrupted. On the other hand, many cerebral palsied children, even those confined to wheelchairs, have fine intellectual powers, which is just one more example of the difficulty in making hard and fast rules about this very complicated organ in our heads.

- Intense stress can be a major disruptor of healthy brain development.

- At least as important as the brain structure with which you were born is its vast network of connections, built over a lifetime of maturation and learning. Many learning problems are associated with inadequate communication (*connectivity*) between one area and another.

- If you exercise your brain well throughout your lifetime, it will retain its abilities longer and may even be able to make new cells, build new neural highways, and activate previously unused connections.

Can I Order Some New Brain Cells, Please?

Until recently, scientists believed that humans could not develop any new neurons after birth, but research has proven them wrong. New brain cells can form even in adults, especially in specialized areas. One area in particular is the *hippocampus*, an important organ in the limbic system that handles the kind of memory needed to retain information or the steps in a procedure. New hippocampal cells can develop even into advanced years, but sustained stress tends to kill them off.

The most dynamic changes happen in childhood, and scientists are excited about new high-tech ways by which to observe and measure this process.

Teaching That Changes the Brain

"We can now see a deficit in the brain and make it go away!" concluded neuropsychologist Marcel Just in a recent presentation entitled "Modifying the Brain Activation of Poor Readers."[14] Just's research at Carnegie Mellon University is only one among an avalanche of studies which use new scanning techniques that can, for the first time, peer inside a child's brain, record, and produce a colored map of its activity while she is safely and happily engaged in a thinking or learning task. While figuring out what these pictures actually mean still raises a number of questions, they are producing some enlightening results with very hopeful implications.

Some of the most exciting findings from these new technologies show how targeted teaching techniques can increase power and efficiency of neural networks. One large group of studies has improved areas of dyslexic brains associated with reading skills. Another line of research targets children's attention skills by teaching the ADHD child to activate the executive systems in the prefrontal cortex and take better control over his brain—and his behavior.

"The limits of neuroplasticity are not known. We don't know the limit to what remedial education can do."

—Marcel Just, Carnegie Mellon University[15]

Revving Up the Brain for Reading

Dr. Just described a study of fifth-grade poor readers who markedly improved their reading comprehension skills after one hundred hours of intensive multisensory remedial instruction (think an hour a day for three months) with specially trained teachers. Such gains are noteworthy enough, but even more interesting is the fact that brain scans done before and after the instruction showed that the children's brains had changed along with their reading abilities. Whereas the "before" scans showed serious underactivation in brain regions specialized for reading, the "after" pictures were completely different. The appropriate connections had been "awakened" and were operating so efficiently that when the instruction was continued for one year, activation levels reached normal. Just's research was particularly exciting because no one knew if there was an age limitation on when such therapies might be effective.

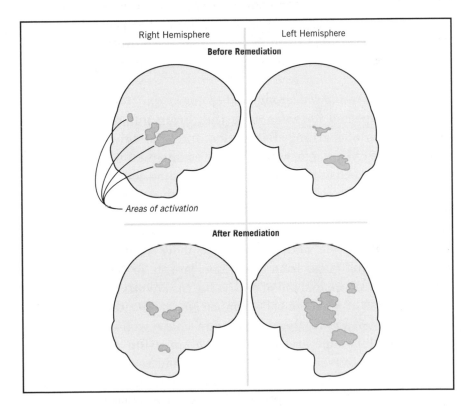

8. *The Dyslexic Brain Changed by Teaching: This brain scan shows dramatically increased brain activation in the left hemisphere language areas of a second-grade poor reader after one year of expert reading instruction. The child's reading scores improved along with the brain changes. Many other studies of this sort have shown the important interface of genetic and environmental factors (type of teaching, in this case) in children's reading abilities. (Adapted from Jack Fletcher et al.* Neuroimaging, Language, and Reading: The Interface of Brain and Environment, *p. 12.) [www.ncela.gwu.edu / ncbepubs / symposia / reading / neuro2,html]*

Sally Shaywitz at Yale has been one of the major pioneers in this type of work. Her book *Overcoming Dyslexia* is a complete description of the programs and their effects. She and many other researchers have used brain scans called fMRI (*functional magnetic resonance imaging*) to determine that dyslexic readers show a distinctive "brain signature" that differs from that of more skilled readers of the same age. Findings center on certain areas in the left hemisphere that are particularly well suited to read ("decode") words quickly and accurately. In the dyslexic brains, they do not activate as strongly as they should, whereas the right sides of their brains appear to be trying to do the job. The right hemisphere, however, is not very well suited for this task. Other areas of the brain also show differences that seem to contribute to slow, inaccurate reading. The specialized instruction appears to "normalize" this pattern.

"I'm sure she's using the wrong part of her brain!" Observant teachers have suspected for some time that brain differences underlie certain types of learning disabilities and that brains can be retrained. Many years ago, with only the scantest knowledge of brain research, I worked with students whose reading sounded something like this (the correct words are in parentheses): *"The gril (girl) worked (walked) up the stars (stairs) and went into the (her) room."*

I thought to myself, "This kid is reading with the *wrong part of her brain!*" The "style" of the right hemisphere would tend to look at whole words and guess from the shape, length, first letter, or some other *visual* feature instead of *analyzing the sounds in order*, which is the purpose of what we call phonics. No wonder these kids don't like reading—it's really hard if you don't have well-developed left-hemisphere language areas or if you're not using your brain efficiently! So, of course you would tend to avoid reading as much as possible and thus fall even further behind than your classmates who are reading for pleasure in their spare time—and strengthening their related brain networks in the process.

In recent studies, appropriate teaching with repeated, systematic practice strengthened the weak areas and moved the action over to where it belonged. We don't yet know if there is a biological limit to the ages when these underactive areas can be aroused, although systematic, multisensory methods can almost always bring substantial improvement, even with much older students. The major problem, of course, is the huge emotional barrier set up by years of feeling "stupid" about reading. It is certainly much easier never to let the problem develop in the first place.

Wired for Trouble? Michael Kilgard, a neuroscientist at the Cortical Plasticity Laboratory of the University of Texas, described research that may explain why some of these networks fail to develop in the first place.[17] Because dyslexia tends to run in families, researchers believe that some children's brains are wired for potential problems. It is also clear, however, that environmental factors can make a problem better or worse—and maybe even prevent it in the first place, even in genetically susceptible children. Kilgard's research goes straight to the source by looking at individual neurons in the part of the brain (auditory cortex) that processes the individual sounds of speech—the very foundation of reading ability.

> The foundation of good reading and language skills lies in individual brain cells that are specialized to quickly and accurately process the sounds in words (their phonology). Early listening environments help determine their power.

Kilgard's research so far has been done with rats, whose brains are remarkably similar to humans' at the level of the neuron—although there the resemblance ends as far as reading skills are concerned. He found that even the auditory areas of rat brains can be "rewired" and strengthened by careful training in listening. One conclusion: early listening experience is a critical factor in the way auditory centers are shaped, and a lack of proper input may result in later problems.

At the seminar where Drs. Just and Kilgard spoke, I couldn't help but jot down in my program notes, "lack of conversation in homes, kids staring at screens even when riding in the car, can't express themselves in words—recipe for learning problems!"

Brains Also Need to Learn to Understand What They Read. Children's brains must also develop the habit of linking the words on the page with what they mean—that all-important *comprehension*. So far, brain scans haven't given us any firm answers about how to connect these circuits—which would be different ones than are used in simply decoding the words. There are many tried-and-true strategies, however, that don't require brain scans to ascertain their value. For example, when a child makes an error in oral reading, ask "Does that make sense?" to get her to *think about what the sentence means as well as how to pronounce the words properly*. Another is to read aloud to the child or listen to story tapes together and talk about what happened and why. When you're in the car together, unplug your children (and yourself) and substitute conversation or other forms of listening. It isn't easy to do, but the earlier you start, the better.

> Replace screen time in the car with audiotapes of exciting stories and your children's reading scores will probably improve.

How to Look at Your Child's Brain

An avalanche of research has followed the advent of scanning devices that can literally "watch" the brain in action. Viewing learning right down at the cellular level has produced some very interesting findings.

Scanners have long been used to see the *structure* of the brain, but they couldn't peer safely into its actual workings, or *function*. Now the brain can be viewed in action with several different techniques that can be used safely with children. Two that are especially popular with researchers studying how children learn are the *EEG* and *fMRI*. Another, called *DTI*, is shedding new light on how brain networks connect. Let's take a brief look at some of the applications of each of these technologies. Although it is unlikely that your child will ever need to be in a brain scanner, you are sure to be hearing much more about such research and its profound implications for teaching, learning, and helping youngsters with neurological disorders.

A provocative and potentially useful purpose for brain-scan studies in children is to determine how various groups of children activate their brains for different types of learning. With this information we might (1) learn more about what "normal" looks like (if there is such a thing) and (2) find out what might be going wrong and how to help in the case of a problem.

Electroencephalography (EEG), which measures brain waves, has been around the longest. The brain emits waves of various frequencies or speeds depending on its level of activity (e.g., Beta waves are a sign of fast mental activity, whereas Theta waves signify deep relaxation or a meditative state). EEG techniques called evoked response and event related potential (ERP) measure the collective activity of thousands of neurons working together throughout the brain as they respond to a given stimulus. Even newborns can wear a cap containing harmless electrodes to measure such activity.

> One study showed that brain wave activity in newborns predicted later school achievement, but the quality of the home environment turned out to be the most critical factor.

ERP studies have shown that brain wave activity, even shortly after birth, predicts later school achievement. Since even very young infants are sensitive to the differences in sounds ("muh" vs. "buh"), researchers have measured brain activation in response to such nonsense syllables. They found that infants showing faster activation in the language areas are likely to have better reading ability after they enter school.[18] This finding suggests that individuals may come into the world with differences in an inborn, genetic talent for language tasks. In follow-up studies, however, the same researchers learned that those brain wave patterns, as well as reading abilities, are also powerfully determined in great part by the quality of a child's home language environment. Youngsters raised in homes where they had lots of involvement with talking, reading aloud, and careful listening improved both their brain responses to language sounds and their reading scores, despite their native predispositions.[19] (Are you getting tired of hearing this message? It does seem to keep coming up!)

Newer scanning techniques that map brain activation from both electrical signals and magnetic fields are called MEG (*magnetoencephalography*) or MSI (*magnetic source imaging*). Dr. Andrew C. Papanicolaou, a noted pioneer of brain imaging, is working with a large team of experts from many universities to look for answers that may help children with dyslexia and other learning problems. They have been studying a group of good readers, a group of dyslexic readers, and a group of young pre-readers who are at risk for dyslexia because of their family history.

This group has come up with a reason why reading skill is so closely tied to language abilities: it turns out they share many of the same brain circuits. When good readers were asked either to listen to or look at a list of words and try to remember them, their patterns of activation were similar for both reading and listening.[20] Every one of the poorer readers, however, had different profiles of brain activation than did those of good readers, suggesting they were not linking the printed words with their spoken equivalents. In fact, as in Sally Shaywitz's research, the dyslexics showed a distinct "neural signature." Their scans showed that they were using inefficient brain networks for the job.

> The best readers seem to "listen" to print as if they were hearing it in their heads, while poorer readers are trying to do it all with their eyes.

What Could Be Lost?

A few researchers have raised concerns about attempts to change children's brain activation by a method of teaching. For example, genetic researcher Jeffrey Gilger recently exhorted an audience of educational therapists and researchers, "I'm concerned that if we have an overfocus on the deficit, you are doing things to the brain that you may not understand. If you 'improve' the left areas, it may affect areas on the right. Don't forget, this is a whole child!"[21] Dr. Gilger is particularly concerned about an issue we will take up in Chapter 8, "Who's Intelligent?"—how learning problems and giftedness so often seem to come together. It would be a shame to jeopardize someone's visual-spatial talents, for example, just so they could read and spell accurately. Or would it? On the frontiers of brain research, nothing is simple!

A Useful Technology Produces Scary News

fMRI (functional magnetic resonance imaging) tracks blood flow of brain activity as the child performs a task, such as looking at a video presentation or listening to pairs of words and choosing the ones that rhyme. As blood and oxygen flow vary according to how much and where the brain is being activated, the brightness of the image changes. It looks like a colored map of the geography of the brain, with some centers lighting up with activity and others remaining quiet.

Although what can be studied with fMRI technology is still limited because the child needs to lie still during the scan, results are already provocative. One study, for example, tackled the controversial question of the effects of exposure to violent media on the brains of thirty-eight children, half with a history of violent and disruptive behavior and half with no behavior problems. ("Media violence" was defined as TV or video games depicting human injury.)

The stunning findings were the first to demonstrate differences in brain function associated with media violence exposure.[22] Viewing violence reduced activity in the prefrontal cortex (the "executive" system), the seat of self-control and attention. The children in the disruptive group were most affected, although even nondisruptive children with previous heavy exposure to violent media were affected. The only normally performing frontal systems were found in those who had not experienced a lot of media violence.

> Heavy exposure to media violence reduced brainpower in areas associated with self-control and attention.

In another study of the brain's response to media violence, young men watched both nonviolent and violent TV episodes while in the scanner, when their brain activity was measured and compared. The results clearly demonstrated that the violent scenes, but not the others, caused brain changes in multiple areas that mimicked the actual experience of engaging in violent behavior, even including the activation of the premotor cortex, where the brain "rehearses" the physical actions involved.[23] We will discuss later why the brain reacts so strongly to witnessing such scenes, and what the chemical firestorm that is released in the brain in such situations may do to children's learning and behavior. At the very least, I think we can safely conclude that repeated exposure to this kind of content is unsuitable and very likely damaging for many if not all of our youngsters' minds.

Looking for Connections

Diffusion tensor imaging (DTI) is a relatively new and welcome scanning technique that can, for the first time, image the brain's white matter. This means, among other things, it can look into the actual volume of connections. Since, as we saw in the last chapter, robust connectivity underlies intelligence, this technique promises some very useful information.

Reality Check on Brain Imaging: Not Yet Perfect

As useful as brain imaging has already proven itself to be, experts caution that we shouldn't accept these results uncritically, as their interpretation is still an imperfect art.

Marcus Raichle, a veteran neuroscientist and pioneer of imaging techniques, advises being especially careful about oversimplifying the brain's workings. For example, the lovely colored splotches that show up in news stories on brain scans are not actual photographs of brains, but rather maps of cortical activity that have been statistically manipulated to show one particular type of firing pattern. The vivid colors can make the image look more dramatic than it really is. As a result, they may tempt us to overlocalize a function that is actually taking place all over the brain. ("Oh, look! That little red area must be where we fall in love." Wrong!) Moreover, because these measurements actually stand for correlation, that is, two things happening at the same time, it does not necessarily mean that activity in a brain area *causes* an effect. Every morning I brush my teeth and my east window lights up, but the brushing didn't cause the sunrise.

"By themselves, imaging studies don't prove that a particular area is the source of a given mental process, only that it's active at the same time," explained cognitive neuroscientist Ed Smith. It takes lots of work with real-life learning and repeated studies to put forth a credible hypothesis linking some specific brain function with behavior.[24]

A third problem of many technologies, including fMRIs, is that they don't record changes quickly enough to capture some of the brain's lightning-speed workings. For example, it takes only about half a second and multiple brain networks to look at, recognize, recall, and name a picture of an animal. The fMRI, which records only every two seconds, might completely miss much if not all of the action. As techniques are rapidly evolving, combining, and being refined, we will no doubt be able to place increased confidence in them. Nevertheless, it will be harder to resolve one final question—the philosophical problem of whether the human mind itself can or should be reduced to the level of a machine.

Caution: Don't Lose Sight of the Child in the Scanner

Drawing conclusions about children and their learning by viewing only the activities of the brain risks reducing them simply to the mechanical workings of neurons and their connections. Don't forget, there is a whole human being wrapped around this circuitry! Scientists and scanners may isolate a single neuron that recognizes your grandmother's face, but they are a long way from truly understanding your entire, unique subjective experience of being with your grandmother.

Biological "reductionism" also carries another risk, according to Dr. Lucy Brown, a neuroscientist at the Albert Einstein College of Medicine. "The risk," she says, "is that seeing the neural activity allows people to take away or excuse responsibility for a behavior—to take away the individual person."[25]

As we evaluate any new development in the science of the brain, it is a good idea to keep in mind that our real purpose—and that of the scientists—needs to be helping living, breathing, wiggling, giggling children who are, thank goodness, very complicated and sometimes difficult.

Teaching Children to Change (and Manage) Their Own Brains

Adult coaching helps children change neural networks "for the better," in psychologist Michael Posner's words, by building strong connections. Some of the most important connections are those that underlie *how* as well as *what* the child learns.

A new type of behavioral treatment for children (and adults) comes from the reassuring news that people can change—and improve—such connections. *Cognitive behavioral therapy, attention process therapy*, and *neurofeedback* are three of the terms used to describe systems of focused exercises that alter brain activity for such skills as paying attention or speed and accuracy of language processing. The best-researched of these is cognitive behavioral therapy (CBT), which has been shown effective for relieving depression, improving attention skills, and alleviating anxiety—test anxiety, for example.

With cognitive therapy, states researcher Dr. Helen Mayberg, a person learns how "to adopt different thinking circuits."[26] Dr. Mayberg's landmark studies showed that behavioral methods can be as powerful as medications in some cases and—surprisingly—that they got results by activating different brain areas than the ones targeted by medication. Psychologists took this as very good news, since cognitive therapies have no medicinal side effects. Because they act by changing brain function from inside rather than from outside, their effects may be permanent. With medications such as Adderall or Prozac, the therapists argue, the positive effects may be lost as soon as treatment is stopped. Behavioral approaches are more time- and labor-intensive, but they are a promising alternative or adjunct to pharmacology.

Many studies have shown the power of conscious mental activity to change the brain itself. Mindfulness meditation or focused prayer have well-established power to cause positive changes in brain wave activity.[27] Cognitive therapies attempt to achieve change by teaching adults or children to become aware of, manage, and alter their unhealthy patterns of thinking or responding. For example, depressed or anxious patients learn to interrupt their habitual negative responses and substitute positive ones. Children with attention problems learn that they have the power to take some control over their own attention and behavior, and they practice new habits, which become ingrained into their brain circuits. Simply teaching children that their behaviors have clear consequences is step one.

> Effective parents practice "behavioral therapy" when they set up appropriate rules and reasonable consequences for children's behavior. Affectionate but firm parental "coaching" is the secret to good results.

School programs targeting specific behaviors for *how* to learn are also effective. In just one of many studies, four sixth-graders diagnosed with ADHD learned how to "self-monitor" because they were taught techniques to keep track of and evaluate their own behavior before and during a lesson.[28] All four increased their preparedness for class assignments. Importantly, the improvement continued after the training ended.

A common rule of thumb for "self-monitoring" involves talking oneself through four steps. Self-talk sends the brain activation up to areas involved in thinking calmly and logically instead of jumping in impulsively. Successful students tend to follow these steps without even thinking about it, but some children need specific help in developing learning strategies that come naturally to others.

Building Attention Circuits

1. *What is my problem?*

    a. "I forget to take my homework to school."

    b. "This math story problem looks really long and hard."

2. *What is my plan?*

    a. "I will put my homework papers into a special folder in my backpack before I go to bed at night."

    b. "I will read the problem very carefully and underline the question words. I will take my time."

3. *How am I doing?*

    a. "I'm doing better since I put a Post-it reminder on the bathroom mirror."

    b. "This really is a hard problem. I need to read it again."

4. *How did I do?*

    a. "I forgot my homework only once this week. I need to keep practicing remembering, but I'm doing better."

    b. "I thought I understood the problem but I didn't know what to underline and I got the answer wrong. I'd better ask my teacher for help. I'll do it at lunchtime."

Obviously, many children need a lot of guidance and personal coaching to learn and firm up such habits, and here is where parents' and teachers' coaching really counts. Remember, every time your child practices this kind of *self-regulation*, he increases those brain connections. (We'll return to this subject in Part Three.) Michael Posner, a strong proponent of behavioral therapies for children's learning difficulties, thinks that schools and even preschools should be taking on more of this responsibility.[29] In a keynote address at the 2003 annual convention of the American Psychological Association, he spoke about "attention process therapy," in which even young children use specialized exercises to improve their focus, planning, and management of attention. His studies show an interesting by-product—an improvement in the children's IQ scores. Posner's book *Educating the Human Brain* describes the importance of environments in promoting all learning skills. He believes that both homes and schools should be much more concerned with inculcating positive mental habits for learning—and life—than with simply filling kids' brains with information. Especially important are solid brain foundations for controlling impulsivity, directing and maintaining attention, and self-management skills.

> *"When a parent or teacher says to me, 'I keep telling him . . . , ' I say to them, 'If your child could do better, he would. Show him, teach him, don't just tell him. If we don't*

teach them these self-management skills, we can't expect them to do it by themselves.' "

—Warren Rosen, psychotherapist in Chicago

Programs that promise to change the brain for the better have to show solid and objective research evidence before they are scientifically accepted for use with children. Researchers are in the process of evaluating long-term effects from numerous recently developed programs. Some, like "neurofeedback," use new technologies to target specific learning weaknesses. Although such brain-training holds great promise, parents or teachers should insist on seeing validated research studies or case reports (i.e., from a reputable outside source) that demonstrate the program's usefulness. Some programs now being marketed are costly and are not always well documented.

Brain Plasticity: The Bottom Line

The bottom line is that any activity, pattern of thought, or feeling that is experienced repeatedly can cause lasting changes in the brain's connectivity. These changes may be beneficial or detrimental. To be effective learners, children need opportunities to use and develop rich networks of connections for language (listening, speaking, understanding, thinking), problem solving, memory, attention, and logical thinking, to name just a few. We give a lot of lip service these days to boosting academic achievement, but too often our culture acts directly against these necessary "habits of mind."

Since "habits of emotion" also become embedded in brain connections, we must also consider the attitudes (such as motivation, willingness to take on a challenge or stick with a difficult assignment, ability to relate to others) as well as the stress levels that we're encouraging. Such qualities depend heavily on an elaborate system of chemical transmission that powers all brain function. That's what the next chapter is about.

CHAPTER 6

How Your Child's Brain Works

"Brain Juice," Emotion, Motivation, Attention, and Medicating Children's Minds

Psychologists are usually happy to be invited to a free meal, and those attending the Annual Convention of the American Psychological Association in August 2003 were no exception. As I entered the enormous ballroom of the Fairmount Royal York Hotel in Toronto at 6:30 a.m., almost every table was already filled. The lavish breakfast, courtesy of pharmaceutical giant Eli Lilly, was put on to promote Strattera, Lilly's recently developed drug for ADHD. As my colleagues and I cleaned our plates, we heard reports from three researchers, each of whom disclosed that they were paid consultants, speakers, and recipients of research support from Eli Lilly.

It was, perhaps, not surprising that Strattera came through the morning with extraordinarily high marks. Its side effects and limited benefit, which were already being recognized in practice, were not mentioned. Nor did anyone discuss nondrug therapies or challenge the implication that medications are the first and only recourse for ADHD diagnoses.

I left the session better informed than when I arrived—about not only the technicalities of medicating children's brain chemistry but also the growing search for a "chemical fix" for troublesome developmental variations. I also acquired a renewed respect for the marketing potential of a slick presentation, a good meal, and paying the right researchers to get out the message.

Brain Chemistry: A New Frontier

Brain chemistry is a hot research field as scientists try to unravel the secrets of message transmission among the brain's billions of cells. These messages travel not only over the trillions of synapses that connect cells, but also, mysteriously, through the "extracellular" space outside neural networks.[1] All learning, memory, motivation, and attention, as well as the biology of emotion, depend on these transmission systems. We still have a lot to learn about how they work—or why they don't. Despite the incomplete state of this knowledge, we now confront a new enigma: drugs designed to manipulate children's brain function.

In this chapter we will briefly review what you need to know about the systems that power brain function, including a child's motivation to learn. We will look at brain effects of drugs like Ritalin, Adderall, and antidepressants, along with some of the implications of "better brains through chemistry." Because brain chemistry is so complex and individual, this chapter is not intended as a guide to making medication decisions about your child. But it should help you ask some of the right questions and find further sources of information.

Quick Take: Brain Function and Learning

1. Brain chemistry regulates learning and emotional state. Many types of chemical molecules control how smoothly and efficiently messages are transmitted between neurons.

2. Neurons in different parts of the brain have receptors for different families of chemicals.

3. Some of these substances also act in other parts of the body, such as the heart and stomach. The brain and the rest of the body are so tightly linked that what happens to one inevita-

bly affects the other. For example, thoughts and emotions may affect the immune system.

4. Your brain chemistry is affected by your genes, by your physical environment (e.g., what you eat or breathe), by your activities (e.g., jogging, reading, playing bingo, conversing with friends), and by your feelings.

5. Although basic brain chemistry is influenced by genes, these systems are shaped by experiences from prenatal into adult life. The brain can "learn" and embed habits of emotion in the same way it learns and grows new connections for language and other cognitive skills. Motivation is one example of a "habit of mind" that is both innate and learned.

6. Medications for children's minds act by changing brain chemistry. New research shows that behavioral treatments can sometimes have similar effects—even without medication.

7. Administering psychoactive medications to children is controversial for good reason. Even if they seem necessary, firm guidelines should be in place.

Brain Chemicals: The "Juice" for the System

"My son acts like he's addicted to his computer—is something weird going on in his brain?"

—mother of an eleven-year-old

"My daughter has test anxiety. She says she just can't think or remember anything when she sees an exam book."

—mother of a high school student

On a day when your thinking is unusually creative and sharp, you can probably thank your brain chemistry for smoothly activating message transmission. Yet brain chemistry is sneaky because it acts below the level of our conscious awareness. I may know I am craving chocolate, but I can't see or hear my synapse crying out for some serotonin molecules. Likewise, a player who gets a rush as he pulls the lever on a slot machine or a teen involved in an exciting video game may not realize that his brain is developing a craving for that quick shot of dopamine.

A student who "loses it" when confronted with an exam may feel mentally paralyzed but be unaware of the "fight-or-flight" instinct that is pouring out stress hormones and neurotransmitters designed to shut down higher-level thinking. Likewise, if you have ever tried to overcome a phobia or chronic anxiety or tried to talk a child out of a hysterical refusal to go to school, you know how powerful these microscopic molecules can be.

A Difficult Introduction to Brain Power in the Classroom

When I was a brand new teacher, I agreed to substitute in a second grade that included a scraggly looking little girl who, I had been informed, was such a "terror" that they couldn't keep a permanent teacher in her class. Since I was both unreasonably confident of my therapeutic skills and badly in need of a job, I accepted the assignment.

"If you can't handle her," the principal told me when I arrived, "just bring her to me."

No way, I thought to myself. I will find a way to teach this child.

Bravado notwithstanding, by the end of the first morning, I acknowledged defeat and carried this poor, screaming, fighting, clawing little bundle to the principal's office. (In those days, there were no psychologists or special services in a financially strapped school district.) Knowing what I know now about learning problems, neurohormones, and the brain's stress response system, I think regretfully of that little girl, possibly abused, maybe learning disabled, definitely angry and frightened. Although I didn't know it at the time, she gave me my first serious lesson about neurochemistry in the classroom. I'm sorry I had nothing at the time to give her in return.

We will return later to why strong emotions are such powerful and unrecognized forces in learning. First, however, we should review a few important basics.

Molecules for Emotion and Thinking

Although you inherited genes that set up management systems for the chemistry of your brain, this balance is continually shifting and is profoundly affected by environmental experiences. Brain chemistry also affects and is affected by internal experiences such as mood and thoughts.

Up to one hundred substances, with various names such as *neurotransmitters*, *neurohormones*, *neuromodulators*, or *peptides,* circulate in the brain and body. It is easy to think of these substances as "brain juice" because they comprise the fuel for neural activity, but they are actually composed of microscopic molecules of proteins, which are carried around by brain fluids. Each type of protein molecule has a different shape that fits, or binds, like a key into a lock, with custom-tailored receptors on neurons. Once activated, the receiving neuron relays the message.

Many of these substances act in other parts of the body as well. Candace Pert, author of *Molecules of Emotion*, once told me, "You simply can't separate the brain and the body, even at a molecular level, because some of the exact same substances are found in both. You may think you're teaching the brain, but you're also teaching the kid's spleen, stomach, heart, and everything else."

> The first symptom of school problems in a young child is often the repeated morning complaint, "Mommy, my tummy hurts!"

Having butterflies in your stomach is one example of Pert's finding. It is also no accident that the first symptom of school problems in a young child is often a somatic (body) one. The mind may not understand the problem, but the gut already has the news. If your child repeatedly fits this pattern, you should schedule a physical exam as well as an appointment with the teacher to discuss what is going on and try to intervene sooner rather than later.

Pumps and Vacuum Cleaners. Because there is disagreement and some overlap in the various terms and categories of brain chemicals, otherwise known as information substances, I will use the commonly accepted terms *neurotransmitter* and *hormone*.

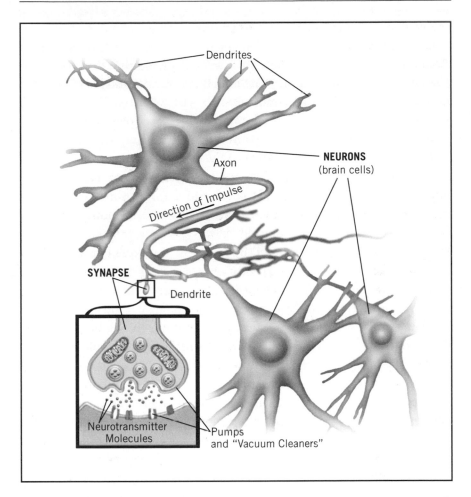

9. The Synapse: Learning Central

The best-researched are *neurotransmitters*, which are pumped into synapses, the tiny gaps between neurons. While in the synapse, they transmit electrical impulses that activate their specialized receptors. Eventually, receptors on either side of the gap suck up the chemicals (a process called *reuptake*) like little vacuum cleaners.

Genetic differences play a role and individual brains have different concentrations of receptors. Some seem either to keep more of certain chemicals in the synapse or suck them up too quickly. Here is where psychoactive drugs like Ritalin, Adderall, Strattera, or Prozac do their work. By altering the function of either the pumps or the reuptake mechanism, they manipulate the amount of neurotransmitter in the synapse. For example, drugs used to affect children's attention have thus far focused on increasing the amount of the neurotransmitters *dopamine* and/or *norepinephrine* in the synapse; drugs to relieve depression block the reuptake of *serotonin* so more is available in the synapses.

What's in That Pill? It is important to discuss two of these chemical messenger families because (1) they are so often involved when children are given medications for either attention problems or depression, and (2) their balance is partially inherited and partially determined by experience.

Serotonin might be nicknamed the "mellow" neurotransmitter. Having enough of it circulating in your synapses makes you feel upbeat, sociable, and competent, whereas a deficit can create feelings of depression or anxiety. It comes in several variations and its network of projections and receptors extends widely, from the primitive brainstem all the way up to the prefrontal executive system. Serotonin may be at least partially responsible for neuronal plasticity, suggesting that it is a critical juice for all kinds of learning.[2]

The building blocks for serotonin transmission, like those of other neurotransmiters, are set up by genes. Nonetheless this system's functions can be dramatically affected by nongenetic factors such as mood, activity level, and diet, among many other things.

> Making yourself smile, thinking of something happy, being sociable, or exercising are simple ways of giving brain chemistry a boost.

Certain foods, such as turkey, have been believed to contain the makings (precursors) of serotonin. Some marketers have capitalized on this notion to create nutritional supplements claiming to improve brain chemistry in children with learning disorders. Because we still have so much to learn about all the neurotransmitters, however, caution is advised.

Serotonin is also vulnerable to disruption by abnormal childhood experience. Abuse or extreme stress early in life can permanantly impair the functioning of serotonin receptors. Studies of monkeys that had been separated from their parents at birth and raised only with peers showed major alterations in serotonin levels, along with symptoms of depression, anxiety, and difficulty with social relationships.[3] Bruce Perry of the Child Trauma Academy is one of several researchers currently investigating long-term neurochemical effects from extreme stress early in human life, especially in children genetically susceptible to disruption of these systems.[4]

Several different varieties of *dopamine* are instrumental in helping us pay attention and sustain motivation. Dopamine is also associated with the rush of getting a reward and is often called the *reward chemical*. For example, when you win at gambling, receive a compliment, or enjoy competing in a game, your brain responds with a rush of dopamine. Since dopamine helps "cement" learning into synapses, the pleasure of these activities is readily remembered, which explains why dopamine is known as a self-generated drug of addiction. For example, exciting and challenging video games increase dopamine release in adult players' brains.[5] Similar studies have not been done with children or teens, but some susceptible children (usually boys), do seem to get "hooked" on this dopamine fix.

> Symptoms of drug addiction include a decreased response to normal stimuli (that "glazed-over" look), but an increased response to stress (unusually irritable).[6] The user gradually loses control of his own behavior and brain, needing increasing doses to get the needed "fix."

The various dopamine compounds act primarily on a circuit of neurons that extends all the way from the prefrontal cortex to some of the deep structures associated with coordinating movement (e.g., basal ganglia) and passes through the emotional brain and some "pleasure centers." Cocaine achieves a "rush" by stimulating the brain's dopamine receptors; repeated use of this drug may actually "burn out" the natural pleasure circuits, making the user even more dependent on the drug.

How Does This Pill Help My Child Pay Attention? ADHD medications presumably stimulate dopamine transmission. The fact that the drugs seem to work for many patients—even if no one knows quite how—is the main justification for their use at present, although they do not cure the basic problem, but simply treat its symptoms.

> Just because your child's symptoms improve on the drug does not mean he has ADHD, because these drugs temporarily sharpen anyone's thinking.

What we call "attention" is actually a complex of many different skills. Stimulants may work by increasing available dopamine in the synapse to

- "wake up" deep-seated mechanisms designed to keep the brain more alert

- increase the level of motivation in the limbic system for work otherwise perceived as "boring"

- and/or activate the prefrontal cortex to take better control over the rest of the brain.

The executive system of the prefrontal cortex is particularly rich in dopamine receptors. Nonetheless, whether or not attention disordered children actually suffer from an inborn shortage of dopamine in the brain is just one source of disagreement among scientists.[7]

Since methylphenidate (Ritalin, Concerta, Methylin) and amphetamine (Adderall) probably act to stimulate dopamine receptors, you may wonder if they, like cocaine, are addictive. This question has not been fully answered. The fact that these pills are "cognitive enhancers"—at least in the short term—has made them a popular street drug on college campuses, where a single pill during exam week may go for the price of several lattes.[8] Parents and physicians must be aware of and guard against this practice, since usage that exceeds prescribed dosage can be habit-forming.[9] Overuse could be especially dangerous for young teens, whose brains are in rapid stages of development.

Some children object to taking the medication. "I feel like I have somebody else's brain, and I lose all my creativity," one aspiring poet told me.

Methylphenidate and amphetamine are controlled substances.

Strattera, which is not, presumably enhances the function of the neurotransmitter *norepinephrine*, a combination hormone/neurotransmitter that is another type of central nervous system stimulant. The Drug Enforcement Administration (www.dea.gov/concern .methylphenidate.html) publishes current information about these substances.

Could drugs for attention deficit have the potential to "burn out" dopamine receptors and create a lifelong motivation problem? This question was raised by pediatrician Leonard Sax in his book *Boys Adrift*. He blames overprescription of ADHD meds as a partial cause of an "alarming rise" in the numbers of unmotivated youths.

Changing the balance of neurotransmitters in the brain may have the unexpected side effect of causing some of the brain's natural receptors to slow down. To stretch an analogy, you might imagine the brain telling itself, "Hey, I suddenly have more than enough dopamine—I'd better stop making so much myself. Reduce production!" Whether or not this effect would be permanent is anyone's guess, but it is well recognized that sudden withdrawal from any of these meds causes a short-term "rebound" effect in which the disorder returns—sometimes more powerfully than ever.

Sax is concerned that we are creating more problems than we are curing by overuse of these medications. He calls for better research to help parents like the mother who, having read his book, asked him, "But is my son's brain damaged forever because he took [an ADHD drug] for three years?"

"We don't know," responded Dr. Sax. "All we know is that young laboratory animals who took those medications were lazy when they grew up."[10]

Whether or not such a finding translates to humans and how long it might take to create such changes are unknown. Yet since ADHD drugs have also been suggested as one factor in the sudden increase of bipolar illness in children, we should all welcome better objective research, not to mention increased public scrutiny and discussion of the trend toward a "medicalization of childhood."[11]

"You don't think it's going to happen to you!" "You don't read this chapter in the baby-care book when you're pregnant—you don't think it's going to happen to you!" I could tell Elena was suppressing tears, but she forced a rueful smile. "I think mothers are

broadsided—it's horrible—it's a critical situation and you're desperate for help and there's nowhere to go!"

Elena and her husband, Tom, had come to talk to me about high-school placement for their son, Darren, a hulking but somehow cuddly looking eighth-grader who could be a poster child for the term *divergent learner.* Creative, original, impulsive, and inclined to physical action rather than mental reflection, he had always had trouble fitting in with the demands and routines of the classroom. Darren showed symptoms of several overlapping learning disorders—disorders of sensory processing, executive function, and reading. What was particularly notable about this family, however, was the scary history of their two-year brush with carelessly prescribed medications. Most physicians would agree that Darren's story represents irresponsible practice, but unfortunately, such situations do occur.

Elena and Tom take their parenting responsibilities seriously and have been fortunate to have the choice—and the energy—to try to help their son in any way they could.

> "We're willing to consider anything that we think might help our child"—Tom was emphatic—"but the schools want the quick fix."

Darren's "quick fix" started in first grade, when he failed to master letter names and sounds. Like many children who don't "get it" and are embarrassed by appearing stupid, he covered his failure by becoming the class clown and soon became seriously disruptive. (Some children go the opposite direction, shrinking and withdrawing into themselves to avoid calling attention to their struggles.)

On the teacher's recommendation, Darren was evaluated by a psychologist and referred to the pediatrician for a Ritalin prescription. On Ritalin, Elena recounted, "He couldn't sleep and was so wired—it was like he was so tired and on a caffeine high, and when he came down he'd be extremely moody—angry, his personality would change on a dime, and he wasn't hungry. That was really different! He was also zoned in school—the teachers liked that, I think."

Concerned, Darren's parents returned to the doctor, who like

Joshua's doctor in Chapter 1, doubled the Ritalin dose. As symptoms worsened ("He was going downhill emotionally"), a sleeping pill was added, and, eventually, Paxil joined the mix. (Paxil is one of a class of drugs prescribed for adult depression that alters the reuptake of serotonin. It can be potentially dangerous for children.) After a few months Darren developed involuntary facial grimaces, called tics, and started to say some very scary things.

"Mom, what would you do if I took this knife and cut off these three fingers?"

Elena shudders. "We were desperate."

They found a new psychiatrist, highly recommended but expensive, and had to make some hard choices to meet this increasing financial burden.

"He told us Darren was on a drug cocktail that was dangerous. When I told him the school insisted on medication, he said, 'I'll deal with the school.' "

When Darren was weaned off his pharmaceutical mix, he slept for three days straight. "This was a big wake-up call for us!" says Elena, who remains adamantly opposed to drugs for Darren. Even as Tom's job has caused the family to move into different school districts, they have resisted pressures to medicate Darren's learning differences. Measures to be discussed in other chapters, such as attention to diet, behavior management, organizational skills, and close communication between parents and school, have all helped. Fortunately, with good professional help, consistent effort by Darren's parents, some very supportive teachers, and hard work by Darren himself, he is learning to adapt his unique mix of talents to the demands of formal learning, and is now thinking about college. And he hasn't lost his appealing, quirky, affectionate, and extremely popular personality.

Parents in a Bind

Clearly, Darren's case is an extreme example. When appropriately prescribed, these medications can quickly change undesirable behaviors. Many parents feel their children have been helped by such drugs, at least as a starting point for a complete program of treatment.

"Frankly, I don't know where to start. I am lost. I am worried that he will be labeled ADHD, ADD. I want to try other routes before they tell me that he needs medication."

—e-mail from a mother requesting advice about her son

Nonetheless, like Elena and Tom, many parents also feel pressured and even bullied by misinformed teachers and administrators who prefer children who learn in the standard ways and conform easily to classroom routines. Parents may be told only about the "quick fix" of a pill instead of much more labor-intensive "behavioral" therapies and lifestyle changes. Moreover, insurance is harder to get for nonpharmacological approaches, such as educational therapy, counseling, and behavior management training. It is a pity that some families are reluctant even to start a process of diagnosis because they fear being pressured to medicate their child.

"That we continue to prescribe drugs to our children in such massive numbers is appalling. There are no historical precedents for a society perpetrating such a travesty on its offspring."

—Joseph Chilton Pearce, author of *Magical Child*[12]

Daniel Burstyn, a parent as well as a psychologist, worries that some parents may prefer a diagnosis to the difficult challenge of a consistent structure and guidance at home.[13] "In the present cultural climate," he states, "it is intrinsically difficult to raise one's children to a wholesome maturity, and many stressed-out, beleaguered parents may prefer to imagine that their children suffer from a neurological disorder. Moreover, many parents are encouraged in this direction by mental health professionals, and are often misinformed about the potential side effects of the medications prescribed to their children."

Even physicians who strongly support the use of medications for attention problems caution that hasty or superficial diagnosis is dangerous. Larry Silver, a psychiatrist in Washington, D.C., and past president of the Learning Disabilities Association, sympathizes with parents trying to find the right dosage of the right medication among the welter of products currently on the market. Dr. Silver recommends chosing a professional who specializes in ADHD, such as a child and adolescent psychiatrist or a behavioral pediatrician, and emphasizes the importance of behavioral counseling for the child as well as family education and counseling.

Teachers in a Bind

In fairness to teachers, I must mention that many of them recommend medication because they feel bullied by parents who fail to take responsibility for providing a healthy, well-regulated home that reinforces the school's academic and behavioral standards.

"If the parents won't do their part by supervising their kids and setting expectations and limits, how can they expect us to 'make' them behave and learn?" is a typical question that teachers ask.

> *"I am a kindergarten teacher in [a midwestern suburb] and I attended your lecture last week on 'Lifestyles and Learning Disabilities.' You said it would be okay to e-mail you, so I thought you might be interested in something I saw which I think may prove your point. Last week my husband and I were having dinner at [a popular steakhouse chain], and two tables away were 2 families with 5 kids, and one of the little boys is one of my students. It was almost nine o'clock and they were just ordering, and it was obvious everyone was having a great time; the parents were yakking it up and the kids were blowing water and soft drinks at each other through straws and stuff like that—not a lot of control, obviously. My little fellow had a hand-held game, so he was punching away at it most of the time. From what I could see, the kids filled up on sodas and fries and by the end of the meal they were getting wilder and wilder except for a really little one who got into his mom's lap and went to sleep. Well, sorry this is so long, but the point is this kid that's in my class—he has been having terrible trouble with his reading readiness, and also is being referred for attention problems. After hearing you, I'm sure that if this kind of stuff in the restaurant is typical, it probably is connected to his*

problems. I know I only saw one night, but this child often comes in really tired and lethargic, and it's hard to get him to concentrate on his work, and you told us that lack of sleep can look like attention disorder. I feel like I should say something to the parents, but my principal says it is none of our business to try and tell people how to raise their kids. Do you agree?

"PS I forgot to say this was a school night."

Medication for Children's Brains: Magic Bullet, Pandora's Box, or Something in Between

If you have a child who is experiencing learning difficulty, especially if he is a boy, there is a very good chance you will be confronted with a decision about whether or not to use medication. By far the greatest proportion of children who take meds for ADHD are male. According to Joel T. Nigg, author of *What Causes ADHD?*, eleven-year-old boys are the most treated group, and the U.S. prescribes far more of these meds than any other country, and some countries ban them. Before agreeing to any psychotropic (brain-affecting) medication for your child, however, I suggest you consult some of the references in the Bibliography, especially Nigg's book and *Should You Medicate Your Child's Mind?* by Elizabeth J. Roberts.

Medications that alter children's brain chemistry are controversial. Although the majority of physicians routinely prescribe them, many doctors feel uncomfortable with what they see as excess prescribing, and many fault the barrage of advertising and one-sided research they receive.

"People are so stressed out, and it's so much easier to say, 'Here, take this pill and go to your room; leave me alone.'"

—Lisa Popczynski, mother of a son
with attention problems[14]

Pediatrician Michael E. Ruff, writing recently in the journal *Clinical Pediatrics*, points out that the enormous influence of a child's environment in the development of attentional skills is being almost completely overlooked. "By distributing 15 tons of stimulants per year, we may be aiding and abetting the burgeoning problem of overcrowded classrooms, overwhelmed teachers and parents, parental deficiencies in discipline skills, escalating academic standards, unreasonable expectations, and a continuance of a culture detrimental to the development of good attentional skills," Ruff states, advocating for more research into proven alternative methods for helping children, families, and schools overcome such learning problems. "Good [research] studies, however, are unlikely soon because there is no money in them," he writes.[15]

Time-pressed pediatricians often prescribe these drugs without gathering the detailed information that should precede any ADHD-type diagnosis. Many are unaware that "best practice" standards include arranging counseling and support of behavioral strategies at home and at school. The American Psychological Association urges that "in most cases," nondrug treatment should be tried first. Pills may relieve symptoms, but they do not cure the problem.[16]

Selling an Idea as Well as a Product

> Q: "If it's in his genes, aren't drugs the only remedy?"
> A: "Actually, no."

In the next chapter you will learn about how the arrangement of neurotransmitters in some families seems to make them more susceptible to acquiring attention problems. But you will also learn that environmental factors in children's lifestyles can change not only brain chemistry but also the activity of the genes themselves.

This debate about "better brains through chemistry" is a cultural dilemma that will not be easily resolved. Whether medicated brains are actually desirable in the long run is not clear. Among many other questions I would like to have answered are possible long-term effects of the rise in blood pressure that stimulants cause in some children. Another unsettling question concerns the effects of such drugs on adolescent brains. Emory University's Elaine Walker recently told a large meeting of psychologists, "the pharmaceutical industry . . . is promoting a range of drugs which may not be beneficial [for some] adolescents and may alter normal hormonal developmental processes in an adverse way."[17]

> Raising children today has become a battle to preserve
> healthy common sense in an out-of-control world.

When one has a child with any sort of developmental difference, the parenting job can sometimes seem insurmountable. As one mother said to me recently, "If you get issued a Ford, it's pretty easy to learn to drive it. But my son is a Mack truck, and it takes a lot more effort." Surely we owe it to parents like this one to come up with a more complete and balanced understanding of how to deal with developmental difference.

In my opinion, expediency, convenience, or outside pressure are very lame reasons for messing around with your child's brain chemistry. While there are certainly times when meds seem to be the best answer—at least in the short term—a decision to medicate your child's mind demands both knowledge and prudent judgment.

Brain Meds—In Capsule Form

1. Medications for children's brain differences are probably being overprescribed as definitions of "normal development" narrow. For example, everything that looks like an attention disorder isn't one; the same symptoms may also characterize normal developmental variation or other problems, such as depression, anxiety, language disorder, or untreated academic problems. These "symptoms" are also found in children with natural talents such as high energy level, unique creativity, or giftedness.

2. School settings may be so restrictive or developmentally wrong for children, especially boys, that normal development starts to look like a disorder.

3. Unless behavioral treatment accompanies drug treatment, any gains made on medication are commonly lost when it is discontinued.

4. Behavioral and environmental treatments take longer and are more labor intensive than simply administering a pill and require a commitment of time and effort at home. Even

the most prominent advocates for medication now agree that environmental interventions, both at home and at school, should be part of any treatment program.

5. The long-term effects of chemically altering the brain's neurotransmitter balances are not well understood. With increasing numbers of children taking psychotropic medications—alone or in combination—we should be demanding more objective research on this issue.

6. It is always wise to get more than one professional opinion before deciding on any psychoactive medication.

7. Before starting any drug treatment, analyze your child's lifestyle factors that may be contributing to the problem and follow the brain-cleaning program described in Part Three of this book.

8. If you are strongly opposed to giving your child drugs for a disorder like ADHD, no one can force you to do so. Rejecting a prescription, however, does require that you inform yourself about alternative approaches and take whatever action you can to remedy your child's situation.

In his very helpful book *A Mind at a Time*, pediatrician Mel Levine adds some wisdom from the physician's perspective:[18]

- Medication should be prescribed conservatively and only after a thorough, multipronged evaluation of all the factors in a child's health and life.

- Whenever possible, a child should be on only one medication at a time.

- Teachers and parents should be actively involved in monitoring the effects of the medication.

- The physician should pursue other therapeutic options if possible before starting medication.

- It is important to schedule regular follow-up doctor appointments to adjust dosage and monitor effects.

Who's in Charge—the Child or the Pills? One final and very important note. Whether or not your child takes medication for attention problems, please make sure he understands that his own effort is still the most important factor in gaining success. Maybe the pills help him get it together and master better learning habits, but they alone do not do the work for him.

If a child feels that someone or something else is in charge of her brain, she is very likely to display a lack of personal motivation. Motivated learners believe they are responsible for their own learning outcomes. They enjoy their successes and are willing to learn from failures.[19]

Motivated Brains

Neurologically speaking, attention and motivation are close cousins. Both are highly susceptible to alterations in brain chemistry, and improvement in one often jump-starts the other. Motivation may also be even more dependent than attentiveness on the values encouraged by the environment. Personal and emotional habits are even more important to learning in the long run than formal academic skills. Study after study shows that students who can sustain a high level of motivation are much more successful in overcoming learning problems and achieving long-term success in school and in life.

Ingredients for "Motivation"

- willingness to take on a challenge or stick with a difficult or boring assignment

- ability to tolerate and learn from failure

- willingness to admit that you made a mistake rather than trying to blame it on someone else

- respect for reasonable rules—even if you don't always like or even agree with them

- placing value on learning

- knowing that your family cares about school achievement

- perceiving yourself as a powerful learner, not doomed to fail

- relating successfully to others—including teachers

- maintaining healthy levels of stress

As with all learning, the brain connections for motivation are developed to a large degree through experience. The best place to learn them is, of course, at home, with parents who model and teach them.

I have often told the story of a little girl I'll call Jessamyn, whom I helped with a reading problem throughout her primary years. Jessie was a dogged worker, but had to struggle hard with reading, writing, and spelling. This child's persistence and grit were due in part to the fact she had received appropriate modifications in the curriculum that made the volume of work manageable—but still challenging—for her. I give most of the credit, though, to her mother (who herself had struggled in school), who gave Jessie unfailing emotional support, empathized with Jessie's frustration, consistently modeled an upbeat, "I won't give up" attitude, and expected her daughter to follow through on appropriate responsibilities at home as well as at school. She was realistic about Jessie's problem without encouraging her to use her diagnosis as an excuse.

> "It's doesn't seem fair, I know," Jessie's mother would say.
> "You're going to have to work harder—but it will be worth it,
> I promise."

One evening, however, the little girl was working very late to complete a science project, carefully pasting pictures onto a poster and laboriously copying the labels and descriptions.

"She was working so hard, I said to her, 'Don't you want me to help you organize that?'" her mother told me the next day.

"No thanks, Mom. I'd rather gut it out for myself," replied Jessie.

Psychologists refer to Jessie's sort of motivation as "intrinsic"—the pursuit of a goal because it feels good to improve, master a hard problem, and gain in real self-esteem through effort. Students with intrinsic motivation don't work simply for external rewards (grades, praise from others, stars, stickers, money), but they give themselves the most satisfying reward of all: pleasure in their own accomplishment. Many excellent sources are available to help your child develop this kind of real motivation (please see the Notes for some suggestions).[20]

A different kind of motivation entirely is the *extrinsic* kind, which comes from being offered a reward or prize.

> Extrinsic rewards (or bribes, perhaps) can have a short-lived and often fleeting effect ("I'll give you a dollar if you can learn the four-times tables").

Likewise, "easy" rewards and unearned praise teach the child little or nothing about long-term, self-generated effort. They may even be counterproductive, reducing overall motivation in the long run. Children born with a more "upbeat" disposition are usually easier to motivate, but how one's emotional, or "affective," circuits develop really depends on experience.

A Few Thoughts About Motivation

- Children want to be successful and please their parents; we can keep that spark going with loving but realistic support. Motivation to learn and improve is built into the infant brain, but repeated failure erodes it. Harsh criticism or punishment is a bad strategy if you want to have a motivated child.

- Doing too much for your child, overpraising, or being too permissive can also damage his personal motivation system.

- The brain is intrigued and stimulated by an interesting challenge—but it needs to be one where success can be gained through a reasonable amount of effort. If the challenge seems either overwhelming or too easy and boring, motivation tends to shut down.

- Many children with learning problems feel inadequate; they need extra boosts of manageable challenges in order to keep trying. Such boosts can come from a perceptive teacher, ac-

tivities outside school, or—most important—loving and supportive family members who let the child know she is valued
for what she is, not only what she does.

- One major reason for "motivation" problems is that school
curricula are often too rigid to accommodate a student's need
to learn differently and to repeat things for mastery. Policy
makers, take note: expecting all students to achieve mastery
without adequate support is a recipe for the ultimate motivation problem, dropping out.

- Even a small success is a powerful impetus to stay in the
fight.

- Telling a child to "get motivated" is a waste of breath. The
brain's limbic system understands feelings, not language.

- False or superficial praise (a smiley face or "good job" when
the student knows it wasn't) is counterproductive. Realistic
and helpful feedback that recognizes effort as well as "results"
is much more useful.

The "Blame Game." Sometimes it is hard to understand why a child
with some sort of learning problem doesn't do better. If a child
has an obvious physical handicap, no one blames him for not being
good at certain skills. The situation is different with problems centered in a brain that we can't see, and the child may absorb a lot of
blame:

"If only you would try harder!"

"I know you can do better if you would just pay attention."

"What's wrong with you? Even first-graders know how to spell
that word."

"He says he does his homework, but he loses it on the way to
school! What kind of way is that to behave?"

"Don't tell me you *still* haven't learned the multiplication tables!"

"Keep on like this, and you might as well kiss college good-bye!"

Students with very high ability in some areas coupled with a disability in others get the most blame. They may have above-average reasoning skills but be handicapped in the "mechanics" of handwriting, spelling, or arranging answers neatly on a worksheet. They don't qualify for special help because they manage to score within the average range on standardized tests even though they are seriously underachieving for their actual ability level.

> Blame games are both scientifically wrong and pragmatically counterproductive.

Consistently feeling like a failure in the early grades has especially serious consequences. Highly stressful early school experiences can alter a child's brain chemistry, setting up enduring roadblocks to learning. Just as surely as a pianist's brain changes as he builds connectivity by practicing, a child experiencing powerful feelings—of fear and anxiety, or pleasure in accomplishment—is embedding "habits of emotion" into the synapses of her brain.

"Learned Helplessness." A very damaging kind of stress comes in situations where we feel powerless. If one is consistently subjected to pain from which there seems to be no escape, it is only natural to give up and start avoiding the cause of the pain. Psychologists call this phenomenon learned helplessness.

It is not surprising that many children with learning problems withdraw from new challenges, particularly schoolwork. Imagine a child with a subtle problem in language expression who goes to class every day worried that she will say something that sounds "stupid" or, when she's called on, not be able to find the right words to answer the question quickly enough—even when she knows the answer. Or the kid who just can't fit in, no matter how hard he tries. A natural reaction is to stop taking responsibility.

"It's not my fault, the test was too hard."

"I never get it right, so why try?"

"People just don't like me, but I don't care."

Children like this are difficult and sometimes annoying. They prefer not even to try in the first place because they are so sure they're going to fail. And they don't want you telling them to "get motivated." Even if they happen to succeed at something, they assert that it was "just luck," not any doing of their own.

Martin Seligman, one of the foremost psychologists in this field, points out that the brain chemistry of learned helplessness is very closely related to that of depression.[21] Instead of using drugs, however, he advises retraining the brain to enjoy and work for success by helping children set realistic objectives and stick to them. One basic strategy from his book *Authentic Happiness* is a technique he calls Best Moments. He or his wife take time to relax with each of their children just before they drop off to sleep at night and review good things that happened that day. With older children, they also set a positive tone for the next day by envisioning good things that will occur.

"The only drawback is giving up fifteen minutes of time after dinner that you might find an adult use for," he comments. "I doubt, however, that you can find many more valuable ways to spend this time."[22]

With a large proportion of U.S. children now surrounded by televisions and computers in their rooms, I wonder how many go to bed with a brain roiling with stress instead of one relaxed by a positive and loving personal send-off for sleep.

> How many depressed, "unmotivated" youngsters are actually reacting with learned helplessness to overwhelming school and homework demands, too much screen time, too much family stress, and too little mellowing human interaction?

The Boy with "No Motivation." I think of Greg, a sixth-grader whose affective circuits as well as learning skills required some major reprogramming. I first met him when I was given an ominous directive: "You need to do something about his math skills," directed the principal, "and by the way, this kid is totally unmotivated—couldn't care less. Good luck!"

In checking Greg's history, I learned that, although he seemed to

have above-average intelligence and no diagnosable processing disability, Greg's overall academic progress had always been spotty. I
also learned that his family—through no fault of their own—had
experienced a great deal of upset during his first- and second-grade
years.

Greg was a husky little fellow whose facial expressions ran the
gamut from belligerent to surly. As he and I walked to the cubicle
that was my "classroom" in that particular school, I tried what I
thought was a positive conversational opening.

"I understand you want some help with your math."

"Nyugh," grunted Greg, eyes glued to his feet.

Once seated, Greg was grudgingly cooperative, and I readily determined that his math skills were, indeed, at barely second-grade
level; he was not automatic even on addition facts (e.g., $4 + 5 = ?$)
and, obviously embarrassed, surreptitiously counted on his fingers
beneath the desk. It was hardly rocket science to understand why
he was in trouble with sixth-grade assignments!

Greg and I spent most of that first meeting talking. I should say
that I actually talked and Greg grunted. Here is an abbreviated
version of our conversation:

Me: "It must be embarrassing for a smart kid like you to need
special help with math."

Greg: "Nyugh."

Me: "Did you know that lots of smart kids have problems like
this?"

Greg: "Nyugh??"

Me: "Yes. You know, math is sort of like a swamp—"

Greg: "Nyugh!!"

Me: "If you don't start out right, sometimes you miss out on getting a solid foundation to build on, and then you just keep sinking
down, and down, like quicksand."

Greg: "Nyugh!" (definite agreement, almost made eye contact)

Me: "I can help you—that's my job, and I've helped lots of kids
with problems like this. But I'm probably going to make you really
mad some of the time. Would you be willing to try if I promise it will
help?"

Greg: Shrugs grudging assent.

Me: "Okay, so you promise you won't get too mad at me—because I am going to give you some math problems . . ."

Greg: "Aargh!"

Me: "But these are really easy and they're really important because we need to rebuild that solid base so you can get yourself out of the math-swamp. [I pull out an addition worksheet that is just beyond Greg's "easy" level.] I warn you, this is going to look like baby stuff to you, but it's important—are you sure you still want to do it?"

Greg: "Give me the paper!" [He snatches it out of my hand, grabs a pencil, and completes the answers.]

Me: "Looks like you finished already. How did you do?"

Greg (looking puzzled): "Aren't you going to give me a grade?"

Me: No, it's your work, not mine. Check your answers and tell me how you did.

Greg reviews the paper. "It's okay?"

Me: "Looks more than okay to me. Maybe you should give yourself a grade or a comment?"

Greg (surprised): "You want me to grade myself?"

Me: "Sure."

We want Greg to start taking ownership of—and pleasure in—this first rebuilding block to success and motivation. Psychologists call this *internal locus of control*.

Greg grabs a red marker from my box and transcribes an enormous *A+* at the top of the paper.

Me: "Is that all you want to say?"

Switching to blue, he grins, looking suddenly childlike. He carefully prints *EXCELENT* (*sic*) *WORK!!!!!*

This, from the boy who had "no motivation" and "couldn't care less."

To make a very long story very short, Greg and I continued to work together that year, and gradually his skills began to catch up with his intellect. Greg continued to receive remediation on and off throughout an intermittently rocky school career. Now a young adult, he has begun to forge a significant career in a creative field that combines math and music.

There are lots of morals that might be drawn from Greg's story, but one is certainly that even the most "unmotivated" kid really craves success. Another is that success, along with the ability to feel ownership of it, is a powerful tonic. I believe that the spark is there in every child; our first assignment is to kindle it by providing the proper scaffolds for relearning success.

CHAPTER 7

Genes, Learning, and the Environment

Biology Isn't Always Destiny

*"I think it's terribly important for people to under-
stand that we can alter something that's genetic."*
—John Stein, professor of physiology, Oxford University[1]

*"The important part of all this is that we're
showing that an attentive caregiver can actually
alter the baby's genes for the better."*
—Allan N. Schore, School of Medicine, UCLA[2]

Some kids just seem naturally to take to school success. Is it because they inherited "good genes" for academic learning? Is there
some environmental magic involved? And what if your child isn't in
this category; how much can you do to improve the situation?

The "nature versus nurture" debate may be the longest-running
argument in the history of science. Which is more powerful—heredity
or environment? Any parent probably understands why this question has been so difficult to settle. For example, our three sons have
looked different and had very different personalities from birth,

and they each experienced a somewhat different environment since we changed our houses, attitudes, lifestyles, and their schools during the years of their development. Yet there are also so many similarities, which are now showing up in our grandchildren. How much did our children and grandchildren inherit, and how much did they pick up from us and from their individual experiences?

One hotly debated question has been what percentage of a person's intelligence is inborn and what part comes from enrichment, teaching, and life experience. After hundreds of studies, most scientists agree that the percentages are probably 40–60, give or take a bit; unfortunately, they do not always agree on which is the *40* and which is the *60*!

> *"There's more and more a proper recognition that you have to understand behavior and genetics and* how they work together *if you want to understand how people stay healthy or become unhealthy" (emphasis added).*
>
> —John Hewitt, behavioral geneticist[3]

But do these questions really make sense? Newer research suggests they are actually the wrong ones to be asking. Instead of arguing about nature *versus* nurture, as if they were somehow at war with each other, scientists are focusing on how genes and environment *interact* to make us who we are. These fields are called behavioral genetics and behavioral genomics. *Behavior*, in this case, does not mean whether we are good or bad, but includes all forms of learning, intelligence, temperament (personality), and anything else we do. A child's experiences exert a surprising degree of power not only over "behavioral" outcomes, such as school success, but even over how genes themselves behave.

As important as this information is, it is not well understood by teachers and parents. Thus we still hear the sort of "genetic determinism" illustrated in the following:

"If this problem is genetic, aren't drugs the only option?"

"How can I be expected to teach this child? Look at his father!"

"Your uncle Ralph never could hold a job and it looks like you got his genes!"

"You must have inherited my bad math gene!"

No one disputes that genes are influential. Do you get an instant buzz from even one cup of coffee while your spouse can consume it right before falling asleep? Do you resist going to the gym while your neighbor is eagerly bounding out the door in spandex? Even such small differences can result from genetic variation. Yet from the moment of conception or even earlier, the environment affects and alters how the genome does its work. By changing your behavior (e.g., resisting the coffee or forcing yourself to go to the gym for a good workout), you can redirect those genetic mechanisms.

If you haven't yet heard the term *epigenetic change*, you should add it to your vocabulary. It is one of the hottest current topics in scientific research. It means alterations in gene function caused by environmental influences. Its enormous implications are just beginning to be recognized.

On the other hand, one's genetic endowment influences one's environment. If you inherit a shy temperament, for example, your natural reticence will elicit different reactions from others than you would get if you were more outgoing. A child who inherits a tendency toward a withdrawn, shy temperament will elicit different reactions from caregivers than will a jolly extrovert. In fact, one's genes (nature) and environment (nurture) are so intertwined that it is impossible to unravel them. As we learn more, the old bugaboo of nature versus nurture seems obsolete. Are genes or environment more important? The short answer is, yes.

Quick Take: Nature and Nurture

1. Genes are powerful, but not always as powerful as most people think.

2. Environments—which include every influence and experience in a child's life—help determine how genes turn on or off, and even whether they turn on at all.

3. So-called epigenetic changes, in which biology is rearranged by life experiences, are responsible for a great deal of who we actually become. Epigenesis acts on a gene like a brake or a gas pedal.

4. Although a few severe disorders are caused by one single gene, all behavior (which includes learning abilities and disabilities, personality, and emotional and behavior problems) is a result of many genes interacting with each other and with environmental influences.

5. Some traits, such as temperament and certain aspects of intelligence, are more heritable than others, but the jury is still out on exactly how or how much.

6. Identical twins are the only individuals born with duplicate genes. Even these identical genomes become different as they interact with the environment.

7. The activation ("expression") of each child's unique genome is part of a much larger system of family, school, and community. To treat any sort of problem, we must first examine the system and its interactions with the child's basic nature. A hazardous or inappropriate culture of childhood may activate or exacerbate a genetic tendency toward a problem.

How Much Can Genes Do?

When Sheila found a seat in my classroom on the first day of eighth grade, she didn't realize—and I certainly didn't tell her—that she was the only student whom I had ever dreaded teaching. Not that there was anything notably wrong about this perfectly presentable girl, but I had already made the mistake of absorbing information about her from my colleagues.

"That child is just downright unpleasant," was the usual verdict. No one agreed on whether Sheila meant to be so abrasive: insulting teachers in subtle but annoying ways, forever rubbing other kids the wrong way, or fouling up assignments because she claimed she didn't "get" the directions—and then criticizing the teacher for doing a bad job of explaining.

Nonetheless, by the end of the first week, I found myself warming to Sheila, who was obviously trying earnestly to please me and get along with her classmates. This poor kid was simply a social klutz, prone to blurting out the wrong thing, intruding on other people's conversations, and often missing the point or taking offense when none was intended. She had similar problems understanding the overall meaning of a reading selection or planning an overall organization for her essays. In short, Sheila's trouble with "big picture" thinking meant she got so caught up with details that she missed the main idea.

By the time parent conferences rolled around, I had become quite fond of Sheila (one more lesson learned by the teacher!) and was eager to have a chat with her mother to share some suggestions about how best to help her at home. A few minutes before our scheduled time, Sheila's mom barged into my office, interrupting the end of my previous conference without apology. Even with this bad start, however, she struck me as intelligent as well as interested in helping her daughter.

I discussed how pleased I was with Sheila's progress, described some strategies that were helping her, and explained how they could be used at home. Sheila's mom nodded and agreed, and as our time ended, I asked my usual debriefing question: "Do you mind summarizing something you got out of this meeting?"

Looking baffled and a little belligerent, Mom hesitated for a moment, then replied, "You said you don't think my daughter is doing very well in your class."

Like mother, like daughter?

Did Sheila inherit a tendency toward abrasiveness and missing the point? The connection between genes and behavior is hard to grasp, since what genes do is instruct the body which proteins to produce in order to keep its cells functioning. How could one gene—or even a huge combination of them—determine someone's personality? Yet it is well recognized that a person's temperament and learning style—including Sheila's particular combination of characteristics—sometimes run in families and may be associated with certain combinations of genes.

> Genes have a seemingly simple job: they tell the body's cells which proteins to produce. Then the proteins work to produce substances that influence very complex behaviors.

On the other hand, perhaps Sheila simply learned these behaviors from her mother—which might also account for why they run in families. Indeed, the attitudes and skills modeled by significant adults in a child's life have powerful long-term effects. Moreover, since young children thrive and learn best with adults who are responsive to their feelings and reactions (contingent caregiving), what was it like to grow up with a mom who, despite her best efforts, simply couldn't read a child's reactions and respond effectively?

The important point, of course, is that we can help Sheila by finding effective behavioral strategies, which in this case are educational activities designed to build social and cognitive skills. The useful question is not, Where did this come from? but rather, What can we do about it?

Genetics Loads the Gun, but the Environment Pulls the Trigger

> *"It is misleading to speak of the genome as a 'blueprint' or to think that genes 'code' for a behavior. Genes simply code for protein structure."*

> —Bruce Pennington[4]

Genes are not a written-in-stone blueprint for behavior. They provide a range of possible outcomes, but the environment—which means anything that happens to you from the moment you are conceived—determines which outcome is likely to occur. In order to understand this important point, let's take a quick look at the complex set of interactions that must take place before any set of genes can influence a behavioral outcome such as your child's learning.

Your Own Personal "Genome Project"

- *The genetic material passed from parent to child is called DNA (deoxyribonucleic acid).* Copies of your unique DNA are found in virtually every cell of your body, setting up a basic outline to make you who you are. You can imagine DNA as a double set of tightly wound, long, ladderlike spirals (the "double helix"), which form twenty-three pairs of chromosomes. You inherited one-half of each pair of chromosomes from each parent. The purpose of DNA is to carry coded instructions for making different types of proteins. A gene is a section of DNA that carries a recipe for one combination of the amino acids that make up a protein.

- *The human genome consists of some 25,000 genes.* Since each gene can be set to either on or off, there about ten billion possibilities for individual variation.

- *The protein code that each gene carries is a long letter string of various combinations of four chemical elements.* Some of these strings contain up to 1,500 elements; even a minute change in one gene's DNA code (e.g., one letter different in a string of more than 1,000 letters) may have measurable results. Most of us simply cannot conceive of the vast complexity of this system, and scientists themselves are awed by what they have discovered so far.

- *These proteins are the building blocks and the maintenance staff for each element of being human.* They set up an initial pattern for everything from the timing of fetal development and the way fetal brain cells arrange themselves, to your height, hair color, the shape of your fingernails, your digestive enzymes, your receptors for salty or sweet taste, the way the brain's neurotransmitters flow, and whether you will be at risk for diseases such as Alzheimer's in years to come.

- *A gene can come in different varieties, just as a food such as ice cream can come in different "flavors." These variations are called alleles.* Different alleles of a gene for height, for example, might account for individual variations.

- *Contrary to what many people think, genes do not stop working after they have done their initial job of arranging our parts.* Genes are constantly at work, and throughout the life-

time, they come on- and off-line, with new genes being activated for new developmental stages.

- *Genes continually interact with and are affected by life experi-ences.* Each gene can be switched on or off either by other genes or by forces from the environment. If an experiential "trigger" is not pulled, the gene may not switch on or "ex-press" itself. Later in this chapter you will read about some provocative animal experiments that suggest how the quality of infant caregiving can either activate or silence a gene re-lated to later problems.

- *Epigenetic changes may affect personality characteristics such as resilience to stress.*[5] These changes cause chemical altera-tions of the DNA depending on various types of environmen-tal experience. Later you will also read about animal studies showing that the quality of early maternal nurturing causes epigenetic changes that make the offspring more or less sus-ceptible to stress, anxiety, and depression. Some authorities believe that epigenetic changes are involved in human disor-ders such as autism, schizophrenia, and depression. If a child inherited a genetic propensity for autism, for example, those genes might or might not express themselves unless some environmental "trigger" caused epigenetic change.

- *How does it know?* If the whole genome is contained in essen-tially every cell in the body, how does a toenail cell, for ex-ample, become different from a brain cell or a bone cell? How, for that matter, do the brain cells in the cerebellum differ-entiate themselves from those in the hippocampus? The main reason is that only some of the genes in a cell get acti-vated. In the same way, a person's physical or emotional char-acteristics depend on which combination of genes is activated (expressed).

Curiously enough, all possible human variation seems to come from only about 5 percent of total DNA; approximately 95 percent is considered "noncoding" because it does not contain any genes. Scientists speculate that we still have a lot to learn about the mean-ing and purpose of all this apparently inactive "stuff."[6]

"The genome is enormously complex, and the only thing we can say about it with certainty is how much more we have left to learn."

—Barbara Caulfield, biotech executive[7]

Nudging Genes Along

Because genes interact both with other genes and with a multitude of environmental variables, they can often be nudged in one direction or other by our "behavioral" actions. These might include changing harmful lifestyle habits or otherwise altering the environment in some way. A frequent example is of people who have a well-recognized genetic susceptibility to alcoholism or gambling but avoid the problem by avoiding its genetic "trigger"—in this case, alcohol or casinos. Genes contributing to addiction do not activate if never turned on by the prerequisite offending behavior.

"I wasn't born with a martini glass in my hand."

—AA member

Another example is type 2 diabetes. Diabetes has a genetic basis but type 2 usually shows up only if the individual eats unhealthily: too many calories, too many refined carbohydrates, and not enough fiber. Type 2 diabetes runs in families, but individual lifestyle changes toward more healthy eating habits may prevent its development. Unfortunately, media advertising and the general acceptance of a fast-food culture present a major challenge for parents who want to model and teach these positive nutritional habits to their children—just one more example of why a parent's job gets harder every year.

Genes That Cause Trouble

Many genes and other influences—both genetic and nongenetic—are involved in children's learning problems.

All specific learning disabilities, attention problems, and emotional difficulties are "polygenic," a result of many genes—perhaps hundreds—interacting with one another, with not-yet-understood aspects of the genome, and with multiple influences from the environment. Reading and other language problems, attention problems, and autistic spectrum disorders have been linked to genes, although no one yet agrees on which of the many candidate gene combinations are implicated or how much is contributed by environmental factors.

At a recent reunion in my hometown, where I taught for many years, I enjoyed delightful conversations with several parents of my former students. The "children" (all now adults with families of their own) were enjoying full and successful lives, but I was not surprised to hear several comments like the following:

"Natty's doing great, and you can probably guess that his three sons are all dyslexic!"

"He's the image of his dad—including being dyslexic!"

"Sheena's still just a bundle of energy—she's running an ad agency—and her daughter sure takes after her! When they visit we're exhausted after one day!"

Fortunately, aware parents and increased emphasis in schools on earlier recognition and better educational treatments for problems are helping a lot. With today's knowledge, there is no reason to let "genetic determinism" get in the way of maximizing children's talents.

Single-Gene Disorders. A small number of pervasive disorders present the most serious challenges. They comprise what you might call an extreme-case scenario—when one single disordered gene insists on doing its damage. This group includes cystic fibrosis, Tay-Sachs, sickle-cell anemia, and Rett syndrome, a rare disorder in girls with some symptoms of autism, which is caused by one gene that fails to give appropriate stop-and-go instructions to other genes. Other syndromes sometimes lumped into this category—fragile X, Down's, Turner's, and Williams—stem from more general chromosome abnormalities.

Recently, I chanced to have two conversations that give poignant evidence of the power of determined and dedicated parents, even in these extreme cases.

Tough News for a Parent to Get. "That was really tough news, the day when Brad was just a few months old and we got the diagnosis of SMA," recalls Jack. I think I detect a quaver in my new friend's voice, but he senses my unspoken question and goes on. "Most people have never heard of SMA and neither had we. Seems Trish and I were each carrying a silent copy of this one nondominant gene; in Brad's case, they just happened to combine. Our other son is fine. Even if, like us, both parents are carriers, there is only a one-in-four chance of the child being affected. It's been tough and it still is, but Brad is the sweetest, smartest, most wonderful little guy, and he's doing really well." Jack proudly displays a photo of a handsome seven-year-old supported by an elaborately engineered wheelchair.

SMA, or spinal muscular atrophy, is a single-gene disorder that affects approximately one child out of six thousand. In SMA, the individual lacks an effective gene for producing a protein that keeps alive motor neurons in the spinal cord. The child's muscles progressively weaken, making him susceptible to a variety of secondary problems that can be fatal.

The severity of SMA and the fact that only one gene is involved make it a potential candidate for future advances in genetic engineering. While geneticists eagerly search for a medical technique to alter the affected gene, extraordinary parents are improving and extending their children's lives with environmental interventions. In talking to Jack and in perusing the SMA Web site (www .fsma.org/), I was impressed not only by the assistive technologies available to help children and families cope with the disease but also by the devotion that surrounds "these wonderful little children," whose parents say things like "We wouldn't trade the time with him for anything."[8]

Outwitting a Problem Gene. A single-gene metabolic disorder called PKU (phenylketonuria) provides an example of behavioral intervention that can intercept the effects of a problem gene. PKU patients have a faulty gene for processing one type of protein enzyme. Unless the child's diet is carefully monitored from the time of birth, toxic substances (phenylalanines) build up in the bloodstream and seriously damage the brain, particularly the prefrontal cortex. (You may have encountered phenylalanines on the warning label of soft drinks or foods containing the artificial sweetener aspartame [NutraSweet, Equal]. Aspartame contains phenylalanine, the amino acid that is brain-damaging for those with PKU. Whether or not large doses of the sweetener might harm others' brains is a matter of debate.)

Anne's daughter Jenny was born with PKU, but she is now a healthy, intelligent, and lively nine-year-old. This is possible because, like all newborns, she was tested for phenylalanines in a blood or urine sample. Because she tested positive, her diet was immediately modified to include only foods safe for her to eat. Such intervention does not "cure" the genetic disorder, but it prevents damage from being done.[9]

"When the doctor called me, he said, 'I have the results of your daughter's PKU test and you need to come and talk to me at once,'" Anne related. "I was sobbing so hard, my dad had to drive me to the doctor's office, and that conversation just scared me more. Thank goodness, another doctor saw the state I was in and said, 'Don't worry. It's treatable.' I could have kissed her."

I asked Anne how hard it is to have a child who can't eat many things that other kids eat without risking brain damage.

"It's not a walk in the park," she replied with a wry smile, "and she doesn't even have the most serious type of PKU. Thank goodness we have a special protein supplement [paid for by state funding] that's safe for her. But there's a lot of effort involved, and it's hard for Jenny, even though she understands. I guess what I would say to other parents is, if you can just hunker down and do what needs to be done—well, you just have to. I've got a child with PKU whose brain needs to be kept intact."

As we parted, Anne added, "At least it puts a lot of things in perspective, and our family is way more conscious of our nutrition, which is really a positive thing."

Obviously, it's not easy to rewrite the genetic recipe, but PKU is clear evidence that even in the extreme case presented by a single-gene disorder, parental diligence can work wonders. Robert Plomin, a prominent researcher in the field of behavioral genetics, likes to use the example of PKU as an "antidote" to the mistaken notion that genetics implies "therapeutic nihilism" (i.e., a hopeless case).[10]

Certainly, for polygenic traits such as learning abilities or emotional development, in which so many genes interact with daily experiences, the words *hopeless case* should never apply. What it takes, of course, are the many dedicated and informed parents and teachers who are willing to "hunker down and do what needs to be done."

Biology Isn't All

Scientists have yet to settle the question—and probably never will—of whether there is something about the human spirit (or "soul," if you will) that transcends the sum of these complex parts. Personally, when working with a real live child, I find it useful to remind myself that I am dealing with a whole little wondrous, feeling person—whether or not he is fundamentally a collection of protein chains and their cellular products. "Biological reductionism" (thinking of people *only* in terms of basic biology) can easily impoverish both our human experience and our professional common sense.

> Thinking of children *only* in terms of basic biology is a dangerous mistake.

How the Environment Pushes Genes Around

A surprising number of studies are starting to show specific instances in which genes respond to the environment. In his fascinating book *Genes and Behavior* Sir Michael Rutter describes both animal and human studies that illustrate such "developmental programming."[11] For example, changes in the diet of a pregnant mouse altered the expression of genes associated with the coat color of her offspring. Young mice in a highly enriched environment showed changes in gene expression that speeded up the development of the visual system. (It is not known whether speeding up a mouse's visual developments will eventually benefit or harm the animal's overall abilities, so please do not interpret this study as a reason to overstimulate your child.) The animal studies described later in this chapter show how the quality of maternal care directly after birth affects gene expression associated either with the stress response or impulsive behavior. In human studies, environmental agents such as chronic stress or smoking have been shown to alter gene expression, as just two examples.

Stressed-out medical students before and during exams experience temporary genetic changes that lower their resistance to infection.[12] "Enriched" rats that have played actively with interesting and challenging toys undergo gene changes that increase their brains' connectivity.[13] Let's look very briefly at the mechanism that actually causes these effects. The active agent in all these environmental effects is a chemical called messenger RNA (mRNA), which carries a translated copy of the protein code to the cells. mRNA, assisted by agents called gene promoters and transcription factors, can even "paralyze" a gene by increasing or decreasing the cell's production of proteins.[14]

"Determinism": Not a Good Idea

Does all this talk about how genes can be altered by the environment make you wonder if we could completely make over children into anything we wanted by applying the right stimulation and methods? Actually, it's been tried and the results suggest caution.

"That Horrible Man." Laura was born in 1933 to a mother who prided herself on being "up to date" with the latest theories of child rearing.

"She believed that horrible man," laments Laura. "Can you imagine trying not to touch or hold your infant and only feeding her every four hours even if she was screaming with hunger? My mother said my dad used to have to hold her down in the chair when I was howling in my crib upstairs and she was afraid that if she picked me up or fed me I'd get spoiled! How *stupid* is that?"

For a hungry infant, very. But at the time when John B. Watson wrote his famous book *Psychological Care of Infant and Child*, Laura's mother was only one of many anxious new parents who feared that disobeying this famous doctor's sadistic version of "mother love" would ruin her child forever. As it happens, Laura is convinced that her enduring problems with stress and a tendency toward depression are a legacy of Watson's influence, since she knows what scientists since Watson's time have learned: that highly stressful early experiences may lay the groundwork for later problems by resetting genes that control chemical balances in one's brain.[15]

Laura claims she chose her career as a pediatrician partly so she could counsel new parents on the importance of bonding—physically as well as emotionally—with their babies. At a time when fads in parenting are more prevalent than ever, I hope she is also advising them that *maternal instinct, wisdom, and common sense should always provide the filter for "expert" advice* (including, I have to add, anything that you read in this book!).

Detrimental Extreme Beliefs. How could a reputable psychologist have given such bad advice? In the early days of psychology, Watson was one of a group of "behaviorists" who insisted that people were primarily a product of their environments. Watson claimed that an infant resembled a "blank slate," which he could transform into almost anything he chose by a process called conditioning.[16] We now recognize the danger of such extreme beliefs, which at one point caused misguided doctors to blame mothers' cold personalities (so-called *refrigerator mothers*) for their children's autism, schizophrenia, and just about anything else that went wrong. Fortunately, the essence of behaviorist theory survives in positive and effective forms of behavior therapy.

The opposite point of view, *nativism* (or, in its extreme form, *genetic determinism*), gives priority to inborn, genetic causes for human traits. It, too, has spawned atrocities, including attempts to wipe out populations deemed "genetically defective." Currently, we should be wary of the insidious nativism promoted by drug advertisements that suggests that if something is genetic, there's nothing you can do except buy their product. Nativism also reduces research funding for scientists searching for natural and effective behavioral interventions for problems.

Of course, the truth lies somewhere between these two extremes. Since Laura has read the research, she must also know that her genes may have predisposed her to be extrasusceptible to early stress experiences, and that children with different genes might have emerged less affected. Responsiveness to stress is one of our most heritable personality factors, but it may be singularly responsive to experience as well.

Individuals Mold Environments; Environments Mold Individuals

Nature-Nurture Avenue is a two-way street. Children are influenced by experience, but bear in mind that their behavior also shapes their experience. A child born with a "difficult" temperament will get different treatment from parents and caregivers than one perceived as "easy." For example, a frazzled, sleepless parent of a neurologically immature infant might react quite differently than they would after a good night's sleep. A restless, high-energy child—especially a boy—in a traditional classroom where a premium is placed on "good conduct" and docility may get very different teacher feedback than a charming, socially skilled child (often a girl) who knows how to say just the right thing to the teacher at the right time.

Genes and the Brain

Genes for Being Human and Genes for Being You

All human beings share genes for certain traits, but, because so many different genes interact, each individual's genotype is also unique. For example, all humans carry genes for height, another very heritable characteristic. Yet there are major differences even among family members; some are due to individual genetic variations and some to environmental factors such as nutrition, health, even a child's emotional state, since severe stress can turn off genetic expression for growth factors.

Language development and its disorders, such as developmental language delay or reading disability, are another important example. All humans come programmed to develop brain structures for acquiring a language of some sort. This ability is so wired into the human genome that even without being exposed to any language, children will instinctively develop one. A number of years ago linguist Susan Goldin-Meadow studied children from a reclusive family whose members were all deaf. Even though the children had never heard language or been exposed to conventional sign language, the youngsters developed an original system of signing with a grammar much like that of a standard language.[17]

On the other hand, individual genes may cause us to differ in the timetable of language development, the ease with which it is acquired, or in the case of a language disorder, whether it might be blocked by some unidentified factor. Families can pass on a greater or lesser risk for language-related learning differences. Like Mollie, the hardworking little girl with dyslexia in Chapter 1, many of my students over the years have come from families whose talents seem to center more on visual, personal, or spatial skills than on reading, spelling, and learning foreign languages. Other students, with diagnoses ranging from Asperger's syndrome to "nonverbal learning disorder," have different types of problems with language that often reflect a family history.

Nonetheless, the *quality* of each individual's language development is very much at the mercy of the environment, since the type of exposure and one's national/local language(s) determine which language sounds, vocabulary, grammatical rules, and level of language competence (reflected, of course, in reading, writing, and social conversation) become embedded in the functioning of the brain. Some families tend to read and talk more with children, while others use more gestures and facial expressions than words. There are even cultural and social-class differences that affect how much and even whether children are encouraged to express themselves or ask questions, which naturally helps determine the way they understand and use language once they get to school.

A "Bad Math Gene"? The human genome endows infants' brains with a basic number sense (can you tell that five objects are more than two?), but whether or not one learns to write numerals, which numerals one learns, and whether multiplication or calculus are mastered depends on culture, experience, and teaching.

I have often had to warn parents (especially mothers of girls, I'm sorry to say) not to let their own "math phobias" become a self-fulfilling prophecy for their children. Despite all our current knowledge, I still meet youngsters like Sandi, a sixth-grader who was absolutely convinced that she couldn't learn percentages and, what's more, that it wasn't necessary for her to try very hard.

"My mother says there's a 'bad math gene' in our family. She says she never could do percent and she got through college anyhow," Sandi gravely informed me after she was referred for special math tutoring. "She won't even take the real estate exam because she knows she'd fail it."

Too bad, because Sandi's mother was obviously a good salesperson, having sold her daughter on the idea, first, that she was doomed to fail at math and, second, that it was okay to give up and stop trying. This double whammy made it much harder for Sandi and for me as her tutor. It took longer, but she did learn percentages, and I hope some different attitudes, as well.

Much more rarely I encounter a parent or caregiver (and do not underestimate the influence of caregivers) who has similar reactions to reading or writing well. We'll talk in a later chapter about the profound impact of adults' models for positive or negative learning habits.

> Children's brains soak up attitudes even more readily than they soak up information. And attitudes are a big part of what enables children to maximize the potential of their own unique combination of genes.

Your Genes and Your Child: A Cautionary Note

> *"When I walk through those school doors, I feel just like a little kid again! And it's not a good feeling!"*
>
> —father of a dyslexic son

Having worked with so many families of children with learning difficulties, I sympathize with a parent who may have struggled with similar but undiagnosed problems and has to revisit this upsetting situation. Consider Bryan, for example. He and his wife had requested an evaluation to help figure out why their son, Matthew, was becoming a serious "underachiever," expert mainly in avoiding reading, written assignments, and homework.

When we met in my office, one of my first steps was, as always, to take a thorough history of the problem and try to identify what might be contributing to it. But uncovering a family history of learning problems isn't always straightforward and definitely requires asking the right questions. So, I don't ask, simply, "Has anyone in your family had a diagnosed learning disability?" to which I am very likely to get the truthful answer "No one that I know of."

Because many adults went to school before learning differences were well recognized, their problems were never acknowledged. So it helps to ask more specific questions if you are interested in uncovering a family history. Because Matthew's symptoms suggested dyslexia, I asked Bryan, "Who, in your family tree, was a smart 'underachiever,' disliked written assignments, and maybe was a poor speller and had trouble with foreign language?"

With such questions, I often hear, "Oh, that was my brother [father, sister, uncle, aunt, etc.]," . . . or, as in Bryan's case, "Why, that's me you're talking about! They always said I just wasn't trying hard enough."

If this situation applies to you, you very likely retain some negative if quite understandable emotional debris about school, teachers, and being called into the principal's office for any sort of conference. It is also not uncommon to blame your child for the same lack of motivation of which you were repeatedly accused. Another natural response is denying that the issue is a problem: "I was the same way, and I turned out fine."

These deeply internalized attitudes can make it difficult to be objective, but if your child is truly miserable, something needs to be done. Your child's curriculum may be more demanding than yours was. The first step is to realize how much your reactions to your child's situation depend on your own previous experience. If you had similar problems and have overcome them, telling your child about your experience, offering constructive and sympathetic support, and explaining how hard work helped you succeed can be a big help. Some parents also find counseling useful for finding positive ways to help their children.

Psychiatrist Warren Rosen, who works with families in Skokie, Illinois, recommends that you evaluate your own "family learning culture" and how well you encourage positive attitudes about school success. "No matter how neurological the problem is in origin," he says, "family reactions are going to make a difference. They affect the child's development, learning, and self-esteem."[18]

"Your child's problems are going to trigger certain emotions in you. Don't be surprised if you have some knee-jerk reac-

*tions of anxiety or frustration. The main thing to remem-
ber is not to assume the child is doing it on purpose or to
annoy you."*

—Warren Rosen

MORAL: Try to put aside your own situation as a child and
be as objective as possible about your child's problem.

Many Ways to Make a Cake. I hope you realize by now that there is
no such thing as a "bad math gene." Genetics and family history can
be *risk indicators*[19] and should be taken seriously because they can
lead to earlier and better treatments. But please remember that
most human traits are influenced by many genes, which combine
in multiple variations. Just as the term *cake* may imply countless
different mixtures of similar ingredients, such terms as *dyslexia,
attention deficit disorder*, or *Asperger's syndrome* signify multiple
variations of certain genetic elements—which are then stirred up
by each individual's particular environment and can be modified
along the way. In fact, similar combinations of genes may result
in quite different outcomes in different individuals. Autism is one
of the most heritable of all neuropsychiatric diagnoses, but some
people who show autistic-type brain abnormalities do not display
autistic symptoms—probably because some experiential trigger
never was pulled.[20]

Identical twins, who inherit identical genomes, do not, despite
their many similarities, always look or behave exactly alike. Since
they start out as genetic duplicates, we might expect complete sim-
ilarity ("concordance") on every aspect of appearance or traits. But
even identical twins experience slightly different environments—
starting in the womb. For example, one twin may have had a more
favorable position before or during birth or be treated differently
after birth. The older they get, different life experiences work subtle
changes on the way genes are expressed. Although the mental disease schizophrenia is considered highly heritable, it is only about
50 percent concordant in identical twins, which means that even
if you have identical genes to a twin with schizophrenia, there

is about a 50 percent chance you will not be affected, probably because your different life experiences have pulled different epigenetic switches.[21]

In a Nutshell: Genes and the Developing Brain

- *At least half our 25,000 genes have something to do with the brain.* With billions of possibilities for individual variation, you can imagine how difficult it is to pin down specific genetic sources of learning abilities, which depend on multiple combinations of genes.

- *Genes tell brain cells what to do.* Brain cells function in tight partnership with their genes. Specialized genes instruct brain cells how to form, grow, and relay the vast number of messages needed for thinking and learning. Meanwhile, outside forces affect these developmental genes in either negative or positive ways. Excess stress, for example, may shut them down at a critical period of development, while good health habits can boost brain activity.

- *Much of what occurs before birth is genetically programmed, yet the fetus is already being affected by the environment of the womb.* Such factors as the mother's nutrition, the quality of the placenta, toxins, viruses, or hormone balances can make big differences in how the brain and every other aspect of the body is structured.

- *With birth and as children grow, environmental factors become increasingly dominant.* The child's home and school experiences—physical, mental, and emotional—help determine how genes play out their roles. Genes are constantly interacting with and being affected by everyday experiences, new learning, emotional states, foods, chemicals, and all the other influences in a child's life.

- *During stages of brain development throughout childhood, adolescence, and adulthood, new genes are switched on and new brain connections form.* Genes direct the rapid formation of proteins that cement learning and memory into synapses.

It is never too late to try to make up for learning that didn't occur properly earlier.

- *Some disorders (e.g., ADHD, depression) may be influenced by genes that affect neurotransmitter activity in brain synapses, but life experiences also affect the same neurotransmitters.*

- *No learning problem should ever be considered a "hopeless case," but effective remedies may take time and effort on everyone's part.*

"Inherited" Characteristics

With compelling evidence that some traits are passed down through families, researchers are zeroing in on those that seem to be most heritable. Two of the most frequently mentioned categories are temperament, or personality, and intelligence.

Personality and Temperament

In study after study, personality traits, or *temperament*, come up as some of our most "heritable" characteristics. Certain genes have been associated with tendencies toward stress, depression, or fearfulness on one hand, and impulsivity, aggression, social problems, and risk-taking on the other. Three examples of strongly heritable traits are *novelty-seeking* (risk-taking, extroversion, impulsivity), *harm avoidance* (fearfulness, stress response, depression, introversion), and *reward dependence* (persistence, attachment to others, sentimentality, warmth).[22]

Please note that these are not descriptions of whole people; they are simply characteristics that may be found in various mixtures in each individual. Since a number of individual genes doubtless contribute to each trait, these temperaments may look quite different in different people. Although we don't usually associate "personality" or "temperament" with learning problems, temperament actually has a close—and possibly even causal—relationship to some types of difficulties.

Novelty-Seeking. If you frequently find your toddler perched on top of the refrigerator or are a veteran of the local emergency room, you may have a child with a tendency to be a risk taker or "novelty-seeker." He may also be an impulsive or extroverted child who has no problem approaching others and will join easily in group play or new situations—and sometimes, in his bumptious enthusiasm, offend other children without meaning to. He may also seek diversions when schoolwork seems "boring" and may be labeled attention deficit disordered. Researchers use the term *disinhibition* to describe such behavior. In some circumstances, this child may be at extra risk for what are called externalizing problems, such as conduct disorders.

Harm Avoidance. When Raina was not quite three, her mother enrolled her in a parent-child program of playing together with large-muscle activities and exercises. But Raina had her own ideas about participation. To her mother's acute embarrassment, Raina—who had been a very late walker—sat solidly in Mom's lap, and, refusing to budge, watched the others play. Although she eventually became a fine athlete and was happy to participate in team activities with her friends, Raina remained "shy," finding it more comfortable to be an observer rather than joining in with strangers. This type of "harm avoidant," "inhibited," or "introverted" personality may also make a person fearful and more prone to stress or depression. Nonetheless, many adults with these characteristics put in extra effort to become socially adept and outgoing and learn to manage their own moods successfully.

Raina's mother says she grew accustomed to report cards that read: "Raina seems to know the material, but she never volunteers in class. She needs to participate more actively."

If a child like Raina also has an expressive language disorder that makes it difficult for her to express her ideas in words even in comfortable situations, this treatable problem may go undetected because everyone simply blames it on being "shy."

Reward Dependence. "Will you be grading the homework?" demands Ryan, knowing full well that he won't put in much effort if he can't see something to reward it. "Reward dependent" people take this natural tendency to an extreme, gaining extra satisfaction from attention, praise, or objective indications of achievement. They thrive on positive reinforcement and are persistent in pursuing it. Children with these characteristics will work hard for grades and the teacher's approval and may have an especially bad year with a teacher who comes across as "cold" and criticizes more than praises.

This trait could apply to many "resilient" children, those unusual ones who thrive despite truly adverse environments, as they know how to extract the maximum amount of attention and positive reinforcement from every situation. Because they are determined to please adults, they may get better treatment than more challenging siblings or peers.

If Ryan grows up in a household or school that places too much emphasis on perfectionism, he may be at risk for emotional problems when he can't meet his own impossibly high standards. This threat is especially acute for reward-dependent youngsters who have a learning difference that causes laborious, "messy" writing or "careless" errors in reading, spelling, or math.

Environment and Temperament

Cross-cultural studies have suggested that temperament traits are universal in humans.[23] Nonetheless, we all know that cultural expectations or family standards of behavior put major restraints on how traits develop.[24] Some immigrant populations, for example, gradually take on different characteristics as a result of societal pressures in the new country.

Temperament traits have been associated with particular neurotransmitters, especially the group called *catecholamines*, which includes both *dopamine* and *serotonin*. Inherited differences in the genes that regulate brain concentrations of serotonin and dopamine appear to be involved, at least until the child's environment exerts its influence.

Early Nurturing Makes a Difference. Rhesus monkeys, which are genetically very close to humans, apparently have offspring with traits—and problems—much like those of humans. Some monkeys have a genetic marker for what researchers term *high reactivity* for either stress and anxiety or impulsivity and social difficulties. Studies have implicated one or more genes that regulate the concentration of serotonin in brain synapses. The crucial finding, however, is that *the troublesome genes become activated only if the infant receives inadequate or inconsistent early nurturing.*

Scientists working with animals use DNA analysis to look for such genetic markers, but they run into problems when they try to separate the effects of these genes from the effects of the type of care the infant receives. For example, monkeys with genetic markers for certain serotonin differences tend to grow up overreactive, nervous, and socially maladjusted (in monkey terms). But are these characteristics caused simply by genes? Or are they caused by the monkey's mother, who shares those genes, and is herself of this disposition and therefore can't provide consistent mothering?

> More effective nurturing seemed to normalize the animals'
> brain chemistry.

To get better answers to such questions, a research method termed *cross-fostering* places animals at birth with foster mothers of different temperament types. In one study, newborn monkeys with the genetic marker for serotonin disregulation were cross-fostered. Those raised by low-reactivity foster mothers, who were calm and expert at soothing and nurturing the babies, showed a surprising outcome. Rather than developing the difficulties—both behavioral and neurochemical—that their genome would have predicted, the expertly nurtured youngsters developed low-reactivity characteristics and went on to take leadership positions in their group. Amazingly, their serotonin brain chemistry was normalized. On the other hand, infants with the same genetic marker who were placed with jumpy, distracted, or fearful mothers showed the troublesome characteristics—as well as the serotonin imbalances—that usually accompany this genetic profile.[25] Steven J. Suomi, the author of this research, thinks it has wide implications. "It is hard to imagine that the situation would be any less complex for humans," he concludes. Indeed, human studies looking at comparable genes that affect neurotransmitters in the human brain suggest that the genes have significant effects on depression and antisocial behavior—but only in people who are exposed to particular life stressors.[26] The authors of this research admit that this topic has such important implications that it demands more definitive research confirmation.

J. Fraser Mustard, distinguished Canadian physician and scientist, is one of many experts who see such findings as having far-reaching implications—not only for individuals but also for public policy. "Brains are brains in rats, monkeys, and humans," he points out, and poor experience in the very early years of life, in utero and infancy, sets biological pathways that make individuals vulnerable to "abnormal neuron function."[27]

> The quality of the early rearing environment made a significant difference in later behavior—and in the associated gene(s) and brain function.

If this research does prove applicable to humans, we should urge that it be used to educate and encourage families—and not as one more blame game to lay on overstressed moms!

Bonding with a Caregiver. Rhesus monkeys may also be able to teach us something important about the lasting neurochemical benefits of forming a positive emotional bond with a caregiver. In another series of studies, infants were either raised by adult monkeys or placed in a nursery and allowed to play and interact with only three or four peers. All infants in the peer-reared group developed lower brain concentrations of serotonin; those who also had inherited the disrupted serotonin transporter gene that made them more susceptible to problems had the lowest concentrations of all. These animals were also more likely to develop social problems, aggression, depression, and impulsivity than those who did not carry the risk gene.[28]

A recent study of variations in maternal behavior in rats came up with similar findings. Like monkeys, some rats are better at mothering newborns than others. Because these mothers tend to groom and nurse more effectively, the infants' levels of stress are lowered, and the offspring are more likely to retain a calm temperament throughout life.

Again, researchers asked, did these "mellow" babies simply inherit their mother's neurochemistry, or is there something about their very early nurturing that interacted with the relevant genes?

As in the monkey studies, they cross-fostered the infants. Those born to stressed-out mother rats were placed with calm mothers; as adults, these babies resembled the normal offspring of nonstressed mothers. The authors conclude that the state of a gene can be established through behavioral interventions that have "tissue specific effects on gene expression."[29]

> Can environmentally caused changes to genes be passed
> down to the next generation?

We can expect much more research on this topic, especially since *these effects may become cross-generational*. Poorly nurtured, highly reactive animals are likely themselves to be poorer at parenting.[30] A tenuous thread of evidence goes even further to suggest that such epigenetic changes can themselves be passed down as alterations in the genome.[31]

Parenting Style Influences Genes. Several different lines of research suggest that the environments created by different styles of parenting can influence genetic expression in human children. One example is the effect of religious homes on traits commonly associated with attention deficit problems. A provocative Dutch study followed nearly two thousand sets of identical twins who had been adopted into separate homes with different religious orientations. Each set of twins naturally had identical genomes at birth. Nonetheless, later tests of traits often associated with attention deficit disorder showed that the religious upbringing tended to suppress these behaviors—as well as the related differences in the serotonin and dopamine systems. The results suggested that being adopted into a home with a religious upbringing tended to modify the effect of genes that cause differences in the serotonin and dopamine systems. The Dutch researchers termed the relevant traits "Experience Seeking," "Disinhibition," "Thrill and Adventure Seeking." Conclusion: the upbringing "not only influences the absolute levels of disinhibition, but also its genetic architecture."[32]

The study does not specify which particular aspects of religious homes may be responsible for this influence, but other studies suggest that the particular belief system may not be as important as the presence of a clear structure of expectations and parental example and support. A great deal of research on intelligence, as well as on personality traits, indicates that in a family atmosphere where genetic effects are completely free to express themselves, they will play a prominent role, whereas in environments where genes are "constrained" by parental expectations and enrichment, the genes lose some of their power in determining how a child develops.

For one example of a constraining environment, consider a child with genetic propensities that could make him an expert chess player. If he grows up in an environment where there are no chess boards and no examples of adults playing chess, his chess abilities would probably remain latent. On the other hand, if he grows up in a household or school setting where chess is played, he might fully develop that talent.

Parental Influence on IQ Scores. The situation appears to be similar for children's IQ scores. In a normally enriched environment where a child is exposed to books, conversation about ideas, a wide variety of experiences, and adults who model lifelong curiosity and learning, the youngster's IQ has an excellent chance of developing to its full potential. In intellectually deprived circumstances, however, the same child's mental development will be constrained, and he will probably end up with a lower IQ than he might have had because the relevant genes were never stimulated.

> *"It may be helpful to think of some genetic factors as constraining certain outcomes rather than determining a particular trait."*
>
> —Jerome Kagan[33]

In the next chapter we will take up the controversial and very interesting topic of what intelligence is and where it comes from— as well as what we can do to help our own children develop it. Before moving on, however, we should conclude this chapter with a few quick words on "genetic engineering" and the potential dangers of trying it at home in your spare time.

Engineering the Learning Brain

Genetic engineering can take many forms: bioengineering crops, selecting a sperm or egg donor on the basis of desirable characteristics, or the as-yet-distant possibility of altering a faulty human gene for a single-gene disorder. (On February 20, 2007, the *New York Times* reported the successful alteration of the single gene responsible for a disorder in mice that is similar to Rett syndrome. This type of intervention is not done in humans, however, because it requires genetic engineering before conception.) Some scientists suspect that it won't be long before genetic testing on newborns might determine if they are at special risk for anxiety or conduct disorders, among other personality variables. The mind-boggling potential—as well as the unanticipated downsides—of all these possibilities suggest that we surely need to be educating our children as thoughtful and critical decision-makers. Let's also include in this category a parent's (or school's) application of extraintense stimulation to a child in an effort to improve on—or even redirect— her genetic allotment.

Some families have long pedigrees of accomplishment in specific fields (think Bach or Barrymore), but can a superstimulating environment make a gifted musician or actor out of any child? Probably not, unless some degree of innate potential exists. Moreover, the resultant pressure, stress, and neglect of certain foundational experiences (that is, natural affection and nurturing) may severely distort the child's development.

Parents determined to engineer the development of a prodigy, a scholarship-level athlete, or a seven-footer are better advised to provide a healthy and naturally stimulating environment while observing and guiding the child's own nature and talents. Likewise, it is sensible to accept the fact that a jumpy, disorganized infant may not become the calmest kid on the block, and a fearful, withdrawn one may never be an effortless extrovert. Nonetheless, supportive nurturance can enable each to succeed happily within the parameters of his or her own temperament.

The following chapters will provide more information and advice about the role of the environment in shaping our children, as well as some serious warnings about how to rescue your child from a culture that too often limits instead of expands mental possibilities.

Capsules of Wisdom

- Your most important genetic engineering job is to provide a nurturing, healthy, brain-appropriate, and stimulating environment at home.

- If you suspect your child may have a genetic susceptibility to any sort of learning problem, you need to be extravigilant in creating a positive learning environment.

- No matter what has already occurred, change is still possible. Genes respond to environmental influences throughout one's lifetime. Skilled parents and teachers seek the fine line between pressuring and providing appropriate support.

CHAPTER 8

Who's Intelligent?

Learning Styles and One-of-a-Kind Brains

*"If I'm so smart, why can't I write as fast
as the other kids?"*
—first-grader after a diagnostic testing session

ere's one for you," challenged my friend Pearl Rieger, a well-known educational dignostician for a Midwestern hospital clinic that specializes in social-emotional learning disabilities and Asperger's syndrome. She also consults with a top-rated private school where she had just been asked for a diagnosis of a little boy.

"Tell me what you think about a first-grader who has an IQ of 142 [which puts him among the top 1 percent of the general population on this particular test]—this kid is just so gifted. He reads at a fifth-grade level, but he's miserable. There are others in that class on his intellectual level, but he doesn't have a single friend. In November he couldn't even tell me the names of any of the children in his class. He has zero social skills, and all he wants to do is brag about how much he knows. He's really aggressive with the other children, and he *bites*!"

"He must be one of your clinic's clients," I ventured.

"Yes, but his father is very resistant to a diagnosis and the child really doesn't fit into any distinct category." She paused. "I'm recommending social-skills training with the school psychologist along with some special help from his teacher and strategies for his parents to try."

At the end of our conversation, my friend, who is defying the usual retirement age, added, "I must tell you, this is the kind of case that keeps me in this business. I think we really need to help this child."

Are We Helping or Hurting?

Each child brings a singular package of talents and a singular challenge to parents, teachers, and diagnosticians. Even our most reliable tests can't capture the whole child, and too much emphasis on test scores and IQ points diverts our attention from the most important question: How can we help?

In this chapter we will take a critical look at some traditional assumptions about testing, about intelligence, and how to test it. We will also address the important challenge of raising "different" brains, and how important but easily misunderstood they are.

Quick Take: Helping Without Hurting

1. No child can be summed up in a set of test scores, especially when the tests themselves may be incomplete or seriously flawed.

2. IQ isn't everything. Success in school and life also depend on many other factors that are not closely related to IQ.

3. Some students have trouble showing their true abilities on commonly used tests, but strategic preparation helps.

4. Traditional ideas about "intelligence" need to change in our new technological society.

5. Each of us has a one-of-a-kind brain, assembled from our genes and our life experiences. One term for these important brain differences is *cerebrodiversity*.

6. *Learning style* is a term used to describe each individual's profile of preferences, strengths, and weaknesses in learning.

7. Some learning styles mesh more easily than others with academic demands but do not necessarily predict lifetime achievement.

8. No one is exceptionally good at everything. High degrees of artistic, mechanical, psychomotor (physical/athletic), or leadership talent often coexist with academic "disabilities"—and vice versa.

What Is Intelligence?

This question, which still causes passionate disagreements among researchers, is especially problematic for parents given an "IQ" score that doesn't match up to the real child they know. It is not surprising that IQ tests alone are not always good predictors of how a child will fare in either the academic or the real world.

In fact, "intelligence" implies a range of talents that are impossible to sum up in one test score. New definitions are reaching beyond traditional verbal and analytic skills to broader aspects of the human brain's potential. This is good news for children with learning differences that may be valuable in a world badly in need of new ideas.

As a newly minted educational psychologist, I firmly believed in the validity of educational testing and, of course, the all-important IQ test. I still use and learn a lot from many different types of tests, but I now understand that a child's long-term success depends on qualities far beyond what any test can measure.

How an Educational Psychologist Learns to Be Humble

As I write, I glance at my study wall to a crudely framed, faded drawing of a vividly colored mountain, accompanied by a smudged but loving note from a fourth-grade girl who was my student for several years, thanking me for helping her "over the mountain." What Carly did not know as she laboriously penned her gift was that her future in our selective K–12 school was being seriously debated by the teachers.

> "She's just so much slower than the others," said her social studies teacher.

"She plods along because she has trouble grasping the concepts. I think we should recommend another school where she won't be so overwhelmed as she gets into middle school," said one teacher.

To my enduring shame, I agreed with this suggestion. Carly was admittedly a sweet little girl, a dogged worker and well liked by her classmates, but I couldn't imagine her succeeding in the academically rigorous environment of our higher grades. I placed a lot of weight on the IQ test in her file, on which she scored significantly below the class average. Thank goodness, her other teachers overruled us, and Carly went on to middle school with her class.

You can probably guess the rest of the story. I watched as Carly progressed through the grades, picking up steam at every turn. By the time she was in high school, she was a class officer, and as a senior she chaired the service organization, managing volunteers and large school fundraisers with charm and aplomb. Never a great student but always known for her dependability, common sense, generosity, and upbeat disposition, she completed a business college degree, joined a small manufacturing firm, and eventually, as a mother of two children, started her own successful business. Boy, was I wrong!

> *"The 'A' students are working for me now."*
>
> —dyslexic father of a dyslexic son

I learned a related lesson from children who scored high "off the charts," in early IQ testing, and then proceeded to blow up in the later grades for one reason or another—poor self-discipline, lack of motivation, stress disorders, or difficulty relating to others. So when new conceptions of intelligence started to come along a few years ago, I was ready to rethink my notions of what "smart" is really all about.

Intelligence, Genes, and Environments

Where does intelligence come from? Specific aspects of intelligence, such as reaction time (i.e., how quickly you respond to a stimulus) and some aspects of language processing, as well as the amount of gray matter in the brain appear to be at least partially inherited.[1] So many factors comprise our "smarts," however, that any number of different genes are probably involved.

Given the lack of agreement on what intelligence really is, most studies have defined it by some sort of IQ score. As long as we understand that *IQ score* and *intelligence* may not be totally synonymous, studies of the "heritability" of IQ are interesting. Overall, the IQs of identical twins, who inherit the exact same set of genes, tend to be more alike than those of fraternal twins, whose genomes are no more similar that those of regular brothers and sisters. So IQ appears to be at least partially heritable.

Yet when identical twins are adopted separately into different families, they are likely to achieve different IQ scores, at least in the short term, as well as different levels of school achievement and long-term success.[2] In fact, when any child from a "disadvantaged" environment is adopted into a "high-quality" home, IQ scores and school achievement tend to rise above what might have been expected had the child remained in the disadvantaged environment.

Intellectually impoverished circumstances tend to depress IQ's no matter what a child's genetic endowment.[3] On the other hand, appropriate early stimulation raises IQ scores and school readiness—*at least for children from disadvantaged environments*. Although these numerical gains fall off somewhat with age, they are not lost. Moreover, data on long-term life outcomes for disadvantaged children in well-structured early enrichment programs show lasting gains in life skills, school completion, social adjustment, self-esteem, and avoidance of trouble with the law, as well as financial and personal success.

There do seem to be limits on what such enrichment can accomplish, however, as advantaged children do not show similar gains.

> Genes set a range of possibilities, not an unlimited field for overanxious parents.

Measuring Potential: IQ and Test Scores Aren't All

In an auto plant or a chemistry lab, testing gives clear answers to important questions. Does the engine run? What is the pH of this soil sample? When it comes to testing children's abilities, however, the situation gets more complicated (e.g., Is Mae "smart" enough to succeed at this school? Will Ronny's "auditory processing disorder" keep him from going to college? How much can we expect from Albert with his diagnosis of "nonverbal learning disability"? Does Freddy have a learning disorder or is he just unmotivated?).

One of the most puzzling questions arises when a seemingly smart child consistently messes up academically. Or, on the other hand, when a child with a nonstellar IQ turns into a superstar.

> In the field of learning differences, clear-cut answers simply aren't easy to come by, and testing for intelligence or for learning problems is still a very imprecise business.

Under- and Overachievers. As we all know, underachievers are those whose performance doesn't match up to their apparent potential. Many "underachievers" actually have unidentified learning problems, often of the type that restrict their ability to write quickly and neatly. If your child's teachers tell you he is "not working up to his potential," your first response should be to find out "Why?" not to start blaming or accusing your child. (Refer back to Chapter 3, "What Should We Call This?" for "differential diagnosis.")

Overachiever is a peculiar term. Is it really possible for a child to achieve more than she has the ability to achieve? Consider Sarita, a popular sophomore who is labeled an overachiever because her excellent grades are much better than they should be according to the IQ and other ability test scores in her school file. Sarita has been diagnosed with dyslexia, but she is an extremely hard worker, "a really neat kid" who gets a lot of emotional support from her family. Determined to become a veterinarian, she is also a talented violinist and fulfills a significant time commitment to community service. Nonetheless, Sarita's guidance counselor is skeptical about her budding college aspirations.

"On the basis of your practice SAT," he advised, "I think you should scale down your choices."

"That's nonsense!" muttered one of her teachers on hearing this verdict. "If anyone can make it, this kid can."

Intelligence: New Ideas About What Matters

> "What all our efforts in neuroscience are demonstrating is that you have many peculiar ways of arranging a human brain and there are all sorts of varieties of creative, successful human beings."
>
> —neurologist Antonio Damasio

Brain research shows that ability comes wrapped in a wide variety of neural packaging. In his seminal book *Frames of Mind*, Howard Gardner enumerated seven separate intelligences, each with its own brain systems. Gardner has added even more "intelligences" to his original list, and his insights have broadened the way many teachers present information, as we will see later in this chapter.

What Matters in the Long Run? "Successful Intelligence"

I thought about Sarita, the so-called "underachiever," when I heard a talk by Dr. Robert Sternberg, a leading researcher of "successful intelligence," who is convinced that traditional tests of IQ are not only incomplete, but also seriously unfair to individuals with potential that lies outside the lines.[4] Sternberg is developing measures that tap a wider range of abilities, which he terms as follows:

- *analytic intelligence:* the traditional kind on which most IQ tests, the SAT, and school achievement tests are based

- *creative intelligence:* imagination, creative problem solving, thinking "outside the box"

- *practical intelligence:* common sense, ability to manage one's life, skill in dealing with others

Sternberg's preliminary findings suggest that his tests predict college GPA just as well as do SAT scores. The most successful people, he points out, are those who recognize and use their strengths in all three areas and correct or work around their weaknesses. For many students with problems due to learning differences, this type of *compensation* is an important key to success.

> Children's brains have a mixture of physical, emotional, so-cial, and intellectual needs. They lose out if we try to boost academic skills at the expense of the other abilities.

A child in the twenty-first century must master literacy and numeracy, and as one who teaches these skills, I never under-estimate their importance. The complexities of our modern world require analytic ability, verbal and mathematical reasoning, and keen scientific understanding. *In fact, the future of our society demands that we start teaching all students—with all kinds of different minds—more effectively. It also demands however, that we honor the importance of personal qualities such as motivation, self-discipline, creative innovation, moral reasoning, and "people skills."*

The ongoing electronic revolution makes new categories of skills important—and profitable. Many dazzlingly successful entre-preneurs, inventors, and other creative types seriously disliked traditional school and even dropped out. Employers evaluate "emo-tional intelligence" and "social intelligence," which include self-management, relationship skills, and innovative thinking, in their prospective employees.[5]

Another contrast between types of intelligence may account for differences between success in school and success in real life. Schools require mainly *crystallized intelligence*—specific information one has learned: vocabulary words, math computation, rules of spelling, facts about history, science, etc. In real life, however, "thinking on your feet," hands-on problem solving, or practical reasoning may count even more. This type of *fluid intelligence* enables us to de-velop solutions to new problems and adapt our thinking to the demands of the situation.

One fascinating study of Brazilian street children provides an example. These youngsters are under great pressure to develop a successful street business, since they risk death if they can't earn money. The successful ones form a business and manage the math-

ematics needed to run it. Curiously, though, they fail completely
when given the same math problems on a pencil-and-paper test
in school. The real world makes sense to them, but they don't understand the school's more abstract way of presenting the concepts.[6]

Many nonstandard learners excel in real-life contexts but fall
apart when the work is a school-type task with no practical rele-
vance for them. They benefit from using concrete materials and
situations—such as manipulative math materials, dramatizations,
simulations, and visual diagrams to organize essays. They benefit
from help with specific memory strategies and direct teaching of
how to express their knowledge in organized written form.

On the other hand, children who shine at "crystallized" knowledge easily recite facts, lists, names of capitals, new numbers of
license plates . . . until the listener sometimes wants to say, "Give
me a break!" They usually do well on memorization tests, but when
it comes to applying their knowledge more broadly, they may be at
a loss. We can help them with such skills as brainstorming ideas,
identifying the main idea in a paragraph, getting the "point" of a
story or discussion, reading "between the lines," looking for an author's point of view, categorizing, and observing how things relate
to one another.

"He Doesn't Test Well"

Some students simply can't "show their stuff" in a traditional testing situation. One reason for these problems is that achievement
tests tap mainly crystallized, as opposed to fluid, intelligence. Another is that repeated failure and frustration creates "test anxiety."
This term can mean a lot of different things, from, *"He should be
anxious, since he didn't do his homework or prepare adequately,"*
to *"He really does know and understand it, but he just blanks out
when he gets to the test."*

Of course, if you're like Amanda's family, it wouldn't be too surprising if your child developed test anxiety. An excellent student but
a very nervous, jumpy little girl who claimed she got "dizzy and
sick" in her stomach when she had to take a test, Amanda came to
me in the fourth grade.

"Can you help me study for the SAT?" she asked.

"The what?" I asked.

"The SAT. My dad says I have to study hard so I will do really well on it."

This from a nine-year-old! Positive strategies—not pressure or nagging—are the way to support your child's brain work for tests. Here are just a few of many practical steps you can take.

Confronting "Test Anxiety"

Setting the Stage: Commonsense Steps That Are Still Important No Matter How Many Times You Have Heard Them

- *Sleep* is one of the best memory aids and is generally more useful than late-night cramming. See Chapter 11, "Brain-Cleaning 102," for age-appropriate guidelines to try to ensure that your child has enough sleep. (No one said parenting would be easy, but this one is especially important.)

- For traditional IQ tests or learning disability evaluations, no formal preparation is possible. For a subject-matter test at school, preparation should have started with completion of the first assignment, but a *well-planned review* of important material right before bed the night before helps set it into memory. If your child requests help, try to help him summarize the important points from the lesson, and list or outline them. This "capsule study guide" will help him review the material efficiently.

- Allow enough time to get the morning off to a reasonably relaxed start; *early-morning rushing or emotional scenes set the nervous system into a stress response*, which reduces thinking capacity and memory. On the other hand, hugs and smiles help.

- Try to have needed *materials assembled the night before*; use checklists if your child has difficulty remembering pencils, notebooks, snack, etc.

- If possible, include some *protein food for breakfast* (milk, yogurt, sausage, peanut butter) and not too much sugar.

- Training in *deep breathing or relaxation techniques* resets the brain for a positive response, improves memory, and calms an anxious student.

- Some schools incorporate *brain-energizing movement activities* (e.g., yoga, Brain Gym [see Chapter 12] or other physical relaxation into the daily routine).[7] You might want to investigate them for home use.

- *Parents can create test anxiety* by placing too much emphasis on the grade as opposed to the student's effort or how much she actually learned. This is a difficult line to walk, but if your child has a serious problem with test-taking, you may want to reexamine your attitudes and remind yourself that you really love this youngster irrespective of the grades she brings home—and don't forget to tell her that, too. Reasonable expectations and accountability are important but sometimes TLC is needed to calm the limbic panic centers and open up higher thinking circuits.

For Subject Matter Tests (finals, unit tests, quizzes, etc.):
- Some students are anxious about testing because they lack effective study skills or have not put in the time necessary to prepare thoroughly. Even if your child has a diagnosed learning problem, he still has to do his share. Ensure that your child has a TV-free and electronic game–free place to study. Some youngsters seem to do better with nondistracting music. When your child tells you she needs to multitask, inform her that experts disagree with her (more about this in Chapter 11). She needs to focus as much as possible on studying one thing at a time. You may have to enforce some clear rules to rebuild neglected habits; the earlier you start, the easier it is.

- Many schools have Study Skills courses for older students. Take advantage of these, or ask the school where you can obtain help or references on where your youngster can learn better study skills for his most effective manner of learning (i.e., some youngsters do better with visual diagrams, charts, illustrations, videos, or audiotapes to get key concepts into memory).

- One important study skill, for middle or high-schoolers, is knowing how to make effective *study guides*. Check with your school or library to find appropriate how-to books. You, the teacher, or a tutor may need to work with your child to help him master making his own.

- A youngster can "study and study" and then get to the test and be unable to answer the questions. This often happens because she did not understand the material in the first place, and when it was rephrased on the exam question, she blanked out. *This is not a memory problem but a comprehension problem* and calls for a conference with the teacher, possible special help, or even temporary work with a tutor.

- If your child has a diagnosed disability in reading speed or writing, you may be able to *request test accommodations* such as an untimed test. Mastering good study techniques is still important, however.

- Some "divergent" thinkers have particular trouble with *multiple-choice questions* because they see the complexity of situations, not the linear path to one right answer. For thinkers like these, I suggest they try to figure out what a less complex mind would choose as the right answer.

- Follow the suggestions in a later section on "brain-cleaning" to send your child into the testing situation with as well-functioning a brain as possible.

Late-Blooming Brains

"I Know I'm Stupid"

Trent was a "late bloomer," just like his dad and his older brother. Nobody doubted he was smart—he was just a little "immature" in some areas of development.

Trent survived first grade, but he finished the year with the absolute conviction that he was "stupid." Never mind his parents' protestations to the contrary.

"But Trent, you're so good at math. Your teacher says you can figure out really hard problems in your head!"

"But Trent, you know how interested you are in so many things ... and you remembered everything from when we went to the museum and learned about China. And you're the best one in the class at fixing the computer."

"But Trent, you always have such good, creative ideas. Remember how you solved our problem when we went to the beach and forgot our beach towels?"

Trent, however, wasn't buying any of the motivating talk. He knew he was "stupid" for one special reason: he was one of the poorest readers in the class. To compound the problem, he also had a terrible time writing neatly and quickly. His teacher hadn't made a big issue of it, but he could tell.

> Trent's first-grade reading program had been absolutely wrong for him and had certainly done him more harm than good.

Trent couldn't tell (nor could his parents) that he was the victim of a lackadaisical first-grade reading program that had short-changed him on important foundations for accurate word recognition. He was also not in a position to understand that many, many children—especially boys—experience later maturation of fine muscles in the hands and fingers and brain connections needed for good handwriting. Trent, like so many others, needed lots of patient teaching, reassurance, and practice before he could be expected to produce written work that reflected his fine intellect. To the rest of the world, Trent was obviously "smart," with advanced verbal skills, but in his own mind he was already a failure.

A trained reading teacher will be able to remedy Trent's reading deficit, and he will eventually learn to write both by hand and on a computer. It will, however, take a lot more time and effort to restore his self-confidence. I know this because Trent is one of many, many such children I have treated over the years, those bright, shiny, and talented little kids who have a developmental lag coupled with a learning difference that was not properly handled. These are kids whose chins gradually begin to droop and their joy to dull because the system has convinced them they're no good.

As an educational therapist, one of my hardest tasks has always been to change negative attitudes embedded in the brain's emotional circuits throughout the formative early school years. Many adults still carry such scars—which, with a "push-down" curriculum, may already be forming in kindergarten or even preschool.

"Developmental Readiness": An Old-Fashioned Idea Worth Revisiting

Teachers used to talk a lot about whether a child was "ready" to learn a certain skill, realizing that "readiness" means not only that the youngster has had the *proper experiences* (such as language development, careful listening experiences, or the training to manage herself in a group) but also that her *brain is mature enough* to handle the skills and concepts involved. Educators are all too familiar with the reality of developmental readiness, but it has gotten a bad name because others have misinterpreted the idea to mean that we just sit around and wait for the brain to get "ready" for whatever we need to teach. Wrong! We have to prepare the brain by providing the right experiences—a foundation that many children today lack.

> Respecting a child's "readiness" does *not* mean just sitting around and waiting for learning skills to mature.

Even with good foundations, however, developmental age makes a difference. An interesting example is found in Malcolm Gladwell's book *Outliers*, which concerns the importance of seemingly incidental factors in life success. Noting that American children born in the later part of the year are underrepresented in college, Gladwell points out that students who are several months more mature when entering school have a much better chance of rising to the top. This is just one example of a reality that causes some parents of children with late birthdays relative to the rest of the class to consider an extra preschool year. (You will find a fuller discussion of this entire topic in my book *Your Child's Growing Mind*.)

"Late Bloomers" May Be Smarter in the Long Run

Parents and teachers who have struggled to bring a "late bloomer" up to speed will be heartened by studies showing that those later developers may have the highest potential of all if allowed enough time to realize it. A fascinating study published in *Nature* in 2006 looked at brain development from childhood to adulthood by periodically scanning the brains of more than three hundred "normal" children.[8] The researchers measured age-related changes in cortical thickness in areas linked to one measure of intelligence and reasoning ability. What they found suggests that the children who ended up with "superior" intellectual abilities were the ones whose brains took longest to mature—as much as four years longer—possibly because the extra time helped them develop richer neural networks.

> As far as the brain is concerned, later maturation may be better.

The scientists conclude, " 'Brainy' children are not cleverer solely by virtue of having more or less gray matter at any one age. Rather, intelligence is related to dynamic properties of cortical maturation."[9] Translation: as far as the brain is concerned, time to mature is important for maximum development.

Does this information make you wonder about everything you have heard regarding the importance of trying to accelerate development from "brainy" babies on up? It should.

One-of-a-Kind Brains

"Cerebrodiversity": Different Brains for Different Terrains

Human brains (cerebrums) are as diverse as our facial features. The term *cerebrodiversity* was coined by Gordon Sherman, former director of the Dyslexia Research Laboratory at Beth Israel hospital in Boston, who now heads the Newgrange School for students with dyslexia. He is a strong advocate for the high potential of youngsters who learn "outside the lines."

Just because an individual is "different" does not necessarily mean he is "disabled."

—Gordon Sherman

Understanding "Cerebrodiversity"

- No one has a perfect brain. Most of us have some sort of "learning disability" or weakness, for which we learn to compensate by using our strong points.

- Whether or not a difference becomes a disability depends on the environment—what it encourages, what it expects. Rigid or punitive schools can turn a difference into a disability.

- As a society, we need to preserve a variety of mental skills, which may become very important in an unknown future.

Dr. Sherman recently shared with me a poem penned by one of his students whose extended family "includes more members with dyslexia than without." Adam's reflections should be a good reminder to all of us:

The Brain Thinking

If everybody was the same
And someone had a thought
And it was wrong,
Then everybody would have the same thought
And everybody would be wrong
So . . .
Everybody needs to be different.

—Adam C., age seven
(reprinted with permission)

Gifted and Learning Disabled: Not an Oxymoron

Back in the 1970s, when I was working as a reading specialist and doing graduate work in educational psychology, I became intrigued by a puzzling subset of my students. Although these children gave every indication of being very bright, they struggled with academics and were often called underachieving or even lazy because of the vast gap between their high tested IQs, apparent quickness, and faltering reading, writing, or math abilities. I suggested to one of my professors that I would like to write a research paper on children who were both gifted and learning disabled (LD).

"Impossible!" she snorted. "There is no such thing."

Fortunately, the world continues to turn, science progresses, and researchers now agree not only that there is such a thing but also that this paradoxical combination is more common than anyone realized. Unfortunately, however, it is still a hard sell for parents, some educators who define "gifted" too narrowly, and—most devastating of all—for the kids involved.

"Colin is simply lazy and careless. If he wanted to write neatly, he could."

"Amy can't be smart. Listen to the mistakes she makes when she reads out loud!"

"Dirk won't remember to turn in his homework and refuses to follow the classroom rules. That's not my definition of intelligence!"

"He can get the answer somehow, but he refuses to write out the equations—and he keeps 'forgetting' the multiplication facts. How is this possible?"

"What do you mean I'm smart? Just ask my teachers—I'm an idiot!"

"Separable Processes"

How is it possible that a single brain can be gifted at certain things and inexpert in others? The short answer is that there are subsystems, or *modules*, of neuronal networks for various types of skills. For example, *math concepts*—such as the ability to reason out answers to word problems—are handled by different neurons than *rote-level memory* involved in repeating the multiplication tables. In reading, these *separable processes* make it possible for a child with *hyperlexia* to read fluently without understanding what she is reading. Many gifted/LD students have poor reading decoding (sounding out words) and spelling compared to their comprehension and language expression. One of my most interesting students ever was such a child—a little girl whose inconsistencies were seriously frustrating everyone, especially herself.

> Sometimes, when a child has a learning problem, the only consistent thing is her inconsistency.

Shanique, "Mistress of Mysterious Ideas." "I think I'm going to need some help understanding this child," reported the third-grade teacher on the first day of school. Since Judy was a skilled teacher and not easily ruffled, my curiosity was aroused: "What's going on?"

"Well, this morning a new student, Shanique, sails into my room and announces, 'I am Shanique, mistress of mysterious ideas.' She got everyone's attention, that's for sure! She's obviously really smart, but her skills—oh, my! I think we've all got our work cut out for us."

Shanique, a winsome little girl with pigtails as unruly as her imagination, certainly did get our attention. Her mother, Vivian, was a visiting mathematics professor at a local university and a single mom who admitted she was desperate for some help and advice. Shanique's previous school in their former home city had transferred her along with a thick dossier of testing results and comments.

Although I was rapidly abandoning my faith in IQ scores, I couldn't help but be impressed that many of Shanique's subtests were the highest I had ever seen, in a range that ranked her as one in a million. Within the profile, however, it was clear that her off-the-chart verbal reasoning skills and vocabulary were not equaled by her "merely above average" abilities at puzzle assembly and other performance skills that require some manual dexterity as well as sustained planning and attention. There are no reading or writing tests included in the IQ battery, but the only subtest that fell slightly below the "average" range was also the only one in which she had to pick up a pencil and copy unfamiliar symbols into a pattern. This extremely uneven profile of differences between very high and much lower scores should raise red flags.

Shanique's previous teachers had noted "poor attention," "poor impulse control," "poor social conformity," "*excessive* self-blame" (often typical of the highly gifted), "poor ego strength," and "aggressiveness."

Shanique's oral language was clear and precise. When her reading skills were tested, she scored right on grade level, but with a large discrepancy between below-grade-level "decoding" (sounding out unfamiliar words) and above-grade-level "comprehension." (Poor word-attack skills combined with higher verbal comprehension signal either inadequate previous teaching or a learning disability. In Shanique's case, it was the latter.) But doesn't a grade-level average mean she's doing just fine? *Absolutely not!* With Shanique's extraordinary verbal abilities, we would expect her to be well above grade level in reading. Moreover, although her creative writing was very advanced in theme, content, and originality, her handwriting, spelling, and spacing of words on the page looked like that of a much younger child. Her understanding of math concepts was quick and insightful, but her written equations lurched unpredictably around the page, and showed many "careless" errors.

Even more troubling than her academic performance, however, was Shanique's emotional and social immaturity. Here are some of the steps in our plan to help her:

1. Shanique was smart enough to understand her own learning strengths and weaknesses. We discussed them with her, applauded her many talents, and let her participate in developing her program of remediation.

2. We sympathized with how frustrating and unfair this situation must have seemed to her and encouraged her to pursue writing her poetry and imaginative stories—with or without accurate spelling, which she could correct later. She received lots of positive feedback from her classmates for her original and entertaining stories.

3. By fourth grade Shanique had developed the prerequisites for mastering word processing skills: sufficient motor coordination and the motivation to practice. This skill ultimately helped a lot with writing fluency.

4. Shanique, who had been smart enough to get by without much effort, needed to take more responsibility for her own learning. She agreed to try to work harder on things she tended to avoid because she deemed them "boring" (e.g., spelling rules, punctuation, math facts). We worked on the idea that frustration was no excuse for being unpleasant or inappropriate with her classmates.

5. At her request, we gave Shanique's mother the name of a psychologist at the university clinic who could help with some of the child's self-esteem problems. (She was acutely embarrassed about letting any of the other students see her "messy" papers.) We also recommended that Mom reinforce some expectations for considerate social behavior and set up a more regular, organized schedule for homework as well as a morning routine to help Shanique arrive at school as "put together" as possible.

> For most children, fourth grade is a time when the brain begins to shift toward more mature development, so it is an excellent time to try new approaches to old problems.

With a terrific teacher, that year was, indeed, one of positive change for this delightful, quirky, and talented child.

I was sad when Shanique's mother accepted a professorship in another city two years later. Before leaving our school, however, Shanique invented a new set of symbols to describe "greater than" and "less than" quantities in math. (Like many children, she had always been confused by the direction of the < and > symbols, e.g., $8 > 5$.) Her "new math" was definitely out of the ordinary, just like Shanique.

Here is a part of one of her stories; perhaps you can begin to see the vast chasm between her mental prowess and her ability to express her ideas on paper.

10. *Translation of Shanique's story (4th grade): "The Snowsnake: The Snowsnake is something all skiers try to avoid. This white, long, hairy, snow, covered creature is said to work for the great forces of the earth, land, sky, sea, and forest. As the saying goes, if you have not been doing good to the earth this will. . . ."*

"Twice Exceptional." Children who come equipped with gifted minds plus one or more major glitches in the learning system are often called twice exceptional. Here are just a few common examples of what this peculiar term may mean:

- Verbally well above average but has relative weakness in oral reading and spelling, mechanics of written language.

- Seriously challenged by handwriting speed and neatness yet the child has a quick mind and becomes frustrated because he can't get his ideas down fast enough on paper.

- Mentally clever but physically clumsy; looks "stupid" because he bumps into things and people, trips over his own feet. May have social problems and/or is the butt of bullying.

- Highly talented in some artistic or creative field, perhaps can play the piano by ear but can't read music; makes mistakes with math computation or other "basic" skills but may excel at geometric design.

- A gifted athlete and leader; falters on subjects that require advanced skills in abstract symbolic learning (algebra, chemistry, grammar rules, reading comprehension).

- A whiz at reading and computing with an amazing memory for facts, but can usually be depended on to say the wrong thing in a social situation.

If you have a child who is "twice exceptional," you have your work cut out for you (as if you didn't already know that!). As adults, and even in college, we are allowed to pick the areas where we want to focus our time and attention. Schoolchildren, however, are expected to be good at everything, mastering the entire curriculum as they lay the groundwork for every field of learning—and perhaps be a good athlete and popular at the same time.

Your main job is to value, nurture, and reassure your child of those talents; seek appropriate help for the needy skill areas; and keep your household as emotionally safe, loving, well regulated, and positive as possible. Many parents attest to the fact that you will ultimately find the effort was 100 percent worthwhile.

> A parent's main job is to try and keep the youngster's self-esteem intact through honest appreciation of his abilities.

In Part Three, we will get more specific about how to accomplish these things. For now, consider an experience I enjoyed last year when I returned briefly to a city where I had previously taught remedial language arts skills. As I was entering a mall, I was hailed by the mother of a former student. To put it kindly, Roxi had been quite a challenge for all of us, and I knew this mom well from innumerable parent conferences, none of which seemed to achieve our mutual objective—to get smart little Roxi, a petite brunette with a wicked sense of humor, to settle down, pay attention, and produce some effort worthy of her clever mind. We also hoped she would stop doing tricks, such as the time she pulled the lever on the school fire alarm system ("Just joking!"). Roxi's parents, teachers, and her physician all preferred to work with Roxi on behavioral management before trying medications for attention deficit, and she was definitely making progress when I moved to another state.

"You remember me," the lady said as she recognized me entering the mall. "I'm Roxi's mother."

"Of course," I gulped. "And how is Roxi doing?" Frankly, despite the many years of hard work by her teachers, myself included, I expected anything up to and including incarceration.

"Oh, she just graduated from law school and passed the bar," my informant said and smiled. "And she's hoping to become a county prosecutor. I guess she finally got it together."

Indeed. As Roxi would say, "Go figure."

Many Kinds of "Clever." We should all be pleased that definitions of intelligence have radically expanded in recent years and that we have learned to view a child as a collection of abilities rather than simply a number at the bottom of a test form. In fact, as Howard Gardner reminds us, being considered "intelligent" depends a lot on what is important in the particular culture into which you are born.

For example, if you lived in an island community or a time when the most important thing was to be a good sailor, those who could "read" the winds and tides—not books—would probably be considered the smartest. Someone like myself, too "stupid" to have a good sense of the sea, who wanted to sit around with a book and a pencil, might be considered quite seriously disabled.

> *Learning style* is a term used to describe a person's unique profile of learning preferences.

We are all familiar with our cultural school values, which favor analytic/mathematical and language skills, often at the expense of others. Gardner shook up the world of traditional education by daring to say that this age-old notion of academic excellence represents only a small section of human ability. Consider types of talents such as these:

- visual/artistic/creative (artists, designers, inventors, software creators, filmmakers)

- musical

- kinesthetic/tactile (body movement and touch, as for athletes, dancers, mechanics, surgeons)

- leadership, "people" skills

- self-knowledge, spiritual

- environmental awareness/enjoyment of the natural world/natural sciences

Gardner's work opened the door to a much fuller understanding of what is now termed *learning styles*. This concept reminds educators that not all children learn in the same way, just as they do not always learn on the same timetable. Simply standing and talking to a class without getting the students actively involved is almost guaranteed to miss a large number of those who learn better through their eyes, their hands, their bodies, or their imaginations than only through their ears.

> I would quite willingly hazard a guess that as many as three-quarters of so-called learning disabilities are actually a mismatch between the child's natural modes of learning and the way that material is presented in school.

A parent whose child is in this sort of situation naturally feels frustrated and helpless, but parents who have informed themselves and banded together are a potent force. In addition to giving your child an extra measure of love and support at home, you can help all children by advocating for developmentally appropriate curriculum, better teacher training, better understanding of "different" learners, and diversifying instruction to meet various learning speeds and needs. Good teaching of this sort is a continual but rewarding challenge that deserves plenty of respect.

"Learning Styles" for One-of-a-Kind Brains

One's learning style appears to be partially inborn and partially developed by what is encouraged and practiced in the child's environment. Sometimes the term *cognitive style* is used.

Gardner insists that teachers and parents should vary their manner, or "style," of teaching to meet the needs of the variety of learners that exists in every classroom or home. Here are a few things you might try in order to boost active learning if, for example, you are trying to help with homework:

1. Instead of simply *telling* your child something over and over again, try to find a way of *showing* it (a picture, a drawing, a personal demonstration such as following a recipe using fractions, graphing family food choices, etc.).

2. Keep *crayons, markers, and paper* on hand so that you can both try drawing pictures, cartoons, or diagrams to illustrate what is being learned. *Play-Doh or clay* might enable the "sculpture" of a spelling word, a model of a map, or the human digestive system. Experiment with different materials. If it works, use it.

3. Some "basics" can be newly mastered with *computer software* that actively involves the child and makes learning, not playing, the point. Computer use is best for students in second grade and above. (See my book *Failure to Connect* for specific guidelines about what to look for.)

4. Try to let the child be the one to choose what sort of *project* she will make if one is assigned. You can help her brainstorm some ideas, but expect her to make the final choice so she feels it is *her* special project. If she can't think of anything, suggest some choices—subject, materials, how to get started—but encourage her to work in her preferred manner, not yours.

5. Get the child involved using *as many senses as possible* ("multisensory learning"):

   - visual (looking)

   - auditory (listening)

- kinesthetic (moving the body)

- tactile (feeling, touching)

6. Encourage active participation by the child:

    - Act out a story together.

    - Dance, sing, or beat a rhythm for the multiplication facts, spelling words, lists of dates.

    - Have the child make up questions about the material. *Who, what, when, where, why,* and *how?* are good question starters ("Why do I have to learn this?" doesn't count!).

    - Build something to illustrate a concept (Play-Doh, Legos, straws, wooden blocks, any material at hand will do).

    - Trace spelling words or math facts with index finger on a rough surface while repeating the item to be learned ("s_a_i_d").

Multisensory input helped our children finally learn the math facts. Our sons still remember the feel of our old living room carpet, where we used to sit in front of the fire in the evening and trace equations with an index finger while repeating the combination ("eight times seven equals fifty-six"), over and over again. Tedious, yes, but it works, and it is much more effective for some kids than flash cards or oral drills (which we also did when riding in the car). Somewhat later, I occasionally observed, as one of the boys was doing math homework, that the index finger would still be "helping the brain remember" by unobtrusively tracing those same combinations on a textured corduroy pant leg.

> Many students do not master math facts by osmosis, and parents often must assume some of the responsibility for practice. We might as well use what we know about the brain to help the process along.

You will find many books with other suggestions for multisensory teaching in libraries, online, or in bookstores that specialize in educational materials.

Learning Styles in the Classroom. Because not all children learn the same way, many teachers use techniques of multiple intelligences. This helps them accommodate students who learn better when they can look and touch as well as listen. Teachers might work with a computer *simulation* (most effective for students in middle school or older), assign hands-on projects to understand concepts in history or science, use dramatized debate, or add artistic interpretations to supplement reading and writing lessons. One high school math teacher was surprised when he experimented with teaching a complex concept through geometry using pictures and diagrams instead of his usual method of algebraic formulas and lecture. To his astonishment, students who had previously failed to understand the material grasped the concept immediately, whereas some of the class "stars" had to work a little harder to master the lesson.[10]

Teachers tend to teach according to their own preferred way of receiving information. Parents with learning-different children can encourage schools to adopt some of these newer ideas about how to address different learning styles while still maintaining academic standards. In some communities, PTAs or other parent groups have raised funds to send teachers to workshops where they can learn how some of these newer techniques can boost scores—and enjoyment of learning—for a wider variety of children.

> *"He needs to get it in through more than one sense—his brain cells seem to need that extra input for him to process it. And if he can touch it or do it, that's what he learns the best."*
>
> —mother of a son with attention problems

Learning-Style Conundrums. Are there actually people who are purely "visual," "auditory," or "kinesthetic" (hands-on) learners? Should we try to teach a child only through her preferred style or "modality"? For example, should so-called visual learners be taught to read through the sight word method rather than by phonics? If a child is highly talented in art but struggling in math class, should we let him escape to the studio whenever multiplication is on the schedule?

Generally speaking, the answer to such questions is an emphatic no! Good teaching tries to incorporate all the modalities. Good reading demands auditory (ear) and phonics skills as well as visual ones. The artist can use his talents to illustrate a book about multiplication facts, but he still needs to learn how to multiply numerals as well as colors. The upshot of a great deal of research is the following:

- The more modalities—visual, auditory, kinesthetic, tactile (feel), and maybe even olfactory (smell!)—you can involve, the better chance you have of getting material permanently into the brain.

- Because the brain is so plastic, we can train modalities to be stronger. Like immobilizing an arm or leg, the child may eventually lose some of her listening skills if she is never required to use them. Likewise, youngsters whose kinesthetic intelligence languishes in front of too much screen time may have retarded development not only in handwriting and rapid keyboarding but also in valuable mental skills that depend on physical coordination and movement.

- One of a teacher's most difficult jobs is to meet individual students' learning-style needs while covering a standard curriculum. Up-to-date school systems give their teachers adequate support and continued training to learn the best ways to diversify instruction while still keeping standards high. They also encourage adequate support services for youngsters who fall so far "outside the lines" that their needs simply cannot be met without specialized help.

One of the most useful books incorporating brain research with practical classroom planning is Pat Wolfe's *Brain Matters* (please see the Notes for other sources).[11]

Learning Styles, Learning Disabilities, and Who Gave the Money for the New Gym? "Will you please come and work with our faculty to help us understand how to deal with students like this—and their parents?" Over the years I have received many such pleas from schools where teachers were bamboozled by a child's learning style.

"How can she draw so well and have such awful handwriting?"

"He's always got to have something in his hands—he fiddles with whatever is around and has a terrible time staying in his seat, but he's the cleverest in the class when it comes to troubleshooting computer software glitches."

"She can remember every detail of the movie she saw last month, but she can't remember the sight words in reading."

"He can find his way through almost any neighborhood we visit, but he can't read a map—now you tell me why!"

One particular type of question comes up in schools that include a number of affluent and successful families. How can we handle a problem learner without alienating his father? (Who just happens to be funding our new science building.)

> "Look at these papers!" a second-grade teacher wailed, thrusting a grubby stack into my hands. "What are we going to do with this kid? His parents refuse to believe he has a learning problem and insist we just need to try harder to make him learn."

The child at issue was Lucien, a second-grade boy, who was obviously very weak in spelling and mechanics of writing. An earnest and hardworking little fellow, he struggled mightily with everything involving written symbols. His reading was also labored and inaccurate, and on math papers he forgot whether he was adding or subtracting. Despite poor writing skills, however, he loved to draw and used his free time to design elaborate war planes in full attack mode, guns blazing, bombs and rockets blasting from every opening. I suspected that the object of this violent assault was probably his own frustration.

As I leafed through his papers, I couldn't help but notice that the little boy's last name was the same as one of the most prominent building companies in town. Aha! Lucien comes from a family with demonstrated high abilities in visual-spatial (designing), kinesthetic (building), and entrepreneurial skills. This package of genetically influenced talents has helped them become very successful, but has also predisposed their son to a learning style that doesn't fit well with this traditional, lecture-based, "academically rigorous" independent school. It's not that he can't learn the skills, but he needs time and a more hands-on approach to handle this deluge of worksheets.

"Children who are virtuosos at building and fixing things—the ones who can visualize three-dimensional space—often have trouble in school, where abstract symbolic learning is favored," explains Sylvia Richardson, a distinguished pediatrician and learning disabilities expert.

> *"These kids can see around corners!"*
>
> —Sylvia Richardson, MD

Later, I had a chance to talk with Lucien's dad. "I know I'm plenty smart," he acknowledged, "but I went to a little country school, and I never had to do the kind of stuff Lucien brings home. But he's a smart kid, and they need to make him learn it."

As I left the campus, I noticed Dad's name prominently displayed over the door of the new athletic building, a stunningly modern structure. A conundrum, for sure. Maybe dads like this one will read this book and use their clout to push for more up-to-date instruction.

Repairing the Emotional Toll of Difference

> *"When you go through the agony of watching the sparkle being slowly crushed out of your child, anything that looks like a solution becomes possible."*
>
> —mother of a nontraditional learner

I recently had the pleasure of visiting a top-notch school for children with diagnosed learning disabilities. As the principal and I circulated through classrooms where every child was not only deeply engaged in the work at hand but also appeared to be working with energy and enthusiasm, I noticed that a great deal of the teaching was being done through "hands-on," multisensory techniques. Instead of just sitting and listening (or, more likely, not listening) to the teacher, these kids were working in small groups at the chalkboard, tracing spelling words, manipulating blocks for math problems, pairing up to create colorful posters for a class presentation, and doing research on topics that were obviously of interest to them. I think of this school as "sunny," not just because of the light coming in the windows, but because of the smiles and thoughtfulness that pervaded the atmosphere.

I asked the principal if she sees major changes in children after they enter this school.

"When these students come to us," she replied, "they are so sunk into themselves, they feel like total failures, and it shows. They've just stopped trying. It takes us a couple of months, usually, to get them on the right track, and then a lot of them just take off—it's the first time they've ever felt success in school, and it's an amazing tonic."

The unfortunate reality, of course, is that only a very small percentage of children are allowed such a positive experience. Such schools are scarce and usually expensive. Some parents who don't have access to such a school decide to remove their children altogether from what they see as a destructive situation and take up homeschooling or an alternative program (see Chapter 9, "Stress"). Others make the decision to move the family to a district with better services and a more suitable school. These seem like drastic measures, but parents feel desperate. The situation is worsened by the fact that often no help is available until the child is seriously behind and a great deal of emotional damage has been done. Yet school services are badly overburdened by the growing number of students needing help.

New Ideas Badly Needed

Educators continually seek better ways of interrupting the escalating numbers of learning problems in today's children. New approaches focus from the beginning on early identification and good, brain-appropriate teaching. Parents are increasingly empowered to advocate for appropriate and timely services for their "different learners." The fact is that all kids can and do learn—they may just not be doing it in the standard way or on the standard schedule. We can all hope that new awareness and research-based strategies will enable us to avoid the situation in which a child concludes that there's not much point in trying because he's sure he will never be any good at anything. What a sad loss of talent that is!

PART THREE

Childhood in the Twenty-first Century

Pathway to Problems or
Gateway to Success?

CHAPTER 9

Stress

The Great *Dys*-abler

A large data analysis in 2000 found normal children in the United States reporting more symptoms of anxiety than child psychiatric patients did in the 1950s.[1]

"When did life for a child get to be so hard?"[2]

—David Elkind

A child in our industrialized world enjoys multiple advantages: food availability, health care, technological and scientific progress, on-demand entertainment and information. Yet children are paying dearly for these benefits. A quiet pandemic of toxic "brain disruptors"—both physical and mental—threatens developing nervous systems and learning abilities.

In this final section of the book we will confront the major dysablers to understand what they are, where they come from, and what parents and educators can do to reduce their impact. We start with one of the worst: chronic stress. As a growing presence in children's lives, it disrupts every aspect of learning by enforcing "a hostile takeover of consciousness by emotion."[3]

Quick Take: A "Hostile Takeover" of Childen's Brains

1. Stress has powerful effects on brain chemistry. "Good" stress can sharpen thinking and motivation, whereas chronic stress may cause depression, learning problems, and erosion of brain circuits.

2. The rise in children's learning and attention problems reflects in part a stress response to current lifestyle habits.

3. Intense early stress, such as abuse or repeated separation from a key caregiver, creates chemical imbalances that cause lasting problems.

4. High expectations and accountability are essential and appropriate for all children, but learning disabilities and emotional disorders can be caused by a "one-size-fits-all" approach.

5. Trying to push kids of any age "ahead of the curve" can damage brains and lives.

6. Some schools cause and contribute to learning problems, and some parents opt out and choose alternative forms of education.

7. There are downsides to being a "winner" in the academic rat race.

Your Child's Brain on Stress:
Direct Route to Learning Problems

The effects of chronic stress on young children's cognitive and emotional development are seriously underestimated, often ignored, and even accepted. Stress sneaks in the back door because it is becoming such an accepted part of adult life. But chronic stress is not a natural state for anyone's brain, and it wreaks special havoc on developing systems.

In a recent survey, almost half of adult Americans reported concern about the amount of stress in their lives, with one-third describing themselves as "extremely stressed."[4] The American

Psychological Association estimates that 43 percent of American adults suffer adverse health effects related to stress. One contributing factor, many acknowledge, is the "merry-go-round" of work and activity deemed necessary to give their kids advantages in life.[5] Ironically, what these parents may also be giving their child is a learning problem.

> People differ genetically in their susceptibility to stress, but if parents are chronically stressed out, they are probably passing on their upset as well as their genes.

Good Stress and Bad Stress

Stress is necessary to keep the human brain tuned up, but only if it comes in appropriate doses. A positive challenge ("good stress") involves a task that is not trivial and for which there is a reasonable chance of success. In this case, the brain fires up to solve the problem, possibly even growing new connections in the process. Children thrive on such challenges and this type of learning tunes their minds and sharpens their motivation to confront new problems in their rapidly changing world.

The most damaging type of stress, on the other hand, consists of an ongoing challenge that is both *threatening* and *unmanageable*— such as feeling like a fool every day in a science class that is far beyond your skill level; having an overly demanding and critical boss, parent, or teacher; or being a small child overwhelmed by a chaotic, noisy, unpredictable family or daycare situation with no relief in sight.

Chronic stress creates a smoldering neural firestorm that can disrupt logical thinking, memory, and attention, not to mention motivation and self-esteem. It can worsen or even cause learning deficits and ADHD symptoms. Although different combinations of genes make people differently susceptible to stress in the first place, repeated triggering of the stress response affects the way these genes are activated and makes the situation worse.[6] A few children, whom we call resilient, seem invulnerable to such forces, but most are not.

The brain's stress response charges up the nervous system to preserve our physical or emotional well-being. It is pretty obvious that we need to respond instinctively, without a lot of conscious deliberation, if we're about to be hit by a car or if flames suddenly leap from the oven. Unfortunately, these useful biological responses also become mobilized, perhaps on a daily basis, by an unfairly demanding boss, a sarcastic teacher, fear of being hurt or socially rejected, a scary movie—or any other of the common stressors of daily life.

What's more, in today's "couch potato" culture, there is often no physical outlet for the body's powerful fight-or-flight response. This factor alone may be causing or contributing to hyperactivity, inattention, or memory problems, given the recent findings about mirror neurons described previously. They cause the brain to respond physiologically to viewed violence as if the viewer were a first-person participant.

> Children and teens exposed to a great deal of violent, arousing content may have a chronic residue of undissipated stress-related energy.

Downshifted!

Stress originates in a set of interconnected organs called the *HPA axis* (hypothalamic-pituitary-adrenocortical). It links the *hypothalamus* in the base of the brain with the *pituitary* and *adrenal* glands as well as the higher levels of the cortex. The hypothalamus keeps our bodies regulated, managing such functions as blood pressure, body temperature, hunger, and sleep cycles. It is busy all the time, exchanging information by way of hormones and neurotransmitters (e.g., epinephrine, norepinephrine) with other parts of the brain and acting as a relay station to the pituitary gland, which then activates the body to quickly adjust our systems to the conditions around us.

One of these many functions is, of course, to prepare us to respond to a serious challenge. For this, the adrenal gland and its steroid hormone *cortisol* jolt our entire system into quick action without a lot of time wasted on intellectual debate. Cortisol is a remarkably useful and versatile hormone, but too much of it can have some nasty long-term effects on the immune system, the brain, and on academic learning.

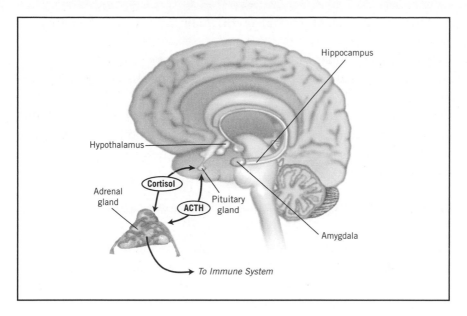

11. Stress and the HPA Axis: A Neural Firestorm

If you will forgive me a personal story, here's an incident that points up the disruptive power of the HPA axis—even for a competent adult and a math problem that should be "easy."

Several years ago, my husband and I took an unguided hiking trip in a remote part of France. At the time, Tom, who holds a graduate degree in engineering, was a middle school math teacher, so I was sure I could depend on him to figure out the maps and distances. What we didn't know beforehand was that our trail descriptions were seriously inadequate, so we often found ourselves walking alone in deserted countryside with little idea of where we were and no available help for several miles.

Late one afternoon, after a long day of trying to follow a poorly marked and sometimes treacherous trail, we realized we were hopelessly lost. Even in the sinking light, I could see that Tom looked just as pale and frightened as I felt, contemplating a night on the ground in an area known for its population of poisonous snakes. (Yes, we were fools.) Finally, we located the trail and then a road with a marker indicating the number of kilometers to the next town, where our reservations had been made for the night.

Greatly relieved, but wondering if I still had the energy to walk that far, I asked my math whiz, "How many miles is four kilometers?"

Tom stared at me, with a sudden look of absolute panic.

"Jane," he croaked, "I can't remember how to multiply by six-tenths!"

It was only a momentary lapse, but I have often recalled this incident when I see a student "freeze" on an exam, when asked to recite in class, or even on the playground when the class bully ambles by.

A Little Organ with a Lot of Influence

What could cause a competent adult math teacher to forget how to perform a simple operation? Plain old fear, which can "downshift" the brain into its most primitive mode. (For the term *downshift*, I thank Renata and Geoffrey Caine and their book *Making Connections*, which details ways in which schools can capitalize on the strengths and needs of their students' brains.)

An almond-shaped organ in the limbic system, the *amygdala,* is uniquely designed to signal to the HPA axis that danger is present. Unlike the hippocampus, which is the memory organ for facts and information, the amygdala registers and remembers things that might represent a threat. It can then trigger an immediate stress response. With upward and downward connections both to frontal systems and to brainstem areas, it can quickly inspire a neural panic when aroused. This necessary type of arousal can cause problems if carried to an extreme. Every repetition of an experience increases the probability that the same cells will again fire in the same pattern. If you know a child who has been severely frightened by a dog and thereafter refuses to go near one—or even near other small furry animals—it should come as no surprise that emotional experiences can become firmly embedded in brain circuits.

The amygdala has trouble forgetting a stimulus that once was threatening, no matter how much we try to talk the child (or ourselves) out of it. When children develop school phobias or "school refusal," for example, the amygdala is probably involved. Sometimes the trigger for the phobia is not obvious, and the child has no way of understanding why this reaction is occurring. Some cases of "test anxiety" may have similar causes.

> Trying to talk a child out of school phobia is probably futile,
> since this part of the brain does not understand logic.

A young child is very much at the mercy of these primitive emotional systems, but as the higher-level systems of the brain mature, they become more capable of taking rational control. Needless to say, after his brief math panic, my husband almost instantly recovered all his mental powers, putting the prefrontal cortex—the brain's "control center"—back into operation.

Cognitive behavioral therapy, described earlier, has been successful in treating attention problems, depression, compulsive behavior, or phobias by teaching patients to activate these higher cortical centers to manage deep-seated but often irrational responses.

High- and Low-Level Stress

The important thing to realize is that a strong negative emotional reaction makes it extremely difficult to use the higher-level thinking/reasoning/memory systems required in school. Some children's brains are conditioned to downshift as soon as they go through the classroom door.

> For many children growing up today, however, stressors
> come in much more subtle form, and may arise more from
> home than from school.

Youngsters in families where adults are under chronic stress are very likely to acquire stress themselves. From infancy, our children are hurried through childhood, subjected to overwhelming noise, activity, inappropriate images, too much excitement, and, in many cases, not enough relaxed relational time with adults able to enjoy having fun with them. Dee Coulter, a well-known author and teacher who has studied this issue, assures me that many of our so-called learning disabled kids are actually part of another "epidemic": that of traumatic stress disorder. They are simply casualties of an adult world that has lost its common sense when it comes to its children.

None of this means, of course, that we should be molly-coddling our children and trying to keep them from any negative input or emotion. Managing stress is tricky, since *the right kind of stress, in the form of manageable challenge, sharpens thinking and motivation.* There is nothing like a little dose of reality to teach important lessons, and children who are shielded too much from the ups and downs of a normal childhood miss important chances for personal growth. The trick is to keep the challenge appropriate for the child's age and to back it up with solid emotional supports. Stress that becomes chronic may have some of the following effects to a greater or lesser degree:

Too Stressed-Out to Learn?

- Quick, reflex response of lower brain centers (fight or flee) takes over from higher brain centers (this loss of thinking ability in the face of stressful challenge has been called downshifting).

- Attention narrows to detect potential threat.

- Child may become hypervigilant, jumpy, hyperactive.

- Child becomes oversensitive to any perceived threat (e.g., strikes out at classmate who accidentally bumps him).

- Visual field narrows (can interfere with eye movements for reading).

- Thinking needed for comprehension of reading, math problem solving, or anything demanding sustained thought can be blocked.

- Digestion is interrupted—stomachaches or "butterflies."

- Heart speeds up; blood pressure rises.

- Memory shifts from hippocampus (for learning facts, school-related material) to amygdala (remembers emotion, what to be afraid of).

- With chronic stress, hippocampus, frontal lobes, and other brain areas shrink, causing long-term effects on memory and learning.

The Vulnerable Growing Brain

Effects of stress depend to some degree on the child's stage of development. The most vulnerable time for stress in the growing brain is in the first year, when serious abuse, trauma, insufficient or erratic nurturing have dramatic, long-term negative effects. Lack of bonding with a consistent caregiver due to disorganized and inconsistent caregiving may permanently change the brain and predispose a child to be stressed throughout life. On the other hand, consistent, loving, and responsive care may suppress stress genes and set even a vulnerable child on a much firmer path toward mental and emotional well-being. Especially important are an *emotionally stable environment*, *eye contact*, and a *familiar face* that responds to the child's needs and emotional reactions.[7]

A seriously disordered stress response resulting from inappropriate or abusive parenting can apparently be reversed when parents are taught more effective child-rearing skills. In an online edition of *Newsweek* ("A Teachable Moment," 4/18/09), Anna Quindlen reported on a study of preschoolers whose family histories as well as their abnormal cortisol levels put them at serious risk for problems including future trouble with the law. After parent training in positive discipline, reinforcement for good behavior, and strategies for engaging children in creative play, the youngsters' behavior—and their stress response—were normalized. *"Having their parents learn the basics of good child-rearing had actually shifted the biology of these kids,"* observes Quindlen.

Infants show abrupt rises in cortisol levels from even minor stressors, such as a doctor visit, but unless the stress is prolonged, this is considered normal—and probably necessary to help the child begin to self-regulate the stress response.

The preschool period is still a vulnerable one for the neurochemistry of the emotional brain. Children under age four show increased cortisol when they are in full-day child care, as opposed to the same children at home on days they do not go to child care.[8] This sign of stress may result from the multiple challenges of adapting to different caregivers and the demands of a peer group. The quality and staffing ratios of the care center obviously count. *It is important to note that these cortisol elevations are not seen when the child receives individualized, supportive care from care providers.* The levels also drop when children in day care lie down for a nap. Although a few children over age five continue to show this stress response in group settings, most do not.

Children are not as resilient as many adults would like to believe. Adults may have learned to screen out and ignore all the assaults on consciousness that are present in our overstimulating, noisy world (although even adults may pay a price in stress-related illness), but children's developing nervous systems have not yet perfected this twenty-first-century survival tactic. Young children, in particular, tend to be *stimulus-bound.* As you have doubtless noticed, they respond to just about every nearby stimulus, especially if it is flashy, loud, surprising, vividly colorful, or moving. Advertisers and children's TV programmers learned long ago that quick takes cause the brain instantly to "alert" to such stimuli and so they use them to shift viewers' immediate attention to whatever it is they want viewers to notice. Flashing ads on Web sites show how hard it is for even the adult brain to use higher brain centers to suppress what is basically a reflex response. Children, whose brains have not yet developed these upper-level screening mechanisms, are even more at the mercy of vivid stimulation of any sensory system.

> *"Sometimes I wonder how we're supposed to teach these kids anything. They're dropped off from a car with the stereo blaring, Mom or Dad's probably on the cell phone, you just know the TV has been on at home all morning, everybody's rushing, and these little ones are so blitzed from all the stimulation that they can't even settle down to an activity. I have to spend the first part of my morning lesson time just getting them focused."*
>
> —teacher at a private preschool

In a recent visit to a preschool in an East Coast suburb, Joan Almon, director of the international Alliance for Childhood, heard the teacher ask each child the following questions, which elicited the same response from all but one of the children in a class:

Teacher to a preschool child: "What did Mommy say to you before you left this morning?"

Child: "Hurry up."

Teacher: "What did Daddy say?"

Child: "Hurry up."

Remodeling Brains by Remodeling Children's Environments

You can vastly improve your child's chances for successful learning by identifying and reducing sources of stress. Let's look at some of the factors in today's lifestyles that are problematic, especially for stress-prone youngsters. Then we will consider some proven stress reducers.

The "Stress Culture" of Childhood

At Any Age

- family conflict

- exposure to violence

- parental anxiety

- divorce, death

- a move to a new home

- excessive noise

- lack of adequate sleep

- the "mean world" syndrome promulgated on television (e.g., It's dangerous out there; lots of people are sick/miserable/unpopular.)

- inadequate physical exercise or other outlet

- separation from nature

- environmental toxins, allergens

- lack of perceived control over threatening or overwhelming situations

- unmanageable expectations

- adults who talk about you in negative tones when you're present

- pressure rather than encouragement for achievement

- excessive media use

- chronic overscheduling

In Early Years

- inconsistent caregiving; poor bonding with a responsive caregiver

- suboptimal day care settings; lack of personal relationship with an adult

- instability and lack of predictability in daily routines (children crave sameness)

- excessive stimulation (child either "shuts down" or becomes overexcited)

- too much novelty (excess of excitement, sensory overload) too many distracting electronic toys

At School

- bullying (by students or teachers)

- peer rejection

- overemphasis on "high-stakes" testing

- lack of mentors and responsive adults

- inappropriate academic demands for age or preparation

- untreated learning disorders

Clearly, some things are more under parents' control than others. Here are some proven tactics:

Buffers for Stress

- Manage your environment (refer to the brain-cleaning program in Chapters 10 and 11).

- Take steps to get your own stress level under control; seek professional help if necessary.

- Pay special attention to appropriate and consistent care arrangements for young children. Make sure infants get lots of loving face-to-face contact.

- Be generous with hugs, cuddling, and body contact appropriate to age and individual needs.

- Remember that massage, yoga, art activities, needlework, singing or playing a musical instrument for pleasure, exercise, movement activities, and nature are stress reducers.

- Encourage free rather than programmed play. Children who look as if they are "wasting" time may be storing up stress resistance.

- If you have a family pet, encourage petting a friendly animal, which reduces stress levels.

- Allow your children an age-appropriate role in any decision making that affects them. Let them hear positive messages when they overhear you talking about them.

- Keep predictable routines whenever possible. Explain changes in routines ahead of time.

- Use hugs and calm reassurance, which work better than logical reasoning, when a child is stressed.

- Try to be a model for doing repetitive or annoying but necessary tasks without irritation.

- Have fun, laugh, relax, and play together!

Kiddie Rat Race:
Who Wins, Who Loses, and Who Gets a Diagnosis?

"In our opinion many young children and their families are living lives enmeshed in pressures that are detrimental to healthy growth and contentment."

—early childhood educators
Bev Bos and Jenny Chapman[9]

One of the greatest stressors for children, parents, and teachers is the current pressure to speed up children's development and make them smarter faster so they will be competitive in the twenty-first century. But even the best-engineered schemes will backfire if they violate the developmental realities of the human brain.

Normally developing children are not the precocious know-it-alls in some movies and TV series, nor do they all learn to read or do algebra on schedule. They are often rambunctious and fail to pay attention to what adults say is important; they have annoying mood swings and even temper tantrums. While genuine developmental problems need timely and effective intervention, overly narrow definitions of "normal" jeopardize all children's development.

Casualties of a "Meritocracy" of Childhood

A "meritocracy" encourages individuals to get ahead on the basis of ability and hard work, and the United States has always prided itself on these freedoms. Like many good ideas, however, this one can be carried to an extreme. When the rat race begins in the cradle, children become its victims. The first casualties are youngsters who are slower developers, have learning differences, or come from disadvantaged circumstances. In the long run, however, "overadvantaged" children are also at risk.

We live in a culture sold on "brainy" infants, "jump-starts" for learning, early specialization in athletics and academics, and building a college résumé before puberty. Children who don't fit the mold may be declared educationally or personally "sick" solely because they don't easily leap onto the fast track. Sometimes it is more comfortable to declare a child "disabled" than to acknowledge that our expectations are hopelessly unrealistic for real children.

There is no "quick fix" for childhood!

No Patience for the "Rough Edges of Childhood"

Pediatrician Mel Levine feels our definitions of "normal" have become too narrow. "The rough edges of childhood or of rugged individuality" are increasingly viewed as indicators of psychopathology, he claims, and very likely to be aggressively medicated.[10]

> "It is ironic that America, whose founding principles emphasized individual rights and freedoms, has developed a culture that demands homogeneity and uniformity in its children."
>
> —Mel Levine, MD[11]

Dr. Levine points out that a weakness or problem at one age may turn out to be an asset later in life. For example, many successful, creative, and high-energy adults would probably be labeled ADHD if they started school today.

The toll of unrealistic expectations was brought home to me when I presented a workshop for elementary teachers in a rural district in Texas. One hot topic concerned the average estimated incidence of organic attention problems in the general population, which is often considered to be 5–10 percent. During the question period, one woman rose from her seat, hands on hips, and belligerently demanded: "What would you say if I told you that half of the children in my second-grade class are on Ritalin? How am I supposed to make these kids learn?!"

Perhaps too candidly, I replied, "I wonder if your school has some source of environmental contamination." I also had to ask what was going on in her classroom that was so developmentally inappropriate that half of her students couldn't pay attention to it.

Needed: Sharp and Stable Minds for the Twenty-first Century. Parents are naturally—and appropriately—concerned about helping their children gain "success." Many are confused, however, by un-substantiated hype about a need to accelerate learning in order to cope with our rapidly changing technological age. In fact, the human brain has certain core needs that hold true in any era—electronic or not. The advanced symbolic and problem-solving skills that will be essential for our civilization to survive the twenty-first century are best built on solid intellectual, moral, and emotional foundations. Children, even very able ones, differ significantly in the time it takes them to establish these foundations.

Childhood: A Journey or a Race?

> *"I feel like I'm on a merry-go-round trying to give my child all the competitive advantages."*
>
> —mother of an eight-year-old

The Tyranny of "The Curve." Most parents do not purposely choose to launch their children into a lifelong rat race. Nor do they realize that some of those "advantages" can cause problems if pressed on children at the wrong time and in the wrong way. But we all want the best for our children, and it is easy to become anxious—and pushy—in the face of such pressures.

Whose Curve? Soon after my book *Failure to Connect* was published, I gave a lecture in a midwestern suburb about the positives and negatives of kids' computer use. I suggested, among other things, that children under age seven should not spend a great deal of time on computers at the expense of hands-on manipulative activities, interactive language, active free play, and socialization so vital for future learning. I also explained the research showing that interaction with a responsive *human* being creates not only the best learning but also the most enthusiastic learners. When I was through speaking, I was confronted by a very annoyed father.

"My three-year-old daughter is on her computer *a lot,* and I en-courage it," he almost shouted. "I buy educational software and she learns way more than I could ever teach her, and besides, this is a technological age and I absolutely will not let her get *behind the curve!*"

What a troubling bill of goods this gentleman has been sold if he thinks an electronic device has more to teach his daughter than he does—or even that early computer use is going to prepare her in any significant way for a future that will demand far more complex intelligences than any software can teach. More important, though, is to challenge this notion of "getting ahead" of some imaginary curve. What curve? Whose curve?

Each child has a special and highly individual curve, which smart parents and teachers know enough to respect. The human brain, too, has a developmental curve for building complex learning skills from the magical glue of a child's experience and imagination. But there's little time for the magic to take place if the subtleties of this complex process escape anxious and impatient adults.

> Pressuring a child to be ahead of some imaginary "curve" guarantees nothing except the likelihood of a learning or stress disorder (or both). There are lots of curves that eventually lead to success.

How Schools Help or Hurt

> *"Two adverse conditions [for learning] are especially dangerous: anxiety and boredom. Anxiety occurs when teachers expect too much from students; boredom occurs when teachers expect too little."*
>
> —Mihaly Csikszentmihalyi[12]

My young friend Alicia could easily have been exhibit A of a casualty from expectations that were unrealistic for her. A shy "young five" when she entered kindergarten, Alicia was a pale little blond with chronic dark circles (which can signal either allergies or sleep loss and have sometimes been associated with learning problems), a tendency to gaze out the window, and a body posture that said, loud and clear, "Let me out of here!" Actually, Alicia's body language was more informative than her lispy and immature speech, and Alicia was also far too shy to tell us how she was feeling about anything.

After several days of careful observation and some informal

testing, Alicia's teacher confirmed that this child was seriously at risk for educational problems, and immediately began to take action.

> Watch the child's body language; it often tells far more than words.

Alicia physically recoiled when asked to participate in simple reading-readiness activities, especially those that involved matching letters with letter sounds (beginning "phonics"). I worked with her as a resource teacher for several years, and she told me much later that, at her parents' request, her babysitter had started insisting when she was about four that she work every day with phonics workbooks. Given her late development of writing skills, unclear articulation, and processing of letter sounds, she found these assignments totally incomprehensible.

"I didn't even understand what I was supposed to be doing! What does 'B' say? It's only some marks on a page—what's she talking about? It was awful!" she related. "I was *so scared* of coming to school, and there were all those alphabet letters and words all over the walls, and I couldn't even think."

Alicia attended a school that had the resources and teaching expertise to get her chugging positively along on her own individual track. In addition, Alicia was tested for allergies, which showed that her body (including her brain) was seriously reacting to both dairy products and the family cat. After her parents modified her diet and found another happy home for the cat, the little girl's energy and attention improved.

By fourth grade Alicia's reading scores were on par with her classmates', and she eventually came into her own in high school as she began to deploy her talented scientific mind. It wasn't easy and it wasn't quick, but patience paid off—especially for Alicia, who is now a Ph.D. biochemist. Who knows what would have happened had we insisted that this vulnerable little girl leap, unassisted, through all the standard hoops.

Far away, in an alternative economic reality, Alicia's story might have played out very differently. At a larger school with overcrowded classes, many children unprepared for formal learning, and insufficient support services, her problems could have remained unidentified until some later grade when "diagnosis by failure" branded her with both an intractable "learning disability" and a high potential for dropping out.

Consider Antony, arriving at kindergarten well scrubbed, wide eyed, a little apprehensive, and trying hard to be "good" and please the teacher.

Antony's brain has lots of potential, but he's already in big trouble. Despite having a quick mind, Antony has lived in an environment that is loving but lacking in the foundations for what's required in the classroom: familiarity with books, careful listening, following oral directions, and taking part in a group or a conversation. His speech is unclear; he can't hear the differences between sounds; lacks age-appropriate vocabulary; can't get his ideas into words, ask a question, or even speak in grammatically appropriate sentences. At this point Antony has a diagnosable language disability. Did it come from genes or a language-deficient environment? Who knows? The fact is that Antony needs immediate educational first aid.

An enriched preschool program might have filled in these gaps, but many children like Antony either miss out on this experience or attend programs lacking adequate staff to deal with the intense degree of need. Nonetheless, Antony's kindergarten curriculum assumes that normal language milestones have already been reached by age five. He is expected to start learning to read—which, of course, depends on all those skills which he lacks. Pity Antony, whose "learning disability" won't be diagnosed until third grade when he gives up trying and starts to cut school and misbehave. And pity the teacher—who is expected to somehow make up lost time and still teach him to read on schedule!

Educators now know how to help Antony by tuning and retraining his brain circuits for language and the related thinking skills. Time is precious, however, for these windows will eventually close, leaving a frustrated, turned-off, and angry kid who has an above-average chance of being at odds with the law and incarcerated by the time he's in his twenties.

Remediating the System as Well as the Students. Serious efforts are under way to identify children at the first signs of failure and institute appropriate remediation. Ideally, all children will have well-trained classroom teachers; as soon as students experience difficulty, specialized instruction will be added in a graduated series of steps to remedy whatever gaps exist.[13] Putting resources upstream before problems develop is a lot more economical in every sense than waiting until the problems do their damage.

Professionals firmly support high expectations for every learner, but they realize that our demands must be based on reality. To expect all kids to learn in lockstep is a recipe for failure.

> If your child shows early signs of difficulty, keep a close watch and do not hesitate to go to the school and—politely but clearly—find out what steps are being taken to remedy the situation. And please don't forget to advocate for those children whose parents lack the resources to do the same.

In a very different scenario, Annette, another entering kindergartener, has already experienced just about every advantage— linguistic and otherwise—that is possible in five short years. Surrounded from birth by enriching and "educational" experiences, Annette demonstrates a near-adult level of spoken language and vocabulary, and her early reading ability gets her a lot of attention. Annette's brain is already a well-honed instrument for academic learning. The problem is that the child appears tense and unhappy much of the time.

"I wish this little girl could just relax and play," said her teacher. "She has trouble interacting with the other children and often looks just worn out," her teacher explained. "I know she has a lot of after-school enrichment and lessons, but she is so concerned about making an error that she's reluctant to try anything new, and she bursts into tears whenever she can't do something perfectly. Is it possible for a five-year-old to have a stress disorder?"

We will return shortly to children like Annette and why they, too, may be headed for trouble. If your child displays the signs of stress cited earlier, maybe it's time to seek a different balance.

Stages of Development:
Doing It Right When the Time Is Right

How much is too much? Or not enough?

Will my child be left behind—or am I expecting too much, too soon?

My child seems to take longer to learn everything; is it better to slow down or keep pushing ahead to try to keep up?

A major source of anxiety for parents in a stress culture is finding the edgy boundary between too much and too little stimulation for their child's brain. I surely wish I could write a simple chapter with an easy procedure that would work for everyone. But I can't (and neither can anyone else). Here are some points to ponder:

Quick Take: "Developmentally Appropriate"

1. Pushing overly advanced academic skills may create or accelerate a learning disability.

2. Trying to plug any type of learning into unprepared or immature brains is a recipe for failure and possibly even botched neural connections.

3. If learning becomes too stressful for children, motivation suffers, and the child may start to avoid challenges—like reading comprehension, math story problems, studying for tests, or advanced science courses.

4. The best way to understand your child's (or student's) readiness timetable is to be a sensitive observer. You are the foremost expert about your own child, and your instinctive wisdom is usually the best guide of all. *If you're worried that it's "too much," it probably is.*

5. Teachers get stressed by the amount of work they have to do to prepare the brains of today's children for the demands of academic learning when skills that we used to take for granted, such as attention, are so often lacking.

6. Age sixteen is often a watershed year in which "unmotivated" or "flakey" students somehow get it together, possibly related to maturation in the prefrontal cortex.

How Brains Grow: A Firsthand View

As a learning specialist in a pre-K through grade 12 school I learned a lot about "developmental readiness." One of my first instructors was a girl named Maddy.

Maddy was a strapping second-grader when she was first assigned to me for remedial math instruction. I remember working very hard with her on solving simple equations, as Maddy seemed bewildered about rule systems in general and math concepts in particular. Maddy's learning style was far more hands-on (tactile/kinesthetic) than abstract; real objects (seven pencils) made sense to her, but the associated symbols (7, $+$, x) simply had not clicked. It was not surprising that first-grade math had not totally "sunk in," and Maddy needed to work with manipulatives (small blocks, rods, balance scales, etc.) to reestablish a solid foundation. She was progressing well until we ran up against that favorite torture device in second-grade math workbooks, the "missing addend" ($3 + \_\_ = 7$). One day Maddy would seem to have it, and two days later she "forgot." (I have since learned that this kind of "forgot" usually means a child didn't really understand it in the first place—or maybe that it is a concept many seven-year-old brains are not prepared to grasp.)

> It is normal for a child to seem to "get" something one day and lose it the next. Solid learning foundations take time and patience.

Maddy went on to third grade, scoring barely adequately in math, and still with some gaps (including that darn missing addend). I didn't reconnect with her until fourth grade when she came to me for help once again, this time in a group working on a writing project.

"Remember when I came here before?" she wanted to know.

"Of course," I replied. "We spent a lot of time on that 'missing addend,' didn't we?"

"But that's so simple!" she exclaimed. "I can't believe I was so clueless! Now I can do long division and fractions and a whole bunch of stuff."

Of course, not every learning dilemma is so readily solved. Yet we would have fewer problems in the first place and more success in remediating the ones that arise if we would only pay attention to how—and when—children's brains are ready to take on certain mental tasks.

Needed: Time and Patience to Rebuild. It would seem silly to try to make a three-month-old infant walk, whereas we would become concerned about a child who doesn't walk at eighteen months. Nature has a clear plan for how development should proceed. If earlier stages are neglected or disordered for any reason, later learning will suffer. If a child can't throw and catch a ball, it is foolish to expect her to enjoy playing baseball. If she can't distinguish between sounds like /b/, /d/, and /g/, it is silly to expect her to complete flawless phonics worksheets. If a ninth-grader is reading at a fourth-grade level, sending him home unassisted with a text at a ninth-grade reading level doesn't make sense. Yet every day, children (and teachers) are put in such impossible situations.

An extreme example was brought to my attention during a recent consultation with a physical therapist. She works in a "problem" school that happens to be located in an area near a toxic waste site. Perhaps unsurprisingly, this school has experienced a peculiar onslaught of brain disorders and developmental disabilities among its students. One such child, a little boy in third grade, was very much on the therapist's mind. Here is a very abbreviated version of our conversation:

Therapist: "This child has so many problems—he's just hopeless on the achievement tests, and his teachers don't know what to do. I'm working with him one hour a week, it's not nearly enough but that's all that's in the budget and we have so many who need help. We're wondering what you recommend."

Me: "What seems to be his most serious problem?"

Therapist: "Well, his writing is so slow, he can't finish even part of the test—but that's just one problem. His whole body is uncoordinated and he seems to have trouble holding his head straight so he can keep his eyes focused on the paper."

Me: "Can this child hold a pencil and draw a square or a circle?"
Therapist: "No, actually, he can't."
Me: "Is it a silly question to ask why he is expected to take a standardized achievement test?"
Therapist: "The state requires it."

So what's the answer? I surely wish I had one. Clearly, this child needs to be in a program better suited to his needs. But in a financially strapped, overburdened school district, with a family unable to advocate for their child, that is easier said than done.

Divergent Views:
Alternative Schools, Homeschoolers, and "Unschoolers"

Some parents are able to rebel against schools that seem out of touch with their children's needs, and increasing numbers seek out alternative schooling.

"Should We Look for Another School?"

This question is a common one from families who are able to make the personal and financial sacrifices for alternative school placements for their children. Frankly, when a child is being systematically destroyed in an inappropriate educational setting, the answer is often "yes."

Every child has different needs, and each state and school district has different rules regarding the way in which they fund and meet the federal mandate that special needs be addressed. Although each youngster with a documented problem is entitled to the "least restrictive" environment for learning, school personnel are often overstretched. Sometimes appropriate therapies are delayed or not available because the problem is not sufficiently "severe."

"We're sending our son to the 'best' school in our neighborhood," one father just told me, "but they don't have enough specialists who understand how to deal with his learning disability. So we're paying for a whole menu of à la carte services outside of school hours, and we're thinking we really need a special school that can make him feel successful instead of like a failure."

"Her school is totally wrong for her, and it gets worse every year. We've got to make a change, and we're thinking of moving."

—frustrated father

Alternative Philosophies About How to Educate Children

For many children, a different educational approach seems to be what is needed. The growing popularity of both alternative schools and homeschooling illustrates the depth of parental concern about current educational practices. A number of alternatives have sprung up for families who are dissatisfied with the local educational services. They are usually costly economically, and in terms of time and commitment. Special schools for children with learning differences often get remarkable results, but their small classes and expertly trained teachers come at a substantial price.

Two growing alternatives are Montessori and Waldorf. Neither method is designed specifically for children with learning differences, but both are founded on a set of well-developed principles about how the young brain grows and the most appropriate ways to support intellectual and personal development. (Montessori education was initially created to teach disadvantaged children, but in the United States it is currently more popular with well-educated parents.) Although they differ in many respects, both have a distinctly articulated system of values based on the principles of a child's developmental needs and the importance of active personal involvement in learning.

Further out on the alternative scale are parents who choose to withdraw their children from school and teach them at home. Most of these homeschoolers follow a curriculum, but a subgroup who call their method "unschooling" have totally opted out of traditional education to let each child invent his own curriculum. They believe that allowing their children the freedom to follow their own interests at their own pace is the best way to ensure active, engaged, and developmentally appropriate learning. This is a difficult notion for traditionalists to buy in to. It is also a serious and life-altering choice to assume all the responsibility for a child's education, one that not many families are prepared to make.

Unschoolers have told me some thought-provoking stories. In one family where both parents enjoyed reading, their son remained totally uninterested, preferring to play outside or build elaborate Lego constructions. (In this household, TV and computer games were off limits most of the time for everyone.) Suddenly, at age nine, this boy decided he wanted to read the sports page in the newspaper, "taught himself" to read within a period of weeks, and reportedly went on to become an avid consumer of all sorts of information from the printed page.

Clearly, this child's household lifestyle provided an enriched language, reading, and thinking environment, so the "basics" were in place. Still, stories like this do tend to give one pause, especially at a time when even four-year-olds are being pressured to learn to read—ready, interested, or not! But current research suggests that early intervention is necessary for many children who are slow to develop prereading skills. So I was highly skeptical about such an approach when I was invited to present a talk at a homeschooling conference in California.

My escorts during the long drive from and back to the airport were two "graduates" of homeschooling, Brianna and Rob, who had become childhood friends in social and sports groups organized by homeschooling parents. As they described their earlier years, it was clear that both had flourished in homes, albeit nontraditional ones, where parents devoted a lot of time, love, and respect to their children, and had themselves demonstrated pleasure in learning. Brianna's parents had followed a fairly standard curriculum, but Rob readily acknowledged he was "unschooled." His story was remarkably similar to the one above.

"My parents never pushed learning on me but they both read a lot—when I finally got interested I found out I loved to read, especially science magazines. I also wanted to read the current events in the newspaper, because I could always talk about that with my parents."

Obviously, we can't draw conclusions from a sample of two, but I must say that any parent would surely be delighted to claim Brianna and Rob—kind, articulate, and thoughtful young people. Both went off to college where, to their shock, they discovered that the other kids—graduates of traditional high schools—actually didn't love their lessons and their homework.

"I was so excited about all the courses I could take—I couldn't wait to learn all that stuff," Rob enthused. (He would soon enter graduate school.)

"Yeah, I found the same thing," added Brianna. "I felt like the world had just opened up to me—it was like this huge buffet table full of learning. And the other kids were complaining about the workload."

"But weren't you terribly behind?" I was skeptical.

Both students assured me they had soon filled in the gaps, especially since their school district had permitted them to enroll in high school and community college math and science classes when they surpassed the level available at home or on the Internet. Moreover, they really *wanted* to learn. Hmmmm.

Lots to Learn and When to Seek Help

As an educator, I keep learning. I am a firm advocate for identifying and treating significant learning differences as early as possible. Yet experiences like this one raise some interesting questions. Above all, they reinforce the power of a positive, mentally enriching environment with parents as models to lure, not push, a child into learning. Clearly, both these young people had plenty of "smarts" to start with, however their brains were arranged. Yet I find myself wondering—if someone had insisted that Rob read at age six, would he be turned off, tuned out, and "learning disabled" instead of on his way to graduate school?

If you are an alternative or homeschooler, you may be wondering how to know whether and when you should seek special help for a child whose reading is delayed. While there are no hard-and-fast rules, check back to Chapter 2, "What's the Problem?," and consider whether your child is showing warning signs of language disorder, in which case you should think seriously about consulting a speech-language therapist for an evaluation. If your child is over seven, is not reading, and rebels against it even though you have encouraged him with reading out loud, models of family reading time, and plenty of opportunities for language development, I would suggest a checkup with an educational therapist. I realize, however, that not all families will agree with this age recommendation and it is, of course, impossible to predict any child's educational future. The most important caveat is not to allow this issue to devolve into a power struggle (which is, of course, one hazard of which most home-schoolers are well aware). We want our children not only to be able to read but also to enjoy it and make it a lifelong habit.

Valued—But for What?

Parents who watch their child struggle to overcome learning defi-cits may justifiably feel a touch of envy for the parents of those "perfect" children who seem to rise to the top in any situation. Yet therapists point out that young adults who have faced and con-quered learning challenges are sometimes better equipped with both self-knowledge and grit than those for whom things have al-ways come easily.

"The best thing that ever happened to me was getting turned down at my first-choice college," a dazzlingly successful business-man once confided to me. "It made me finally confront the fact that as a dyslexic I simply had to buckle down and work harder—I think it made all the difference in my life!"

Life as Performance

In a high-pressure meritocracy, the "stars" face special risks. In her famous book *The Drama of the Gifted Child*, first published in 1979 but very relevant today, psychiatrist Alice Miller talks about her "gifted" adult patients, highly successful achievers far ahead of the curve, but plagued by "dark feelings" of anxiety whenever they fail to be the "superstar."[14] Their constant seeking for recognition is of no avail, because when the "drug of grandiosity" fails, they are over-whelmed by emptiness and depression.

Miller traces this angst to parents whose high expectations failed to give the child what he needed most, "to be regarded and respected as the person he really is at any given time ... and as the central actor in his own activity." In other words, accept and love your child in her beautiful and precious childishness, observe and follow her interests and needs, and forget about trying to make her into a product of your own wish fulfillment.

Miller's message has apparently not penetrated, however. "Many of today's most unhappy teens probably made the honor roll last semester and plan to attend prestigious universities," begins a recent article in a psychological journal.[15] It cites research indicating that teens whose parents overemphasized their accomplishments were most likely to be depressed or anxious and use drugs. Excessive fear of failure is a powerful stressor, and parents obsessed with grades and achievement set children up for trouble.

> Praise your child, not just her accomplishments. Families in which children feel they are valued for what they *do* rather than what they *are* pose a particular risk.

Winners or Losers?

In an article published in the *Atlantic*, columnist David Brooks reported on interviews in which Ivy League students—highly successful meritocracy survivors—candidly described their exhausting race to stay ahead of a rapidly accelerating curve.[16] Double and even triple majors combined with extracurricular achievements that leave so little time for personal life that it's necessary to make an appointment for even a casual chat with a friend—often in the early hours of the morning. One young lady apologized for her need to sleep five hours each night, although she claimed to be able to study in her sleep.

> *"Sometimes we feel like we're just tools for processing information. That's what we call ourselves—power tools."*
>
> —Ivy League student

A few youngsters, of course, seem to thrive on relentless competition, despite the long-term emotional and personal costs. For most, however, these values translate into unrealistic expectations and potentially unhealthy alternatives. Perhaps even more worrisome, this emphasis on competition and achievement can push values and moral guidance into the background. "When it comes to character and virtue, these young people have been left on their own," Brooks concludes.

Is this really what we want for our children?

Definitely Behind the Curve — or Was He?

"He cared not for books or study, and saw no sense in talk of college. . . . Recalling his childhood in later life, [he] wrote of the unparalleled bliss of roaming the open fields and woodlands of the town, of exploring the creeks, hiking the beaches, 'of making and sailing boats . . . swimming, skating, flying kites and shooting marbles, bat and ball, football, wrestling, and sometimes boxing . . . shooting at crows, ducks, and running about to quilting parties and frolics among the boys and girls.' 'The first fifteen years of his life,' he said, 'went off like a fairy tale.' "

—from *John Adams* by David McCullough[17]

CHAPTER 10

Brain-Cleaning 101

Banish Brain Disruptors

"You can't clean up everything, but a lot of little changes can add up to a big difference."
—Claire Coles, Emory University School of Medicine, at a conference sponsored by the Learning Disabilities Association (LDA)[1]

couldn't miss the urgency of the hand insistently waving in the middle of a crowded auditorium where I was presenting a workshop entitled Brain-Cleaning 101: How to Help Your Child Learn Better. The topic had evidently hit a nerve with both parents and professionals—a very raw nerve for some, I discovered, as the person attached to the waving hand spat out her question.

"This is just too much! I can't do it all. I've got two kids, two jobs, and what you're suggesting takes time and energy. I know it's important, and I know it would help my kids, but where do I start?"

Where, indeed? This earnest lady, like so many overwhelmed parents today, is coping with a frontal assault on her children's healthy learning. She knows all too well that she really has three jobs, not two, and that the most important one is to structure a loving, supportive, and brain-building environment for her children. As a new wrinkle in parenthood, moreover, she must also stand as a bulwark between her children and the innumerable distractions and potential hazards in kids' lives today.

Many things that we take for granted have the potential to stunt the growth of key brain systems. Hidden toxins, both physical and mental; too much of the wrong kinds of food and drink; super-stimulated, overscheduled, stressed, and sleep-impaired lifestyles; too little brain-training in sustained attention or concentration; overwhelmed parents; inconsistent caregiving; insufficient time to play, relax, explore nature; little practice in learning to use one's own mind reflectively—all add to the accelerating toll of learning problems.

Where to start? Somewhere! Anywhere! Even small steps can make a huge difference. Lifestyle-induced damage can be prevented or reversed. Determined parents, armed with knowledge, can little by little reprogram children's daily habits along with the brain functions affected by them. It does, indeed, take time and energy. Is it worth the effort? That's your call. The remainder of this book lays out a five-step program to help you get results.

> Educators as well as parents need to pay attention. They can play a major role in combating brain disruptors.

Quick Take: Combating "Brain Disruptors"

1. Homes and schools are potential sources of "brain disruptors."

2. Environmental toxins are a significant problem. You can't create a toxin-free environment for your home or classroom, but small, manageable steps add up to big differences and are definitely worth the effort.

3. Healthy, loving, and well-regulated home lives build "cognitive reserve" that helps children withstand toxic influences.

4. Sleep habits, food and beverage choices, amount and type of physical exercise, and media all impact the growing brain and learning abilities. Attending to them can dramatically

improve achievement and reduce or even eliminate the need for drugs like Ritalin.

5. The best prevention starts before the child is conceived, but dramatic changes are still possible even if you're a late starter.

6. Be sure that all caregivers understand the importance of following your guidelines.

7. Be aware and be informed. Helpful publications and Web sites are listed among this book's references and new information is constantly available.

8. Remember: "No evidence" of harm does not mean that a product or activity is harmless. It simply means we don't know.

9. A good motto when dealing with all hazards is "prudence without paranoia." There's no point ruining your life with anxiety, but reasonable safeguards make good sense.

10. You may have to be firm and even temporarily unpopular to cleanse your child's brain of some harmful—but all-too-common—substances and habits of life today. It's too bad that responsible parenting takes so much grit.

Understanding "Cognitive Reserve"

I overheard a frazzled-looking mom a few days ago while grocery shopping. As she attempted to decipher the ingredients on a box of cereal, she remarked to her friend, "There's so much to worry about that I just can't even deal with it! It's impossible to be perfect, so why try?"

This reaction is totally understandable. It is easier to deny a problem and hope for the best than to take the necessary action, especially if it means extra time, extra hassles, and perhaps extra expense. But every little step you can take is important for one particular reason: it will build up your child's all-important cognitive reserve.

Cognitive reserve is defined as extra brain connections, thinking power, and mental resilience. This sturdy buffer against damage, stress, and even brain disease is accumulated through a lifetime of healthy brain activity fostered by wholesome lifestyle choices and nurturing environments. The more you have, the more you decrease the possibility—or the effects—of problems.

The medical notion of "total body (or brain) burden" is an important concept to understand here. Each of us inevitably picks up and carries a certain toxic load—both chemical and psychological; the point is to keep the total residue as small as possible by reducing manageable risk factors. In doing so, you can minimize your child's problem potential—not only for learning difficulties and attention and mood disorders but also for long-term threats such as Parkinson's or Alzheimer's disease.

Working to build a strong and healthy brain is especially important if your child is at risk for any kind of problems. As we launch our assault on brain disruptors, we should remember that perfection is an impossible goal. It's the total sum of your everyday efforts that will make the difference.

Step 1: Disrupt the "Disruptors" in Everyday Environments[2]

As I emerged from a full-day session at the Annual International Conference of the Learning Disabilities Association, I noticed that the participants' somber facial expressions mirrored my own feelings. This had been my first full-bore introduction to environmental toxins as "brain disruptors" that cause both pre- and postnatal damage and contribute to a surge in children's learning disabilities. Frankly, I felt completely overwhelmed at the magnitude of identified threats to children's development. But there were hopeful notes:

1. The human brain has considerable capacity to defend itself against toxic assaults.

2. The more cognitive reserve you can build in your child, the better these defense systems will work.

Environmental Learning Disruptors. Despite scientists' warnings about their potentially damaging effects, environmental toxins have infiltrated homes, neighborhoods, and schools. Autistic spectrum disorders, attention deficits, and lowered IQ scores are just a few of the suspected outcomes. Fortunately, understanding the problem leads to constructive action.

Since World War II, haphazard regulation in the United States and other countries has allowed tens of thousands of potential neurotoxicants (chemicals poisonous to the nervous system) to be released into the environment. Many of these substances are useful in our industrial economy, but their sheer volume and lack of regulatory control represent a threat to the mental well-being of our children. Whereas drug manufacturers are required to test and demonstrate safety of new products, no such proof was required until recently for new chemicals, and a product already on the market must be proven dangerous (a difficult and infrequent process) to be subject to regulation. As a result, fewer than half of the 2,800 most popular chemicals expelled into our children's world every year have been studied for toxicity.[3]

> *"[Multiple] chemicals are known to cause clinical neurotoxic effects in adults. Despite an absence of systematic testing, many additional chemicals have been shown to be neurotoxic in laboratory models. The toxic effects of such chemicals in the developing human brain are not known and they are not regulated to protect children."[4]*

> —P. J. Landrigan, chairman of the Department of
>   Community and Preventive Medicine and director
>   of the Center for Children's Health and the
>   Environment of the Mount Sinai School of
>   Medicine in New York City, in *The Lancet*

"Bluntly put, potentially toxic substances should not be released into children's environments and developing nervous systems until they are proven safe," argues Joel T. Nigg, author of *What Causes ADHD?*[5] Parents who are justifiably outraged about this situation are demanding new legislation to prohibit the release of suspicious substances until satisfactory proof of safety is available. In the meanwhile, every parent should be informed about known risks and how to avoid or minimize them.

Special Risks for Children

Before birth, toxins can cross the placenta and cause genetic and brain alterations that interfere with normal development. Malformed brain structures and disruption of neurotransmitters such as dopamine and serotonin may have effects that show up at any time during the child's life span. The blood-brain barrier, a shield that filters and protects the mature brain from some toxins, does not form until about six months after birth.[6]

Young children are especially vulnerable because of their small body size, rapid metabolism, tendency to put things in their mouths and time spent near the floor, inhaling vapors from products such as household cleaners or pesticides. Young brains are growing at a very rapid rate, and any disruption may have wide-reaching effects. The major bright spot in this unsettling picture is the fact that the quality of nurturance and appropriate stimulation in postnatal environments can be even more powerful than most brain disruptors, and this is something you can definitely influence.

Toxic Classrooms? When a child enters a day care or school setting, additional hazards present themselves. Many years ago, when I was a primary school principal, I was seated at my desk late one afternoon when my eyes began to smart and my throat to choke up. Peering into the hall, I observed two men with face masks who were holding hoses and spraying around the edges of the carpeting.

"What are you doing?" I screeched.

"Spraying for bugs," one replied.

Needless to say, the next morning I arrived early at the office of the powers-that-be with a rather strident request that pesticide application be reserved for times when children were on vacation for several days and the fumes could have a chance to dissipate. Many schools have made progress since then, and good information is available for administrators about various hazards in school buildings. Yet too many schools are still exposing children to environmental poisons. One more responsibility for the principal, but an important one, indeed!

At a workshop for a school district in central California, teachers solemnly agreed that on the days when aerial crop spraying was in progress, their students were "bouncing off walls" even more than

usual. Environmental guidelines indicate they were right. Detox-
ifying schools and protecting the surrounding environments needs
more careful attention. For example, we may need to sacrifice
perfect green lawns rather than expose students to potentially
neurotoxic herbicides and pesticides. Many communities have
stopped using pesticides on public parks and recreation areas.
See www.beyondpesticides.org to find out how to take steps in your
community.

With the list of potential dangers growing longer every year,
parents and teachers should not only stay as well informed as possible, but also start speaking up and demanding changes. Joining
together with other parents in school, play group, or community as-
sociations can effect big changes. Below is a summary of current
suspected brain toxins, followed by practical steps you can take to
avoid them. (Much more in-depth information is available from the
sources cited in Appendix D; the list of potentially hazardous chemicals is so long and so full of complicated chemical terms that one's
natural reaction is "Help! We're surrounded!" The best approach is
to be on guard against the major categories of proven culprits and
stay informed about new findings.)

A Neurotoxin Primer

1. *Metals* such as lead, arsenic, methylmercury: may be found in
   products as varied as children's toys and paint in older
   homes

2. *Organic solvents* such as acetone, benzene, ethanol, toluene
   used in cleaning products (e.g., carpet or upholstery cleaners), paint thinners, etc.

3. *Dioxins and PCBs* (polychlorinated biphenyls) used in electrical equipment and insulators

4. *Pesticides:* insecticides, fungicides, rat poison

5. *Flame retardants:* used in some fabrics

6. *Formaldehyde:* used in some fabrics, art supplies

7. *Nicotine and alcohol*

8. *Bisphenol A and phthalates (plastic softeners):* have been used in some infant bottles, pacifiers, children's toys, drinking bottles, food containers

9. *Over-the-counter drugs:* excessive or inappropriate use may affect brain chemistry. Watch your child for signs of a negative reaction. Keep all drugs and other toxic products away from children's reach and/or in a locked cupboard.

10. *Electromagnetic radiation(?):* currently controversial, unproven effects. More research is needed about degree of danger and size of dose necessary for adverse affects. Possibly implicated: microwave ovens, cell phones, electrical appliances, high-tension power lines, computers, game consoles, and cell phone towers. Some parents who believe their children's learning has been affected by high-tension power lines have requested that children's classrooms be moved out from under them. Environmental consultants offer screening for private homes to determine risk level and suggest action steps. Look for current books or articles to keep up with this controversial topic.

A Few Practical Steps to Reduce Risk

- Stay informed. New information is always coming out. Check out books and Web sites. Invite reputable experts to speak at PTA or club meetings. Contact the Learning Disability Association of America for current information. Their *LDA Newsbriefs* is informative and helpful.

- Survey your house or apartment for potential toxic products (lead paint, carpeting, pesticides, furniture coverings or other areas containing formaldehyde). Replace with less toxic products when possible.

- Read labels and check ingredients against published lists of toxicants. Dispose of toxic products properly at a hazardous waste site.

- If you have questions or concerns about a product, ask questions and press for answers. "Better safe than sorry" is always a good motto. Useful Web site: www.checnet.org.

- See the classic books by pediatric allergist Doris Rapp.[7] Some authorities believe that environmental toxicants trigger allergies that, in turn, impact the brain and learning abilities.

- Use natural or organic products—e.g., wool, cotton, linen, wood, glass—whenever possible. Until we have more research, avoid nonstick coatings on cookware and excessive exposure to electromagnetic radiation (e.g., children's frequent cell phone use, aging microwave ovens with loose seals). Avoid heating or microwaving food in plastic containers.

- Make a survey of your child's toys, school supplies, and jewelry (which may contain lead) for potentially harmful ingredients. Stores and manufacturers should be held accountable for products sold for children's use.

- Consider switching to natural cleaning products whenever possible.

- Keep your child away from lawns where pesticides have recently been applied; it takes forty-eight hours for their effects to dissipate. Be cautious about any pesticide, herbicide, or fungicide use.

- Join the growing numbers of parents who are fed up with lax attention to this "hidden pandemic" and want to take action. Parent groups in several states (for example, Maine) have already succeeded in influencing legislation to make their children's brains safer.

What Schools Can Do[8]

- *Indoor air quality:* Obtain the "Indoor Air Quality Tools for Schools" materials (www.epa.gov/iaq/schools).

    - Is the school clean and are carpets, floors, ceilings, and air intakes free of water stains and mold?

- Do classroom windows open and are heating, air-conditioning, and ventilation systems in order?

- Are excess dust, fumes, and noise under control?

- Are *toxic products* that contain lead, mercury, formaldehyde, or solvents avoided in favor of safer ones (e.g., in cleaning supplies, science labs, and art rooms). Is a nontoxic purchasing policy observed?

- *Pesticides:* Some states have enacted no-spray zones for pesticides around schools. Find out your school's and your state's policies and determine whether existing laws are being followed.

- Is *diesel bus exhaust* minimized by no-idling zones or located well away from the school?

- Are *drinking water, paints, and playground equipment* free of lead and arsenic?

- Is the *food* served to students wholesome and nutritious?

If you find it appalling, annoying—or infuriating—that busy parents have to take on these concerns and become police officers regarding yet one more aspect of their children's lives, you are not alone! Outraged parents are always a force to be reckoned with, so don't be afraid to speak up.

Moreover, toxic chemicals are not the only brain disruptors in children's lives today, and minimizing other more controllable threats to healthy development is something any parent or teacher can do.

Early Environments

If all newborn babies were alike, it would be easy to figure out how to raise them most effectively. As we all know, however, some take a lot more effort than others. A learning-power environment takes each child's individual schedule of development into account. For example, some children can handle overstimulation better than others who decompress if their schedules are even slightly disrupted. Children also seem to respond differently to various toxins, to media exposure, or to all the other forces that currently assail the growing brain. In *Your Child's Growing Mind*, I explain how to assist your child's individual developmental schedule, as well as recognize any significant irregularity signaling a need for special attention.

> Many children who later show up with learning problems start out with vulnerable nervous systems. They require extraspecial care.

Breast Milk and the Brain. In the best of all possible worlds, all mothers would enjoy the special closeness and mutual benefits of breast-feeding their infants. Many components of human breast milk are protective: they enhance brain development, particularly certain long-chain polyunsaturated fatty acids (PUFAs) that particularly benefit the growth of neural wiring. Breast milk is also a source of important hormones and nerve growth factors.[9]

As it happens, many fine, capable mothers are, for one reason or another, unable to nurse. Some are also alarmed by the suspicion that their breast milk may be contaminated by environmental toxins accumulated over the years, stored in body fat and excreted in breast milk. Nonetheless, the balance of opinion at this time is still strongly, if possible, "breast is best."[10]

The very fact that we even need to question the potential toxicity of mother's milk, however, is shocking. No wonder many thoughtful nursing mothers are both confused and justifiably furious about the situation!

It is far beyond the intent of this book to give breast-feeding the detailed treatment it deserves. However, based on current professional advice, a few clear suggestions have emerged:

1. Give breast-feeding your best try. Some of the most important nutrients are available in the earliest days of a newborn's life. Be patient and persistent; sometimes it takes some time for you and your baby to adapt to each other.

2. If you cannot nurse, be sure to check with your pediatrician about obtaining formula that has been supplemented with brain food such as the long-chain fatty acids. These products

tend to cost more, but please remember that it is much more important to endow your child with strong brain cells than with infant furniture, a large layette, or toys. We may hope that your doctor and your insurance company will think so, too.

3. Make bottle-feeding, if necessary, as close a bonding experience as you can. The baby's emotional brain is also growing by leaps and bounds (and so is yours, just not quite so quickly).

Lifestyle Differences That Make a Difference

"These days you have to be assertive if you want your child to have a healthy body and a healthy brain. There's so much out there that makes it easy not to do it right!"

—mother of two successful students

In the remainder of this chapter and the next, we will consider brain disruptors that, although they cannot be tested and measured in a chemical laboratory, are hazardous to children's brains and their learning. These specific steps will help you minimize the damage and build your child's cognitive reserve.

Step 2: Feed the Learning Brain

"There's so much out there that I can't protect them from. At least their home and the food they eat should be as safe as I can make it."

—Cameron Lilly, in the *New York Times*[12]

One of the biggest favors you can do your child's brain is to bite the bullet (a vitamin-filled one, of course) and become nutrition-conscious. The current catastrophe of obese children is clear evidence of our unhealthy nutritional habits. Obesity gets a lot of press, but the equally alarming public health implications of children's poor nutrition—negative effects on their learning—get relatively little attention. Scientific evidence is mounting that many learning, behavior, and mood disorders stem at least in part from careless or uninformed food choices. Families and schools that have improved their children's meals report positive results.

TIP: Do your child's brain a favor: become nutrition-conscious.

Informed parents have long since taken nutrition to heart; they monitor and guide their children's food consumption and try to teach them to make good choices (an uphill battle these days). Many also lobby the local school to clean up its own act by removing soft drink and snack machines and offering healthier food choices. Since there is a very cozy relationship between what goes into your child's stomach and what comes out of her brain, this concern makes serious sense.

Food and Your Child's Brain

Everything that happens to the human body eventually affects the brain in one way or another, but the two-way highway between the brain and the digestive tract (or "gut" as the doctors say) is especially busy. To understand how interactive this system is, consider the following:

- *Brain and gut work together.* The brain launches fleets of hormones and other neurochemicals that are transported to the rest of the body. Most of us have felt excited, nervous, or frightened and had the effects show up a long way from where the feeling originates—a fluttering in your heart or clammy, sweaty hands, for example. Even more likely is some sort of reaction—either temporary or chronic—in the stomach or intestines. The reason is that neurotransmitters and neurohormones have multiple receptors in the digestive tract.

- *Food's nutrient bundles are unpacked and sent throughout your body—including your brain.* If you have ever been extremely hungry or crashing after too much sugar, you may recognize the feeling of weak or "foggy" brain function.

- *The brain runs on glucose*, which the gut extracts from most kinds of food; in fact, the brain gobbles up 20 percent of the food energy we consume even though it comprises only 5 percent of body weight. The most usable form of glucose comes from complex carbohydrates such as whole grains, fruits, and vegetables—*not* sugar itself.

- *Too much glucose, too fast* causes a peak (a "sugar high") followed quite rapidly by a deep valley, which is really a state of *brain starvation* in which a child cannot think clearly, loses some memory function, and may feel physically weak or dizzy. Some children are more susceptible to this problem than others, but if your child crashes in midmorning, you should recalculate her breakfast choices. Caffeine, found in some soft drinks, can make this situation worse. Some authorities speculate that some cases of ADHD are actually a blood sugar imbalance.

- For good functioning, *the brain needs adequate amounts of protein, iron, vitamins (especially B vitamins), and trace minerals such as zinc.*[13] These ingredients are best consumed in a healthy, normal diet. Overdosing or experimenting with extreme and unproven nutritional therapies can do more harm than good. Check with current reference books, your pediatrician, or a dietitian if you have questions.

- *Essential ingredients for brain health that are often lacking in children's diets are essential fatty acids* (EFAs) containing omega-3 and -6 (described in more detail later in this chapter). These EFAs build and repair the brain's connections; lack of EFAs has been blamed for everything from reading problems to attention deficits to autism to mood and psychiatric disorders.[14]

- *Toxins in food also find their way into the brain*, where they can have subtle or disastrous effects. A "blood-brain barrier" screens out some nasty substances, but not all. Watch your child's reaction to various types of foods to determine which might be causing trouble.

- Some children have *undetected food allergies* that create temporary brain problems. Outspoken pediatrician Doris Rapp shows videotapes of children who have dramatic and sudden personality changes, crying jags, or mental lethargy after being exposed to an allergen.[15] She lists the following risk factors to look for:

- child has allergic relatives

- child has other allergies

- child is pale with chronic dark circles and runny nose

- child's disposition "flips" suddenly

- child has many infections and has frequently taken medications

The question of what, specifically, your child may be allergic to is best left to an allergy specialist, but Dr. Rapp does suggest a quick test for a food you suspect might be a problem: Have the child write his name, then have him eat one specific food, wait forty-five minutes, and have him write his name again. If you see a dramatic deterioration in his handwriting, you may want to consult an allergist or wholistic physician for more complete testing.

- Some children with unusually sensitive nervous systems adamantly *refuse to eat anything except a very limited menu*— all white foods, for example. They may gag on foods with different tastes or textures. Parents of a child like this would be wise to seek advice from a professional as to how maximum nutrition can be obtained while still accommodating and, one hopes, expanding the child's preferences.

- *Diet may be a critical factor in the expression of genes related to learning problems.* Much more research is needed, yet provocative clues exist. Consider the youngsters whose symptoms of ADHD have improved dramatically after their diet was changed. Dr. Joel Nigg suggests there may be subgroups of children whose brains are sensitive to different types of dietary substances or combinations, resulting in subtle neurodevelopmental deficits. He thinks the disturbing lack of information on this issue should be "an important public health concern."[16] At Harvard, Martha Herbert conducts cutting-edge research on autism.[17] She concludes that genes alone do not account for it. She notes that children on the autistic spectrum have an unusually high incidence of gut-related disorders, suggesting that food allergies triggering immune system response may be partially implicated.

"I think what we are looking at [in autism] is a transition from a behavior disorder and brain disorder to a whole body condition."

—Martha Herbert, Harvard Medical School[18]

- *Obesity* is not a natural condition for children; an unhealthy body places extra strains on the learning brain.

Despite mountains of information linking brain function with what we eat and drink, however, many parents still seem remarkably clueless on this issue. An outraged third-grade teacher recently bent my ear about an incident she had just witnessed in a supermarket.

"Here was this mother—well dressed and she was really doing her best, but she had these two little kids who were totally out of control— the kind I whisper to myself, 'Please, please, don't let them end up in my classroom!' They were all over the place, no matter what she said or tried—and she really was trying to get them to behave. So we ended up in the check-out line together, and she rolls her eyes and says to me, 'I'm sorry, but these kids are driving me nuts!'

"So I looked at her cart, and the whole bottom shelf was filled with cans of soft drinks—all different kinds, sugar and artificial sweeteners, full of food colors and heaven-knows-what. And there wasn't a single piece of fresh fruit in that cart, but you should have seen the bags of snacks! I'm thinking, Lady, don't you know anything?, but I kept my mouth shut. She probably wouldn't get it."

It's Not Easy to Buck the Taste-Good Tide

The all-too-familiar "typical American diet" of fast food and overprocessed, undernutritious food is not brain-healthy for anyone, but children and teens are at special risk because their neuronal connections and neurotransmitters are in such formative stages.

"The overwhelming majority of food-product advertisements seen on television by American children are of poor nutritional content."

—Lisa M. Powell, Institute for Health Research and Policy, University of Illinois in *Pediatrics*[19]

You would never know it, however, from children's television content, which is designed to form lifelong attitudes and preferences. Concerned parents are forced into battles with their own children, who have been lured by a barrage of ads for sugary, fatty, salty, additive-laden treats. Two recent studies, one by the Kaiser Family Foundation and the other by the U.S. Federal Trade Commission, found that in 2004 and 2005, young children were exposed to an average of about 5,500 food ads a year—with the numbers rising.[20] Almost all ads were for processed snacks, candy, or sugared cereals; children's food ads for dairy products and fruit juices comprised only 5 percent of the total, and there were none for fruits or vegetables. Many foods were linked to popular TV icons and often included mention of a Web site containing more advertising or subtle product exposure.

Young children and teens consume quantities of soft drinks containing either heavy sugar content or artificial sweeteners, both of which are potential brain disruptors.[21] Middle and high schools make profits from soft drink and snack vending machines—and then lament their students' academic ineptitude. Fortunately, some have realized that there is something very wrong with this picture, and have taken measures to correct the situation.

Being a nutrition-conscientious parent is far more difficult than it should be. Yet any positive step you take is important.

Nutritional status and learning status go hand in hand.

What You Can Do: A Beginning

Major change is difficult, but many sources are available for help in getting started. Numerous books and online sources give up-to-date information on children's nutrition with tips for making good eating habits a part of your lifestyle.[22] I have listed just a few in the Notes. Keep alert for new research. Improving your child's brain by revising the family diet takes fortitude, but even small changes will benefit everyone in the family. Some authors suggest a complete clean-out of all questionable products for starters, but older children should be part of any negotiation about major changes in cherished habits.

Until we know more or get better regulation, try to rearrange your budget, if possible, to include organic products when you can. Read ingredient labels, and if sugar in any form (such as fructose or corn syrup) is near the top of the list, be wary (ingredients are listed in order of their quantity in the product). Remember that the brain runs best on a steady supply of glucose from many sources, and sudden jolts of sugar throw off this cycle. Be especially alert for artificial colors and sweeteners (aspartame, Equal, NutraSweet) that, according to physicians, can upset the body's balance of neurotransmitters, causing a range of neurological symptoms—a fact about which the general public has been substantially underinformed.[23] Beware, also, of labels that read like a course in chemistry. As Michael Pollan suggests, a product with more than five ingredients is probably not food![24]

Many pediatricians have long doubted parents' firsthand evidence of negative effects of some food colorings and preservatives on their children's hyperactive behavior. Recently, however, a convincing study has caused them to rethink their position on this issue. For six weeks children ate an additive-free diet. When they were then "challenged" by being given foods that contained the substances, their behavior problems worsened.

> "The overall findings of this study are clear and require that even we skeptics, who have long doubted parental claims of the effects of various foods on the behavior of their children, admit that we might have been wrong."[25]

Many American and European children skip breakfast, which puts them at risk for blood sugar fluctuations, "fuzzy" brains, and poorer school performance. Try hard to get something wholesome into your child in the morning. Don't forget, the brain runs best with adequate protein—and this includes parents' brains as well!

Perhaps one of the easiest prescriptions to implement is to re-member that the brain needs water. Juices or soft drinks are not a substitute. Teachers, please take note: water breaks may improve your students' learning and behavior.

Schools Take Action for Better-Functioning Brains

Would you be surprised to see your school principal strolling the hallways with a bowl of fruit? A national survey by *Health Magazine* found that increasing numbers of schools, concerned about students' achievement scores and behavior problems, have instituted plans to revise their nutritional habits.[26] Parents, too, have spoken up to ask that teachers enforce a "healthy treat" rule for students' birthdays and class parties. After revision of school lunches and snacks as well as educating students and parents about the importance of healthy food choices, schools from preschool to high school have seen improvement not only in physical fitness but also in academic achievement and attention abilities, as well as reduction in negative behaviors such as bullying.

These results are not surprising. In addition to the possibly toxic effects of some food additives, poor nutrition is just one more stressor for children's already overblitzed brains.

> A healthy body is the best home for a sharp, well-functioning brain. Parents and teachers who really want to help kids learn better can insist that food choices at schools are designed to sharpen, rather than dull their student's minds.

Food Alters Genes

Food choices are one of the environmental factors that can trigger *epigenetic change* in genes. As we saw earlier, such changes can determine whether a gene does or does not turn on (express itself). In rodent studies, diet is so powerful that changing a pregnant mouse's diet can change the genes that determine the color of her baby's coat. A different line of research suggests that diet may predispose certain people to cancer by silencing genes that could suppress growth of tumors.[27]

Families with genetic susceptibilities to brain interference from food substances (e.g., sugar, food additives) may be told that their learning problem, such as ADHD or autism, is totally genetic when it is, in fact, an intricate interaction of genes and environmental triggers. We can also observe people with a genetic constitution that seems to allow them to get away with nutritional murder and remain slim, healthy, and mentally sharp—at least for a while. It seems likely, too, that some children can eat poorly and still function well. It makes sense, however, to avoid guesswork about this serious subject.

In the next chapter, we will continue our brain-cleaning with strategies for two other factors that increasingly disrupt children's lives and learning.

CHAPTER 11

Brain-Cleaning 102

Tackling Lifestyle Factors

For a culture skilled in giving lip service to the importance of achievement and brainpower, we are remarkably careless with the brains of our children.

Toxic chemicals and unhealthy eating habits are not the only brain disruptors in children's lives today. Reducing other more controllable threats to healthy development is also important. Remember that most of these risks are cumulative, which means that any steps you take will add up. They may not show up right away, but persistence and patience will very likely pay off.

Because of neuroplasticity, physical, intellectual, and emotional environments have enormous power over the way children's brains develop. They also influence whether or not risk genes express themselves in learning disabilities, attention problems, or emotional disorders.

Implementing these brain-cleaning steps can sharpen brain function and may reduce or even eliminate your child's need for medication to improve learning or attention.

It is hard to be firm—even about what you know to be right—in the face of "Oh Mom, all the other kids are doing it." Mass marketing of bad habits and unhealthy values doesn't help. But none of the "other kids" have your child's particular brain chemistry, and some of them have problems, too. I suggest you start as early as possible. With older children aim for manageable changes in small steps. Discuss with your child why these actions are important in making school learning easier and family life happier. Remember that when given a choice—treats, electronic amusements, toys, or more time with their parents—children choose their parents. This is a reward you have the power to bestow joyously—for your own benefit as well as for that of your child.

Teachers face an uphill task to maintain learning standards when so many of their students have problems. Educators can tactfully but firmly provide information to guide parents and inform them of the basic "rules" for raising strong and effective learners.

Here are two other important steps in your brain-cleaning program.

Step 3: Take Sleep Seriously

"Please, please, please tell our parents this!"

—teachers at many workshops

Brain function is the first casualty when a child isn't getting enough sleep. Research documents a strong relationship between insufficient sleep and children's learning, memory, mood, and attention problems. Yet teachers cope every day with tired, mentally listless, or hyper students who arrive at school chronically sleep deprived. Sleep deprivation is an accepted downside of contemporary adult culture, and its effects on both performance and emotional well-being in vulnerable children are even more virulent. For the most part, these problems are also preventable and treatable—an obvious starting point for a child who is experiencing difficulty with any form of learning.

Sleep deprivation mimics the symptoms of ADHD and mood disorder.

Why Is Sleep So Important for the Brain?

Getting enough sleep helps every part of the brain and affects both cognitive and emotional functioning. It restores the mental energy that children use up every day in school. *Students with learning problems, especially, need to use many times the normal amount of mental energy to compensate for processing difficulties* and a day at school is extremely tiring for them. For example, they may take longer to grasp (process) the meaning when a teacher gives directions, when required to understand a paragraph in a science textbook, to figure out how to respond appropriately to a teacher or peer, or to inhibit inappropriate behaviors or emotional crashes. A well-rested student with such problems has more *cognitive reserve* (extra brainpower) to use her talents and the methods she has been taught to compensate for the problem. When she's worn out, however, that reserve simply isn't available.

Adequate sleep provides the following brain benefits (this goes for adults, too!):[1]

- resets the learning machinery to be revitalized for a new day

- replenishes energy stores in the synapses

- repairs metabolic damage from stress or overload

- accelerates neural growth in learning networks

- consolidates memories of events and material learned during the day; may repeat patterns of firing of neurons connected to memory centers

- stimulates insight and creative applications of new learning

- helps link separate areas of the brain

- helps restore the brain's emotional resilience

- sharpens psycho-motor skills and coordination (e.g., athletics, handwriting)

> Middle schoolers are particularly at risk for chronic sleep
> deprivation because they need far more sleep (about nine
> hours, on average) than most parents realize.

In a 2004 study of more than two thousand children ages 11 to 14, the youngsters who got the least sleep had lower grades, lower self-esteem, and more depressive symptoms. The researchers acknowledge that cause and effect are difficult to sort out in these cases but speculate that the relationship between emotional distress and sleep goes both ways. University of Massachusetts professor Jean E. Rhodes, author of the study, said in an interview that parents could help their children "figure out how to schedule and manage their time in ways that incorporate all the necessities of middle school life" and still try to fit in a good night's sleep.[2] Clearly, not the easiest of parental responsibilities, but an important one. It is better not to wait until middle school to start, however.

How Much Sleep Do Children Need?

A survey of fact and expert opinion on this question yields remarkably consistent conclusions about the amount of sleep needed in a 24-hour period:

Infants up to 6 months: 16–20 hours

6 months–2 years: about 15 hours

2–6 years: 10–12 hours

7–13 years: 9–11 hours

14–18 years: 8½–9½ hours

Children do not always act sleepy when they are. In fact, overtiredness often produces excess activity—a sort of unnaturally "hyper" state. Parents must exercise judgment in managing outings and evening events, because overexcited children do not recognize their own needs.

Sleepy Kids: What Can Be Done?

Children chronically dulled by loss of sleep are a cultural by-product of our stressed-out, overcommitted lifestyles. How many learning disorders and emotional upsets would be avoided if it were otherwise? Who knows? At least there are concrete steps you can take that may help with any such problem that exists in your house.

- Do your best to respect your own health and sleep needs. Children model their behavior after the adults in their lives.

- Establish and try to stick to a regular bedtime. Be clear with your child about why it is necessary to enforce basic bedtime rules. Explain the effects of insufficient sleep, and be firm.

- Some children, especially if they are very keyed up after the day, have difficulty falling asleep. For help, stick to a bedtime routine—relaxed time with a parent or caregiver, a warm bath or a calming back rub, a story or song. I like Dr. Martin Seligman's idea of talking about pleasant things that happened during the day and that will happen tomorrow. If anxiety or stress is a serious problem, you might want to re-evaluate the pressures on this child or the possibility of over-scheduling. For a chronic problem, you may also want to talk with a psychologist—one hopes you will get something more than a knee-jerk prescription for sleeping pills.

- Use common sense. Avoid rowdy play, exciting or frightening TV, family arguments, or hearty meals directly before bedtime.

- Be wary of allowing a TV or computer in your child's room. Media and cell-phone use into late evening hours are growing problems at all ages and especially for older children. (See the later section on media for more information on reestablishing control over this potentially disruptive force.)

> Five- and six-year-old children who watch TV programs meant for adults have a markedly increased risk for sleep problems. Watching TV at bedtime or alone can be especially hazardous.

- Be aware of the fact that some children have organic sleep disorders. If your child snores excessively, has labored breathing in sleep, or shows other signs of a medical problem, alert your physician.[3] *Some authorities now suggest that any child referred for an attention deficit should first be checked by a sleep clinic.*

- For middle schoolers and teens, do your best, and work with your child's school on correcting factors of special risk for this age group, which include

  - an early start of the school day (some districts start middle school later than elementary school because of young teens' extra sleep needs)

  - part-time jobs

  - an excess homework load (of special concern for children with slower processing speed or lagging reading or writing abilities)

  - extracurricular activities, social networking, video game addiction

Step 4: Manage the Media

"Could the intellect that produced the digital revolution also be destroyed by it?"

—Edward Tenner, technology innovator[4]

I am seated at lunch in a diner in New York City, picking the brains of James Mendelsohn, a popular tutor for middle-school and high-school students and author of *A Parent's Guide to Tutors and Tutoring*.[5] Dr. Mendelsohn is both experienced and obviously effective, as his schedule is crammed with students whose parents pay for this extra help, often on top of private-school tuition. As we prepare to leave, I ask him if there is one thing he would tell parents about helping their children succeed academically.

"Tell them to limit TV and computer games!" he exclaims.

Managing the electronic media that increasingly invade the lives—and the bedrooms—of schoolchildren, teenagers, and even infants is a tough parental balancing act. What is a responsible parent to do, given the fact that unbiased research on this issue is minimal but potentially alarming? How should one sort facts from advertising claims from companies with millions to spend on promoting themselves? What does screen time really do to the growing brain? Can all these gadgets make kids smarter or better students, as some have claimed? Can too much electronic stimulation cause learning disabilities, attention deficit disorders, or even autism, as others have suggested? How do different types of media affect children of different genetic vulnerabilities? And how do we help children resist programming that is especially designed to entice their brains into more and more screen time? At this point we still have more questions than solutions.

When I use the term *media*, I include TV, computers, hand-held devices—essentially anything on a screen. Scientists now agree that the habitual use of any electronic media affects the development of the human brain, mainly depending on type of content and usage.[6] The real question, of course, is how the device is being used and whether the resulting brain changes are good or bad. The following section will summarize some important facts and suggest commonsense guidelines. In a hypertech climate, where good research lags far behind children's media usage, you have to become judge, role model, and—if necessary—enforcer of your child's media health.[7]

> If your child starts to show a learning problem, one of your
> first steps should be to conduct an honest evaluation of the
> child's media use and take corrective action if either amount
> of time or type of content appears to be a factor.

Media and the Learning-Different Child

Children with "different" brains are often uniquely well adapted to the type of mind-work inherent in media use. For example, many self-proclaimed dyslexics have achieved success in computer graphics or system design. "Aspies," as individuals with Asperger's syndrome sometimes call themselves, find the interface with an electronic screen much less taxing than the interface with human faces, and some consider themselves unusually well adapted for programming. Here are a few observations on technology and learning differences:

- Children with learning differences may be adept with new technologies and are often strongly drawn to them.

- *Different learning styles lead to different types of tech talents and liabilities,* just as with any other type of learning. A child who is "slow" in reading and spelling class may become class troubleshooter for other students' botched-up computer files. Someone who instinctively understands programming might have trouble coordinating his fingers for standard keyboarding.

- *Many children with learning problems* seem to be unusually fascinated by screen time. They may also have a higher-than-average susceptibility to screen addiction, although research is only starting to document this hypothesis.

- *Children on the ASD (autistic) spectrum* may obsess over screen images and act out in a tantrum if the screens are turned off. Nonetheless, as discussed earlier, they especially need practice time with human social skills. On the other hand, computer applications may facilitate their learning in later years, a subject that is still under exploration.

- *On-line gaming* is of special concern for any child who feels socially rejected by his real-life peers because the satisfactions of a virtual world can become addictive.

- *Children with a familial risk for attention problems* need especially firm attention to guidelines for amounts of screen time. (Attention-impaired parents may have more-than-average difficulty organizing these limitations, however.)

- *Every child needs face time and not screen time during the first few years.* This necessity goes double for a child from a family with a history of social and emotional disorders.

- *All children also need interactive human language* with responsive adults. They cannot get this from any electronic device. *To avoid potential language disabilities,* ensure a rich language environment for your child starting with birth.

Media and Learning Problems

> *"When you see your kid just sort of catatonic—you call his name, 'Travis . . . Travis . . . Travis'—and you get nothing, you know something has to be wrong. Now our boys get screen time only on the weekends, and that includes handheld games."*

—father of three school-age sons

Teachers have long suspected a close relationship between screen time and the severity of learning problems. Parents who are dialed into their children's development (instead of their own favorite program or e-mail) also sense that something is seriously amiss in the relationship some kids develop with electronic media. Now that objective researchers are finally taking a look at these concerns, we are starting to find out that they are all too real.

Television has been the most-studied medium in relationship to children's development because it has been around the longest. In fact, some types of computer use may have even more dramatic— and potentially more negative—effects that have yet to be investigated.

Four areas of concern relating to overuse of technology have emerged that particularly impact learning difficulties. They are attention, language development, "people" skills, and problem solving/imaginative thinking. These abilities are not "old-fashioned" ones that will be out of style in a technological world. In fact, they will be more important than ever for success in a technological world.

Attention. Several studies have linked television exposure to attention and learning problems.[8] It is widely recognized that exceeding a certain number of viewing hours causes school grades and achievement scores to drop. The "safe" amount of viewing seems to vary from child to child, but it is generally less than many U.S. children watch. In addition, new research implicates even preschool TV exposure in later problems.

> "Background TV [for young children] is a disruptive and distracting influence. Our evidence is that TV keeps the children from sustaining their attention at a time when developmentally, they're beginning to organize their attention skills and sequencing behaviors."
>
> —Daniel Anderson, Ph.D., University of Massachusetts[9]

Nearly three-fourths of young children in the United States grow up in households where the TV is on almost all the time.[10] Even if young children don't seem to be paying attention to the screen, having TV on in the background interrupts the brain-building effects of their play. It doesn't matter if a parent is in the room or whether the dial is turned to a children's program or an adult one that they don't understand, such as *Jeopardy!*. The problem is that the children periodically switch their attention away from their play to glance up at the screen, thus interrupting the "flow" of thought and attention, along with related brain circuits for language, self-monitoring, and problem solving. No one has looked at similar effects from adults' computer use around young children.

Periodic interruptions of play may seem unimportant, but they can have big long-term effects. One of the main functions of children's play is to help them develop habits of *sustained attention* to an object, such as manipulating a toy, or to an activity, such as block play or dress-up. Natural play also involves *independent problem solving* ("That shape didn't fit into that hole, this hole looks better"); *planning* ("My tower won't stay up, maybe the big block should go on the bottom"); and imagination ("I'm the mommy getting dressed for work"). Many adults don't realize that quiet, hands-on "child's play" builds the skills that good students use in school (and good workers and innovators use in the adult workplace).

Here are just two of the questions we should be asking about effects on attention before we plunge our youngsters into electronic worlds:

Question 1: Whose Brain Is in Charge Here? The rapid-fire, epi-sodic nature of most children's media may contribute to shortened attention spans. Television and computer games (including many "educational" ones) rely hevily on distracting features (e.g., zooms, pans, quick movements, flashy colors, sudden loud noises) that alert lower centers of the brain. In these examples *the medium is taking control of the child's attention system rather than allowing the child to learn to manage his own attention system.*

> If we hand our children's minds over to an electronic brain, we should not be surprised if their own brains become impaired.

Question 2: Is My Child Reacting or Reasoning? Most currently available screen media activate *posterior, sensory lobes of the cortex* as opposed to the *executive frontal systems.* Many popular computer applications, even those intended to improve academic skills, re-quire quick response that encourages an impulsive "guess-and-test" strategy, mimicking the primary problem of ADHD. As important as sensory areas are, frontal systems are even more critical for life success. As we saw in earlier chapters, the frontal control/organiza-tion/planning centers mature slowly throughout childhood and ado-lescence and need appropriate care and nurturing throughout these years. Executive function disorder is a relatively new but surpris-ingly prevalent and growing problem. *Is this because we have al-lowed electronic media to idle the control centers of our children's brains?*

There is no inherent reason why today's technologies need to limit rather than expand children's mental development. Any me-dium can engage the brain in complex, deep, and meaningful prob-lem solving, especially if the experience is mediated by thoughtful adults. Unfortunately, however, too many children spend a great deal of time with superficial, flashy, and engaging (and readily mar-ketable) but inferior content. Parents and educators can help by being critical consumers and careful monitors for all media use as well as demanding more intellectually satisfying products.

Language Development. Most children's media use seriously neglects— and even subverts—language use during critical periods for its de-

velopment. Children over age two may pick up vocabulary words and concepts from well-crafted programming, especially if a real adult "coach" is around to help them understand and talk about the experience. To really learn language properly, however, children need to talk and listen carefully—neither of which they do when they are engrossed in visuals on a screen.

It is only from responsive interactions with real people that youngsters learn to understand and use language effectively, which includes forming intelligent, grammatical sentences and understanding gestures and facial expressions. Since language development affects reading, math, and almost every aspect of academic learning, the escalation of screen time is of particular concern for children who lack sufficient face time with verbally responsive adults and good models of the type of language found in books (often gained from parents or teachers who read aloud to children).

Attention and language development are closely tied together in the brain, because the higher thinking centers of the brain use language—known as *inner speech* or *self-talk*—to plan, monitor their own behavior, and focus attention. *("This block needs to go on top— careful, careful, don't fall over . . .").* Screen time misses this critical developmental stepping-stone.

> *"As a cognitive neuroscientist and scholar of reading, I am particularly concerned with the plight of the reading brain as it encounters this technologically rich society."*
>
> —Maryanne Wolf, author of *Proust and the Squid: The Story and Science of the Reading Brain* [11]

"People" Skills and Autistic Spectrum Disorders. Adults accept the fact that screen technologies change the character of their interactions with other people. Yet most of today's adults developed the parts of their brains that make them capable of carrying on and valuing basic social relationships in a different world, before loving adult faces were supplemented—or even replaced—by screens and electronic voices.

> For every hour adults spend on computers, they lose sixty minutes of traditional face-to-face interaction. What are the

effects on children, especially those at risk for autistic spectrum disorders?[12]

As we discussed in Chapter 3, "What Should We Call This?," questions have been raised about whether excess screen time might contribute to a worsening of autistic spectrum and other social
communication disorders, although no research has directly investigated the possibility. In a chapter entitled "Development of Social
Brain Circuitry in Autism" in their book *Human Behavior, Learning, and the Developing Brain*, Geraldine Dawson and Raphael
Bernier point out the importance of direct and interactive language
experience for all children, and especially for those potentially on
the autistic spectrum. "Simple exposure to language does not necessarily facilitate the development of brain circuitry specialized for
language," they emphasize. "Language needs to be experienced by
the infant within a socially interactive context."[13]

> Children need to interact with responsive people—not
> screens—to develop brain circuits for social and communi-
> cation skills. Children on the autistic spectrum especially
> need direct, guided language and social experience.

Dawson and Bernier cite one interesting study in which three-
and four-year-old children with autism preferred listening to
mechanical-sounding, computerese rather than their mother's
voices and had correspondingly different brain wave responses from
typically developing children. The more severe the autism, the
greater the preference for mechanical speech. The authors do not
draw implications from this finding.

While it is highly unlikely that any amount of screen time could
cause autistic spectrum disorders, including Asperger's syndrome,
it could be one factor in the expression of this syndrome in sensitive
individuals. Moreover, as we discover the latent power of video
addiction for young people with interpersonal difficulties, careful
monitoring becomes even more important.

Problem Solving, "Ideation," and Making Your Own "Mind Pictures."
When chemist Friedrich Kekulé was struggling to discover the
structure of the benzene molecule, he had a dream one night in

which he could "see" snakes dancing while holding their tails in their mouths. Aha! he realized. The structure is circular! And Nobel Prize–winning research was born.

Children of the screen absorb innumerable images, icons, advertising logos. In this sense, they are a very "visual" generation. But these images have one limitation—they are all other people's. Will our children be short-changed in creating their own? Will they be able to think abstractly and imagine a concept or a solution that has not been brought to them ready-made in living color? Do they even have time to create a coherent idea?

> Teachers find that one of the greatest weaknesses of today's students and especially those with learning problems is weakness in problem solving, which means being able to imagine and develop strategies to solve a new or unfamiliar problem.

A memorable example of a failure in problem solving was once related to me by a preschool teacher who had taken a small group of four-year-olds out to the woods behind the school for a nature walk. The children's progress was interruped by a fallen tree trunk lying across the path. Instead of climbing over or scampering around it, however, the two boys in the lead stopped dead and looked helplessly back at the teacher. "What shall we do?" they asked. "I couldn't believe it," the teacher told me. "If these kids can't push a button or someone doesn't tell them exactly what to do, they're helpless."

"These remote-control children do not see themselves as problem solvers," asserts psychologist Diane Levin, who calls this condition *problem-solving deficit disorder.* Traditionally, if you gave children lumps of Play-Doh, they would soon manage to create something out of it, she explains. Now they're more likely to scratch their heads and ask, "What does it do?"[14]

Such trends are worrisome, since the ability to initiate problem-solving strategies is arguably the most essential skill for powerful learning. It is also the core of a nation's success in a world of new discoveries and new ways of thinking. Problem solving involves envisioning both a solution and a plan for how to get there, requiring a mind that can move beyond what it has previously seen and done before to envision an original solution. Imaginative play incor-

porates these skills, whereas staring at screens or following someone else's programs do not.

I believe that the media hazard we should be most concerned
about—and that may explain the correlation between a lot of media
use and academic decline—is something we might call *ideation*.
This term means "forming ideas," often abstract ones, and often
with some sort of self-created visual "picture" in one's mind. Think
of (and picture, if you can) Copernicus *envisioning* the sun as the
center of our solar system instead of the earth, or a child creating a
mind-movie of a story or a history lesson she is reading about. Remember, learning disabled children often have problems with reading comprehension or math story problems because they have
special trouble "seeing" the events they are reading about in their
minds. What relationship does screen time have to this important
mental skill?

Without trying to summarize a great deal of abstruse research on
concept formation, abstract thinking, and "mental imagery," let me
just repeat that one way to encourage abstract thinking abilities
is free, unprogrammed, imaginative play along with enough quiet
time to pursue some original flights of fancy. Many of today's children lack opportunities for independent problem solving and unprogrammed (in every sense) time in which to discover that their
own minds and imaginations can be pretty interesting places to
explore. Without such foundations, problem solving suffers along
with the ideational ability to understand benzene molecules or just
about anything more complicated than a Ronald McDonald icon.

Setting Limits

I think I can safely assume that most readers of this book are already well informed about the need for parental oversight of all
media. The question I receive most often is, "How much is too much?"
Ah, if only there were a simple answer, both my job and yours would
be much easier. Each family and each child are different. The most
important caveats are these:

- Watch your child. Stay in touch with and monitor usage of all
  electronics. "A little" has a surprising way of becoming "a lot"
  before you know it. If a learning problem crops up, media use

is one of the first things to address, and you may need to become the adult control system that your child's brain still lacks.

- The way you yourself use media will have major effects on your child's attitudes and management abilities. A parent texting during family dinnertime needs to rethink some priorities.

- The earlier you start establishing good media habits, the easier it will be. Just because everyone else is putting a TV or a laptop in the baby's room does not mean either that it is a good idea or that you need to follow the crowd.

- Think twice before purchasing electronic gaming devices, especially if your child is having academic troubles.

- If you have already let media use get out of hand, work with your child to establish mutually satisfactory guidelines. Professional help from a counselor or psychologist is a back-up resort.

In a recent op-ed piece in the *Wall Street Journal*, Daniel Akst, who obviously takes his children's learning very seriously, issued a challenge to his fellow parents to do a better job of managing achievement-related factors in the home.[15] One of the foremost, he believes is "a tight lid on media." "Too many kids are growing up in homes with little emphasis on reading, learning, or culture," Akst accuses. "Nielsen Media Research reports that Americans aged two to seventeen spend an average of three hours a day watching television, *which is too much for any good student*" (emphasis added). With both video games and weekday television strongly correlated with poor school performance, Akst advocates: "[Nonhomework] computer time is limited, there's no gaming system, and during the school week, virtually no television. Extracurricular reading is constantly encouraged, and we choose movies with care." Akst is careful to point out that his family also has a lot of fun and good conversations together.

Too Much and Too Soon

> *"As a society, we are in the middle of a vast uncontrolled experiment on our infants and toddlers growing up in homes saturated with electronic media."*
>
> —Daniel Anderson, Ph.D., prominent researcher on children's media[16]

With every new study of electronic media in children's lives, amount of usage escalates. Many Europeans have trouble believing that U.S. preschoolers commonly have TVs and/or computers in their bedrooms, with even infants under one year developing screen habits. Evidently most parents do not take seriously the American Academy of Pediatrics' concerns that far too little research has been done on the downside of early media exposure. The AAP recommends *no screen time for children under age two*, with only an hour or two a day of "educational, nonviolent programs" for older children.[17] (Clearly, with older children and when school assignments require screen time, the rules become more flexible, but parental judgment is still needed.)

Young children can now even get their "nurturing" from electronic devices. As only one example, an infant seat featuring calming vibrations and eight soothing songs is a big seller, doubtless saving worn-out parents a lot of cuddling, rocking, and 2 a.m. floor pacing with a fretful infant. Yet these early months are a critical period for social and relational bonding that cements the foundation of important frontal brain centers. It is hard to believe that a warm, responsive human body isn't an important part of this equation. Moreover, one of the brain's major jobs in early life is to learn to self-soothe, laying the groundwork for top-down systems of personal control and management of one's own brain. The long-term impact of inviting what some see as "electronic mind control" into the nursery is still a very vexed question.

Older children's media use escalates until, by the time they leave high school, U.S. youngsters have spent more time with electronic amusements than they have in school. Many spend homework time multitasking among a variety of electronic distractions, despite growing evidence that this habit reduces quality of work and may even interrupt development of higher-level reasoning.

> *"I am a counselor at a local mental health center working with children who struggle in school. I have been over-whelmed by the number of students with TVs and comput-ers in their rooms. I can't begin to tell you the times children have told me they are tired from not being able to sleep, so they turned their TV on . . . and of course just got more tired and more stressed! Additionally I have sat in the living rooms of homes where the TV is front and center and have had to ask people to turn it off while we talk."*
>
> —Ralph, in an e-mail

Something has to give, and increasingly that neglected some-thing includes sleep and everyday activities that build children's learning skills, personal values, and interpersonal abilities. Screen time has pushed aside family conversations; reading; board, card, or word games; creative play; restorative activity outdoors; exercise; unprogrammed social learning with other children. Perhaps even more worrisome is children's lack of unprogrammed time to reflect, imagine, dream, and get acquainted with how to manage their own minds. Neuropsychologists call this *self-regulation* and *executive function*; philosophers and authors of self-help books call it personal fulfillment.

Digital skills will obviously hold a prominent place in twenty-first-century life. But we may hope that human skills and the cre-ative, imaginative properties unique to the human brain will also survive. We don't want to lose what is so important for children with learning problems: unstructured family play, close human relationships, and real, spontaneous laughter, silliness and fun that doesn't come from a screen.

A Horror Story: Told at a Mother's Request

Screen time intrudes into the brain's development in both subtle and not-so-subtle ways. Although I had already published two books on the effects of media on children's brain development and learning, I didn't realize how powerful this intrusion can be until I got an eye-opening example. I was on a book tour promoting *Failure to Connect*, a guide to many constructive applications of computer technology as well as a warning about its harmful downsides, when the escort driving me around explained why she was particularly interested in my books. Her seventeen-year-old son had just been diagnosed with online video-gaming addiction.

"He flunked out of school last year," she related. "He had never had academic problems before, so we weren't looking for trouble. He never had a lot of friends, but he gradually lost all contact with the few he had; he stopped sleeping—he stayed online all night—and finally threatened suicide. We were all total wrecks, but he couldn't break the gaming habit. We finally found a good psychiatrist who specializes in addictions (we've paid out a fortune!) and our son is just now enrolled very part-time in community college. He's still sort of a mess, but we think maybe we're starting to get out of the woods. The psychiatrist said this is a real illness that had screwed up his brain chemistry and the only treatment was to go 'cold turkey'—absolutely no more gaming—so you can imagine what that's been like!

"But, please, please," she went on, "tell other parents just how dangerous this can be! That's why I particularly wanted to be your escort—you talk to parents and they need to know about this! If only we had known, we would have been so much more careful earlier on. I guess we just didn't realize how much it could affect his actual *brain*!"[18]

I tell this story not to sensationalize a serious subject, but to emphasize a fact handily overlooked in an entertainment society. None of the newer technologies so prevalent in children's worlds is completely benign. Video addiction is a growing reality (and a lucrative new psychiatric specialty). But any frequently used technology, even books and pencils, has profound effects on the very "plastic" growing brain.

Connected or Disconnected?

Your child's media use will help shape her brain. The question is—
will it be for better or for worse? With media of various types so
influential in many children's mental development, it is surprising
how little substantive research exists on this issue. Nonetheless,
here are some things to think about:

- Children differ enormously in their response to any stimulus;
  the same degree of media exposure may have widely different
  effects in different individuals.

- Boys and girls tend to differ on both type and amount of usage; boys may be more vulnerable to damaging effects on
  learning.

- The effects of media will vary depending on the age of the
  child involved. Very young children are in a critical period for
  many foundational skills and too many electronic distractions can short-change their development. We do not know
  yet whether the very early introduction of entertainment media into the nursery sets a course for later addiction, but at
  that age, parental caution is clearly called for.

- If parents themselves have a powerful media habit, it may be
  harder for them to maintain sensible controls or even to give
  children adequate amounts of face time.

- The educational value of any medium can be improved when
  adults help children understand, analyze, and discuss it. Mediating the child's experience helps develop critical thinking
  skills.

- Different media will have different effects, depending on type
  of content and how much adult mediation goes along with the
  experience. Computers are not necessarily better for children
  than TV and may be more harmful because they tend to be
  more engaging and sometimes even addictive.

- The best way to gauge your child's reactions to any experience is to be a careful and objective observer. Let your own

eyes and intelligence—not the claims of advertisers, neighbors, or your own need for an electronic fix—be your guide.

*"When I see these parents driving up to drop off their kids,
and they're so busy on their cell phones they can barely kiss
them good-bye, I really wonder . . ."*

—director of a suburban nursery school

Techno-Learning: The Upside

If used appropriately, visual media in general and computers in
particular seem to interface neatly with some learning-different
brains. Benefits differ, however, according to the age of the student
and are very questionable for children under seven.

Students with dyslexia, for example, often tend to think and visualize better in wholistic, three-dimensional space than they do in
the more linear forms of language. Thus they may quickly grasp
computer graphics (e.g., graphing equations, computer-assisted design) and learn better if a teacher's lecture is backed up by a good
computer simulation. Many such students have particular trouble
becoming "automatic" on routine skills like handwriting, spelling,
punctuation, and rapid math calculations. Applications such as
word processing, databases, and spreadsheets ease the pain of getting good ideas down onto paper, organizing information, performing routine calculations. They may facilitate the release of the
poet, author, or math/science theorist who lurks behind that "sloppy"
handwriting and those "careless" errors.

Software for elementary grades and up can also make necessary
drill work more interesting, less embarrassing, and better cali-
brated to individual skill levels. It can act as a motivator, aid planning of essays or reports, simulate complex concepts in interactive
visual as well as verbal modalities, to name just a few uses. For individuals with social learning problems, the computer is a far more
comfortable learning companion than the confusing world of people
with their unpredictable reactions and incomprehensible facial expressions. Yet managing some degree of interpersonal experience is

important for getting along in the world. Finding a balance between teaching computer skills and teaching people skills is a continuing challenge.

Educators must also find a new balance between hands-on, multisensory learning and tech proficiency. For example, young children should learn and practice letter formation before word processing, since the physical act of handwriting also helps them learn to read. So does practicing spelling patterns. Using hands-on manipulative math materials (cubes, counters, etc.) and working out equations by hand on paper helps children understand what numbers stand for. Without this understanding, numerals on a screen are a hollow exercise and may contribute to math disabilities. Before introducing software "tools" (word processing, spreadsheets, etc.), we should work to establish automaticity (quick and accurate recall) of math facts, spelling rules, and reading fluency.

Appropriate technology use provides a needed counterpoint to the "chalk and talk" environment of the traditional classroom, but it must be used in the right way, and at the proper ages.

Media: Not All Good, Not All Bad. Clearly the upsides or downsides of any technology depend on how it is used. As Steven Johnson makes clear in his interesting book *Everything Bad Is Good for You*, any medium that "forces us to be intelligent" by asking us to solve complex problems may have beneficial effects. After about age seven, any medium that causes children to stop, think, plan, reflect, or evaluate may improve thinking skills.

Many "differently wired" children have the potential to be leaders in what will probably be a differently wired world. Perhaps some of today's so-called learning disabled kids will be the ones to develop new and challenging techno-applications to expand human mental abilities. But, I venture to say, they will do a far better job if they experienced as children a solid balance with spontaneous, three-dimensional, nonvirtual experience.

A final reality that gets little attention is the sociocultural divide in children's use of the medium of television. Less privileged youngsters log in far more viewing hours with far less control of content than those in higher socioeconomic groups. In dramatic contrast, many parents of the "haves" either limit or prohibit television use altogether.

> *"Television? Why,* our *friends don't allow their children to watch it!"*
>
> —mother of a six-year-old in an upscale
> urban neighborhood

Savvy educators now provide education for both students and their parents on "media literacy."

Multitasking: The Upside and the Downside

> *"She'll be up there trying to write a paper and all I hear is 'BING-BING-BING' her friends texting her. . . . She already has enough trouble focusing her attention and I just think this can't be helping."*
>
> —father of a fourteen-year-old

Parents tend to watch their children manipulating four or five media at once and wonder, Does this ability represent some sort of "new intelligence"? If multitasking is a new type of intelligence, however, research suggests it is inferior to the older forms. When Marcel Just, director of the Center for Cognitive Brain Imaging at Carnegie Mellon University, conducted brain scans on multitaskers, he found that trying to do more than one thing at a time reduced brain activity for each task. "Multitasking is inefficient," concluded another study in which college students repeatedly switched between two tasks. Every time they switched back and forth, they lost time and reduced the mental energy available for each task. It's like trying to run the toaster, coffeemaker, and hair dryer on the same circuit, Just explained. "There just aren't enough resources to support it."[19]

The more similar two activities are in terms of the modalities used (e.g., trying to pound a nail while cooking or solve an algebra problem while following the plot of a TV show), the harder it is to do them at the same time because they call on similar brain circuits. Kids may be able to do homework with background music or listen to a lecture and doodle, but they can't simultaneously read intelligently, text-message, and talk on the phone—all verbal (word-based) activities. Having to physically shift between ideas or implements (e.g., from a computer to a phone or one screen to another) also reduces efficiency.

Many "memory" disabilities actually have to do with the fact that the information was never properly taken in and stored in the first place (*encoding*). This crucial stage in the learning process is a core issue in learning problems, and probably the first disrupted by multitasking.

Psychologists refer to "central learners," who tend to focus intently on one thing at a time. Do you remember only the face of the person you were talking to (central learning), or did you also notice the flowerpot on the table and the fact that there was a lightbulb missing on the fixture above the person's head (peripheral learning)? Multitasking may be much harder on central learners than on people who naturally take in lots of items at a time.

No one knows the long-term effects of this type of brain-training, especially on children who have constitutionally errant memory and attention. Some preliminary research suggests that chronic multitaskers develop skills to rapidly sort and prioritize information— even though they don't usually stop to think about it. As useful as this skill is, being constantly at the beck and call of multiple conflicting stimuli has some ominous implications.

In his book *CrazyBusy*, attention expert Edward M. Hallowell likens modern life to "playing tennis with three balls." He is convinced that unless we set healthier boundaries between humans and our electronic adjuncts, we—and our children—are in not only for attention problems but also for *damaging levels of stress*. Since television viewing and computer use can both increase stress levels, and stress can both cause and worsen learning problems, this concern must join the seemingly endless parade of hazards for vulnerable children in our modern world.

> Intelligent media use means putting children's brains in charge of their media instead of vice versa.

Minds for the Future

The most successful minds in the twenty-first century will be strong and flexible ones that can remain smarter than and independent of their digital companions. Allowing—or even encouraging—enslavement to electronics is a poor way to begin.

In a Nutshell: Mediating the Media

- *Use caution and set clear limits on both time and content.* Every child and every family is different, and parents have to use their common sense in establishing guidelines.

- *Monitor children's use.* When confronted by a seductive entertainment, children are not good judges of what is best for them.

- *Keep television and computers out of young children's rooms* and keep them in a central place where you can track the amount and type of use.

- *Lend your child your adult brain* as you watch or play along with your child. Use conversation to expand understanding and help the child be a critical user.

- *Insist on balance* with time in nonelectronic play, outdoor activities, exercise, social fun, and unprogrammed quiet time.

- *Turn off the media at mealtime* and have a family conversation.

- *Get help* if you yourself are addicted.

- *If you suspect trouble,* do not wait before taking action or seeking outside help.

- *Be firm.* You are confronting a formidable industry that may or may not have your child's best interests at heart.

"Brain disruptors" are, sadly, omnipresent in the everyday lives of today's children, but committed adults can significantly mitigate their effects. Fortunately, research has also given us clear directions for developing positive learning environments both at home and at school. That will be the subject of our final chapter, and it turns out to be the most important topic of all.

CHAPTER 12

Successful Environments for Successful Children

M any children who start out with developmental learning problems become successful, happy, and self-confident adults. Meanwhile, kids who seem to be chugging along on the fast track can all-too-easily lose their steam along the way. Home and school environments make the critical difference. This book has addressed many of the reasons why even so-called privileged environments are placing children at unnecessary risk. Creating a truly privileged environment for a child's mental and emotional development takes effort, but the ingredients are straightforward. Here are some final thoughts about what is important for true success.

Quick Take: What's Important?

- "Self-regulation" is at least as important as intelligence for success in school and in life.

- Parents, teachers, and caregivers determine how well children learn self-regulation, and they can learn to do a better job of teaching it.

- Keeping a lid on sensory overstimulation helps children's brains establish foundational learning skills.

- Adults who "mediate" children's experience with language help them develop intelligence and self-control.

- Physical exercise, play, and experiences with nature and the arts are underestimated as sources of successful development.

- Thinking of a child only in terms of genes and brain cells misses the core of being human.

- There is more to success than money, grades, or achievement. A strong sense of self is the starting point for full personal growth, which psychologists term *self-actualization*.

- Quiet time starts children on the path to self-actualization and helps them discover who they are and what is important to them.

Step 5: Teach Self-Regulation, The Key to Success

"Self-regulation," which is simply an expanded version of self-control, is a major ingredient for success in learning and life. Children who develop good self-regulation skills have extra ammunition for overcoming problems and capitalizing on their particular combination of talents. The ingredients for self-regulation depend on home, school, and community. These ingredients are

- a strong belief in one's own abilities and potential

- self-control

- positive relationships with others

- motivation and persistence

Psychologists find these qualities to be at least twice as influential as IQ for both academic and life success. They will determine in great part whether your child overcomes innate problems or succumbs to them, and may even determine whether or not problems develop in the first place.

Failure to attain self-regulation is a core problem that accompanies many learning, attention, and emotional-social problems. Environments strongly influence development of self-regulation.

Self-Control: A Casualty of Childhood in the Twenty-first Century?

"If forced to choose, we would all rather our children be poor with self-control than rich without it."

—David Brooks[1]

Self-regulation is an "executive" skill that depends on a widespread system of brain connections dominated by anterior (frontal) brain areas. Because the frontal brain areas have an extremely long course of development, executive skills are very susceptible to environmental influence. Frontal lobes are very plastic up until eight years but continue to mature throughout the teens. Here are some of the factors that impede their development:

- *stress overload* from unsafe or disorganized environments, which block the brain's ability to utilize higher cognitive and control centers

- *media* that pull the child's attention and control out of her own brain and hand it over to whatever is on the screen

- *intrusive sensory environments* (e.g., noise, visual stimuli, too many toys and excitement, pushy adults) that distract children from learning to manage their own minds

- *adults who are unable or unwilling* to spend the time to model and teach self-control, attention, thoughtful behavior, forward planning, delay of gratification, persistence

- *schools that focus on the back of the brain* (memorizing information, academic acceleration, scores) *at the expense of the front* (*how* to learn, reflect on ideas, and develop positive strategies when confronted by a problem)

- *overmanagement* that reduces a child's personal sense of control

As we have seen, executive skills come more easily to some brains—and some families—than to others. Research shows, however, that even constitutional weaknesses can be remedied by providing a safe, extracaring, sensibly structured physical and emotional environment while actively teaching skills of self-regulation.[2]

Safety and Structure: Firm Foundation for Learning. We know that a stressed, frightened brain isn't much good at thinking. Children don't have to be lost in the woods to feel unsafe, however. One all-too-common daily stressor for many children is a lack of structure.

Safety Need A: reasonable structure. "Hurry up, Ben!" Mom grabs her son by the arm, abruptly pulling him away from his new Lego invention. "I forgot your dentist appointment! And you'll need your hat—where the heck is it? Oh, d__, the dog's peed on the rug again. Who forgot to lock him in his cage? And I've got to pick James up at practice in half and hour. . . . Hurry UP!"

I'm reluctant to admit that this scene sounds awfully familiar to this veteran working mother. We all have bad days, and most children manage to survive our mistakes. But if Ben's life is overbalanced with chronic confusion and upset, especially if it isn't offset by relaxed, fun, family time and obvious affection, his learning abilities may suffer.

> *"These new habits are so hard and we're such an instant gratification society. It's a commitment and everyone has to be on board to change the rhythms of a family. For example, getting up twenty minutes earlier to have a more relaxed breakfast and getting everyone out the door on time helps all the children in a family."*
>
> —behavioral therapist for parents and students with ADHD

Anything *persistently* perceived as a threat—such as unpredictable family upsets or being abruptly dragged away from play—can downshift the brain into low-level reflex responses ("No, I won't go! Leave me alone!"). Obviously, surprises and upsets are part of any normal life, but chronically hectic, unpredictable, or even dangerous lifestyles make it very difficult for youngsters to mobilize both self-control and academic learning abilities.

An unregulated classroom can have the same effect. I once observed the first-grade classroom of a little boy who had recently begun to show signs of attention problems. I was immediately struck by the fact that many of the children were very unruly and that the physical space, although large and well lit, was, frankly, a mess. Bookcases overflowed with uneven piles of outdated teaching materials and worksheets, children's folders cascaded from the teacher's desk, and a general atmosphere of disorder prevailed. Children wandered without any visible purpose; some "accidentally" bumped, pinched, or tripped others. No surprise that a child with a tendency toward distraction might be pushed over the edge into "problem" behavior in such a setting.

A firm but loving external structure helps a child feel safe, reduces stress, and begins the process of internalizing these all-important controls. Obviously, being a neat freak or hypercontrolling adult is not what is meant by *structure*. But parents who recognize their own need for help in "getting a grip" on home life will undoubtedly help their children get a better grip on learning.

> One of the first prescriptions for a child in behavioral therapy is a well-regulated, predictable home and a school environment with well-stated rules, expectations, and limits.

Structure for the Unstructured.

> *"She needs better structure at home? You're kidding! I can't even organize myself!"*
>
> —self-described "ADHD" mother of a child
> with a learning problem

Young brains need and respond to predictable routines. "Patterned, repetitive experience in a safe environment can have an enormous impact on the brain," advises Bruce Perry.[3] Achieving a well-regulated home life is difficult under the best of circumstances but for the chronically fragmented, it presents a real challenge. Moreover, our overcommitted lives and crowded schedules are poison to predictable routines, calm mornings and bedtimes, leisurely family conversations, and well-regulated, quiet space and time for homework and reading. Nonetheless, getting better control over family schedules, planning ahead, using organizational aids (wall calendars, lists, electronic reminders), and having reasonably consistent rules and clear consequences are truly step one in helping your child's learning.

Safety Need B: A consistent, competent, caring caregiver. In his wise and comprehensive book *Genes and Behavior*, Sir Michael Rutter emphasizes the importance of early rearing environments in either moderating or exacerbating "risk" genes. High on his list of factors that may activate "risk" genes are:

1. lack of stable, ongoing, and "harmonious" relationships with caregivers

2. lack of cohesion or frequently inappropriate adult behavior (e.g., drug use, out-of-control emotional scenes) in family and community

3. too little "reciprocal conversation" and play

Children who are tossed around emotionally by inconsistent, nonresponsive, or untrustworthy environments are at special risk for just about any learning problem you can name. A lot has been written about the ways in which insecure early attachment distorts emotional adjustment, but we need to realize that such emotional insecurity has academic consequences as well.

Wounded Child, Wounded Learning. I always felt that Clemmie appeared in my life one summer much like a foundling left in a basket at someone's door. Slightly built and wistful in expression, she might as well have been an orphan—albeit a very wealthy one—considering all the different caregivers she had experienced in her first eight years.

Clemmie had just teetered into grade three "by the skin of her teeth" and was referred by her headmistress because of a suspected attention disorder and a "reading problem." This was a definite understatement, since I was appalled to discover that this child could not read a single word. Even more appalling was that neither her teacher nor her mother knew it. Clemmie, who was clever despite having both dyslexia and dyscalculia, had somehow charmed and faked her way through the baffling world of letters and numerals.

"I knew she had a problem, but I didn't realize it was *that* bad!" exclaimed her mother when she managed to break away from her office long enough for an initial conference. "I always just blamed it on emotional upset—Clemmie's had sort of a discombobulated life. I had this terrific nanny when she was born, and Clemmie got so attached to her Dodo, as she called her. But after three years, Dodo had to move back to Scotland to take care of her own mother. It was hard on everyone, and Clemmie was inconsolable—cried and cried for 'my Dodo.' She was just so sad all the time. Then we got Casey— we finally got used to her, Clemmie warmed up, then Casey ups and leaves to go back to graduate school. I was in the middle of a second divorce, and my business was really taking off, and it's been just one nanny or sitter after another—you can imagine how hard that's been on everyone. I beat myself up for being such a rotten mother, but I just don't have the answer."

Clemmie was, indeed, an anxious and wounded little girl. She began our work together convinced that she was a hopeless, worthless failure. That summer we got a good start on attacking her reading and math problems, which the school then finally began to take seriously. But she remained a helpless problem solver, easily distracted and prone to giving up at the slightest hint of difficulty. Eventually Clemmie went off to a very costly boarding school that specialized in helping students with learning disabilities. There she began to feel competent—and maybe even a little bit powerful—for the first time in her life.

There is little doubt that Clemmie would have had some type of learning difficulty even in the best of circumstances. The difference is that a solid foundation of early bonding and dependable emotional support would have equipped her with much firmer personal resources to meet challenges and overcome or compensate for them.

> If you were to write only one research-based prescription to buffer children from academic, social, and emotional problems, it would have to be for consistent, high-quality care in a child's early years.

Self-regulation and motivation are among the benefits children gain from good nurturing. In a stable and supportive environment, infants begin to internalize self-control as well as emotional resilience. For example, a quality termed *maternal warmth* has been shown to mitigate both genetic and environmental risks for attention problems. "Our study suggests that in Britain, where drug treatment of ADHD is rare, low-birth-weight children develop fewer ADHD symptoms if their mother feels warmly toward them," writes Terrie E. Moffitt of King's College London.[4] She makes it clear that she is not blaming parents for a child's genetic or biological problems, but rather encouraging them that their efforts can, indeed, make a significant difference in either case. We may assume that warm caregivers other than the biological mother will also have a positive effect.

How much the fractured nature of much early child care today contributes to rising rates of problems is a question worth contemplating. Here are essentials for good caregiving for the growing brain:

- assurance of safety and establishment of trust

- emotional warmth; contingent response: the caregiver "tunes in" to the child's signals, listening, emphasizing, and responding appropriately

- predictable, structured routines that are flexible enough to adapt to the child's needs

- management of physical stressors and appropriate stimulation levels—both sensory and intellectual

- "mediation" of experience (more about this later)

Sensory Experience Is the Foundation of Self-Regulation

We all love to watch an infant learning the joys of sensory experience as she moves, touches, feels, looks, listens, smells, or tastes. Responsive caregivers provide appropriate stimulation (interesting faces and toys to gaze at and make sense of, loving voices and music to respond to, warm baths, brushing, massaging, cuddling, etc.). Sensitive adults learn very quickly that stimulation has its limits, however, as too much causes the child either to shut down or become overexcited and eventually dissolve into shrieks.

It is important to remember that sensory experience is the raw material for academic learning. In addition, responding to and organizing sensory input is the first step in self-management. Children whose senses are too frequently overwhelmed may learn to shut down and screen out experience instead of actively learning from it—a sure start for a learning problem. Because children vary in their thresholds for "appropriate" or "overwhelming" stimulation, wise caregivers watch the child and follow her cues in managing the amount and quality of sensory input from the environment.

Some developmental problems such as autism or sensory processing disorder involve difficulty at this foundational level. Any child needs caregivers who will protect, moderate, and soothe, but extrasensitive children require more than most. Their caregivers may even need professional guidance to help their child adapt to normal levels of sensory stimulation. (Refer back to Chapter 3, "What Should We Call This?" for some possible therapies.)

Overstimulating Environments and Scrambled Brain Circuits

A glaring (actually, blaring) example of our culture's failure to provide appropriate habitats for growing brains are the unregulated noise levels in children's environments.

> "Children are spending their early years in habitats designed for adults instead of spaces or places that honor and respect the needs of growing, learning, exploring children."
>
> —Bev Bos and Jenny Chapman in
> *Tumbling Over the Edge: A Rant for Children's Play*

Carleton is very tired when his dad picks him up from day care. All day long, his classroom has resonated with the hubbub of active toddlers on a rainy day in a relatively small space. Courtney has had another one of her screaming tantrums. Babies cry in the nursery room next door. Children run around. And the teachers shout directions. Even at rest time when they play a video, the sound is turned up to subdue the crowd. Carleton gets into Dad's car, where the stereo pulses with light rock. Dad is talking loudly on his cell phone; he seems mad as he blasts his horn at a car blocking the exit. Carleton is just so tired; he lays his head against his car seat, but he is too keyed up to sleep.

OUCH!

Adults complain about "noise pollution" in modern life, but few realize that what constitutes an annoyance to them may be a real impediment to their children's rapidly developing brain circuitry.

- I am seated in a multiplex with two excited six-year-olds, waiting for the movie to begin. Suddenly, the theater is engulfed in piercing sound as the previews flash into view. "OUCH!" I think, instinctively covering my ears with my hands. My little companions seem unfazed, but I wonder, what is this all-too-typical auditory assault doing to their ears—and their brains?

- As my husband and I are being seated in a popular restaurant, I notice a mother and father at the next table with an absolutely adorable child of about one year asleep in a sling on her mother's lap. I also notice that the music piped in for our "dining enjoyment" is so loud that, combined with people's conversations and the clatter of dishes, we need to shout at each other over the table. But the baby sleeps blissfully on. Could the noise possibly be damaging for her?

- In a toy store, I watch a toddler investigating a new toy. As he activates a button, the toy "speaks," revealing a strident electronic personality. Other children are activating other toys, all of which add to the general din.

Noise Pollution and Self-Regulation. In each of the above examples, research has answered the question "Could this be damaging them?" with a definite yes. The loud and intrusive noise level that is all too typical of a child's experience may harm not only his hearing but also his language, attention, reading abilities, and mental development. As if that weren't enough, the unrecognized but constant level of stress generated by an unnatural sensory stimulus may multiply the effects of other stressors in the child's environment. As you may recall from a previous chapter, even low-level stress, particularly if it is outside the child's control, has a profound negative impact on learning and general well-being. For children with vulnerable nervous systems, extra stressors add up to trouble.

Overly noisy environments can harm learning in several ways:

- The brain's emerging systems for making sense out of sounds are especially sensitive during the last three months of pregnancy and the first few months of life. *Unnatural levels of sensory stimulation* (yes, a fetus can hear that heavy metal or loud industrial equipment) *may "scramble" brain wiring* at a time when it is trying to self-organize.[5] Malfunction may be implicated in autism, according to researcher Michael Merzenich. He is especially interested in the effects on children's brains of ambient noise in modern life, particularly in childcare environments. "There is so much more exposure for infants than there used to be," he points out: blasting radios, power mowers, TVs, stereos, sirens, or even loud air conditioners or fans. "Even little things can add to the risk."[6]

- *Extreme loud noise* can damage hearing at any time in life. Reporting in the *New York Times*, health guru Jane Brody cites findings that one U.S. child in eight has noise-induced hearing loss, "an entirely preventable disability that will stay with them for life." Often the problem is not detected until signs of learning or behavior problems show up. Noisy toys and personal listening devices are among the everyday culprits that can permanently damage hearing. "Before buying noisemaking toys, parents would do well to listen to how loud they are," she advises, since even government-approved toys can produce sounds as loud as a jet taking off. Workplace rules for adults mandate ear protection for sounds over 85 decibels, but some toys emit up to 138 decibels.[7] Five minutes of full-blast exposure to a personal listening device can also affect hearing.

- Locating schoolrooms near airport noise created learning deficits in nine- and ten-year-olds, according to a large study conducted in the U.K. The louder the noise, the greater the deficits.[8] One commentator suggested that parents get sound meters to monitor their children's environments.

- Sudden, loud sounds such as a car horn have specific effects on the brain. They alert posterior (back) parts of the brain at the expense of the higher-level control centers in the prefrontal cortex. They also unleash a storm of neurotransmitter activity that puts the brain on alert for potential danger. As we have seen, a brain in this hyperalert state is in very poor shape for complex reasoning, and there's no room at all for reflective thinking.

- A constant level of background sound, such as TV, may interrupt the child's development of "self-talk"—that critical inner voice by which we regulate and organize our attention and behavior.[9] Self-talk is the silent partner in attention, motivation, and self-regulation.

- When children need constantly to "screen out" unpleasant or irrelevant noise, they may develop a bad habit of screening out human voices—all at a time when brain circuits for intelligent listening are in a critical period of development.

Noise has been the best-researched hazard in children's sensory environments. It may not be the only one, however. It is well known that extended periods of computer use can create eye and brain strain in adults. Although I hear a great many anecdotal reports from eye doctors about visual difficulties, eye-tracking, and related reading problems from television and video games, definitive research is still lacking. What are the long-term effects of the countless hours children spend hunched, unblinking, over their hand-held devices? And what important experiences are being crowded out?

The long-term effects of this increasingly unregulated sensory assault on children's brains are unknown. Any sensible parent these days must serve as gatekeeper on sensory overload, whether their children agree with them or not.

Parenting or Caregiving Styles for Self-Regulated Learners

The adults with whom children spend the majority of their time have an alarming degree of influence in shaping brains around self-regulation abilities. I say "alarming" because research has demonstrated over and over again that (1) most child care in the United States is seriously below par; (2) some parents themselves lack the knowledge, skills, or time to promote effective learning habits; (3) the general culture—media, social attitudes, even school culture—actively promotes examples of poor self-control.

On a hopeful note, research also shows that adults can learn to do a more effective job. Parent training programs have shown remarkable effectiveness in improving children's self-management and learning. In one Australian study, families receiving such instruction significantly reduced preschoolers' disruptive behaviors and attention/hyperactivity difficulties at the same time they improved "parental competence."[10] Another program, called Tools of the Mind, teaches adults to use specific mental exercises such as gradually teaching children to resist distractions and wait for desired treats or to complete a job before starting another to build rudimentary skills of executive function.[11]

Psychologists Peg Dawson and Richard Guare, after thirty years of working with children who have attention, learning, and behavior difficulties, target executive skills as the most important factor in their patients' outcomes—both in school and in later life. Their book *Smart but Scattered*, listed in the Bibliography, lays out specific steps parents can take to remedy this growing problem.

An important caveat is to spend enough face time playing and interacting with your child (or charge) to get an idea of his individual learning style and interests. "Intrusive" adults (or intrusive media) interrupt children's naturally motivated learning (including play) in order to take control of the interaction, but following the child's lead is a better plan. A child can extract a surprising amount of brain stimulation from even simple activities. An infant intent on tracking a sunbeam's passage on the nursery wall instead of playing with her "brainy" toys, a toddler's repeated (and "boring" to an adult brain) demand for the same story over and over again or a drive to pour sand or water in and out of the same containers over and over again, a first-grader's yen to attack the climbing bars without assistance, or a middle-schooler's repetitiously annoying questions ("How come you're allowed to make rules about my Internet use when you break traffic rules all the time?") may be frustrating to adults, but they happen for a reason. Each represents the brain's need to refine, practice, and expand cell networks at a new stage of development.

When we must intrude ourselves into the situation, it is usually wise to follow the child's lead rather than seizing control, since our adult brains simply don't "get it" from the child's perspective. Through training, however, adults can learn to help the child expand on those natural interests and develop effective learning strategies. One of the first things we should teach adults is how to help a child feel like a powerful learner who takes responsibility for her own behavior and success. An adult who grabs control of every encounter steals a child's chance to develop creative and confident problem-solving. There are subtle but important differences between "Here, let me show you how to do that" (taking control) and: "You try it first, and I'll help you if you have trouble" (giving the child a chance to problem-solve).

Instead of "Write the rhyming words in neat rows, like this" (adult's brain does the organizing), try "Show me how you could arrange your words on the paper to make it look neat" (child is invited to develop an organizational strategy).

Discipline techniques can also promote self-regulation: Reconsider "I'm ashamed of your behavior while Aunt Julie was here. If you do that again, I'll . . ." (control of one's behavior comes from outside) in favor of: "I know you realize you hurt Aunt Julie's feelings. How could you let her know you're sorry?" (child is expected to find a way to control his own behavior).

The above examples are clues to why the children of overly permissive or overly authoritarian parents tend to have problems with self-regulation and motivation. Parents and caregivers who demonstrate, expect, and support personal responsibility generally get much better results.

Secret for Success: Who's Responsible? A related concept called *attribution theory* helps explain a great deal of life success as well as academic achievement. In an article titled "The Secret to Raising Smart Kids," pioneer researcher Carol Dweck explains that the secret lies in the child's belief about what is responsible for his success or failure.[12] Children who attribute their performance to their own intelligence or talent (or lack of it) as opposed to their personal effort tend to be lower achievers. Consider these statements:

"I'm stupid, of course I failed the test."

"You're either born smart or you're not."

as opposed to these:

"I could have done better if I'd gone for extra help."

"Being smart is a matter of working hard to learn and improve."

International researchers have found that parents in the United States tend to believe that intelligence lies in the luck of the genetic draw, while Asian parents teach their children that their achievement will depend solely on how hard they work.

"Our society worships talent," says Dr. Dweck. "In fact, thirty years of scientific investigation suggests that an overemphasis on intellect or talent leaves people vulnerable to failure, fearful of challenges, and unwilling to remedy their shortcomings."[13]

Many adults who have triumphed over learning differences attribute their success to the fact that they knew they had to work extrahard and develop strategies to bypass their difficulties. Here are just a few examples of how parents and teachers can use attribution theory:

Attributions for Success

- *Emphasize hard work and persistence* ("You really tried, and look how you improved") *rather than intelligence* ("You're so smart!").

- *Focus more on the value of learning than on grades.* "What did you learn that was interesting/important/useful?" gets better results in the long term than "What did you get?"

- If children take medication for attention problems, encourage belief that the medication *helps them manage their attention* rather than that the medication does it for them.

- *Be a "social skills coach."* Try to help children with social skills problems understand how their actions and comments elicit reactions from other people. Therapists use videotapes to help a child understand how he might have gotten better results in a social situation.

- Enforce the need for *basic good manners*, kindness, and concern for other people.

- Help children set *realistic goals for continued improvement* ("This week I will master five words from the spelling list; when I can do five, I'll go for six").

"Mediating," Not Managing. In addition to encouraging the child to take the lead (e.g., in games or schoolwork) successful learning coaches mediate experience by supporting, expanding, and stimulating the child's thinking. Kathy Hopkins, director of the National Institute for Learning Development, calls this "helping the child frame, focus, and filter" experience.[14] She confirms that many of today's children badly need to be taught *how as well as what to learn.*

Mediation and "Enculturation." An odd thing happened when human "coaches" mediated experience for chimpanzees. Scientists practiced interactive teaching with the animals which featured "constant, nurturing communication." Chimps are naturally among the smartest of animals, but adding the kind of enrichment that humans give small children made them even smarter. The chimp's human caregivers communicated with body language, gestures, and even words as they taught the animals activities such as looking at picture books and playing naming games in which the coach would say a word and the chimp would point to a picture. The chimps "just blossomed," in this rich cultural environment, adding brain capacity for paying attention to conceptual and memory tasks, reports Ohio State University psychologist Sally Boysen.[15] She speculates that the enrichment enhanced neural pathways in their frontal lobes.

The powerful process of this kind of "enculturation" needs to happen early in life. For human children, the critical period is between birth and three to four years. Dr. Boysen's next remark is one with which many teachers may agree:

> "Our schools likely have many children who have not had
> the benefit of that kind of socialized attention and directed
> learning, and I think once you go past what might be a sen-
> sitive period without rich communication with kids, it may
> be too late. They're going to have challenges for life."[16]

Mediating with Language

Just as with chimps, brain-building potential expands when adults
use language to mediate experience for children. Things also get a
lot more complicated as we move beyond picture books and naming
games. To understand how and why language mediation works, let's
observe two hypothetical caregivers in a supermarket. Each is pushing a shopping cart in which rides a child of about three or four.
Each is conducting an important lesson about self-control, learning
strategies, and higher-level thinking (or not).

Caregiver #1 is in the cereal aisle when her charge reaches out
and snags a box of cereal.

"No!" snaps the nanny, gently smacking the youngster's hand.
She replaces the box on the shelf and proceeds down the aisle.

Caregiver #2 has a very different response. She uses language
instead of physical intervention:

"That cereal looks good, Bethany, but remember, we still have
two full boxes of cereal at home in the pantry. Next week when we
come to the store, we can put cereal on our list. What shelf do you
think we should put it back on?"

The vast differences between what is being taught in these two
simple exchanges bears some deconstructing:

Caregiver #1: The child feels powerless and probably "bad." Aggressive physical action is the way we deal with problems. Experience is in the here-and-now; no self-control, planning, or reasoning
is modeled. Children who internalize these beliefs are on a fast
train to school problems.

Caregiver #2: The child and her wishes are valid, but impulsive behavior is not the best way to succeed in getting what you
want. The child is expected to share responsibility ("What shelf do
you think . . ."). Language is the way to solve problems. Decisions
are made on the basis of logic (we already have enough), active use
of memory ("remember, we have . . ."), use of symbols (in this case

words) to represent something that is not here right now—an introduction to abstract thinking: ("two boxes," "at home in the pantry," which also encourages picturing the shelf in the pantry)—and the importance of future planning ("next week . . .").

Caregiver #2 is promoting both personal and academic skills. Many youngsters, unfortunately, go off to school without them and are at high risk to end up in the "disabled" column.

Research has shown that this "style" of adult-child interaction is closely related to socioeconomic factors, particularly the educational level of the adult.[17] It should motivate you to pay very close attention to the quality of caregiving you choose for your children, especially in light of the research suggesting that this kind of responsive parenting (and/or caregiving) is much better delivered *before age six*.[18]

Peter Isquith, developer of widely used tests of children's executive function, practices mediation of language use in his own home.[19] At a recent conference he recounted this interaction with his five-year-old daughter at dinner one night:

Child: "Daddy, catsup!"
Isquith: "Wait a minute. Will that work?"
Child (hesitantly): "No . . ."
Isquith: "What's another way?"
Child: "I go get it myself?"
Isquith: "Yes, and is there another way?"
Child: "Daddy, will you please reach me the catsup?"
Isquith: "Sure, honey. Thanks for asking so politely."

Another Way to Stimulate Brainwork: Get Physical

How can we focus so hard on kids' heads and forget all those other body systems that make heads operate efficiently?

What a peculiar world we live in where we have to be reminded to get children active and moving! Neither lassitude nor obesity is a natural state for kids, and learning and attention are collateral damage for a sedentary generation.

Several years ago, in response to falling test scores, the governor of a southern state justified his decision to eliminate recess from the school day with a comment like the following: They'll learn a whole lot more at their desks than they will hanging upside down from some tree. Actually, children's brains need both physical and intellectual input to keep functioning well. Imagine, too, all those poor little restless bodies lacking an outlet, half-starved for oxygen and a refreshed cerebral blood supply to keep paying attention all day. As a matter of fact, hanging upside down from a tree—or from anything else—may stimulate some very important brain connections, both cortical and subcortical.

If the governor's ignorance was implemented, you can be sure that the incidence of problem referrals—and ADHD prescriptions—would have increased shortly thereafter. The students would be statistically at greater risk not only for learning problems and lowered test scores but also for mood disorders and sagging motivation.

It bears repeating that helping the body work better helps the brain work better. This fact applies across the age span, but children learn first and foremost with their bodies, which naturally crave *physical safety, appropriate levels of multisensory experience, movement, and play.* These "simple" requirements build lifelong brain connections and sturdy neural foundations for everything from basic skills to abstract learning to prize-winning invention and creativity. Physical activity and play regulate attention and emotions, teach social skills, sponsor imagination, create mental "hooks" for improved memory, and even incubate new brain cells.

Thinking Starts with the Body

> *"I am absolutely convinced—I see the difference in my classroom every day. They simply concentrate, learn, and behave better when I start with the exercises. Some days it seems like magic!"*
>
> —elementary school teacher

Frankly, I was a bit skeptical when I began to hear comments like this from teachers at different grade levels who are using a series of physical movements—in this case Brain Gym—to sharpen students' thinking.[20] After hearing the same story numerous times, however,

I enjoyed talking with Carla Hannaford, a biologist, teacher, and popular workshop presenter who explains the science behind such "magical" results in her book *Smart Moves: Why Learning Is Not All in Your Head*. Dr. Hannaford is herself a bundle of energy and a forceful salesperson for paying far more attention to the bodily systems that support the learning brain. Her main focus is on "integrative movements," patterned exercises done in a "playful" context, where they can become an "effective, profound, commonsense, non-drug option that greatly facilitates lifelong learning."[21]

Science does indeed support the notion that physical movement and hands-on experience underlie human mental capacities. "I am convinced that mental processes are grounded in the brain's mappings of the body, collections of neural patterns that portray responses to events that cause emotions and feelings," writes Antonio Damasio, a philosophical neurologist whose research has reinforced the firm connection between our visceral, sensing, feeling bodies and our higher-level thinking abilities.[22]

> **MORAL:** It is simply impossible to teach a child's academic brain in isolation. If you don't get the body on board, learning is bound to suffer.

Grounding the Virtual in the Real. Many children with learning problems have never managed to integrate touch, feel, and movement in the three-dimensional world. This deficit may begin if young children are too often carried, pushed in strollers, or restricted because of convenience or safety fears. It is extended when schoolchildren are deprived of regular exercise times during the day. In addition, a substantial decline in the amount of small-muscle manipulative experience has cut off children from important benefits of object play, hobbies, experiments, needlework, and non-electronic games.

A developmental gap occurs if a child is restricted in moving freely to explore, navigate, and master environmental space. Consider an infant crawling to investigate a new play area, a child ranging through her house or apartment to get a "feel" for the arrangement of rooms, or children playing chasing and hiding games in a park. Exploring physical spaces through movement contributes to higher cognitive skills that depend on spatial abilities, including math, science, the arts, and memory.

Learning to navigate one's body in the world of physical space confers a valuable sense of self-confidence in tackling new problems. I personally remember the first summer I went to day camp. A shy child, I felt totally overwhelmed by new people and large, unfamiliar spaces. I also remember vividly the day when I suddenly realized that I felt in control of myself and this environment—a physical sensation of confidence from "knowing" something with my feet as I walked between activites. It was probably not a coincidence that I was about to turn seven at the time, since this would be a period of rapid cortical maturation for the related sensory association areas.

Scientists believe that the human brain contains *spatial organizers* called grid cells that account for our ability to "place" objects, events, and even abstract concepts in memory.[23] When I abruptly ask a roomful of teachers, "Where is Russia?" about half the audience inadvertently points in one direction or another (most to their upper right).

Grid cells develop as a result of physical movement in real physical space. Likewise, emotional, personal, and attentional control are grounded in mastery of a physical self. How many "disorders" are really cases of children today being cut off from this fundamental mastery of personal space?

Exercise Builds Brains. Smart parents understand that exercise is a family affair. Everyone's brain will be better off after a vigorous family outing in open spaces. After a long, stressed-out day when you feel as if every ounce of energy has been sucked out of your brain, you might try replenishing a few cells by tango dancing. In a recent study, such complex, patterned movement stimulated production of a substance called BDNF (*brain-derived neurotrophic factor*), which caused genes in the brain's central memory center (hippocampus) to create new neurons.[24] Vigorous, fast dance routines may even quicken your—and your child's—overall speed of information processing. If you're also having fun, the positive effects will be magnified.

While tangoing may not be on your wish list, any kind of vigorous exercise will make a difference. What works for adults seems to work even better for children. In his best-selling book *SPARK,* Harvard psychiatrist John Ratey describes innovative school programs in which students not only have fun getting fit but also improve their test scores, attention, and interpersonal relationships. It sounds like an improbable miracle to arise even from a special sort of PE class, but Ratey gives us the neuroscience to explain it in the following excerpt: "exercise improves learning on three levels: first, it optimizes your mind-set to improve alertness, attention, and motivation; second, it prepares and encourages nerve cells to bind to one another [thanks to that increased BDNF], which is the cellular basis for logging in new information; and third, it spurs the development of new nerve cells from stem cells in the hippocampus."[25]

Ratey believes that in a few years we will have more specifics about the most effective kinds of exercise.

> Experts suggest at least sixty minutes a day of vigorous exercise for children.

Movement activities help children with learning disorders. One study showed that twenty minutes a day of "very vigorous" exercise such as running significantly reduced autistic "self-stimming" behaviors such as arm flapping.[26]

Exercise regulates neurotransmitters that control emotional brain work and it acts as a chemical tonic that is potentially as effective as medication for mild to moderate depression.

If your child avoids this type of physical activity, you might gently start family walks and encourage whole-body movement games such as hide-and-seek in the park, along with other types of physical exploration (it will benefit your brain, too!). Teachers who can somehow arrange active, regular, supervised playtimes for their students will experience fewer attention and discipline problems. Enlightened administrators will ensure that the schedule includes such activities.

For children with severe movement disorders or sensory processing problems, specialized therapies are available from occupational or physical therapists.[27] The combination of music and patterned movement may be particularly beneficial.

> Did you know that a toddler picking up Cheerios from his high chair tray is laying neural foundations for language development or that a high-schooler running laps may improve his test scores?

Exercising Fingers and Imaginations. Don't let your child skip the important stage of "object play." I once heard a noted heart surgeon comment that he believed he got his visceral "feel" for the workings of the human heart from a childhood fascination with constructing pumps for water play. Even adults who depend on advanced technologies to image bodies, buildings, or bridges are better equipped if they have a gut-level understanding of how things fit together, gained from hands-on play in childhood.

The hand and finger motions used to manipulate toys, puzzles, locks, and other play materials are also tied to language development, probably because they share adjacent circuits in the brain.[28] Similarly, children who gesture when they are figuring out a math problem tend to understand and score better, showing how basic hands-on brain work gets translated into achievement test scores.

Abstract thinking and complex problem solving are also grounded in children's manipulation of physical objects. In a *New Yorker* interview, Will Wright, breakthrough video game designer (e.g., The Sims, Spore) attributes his creativity, talent for problem solving, and self-motivation to the hands-on curriculum at his Montessori school. (The Montessori curriculum is based on the child's self-motivated use of methods and materials designed specifically to build skills and concepts appropriate for the needs of the growing brain at different ages.)

"Montessori taught me the joy of discovery. It showed you can become interested in pretty complex theories, like Pythagorean theory, say, by playing with blocks." Wright, like many breakthrough video creators, is also an avid reader who credits ideas and plots from books for many of his game ideas.[29]

Disciplining the Mind with Motor Planning. Patterned, rhythmic activities are also excellent brain-training. "Motor planning," the complex brain work needed to execute a sequence of movements, stimulates executive brain centers to plan, monitor, and control the movements. Examples are patterned dancing (e.g., tango, tap); tai chi; karate or other martial arts; calligraphy; maze puzzles; and games involving a complex series of finger movements. Such activities encourage connections in frontal systems for motor control. These centers are next-door neighbors of the executive centers for academic attention and self-regulation.

It is well known that children with ADHD tend to have difficulty executing complex sequences of movements (e.g., tying knots, handwriting). They may be good at such sports as running or swimming, which involve less complex movement sequences, but less adept at diving or gymnastics. Motor planning skills are strengthened over many years of practice, yet many children today have forgone such activities as constructing models from scratch, playing games such as Pick-Up Sticks, embroidering, knitting, doing carpentry, and manipulating clay or other hands-on materials. Is there a message here? Can rapid texting or electronic game play do the trick? I wish I knew—but don't count on it.

> Should we be prescribing dance, martial arts, and knitting
> for ADHD?

"Patience. What's That?" I find it interesting that one of Albert Einstein's favorite activities as a child was building elaborate card houses, perhaps practicing the patient, step-by-step concentration and persistence of scientific experiment and mathematical problem solving. Has patience become outdated in a fast-paced electronic world? Will the children who have learned to discipline their fingers and their minds around play materials prove to be better equipped than those who haven't to surmount life's challenges?

I once observed a class of eighth graders in a Waldorf school, which made me, as a former middle-school teacher, take notice. At an age when we expect (or do we encourage?) children to be restless, unfocused, and distractible, these young teens spent the better part of an hour seated in a circle, deeply engaged in a long-term project in which each child whittled a solid block of hard maple into a smooth, even ball—using very sharp knives. No extraneous conversation, no silliness, and certainly no failure of attention here! The students approached their tasks with the utmost seriousness, skill, and obvious dedication to and pride in the quality of their individual projects. The school director explained to me that this is one of several capstone activities in a planned curriculum that includes hands-on projects in which students develop and demonstrate the ability to handle such a challenge. Waldorf values include respecting and enriching the natural developmental cycle of the child with personal and artistic qualities as well as academic ones.

Perhaps these were very unusual kids. Or perhaps popular expectations underestimate the potential of this age group? Historically, teenagers have assumed responsibility and contributed to society through hands-on apprenticeships with adults who modeled and expected mature, constructive behavior. Does isolating teen culture—or children of any age—in extracerebral space simply encourage problems by degrading their natural potential?

Incidentally, I am often asked if I recommend Waldorf or Montessori education. I do not recommend any one educational philosophy because every child and every family differ in their preferences and needs. Any parent considering alternative schooling should visit the school, obtain all available information, and evaluate the program both philosophically and for the specific child.

The Playful Brain: On the Road to Achievement

> *"It seems to us that the division between childhood and adulthood has tragically blurred. This blurring means that the time and space in which small children can play, unfettered by the demands of the adult world, is disappearing."*

> —Bev Bos and Jenny Chapman,
> in *Tumbling Over the Edge*[30]

The rapid disappearance of free, joyous, unstructured, creative, and imaginative play is creating a landscape of childhood that is one of the most barren in history. If you noticed that this subject has appeared frequently in this book, it is because there is good reason for concern.

"Eight is the new thirteen" I was told at a conference of independent toy retailers who (figuratively) swim upstream by attempting to stock only wholesome, nonelectronic products that require the child's brain to be in charge of the toy, rather than the other way around. Children whose imaginations are alive don't even need toys—they can create a game out of whatever materials happen to be at hand or out of ideas alone. Yet the age period during which children play freely, creatively, and imaginatively is—like school curricula—being pushed down, down, down into younger years and sometimes neglected altogether. The long-term cognitive effects of this change are unknown, but many authorities fear that this loss translates into problems for the children themselves and for a society badly in need of creative thinkers and adept problem solvers.

"A good toy is 90 percent child and 10 percent toy, but children's play today has those percentages reversed," says Joan Almon, director of the Alliance for Childhood, a grassroots organization dedicated to children's well-being. These professionals from all over the world are so concerned about diminishing amounts of playtime that they have begun a campaign to restore active, unstructured play to childhood. Hundreds of research studies support their contention that play is a natural and essential "food" for brain development and academic and personal skills.

A position paper published online (www.allianceforchildhood.net/) and entitled *Crisis in the Kindergarten* states, "Child-initiated play lays the foundations of learning. Through play, children learn to interact with others, to recognize and solve problems, and to feel the sense of mastery that results. In short, play helps children make sense of and find their own place in the physical and social world."

Play and Adult Brilliance. My observations suggest that our "different" learners, many of whom are extremely talented, may require a larger quotient of play in their lives than do other kids. Even after they are grown up and, in many cases, highly successful in creative or innovative fields, their novel ways of thinking keep them mentally and physically "playful." What a wonderful gift that is to retain (and to communicate to one's own children) in our super-serious, dog-eat-dog world!

Here is an important note for those parents or teachers who fear that allowing children time to play will distract them from academic progress and preparation for adult success. In study after study of highly successful, brilliant, and creative adults—from Nobel Prize winners to artists, screenwriters, directors, and developers of killer software applications—these individuals have described their work as a form of play and often refer back to the imaginative games they invented as children. When teachers tell us that young children can no longer think of something to do with a lump of Play-Doh, are at a loss when they have "nothing to do," or are unable to pretend that a block is a loaf of bread when playing "store," I think we should all be worried.

Nature and the Outdoors

> *"I think if you really want your children to learn what it takes to be successful, you should go out and live in the woods for a while."*
>
> —Texas software executive

New research suggests that playtimes will be even more valuable if they take place somewhere in the great outdoors. In 2005 Richard Louv published a book called *Last Child in the Woods* in which he attributed much of the malaise among today's youth to a substantial lessening of the time children spend outdoors interacting with nature. Coining the term "nature deficit disorder," Louv set out a clear prescription: take your kids and your students outside where they can walk on grass instead of pavement, see the sky, inhale brain-restoring oxygen, soak up the natural hormones stimulated by sunlight, and roam freely in the natural world.

An impressive amount of research demonstrates that we humans not only benefit from but actually require contact with nature for optimal physical, mental, and emotional/spiritual well-being. Even having a window in a classroom can improve academic achievement, not to mention children's behavior. Behavior also improves when children play on grass instead of on asphalt playgrounds, and children in a natural setting tend to treat one another more kindly. The presence of trees and running water have been cited as especially beneficial.

Children seem to gain the most positive benefits from nature when they are permitted to explore and enjoy according to their own inclinations—not under the rule-based adult structure imposed on, for example, a soccer field. Organized sports and even the simple fact of being active outdoors have their benefits, but unstructured, restorative interactions with nature are in a different category.[31]

Louv and others cite benefits of natural environments for children, which include

- improved academic achievement

- reduction in attention problems

- stress reduction

- improvement in mood and resistance to depression

- enhanced use of senses

- physical health (exposure to sunlight and oxygen; reduced obesity)

In light of this research, perhaps everyone's homework assignments should include organizing picnics at the park, the beach, or the country; arranging play spaces in natural areas near schoolyards; substituting outdoor time for media time; and, for urban youngsters, expanding experience with nature. It is good advice for any family or school district to seek opportunities for putting everyone's minds back in touch with restorative green spaces.

Playing (and Learning) with Creativity: Don't Forget the Arts! The first item usually chopped in a school budget crisis is funding for art, music, dance, drama, photography, creative writing, debate, and other "frills" of unrecognized or underappreciated value. Now research is finally beginning to document the fact that the arts are anything but "frills." They play an active role in expanding and even healing young minds.

Specific training in the arts has been shown to increase academic skills, such as the well-publicized relationship between music training and mathematics. Less tangible are the benefits for critical personal qualities, which include attention, systematic and creative problem solving, and motivation. Musicians have taken the lead in promoting research to document the profound physical effects of music on the human brain, but the reasons to expose children to the arts go far beyond making them "smarter."[32]

In the words of one neurobiologist, a "cafeteria of experience" benefits overall development, especially when families enjoy varied experiences such as museum visits, art shows, concerts, and theater together.[33] Resourceful parents and teachers can find many inexpensive or free events to upgrade their children's taste beyond cartoon icons. A follow-up discussion—what did everyone like or dislike, and why—adds a dimension of thoughtful analysis.

Many children with different learning styles have talents in one or more artistic fields; encouraging this important dimension of development can often make the difference between a turned-off, tuned-out student and a successful one.

A Quiet Mind: Fertile Ground for Getting a Life

"All men's miseries derive from not being able to sit in a quiet room alone."

—Blaise Pascal

If your child never has a chance to be alone and quiet within his own mind, how can you expect him to learn to use it well?

The notion of a "quiet mind"—whatever that is—seems a little far-fetched in our stressed-out, time-pressured culture. Equally bizarre is the idea of enticing distractible children to calm and direct their thoughts. Yet focused mental training is possible—even with children—and it is a remarkably effective tool to reduce stress, improve physical and mental health, lift depression, and hone attention and memory.[34] Practices that range from prayer to meditation to mind-centering and calming physical postures have helped both adults and children learn to direct their attention and improve their brains. Quieting one's mind is also a method of gene control. Meditation and other relaxation techniques work within the body's cells, turning on and off genes that are associated with positive and negative health effects and brain processes.

The highest levels of human creativity and achievment arise from a place of what Eckhard Tolle calls "inner stillness."[35] But any kind of "stillness" is hard to come by in a society that pipes radio ads into children's school buses and where a "quiet" walk keeps pace with a demanding beat from earphones.

Different approaches work for different individuals. For anyone, the first step is simply to have some unprogrammed time. For many of us (children included), however, separating from continual distraction is difficult and even anxiety producing. Some commonly used approaches for retraining the body and brain to settle down and focus include spiritual practices within the church or family, quiet walks and talks, training in disciplines such as simple yoga, guided meditation, or quiet time outdoors in nature. Schools that have piloted a range of different options report promising results, and although applying these ideas is relatively new, we can expect to hear more about this counterbalance to the distractions and stressors that are causing so much trouble for children today.

> "Boredom" is not a disease. The brain needs quiet time,
> which can be an opportunity for growth.

Parents and teachers should keep in mind that the fully developed learning brain needs more than pure mastery of subject matter. It also needs sufficient time, mental space, and thoughtful nurturance in which to lay the foundations of wisdom and insight. Children allowed the precious opportunity to learn to be comfortable within their own minds will be buffered from the ups and downs of achievement and fortune. Without internal exploration and reflection, children's self-development and their learning will be shallow processes, indeed.

Getting a Life: What Really Counts?

> *"It's not for us to say what our child is supposed to be. Great gifts usually come with great gaps. There aren't any perfect solutions, and you just keep trying."*
>
> —mother of a very "different" learner

Let's now finally return to the most fundamental question of all: *What is really important for your children in the long run?*

Having put this question to many, many parents, I can tell you the usual answer: they want their children to be rich. But this kind of "rich" doesn't refer to money. It means "self actualizing," or being happy in the fullest sense: emotionally grounded and able to use one's talents both for one's own satisfaction and for the benefit of others. As we have seen, kids who have experienced bumps in the developmental path—such as having overcome or compensated for a learning problem—may have a head start on this kind of self-knowledge and resilience.

The ability to self-actualize, which is attained by probably fewer than half of all adults, is not measured in quantity—of brain cells, test points, or possessions—but in quality. It requires going inside to reflect on and discover one's own life purpose. Yet many children in our edgy adult world are living on the cusp of externality, their minds distracted and often overwhelmed by relentless activities, entertainment, and the acquisition of "stuff."

In this century of dramatic change, we all have the opportunity to retrench and reevaluate what is truly important. Re-creating environments to help children grow a self as well as an intellect should surely be at the top of the list.

Summing Up: Do We Care Enough?

The purpose of this book has been to explore the reality of children's learning problems, how contemporary culture is contributing to them, and what we can do to help. As humans, we have the unique ability to use our minds to modify our—and our children's—biology. Yet overemphasizing the role of "nature" (in the form of genes and the products of brain cells) and neglecting the role of "nurture" is scientifically incorrect and morally hazardous. Our children are not standardized performance machines; each is an uneven assortment of talents, liabilities, and human potential that develop and change, subject to the influence of home, school, and community environments.

The previous chapters have emphasized the extraordinary plasticity of human development. What we do with and for children makes a difference. And much of what we are doing today is physically and intellectually unhealthy. Reevaluating and rearranging adult habits and priorities is both annoying and inconvenient. It is worth it.

A little girl was taken to her aunt's house for dinner one night. As Auntie was serving the plates, she asked the child, "Do you like Brussels sprouts?"

"Oh, yes," came the reply.

As dinner ended and the aunt began to clear the plates, she noticed that her guest had not touched a single sprout.

"I thought you said you liked Brussels sprouts," she remarked.

"Oh, I do," said the little girl. "Just not enough to eat them."

We say we care deeply about our children's learning. But do we care enough to do what needs to be done?

Terms of Dysfunction:
Learning Problems, Seen and Unseen

Ideally, we can offer effective treatment for a child's problems within the context of his home and school environments without having to label him with a disorder. (See Chapter Two for a fuller discussion of this issue.) In reality, however, obtaining insurance or special educational services often requires a specific diagnosis of a recognized "handicapping condition."

This chart lists most of the common diagnostic terms currently in use. You will note that many overlap with each other. There is considerable disagreement about exact definitions or even the validity of these terms and the many others you may run across. Note that this list is not intended to be complete.

Specific Disabilities in Academic Learning
(Learning Disabilities)

Learning disabilities are usually defined as specific problems with some aspect of a school subject:

Reading Disorders (see text for more detailed information)

    Dyslexia, sometimes called *phonological reading disorder*

    Hyperlexia

    Unexplained ("Garden-Variety") Reading Disorder

Other Learning Disabilities

Dysgraphia: writing

Dyscalculia: math

Nonverbal learning disability: math concepts, reading comprehension, difficulty with social relationships

More General Developmental Problems That Affect Academic Progress

Language Disorders and Auditory Processing Problems: difficuty with accurate listening, understanding, remembering what is said; difficulty expressing oneself orally or in writing

Phonological / articulatory disorder: "slushy" speech; inaccurate processing of sounds in words

Difficulty or slowness in understanding and processing spoken language is sometimes called *central auditory dysfunction*, although this diagnosis is still controversial and should be given only by audiologists.

Pragmatic language disorder: difficulty understanding or communicating appropriately with others; poor understanding of facial expression and gesture

Problems with Sensory and Motor Development: delayed small- and large-muscle coordination: shows up in activities such as handwriting, sports, keyboarding, feeling comfortable in one's body. Also called the following:

Perceptual-motor problems

Developmental coordination disorder

SPD: Sensory Processing Disorder (also called *sensory integration disorder*)

Visual-Spatial Skill Deficits: understanding how things relate to one another in space; perceiving shapes accurately and manipulating objects in one's mind

Social Skills Deficits: (see *pragmatic language disorder*, above) problems understanding and dealing with others; may have trouble interpreting facial expressions or gestures; tendency to "say the wrong thing" without understanding what's wrong. This is a prominent aspect of ASD syndromes (see below).

Pervasive Developmental Disorder (PDD)

Autism Spectrum Disorders (ASD)

Autism: severe problems with social communication; abnormal processing of/response to sensory stimuli such as loud noises, human eye contact; repetitive movements (e.g., flapping, spinning); intense preoccupation with specialized learning (e.g., memorizing license plates, baseball statistics); may exhibit unusually advanced development in specialized areas ("splinter skills"), advanced spatial relations abilities

Asperger's syndrome: thought to be a "high-end" variant of autism

PDD: NOS (not otherwise specified) means no one quite knows what it is or where it came from

Sometimes *Hyperlexia* is included in the ASD grouping.

Executive Function Disorder

Difficulty in managing one's own brain and behavior; problems in attention, planning, organization, social skills

Disorders of Managing Attention

Attention deficit disorder (ADD)

Attention deficit with hyperactivity disorder (ADHD)

Other Disorders of Executive Function

Developmental output disorder: shows up in inability to organize a project, organize and write a theme, or complete homework

Behavioral Problems

Attention problems (*ADD* or *ADHD*) are often grouped here

Conduct disorder: serious difficulty behaving appropriately

Motivation problems: a vague and undefined category

A Few Thoughts About When to Worry

In the anxious parenting culture of today, it is all too easy to panic when your child shows the slightest deviation from what you believe to be "normal" development. Please keep in mind that there is a wide time range in which children acquire various skills and that anxiously hovering over your child's every development or trying to hurry him along the learning curve are short routes to neuroticism for both of you. Here are some very general suggestions about how to maintain perspective while recognizing when help is needed:

- Do not automatically assume that your child has some sort of "brain disease." Follow the guidelines in this book to analyze lifestyle issues that may be contributing to the problem and make needed changes. *Note:* If your child shows early symptoms of autism, you should promptly consult your pediatrician.

- Your pediatrician is an important line of defense in any case. Explain your concerns, and back them up with specific examples. Make sure your child has a thorough physical exam to check for any sensory deficits (hearing, vision) or other physical problem. Be aware, however, that your doctor may not be trained to understand learning disorders, so request a referral if your questions are not answered to your satisfaction. "He'll grow out of it" is not usually a satisfactory answer.

- Seek out references to inform yourself about the developmental milestones that signal a child's progress during the first few years. (Amy Egan's *Is It a Big Problem or a Little Problem?* and my *Your Child's Growing Mind* are among many such sources.) If you observe persistent lags in one or more areas, there is no reason to panic, but you probably should start asking questions.

- Observe your child among peers of the same age; if you *repeatedly* notice *major* differences in some important aspect of behavior (e.g., language, motor skill development, socialization), tell your doctor and follow her suggestions.

- Don't make the mistake of concluding your child is defective simply because other children are ahead in a few specific skills ("Latisha can count by tens!" "Bryan already turns cartwheels!").

- Family members such as grandparents who have firsthand experience in child development may offer a useful perspective.

- Try not to communicate your anxiety to your child (this is hard). Don't forget to smile, as a worried-looking parent is understandably scary to a young child. Ask the professional for the best way to explain the situation truthfully but tactfully to your child.

- Check out Appendix C for options in evaluation and treatment.

A Primer on Getting Professional Help
for Your Child

We can hope that your own common sense combined with the information from this book plus your efforts to work constructively with the school will put your child's learning on track. If the problem persists, however, you may want to seek a more professional evaluation. This can be a daunting job. Problems and problem categories are not always clearly defined, they often overlap, and the current state of the diagnostic art is admittedly "fuzzy."

Appendix A contains a list of commonly accepted diagnostic terms. In Chapter 3, "What Should We Call This?," we summarize research on the major diagnostic categories that are currently recognized. However, new terms keep cropping up. I am periodically asked about some "disorder"—often a set of initials—of which I have never heard. Occasionally they are research based, but many turn out to be a "diagnosis" created by someone with a product or a program to sell. Some are well intentioned, but be cautious. The same goes for the confusing array of treatment options you are likely to be offered. With the profusion of Internet resources, parents have access to a lot more information—and misinformation. It is wonderful to be able to find helpful data and commentary, but in this field we must always be on guard against the venal or misguided creeps who profit from selling "cures" to desperate families.

Here are just a few preliminary steps toward getting a useful professional diagnosis:

Steps in Obtaining an Evaluation

- Work with the school as far as possible to identify specific steps that can be taken in the classroom or on the playground. Follow up at home on any recommendations from the teacher, school psychologist, or learning specialist.

- If these measures are ineffective, you may request special testing from the school psychologist. Do not be surprised if the waiting lists for such services are very long.

- Keep your pediatrician informed of your concerns and any measures that are being taken.

- States, districts, and even individual schools vary dramatically in the types of services available and how they are paid for. Check out the national organizations in the Reference List (Appendix D) and their local branches for information pertaining to your area.

- If any testing is done at school, ask for a follow-up conference to get a thorough explanation of (1) what the test(s) mean and (2) what specific recommendations are made for treatment. You are entitled to a written report on any results or recommendations. Take someone you trust with you to take notes and be objective in remembering what was said. Any parent is likely to feel very emotional in such a situation and may not think clearly on the spot.

- If you are unable to get reasonable satisfaction from the school, you may need to seek an independent evaluation. The most qualified professionals are usually at a hospital or a clinic that offers a complete *psychoeducational or neurodevelopmental evaluation*, preferably a multidisciplinary one, meaning that several professionals from different areas of expertise may be involved. Please do some preliminary checking on the credentials and level of experience of the people who will be working with your child. If you need to travel a distance to locate a reputable clinic, this is money well spent in the long run. If you can't get to a clinic, look for a local professional who has credentials, an established track record, and good recommendations from schools and from other parents.

- Be a prepared consumer when test results are given at a clinic. You have a right to a complete explanation of results, a written report, and specific recommendations for steps you can take both at home and at school. Don't be afraid to ask questions, and take your observer/note-taker along to make sure you record all the information.

- If you are skeptical about the results or any of the recommendations, you can seek a second opinion.

- Reevaluate your home environment, your child's lifestyle, and his school or care setting in light of this new information. Grit your teeth and make any changes that might be needed. Changing lifestyle habits is difficult, inconvenient, and takes time.

- The professional organizations in the Reference List (Appendix D) may be able to help you find information on competent evaluators or well-validated treatment approaches. Please do not fall for any of the "quick-fix" commercial products or services that promise results (if you spend money, of course). In this field, no reputable professional will promise you anything, because there are no easy answers.

It is impossible to recommend treatments that will be appropriate for everyone, but the information in the previous chapters should equip you to ask the right questions and understand the answers. Trust your own parental wisdom, and you can become your child's best advocate. In addition, a relatively new specialty, which goes by various terms on the order of "learning disability advocate," attracts experienced professionals who become case managers to help parents find and obtain appropriate testing and treatment.

Steps in Finding Effective Treatment Options

- Before you sign up for a program of remediation, do your homework. Check with your child's school psychologist or other professionals, consult books or reliable Web sites on your child's specific condition, and talk to other parents whom you trust. You can also get a lot of information on the Internet, but remember that anyone can say or claim anything they want to there. Evaluate the sources of the information (i.e., *.com* Web sites are commercial, while *.org, .gov,* and *.edu* may have more credible information). Ask questions and be a critical consumer.

- If anyone promises you anything in the way of a "cure," avoid them.

- Ask for research studies validating treatment effects.

- Inquire about past experience with children with the same type of problems as your child.

- Be wary of treatments that claim to do everything for everyone; neurodevelopmental disorders may require specific approaches.

- Ask for referrals to other parents who have faced similar problems, but again, be skeptical. When parents have poured a lot of money into a treatment, they are sometimes over-eager to believe that it has "worked."

- Do not accept any ideas that violate you own common sense. You know more about your child than anyone else does.

- The best remedial results are obtained mainly because of the skill and empathy of the therapist, combined with her level of training. Look for someone who is professionally skilled and also relates well with your child.

- As always, spending time on thorough research and giving your child extra love and support are your best strategies.

APPENDIX D

Reference List

Useful Web Sites: Organizations

Alliance for Childhood: an international organization that supports the healthy development of young children, including developmentally appropriate curricula and appropriate media use; www.allianceforchildhood.org

American Speech-Language-Hearing Association: A professional organization for speech/language therapists, also publishes information for parents, including checklists of age-appropriate skill development; www.asha.org

Autism Society of America: funds research and publishes current information about new findings; www.autism-society.org

Association of Educational Therapists (AET): the national professional association for educational therapists, defines and sets standards for therapists; www.aetonline.org

Autism Speaks: specializes in information for parents; www.autismspeaks.org

First Signs: information and resources for early identification of autistic spectrum disorders; www.firstsigns.org

Incredible Years Programme (for behavior management); www.incredibleyears.com

International Dyslexia Association (IDA): extensive information about reading development; reading, writing, spelling, and mathematics difficulties; and approved treatment strategies; www.interdys.org

Learning Disability Association of America (LDA): provides support and current research to people with learning disabilities, their parents, teachers, and other professionals; www.ldanatl.org

Lindamood-Bell Learning Processes: conducts certified professional training for remediation of reading and language problems, including reading comprehension difficulties; sponsors clinical trials of therapy programs; www.lindamoodbell.com

National Institute of Learning Development (NILD): conducts certified training courses and conferences for educational therapists; www.nild.net

Useful Web Sites: Sources on Combating Toxins

The Green Guide: reviews potentially dangerous chemicals: www.thegreenguide.com

"Indoor Air Quality Tools for Schools" materials: www.epa.gov/iaq/schools

Institute for Children's Environmental Health: www.iceh.org

Learning Disabilities Association Project: www.healthychildrenproject.org

Physicians for Social Responsibility: www.psr.org

NOTES

Chapter 1. Too Many Dyssed Kids

1. Robert J. Sternberg and Elena L. Grigorenko, *Our Labeled Children* (New York: Perseus Books, 1999).

2. One of many articles on this subject appeared as "The Dyslexic CEO," a cover story in *Fortune*, May 13, 2002.

3. The Centers for Disease Control publishes current statistics on childhood disorders, www.cdc.gov.

4. Robert Pasternack presented data on special education at the Lindamood-Bell annual conference in Anaheim, California, March 18, 2005.

5. Nanci Bell reported these statistics on a high incidence of reading and learning disorders in prison inmates and school dropouts in her keynote address at the Lindamood-Bell annual conference in Anaheim, California, March 13, 2008.

6. W. S. Gilliam and G. Shahar, "Preschool and Child Care Expulsion and Suspension," *Infants and Young Children* 19 no. 5 (2006): 228–245.

7. Judith Ripke, personal communication, June 18, 2008.

8. "2.5 Million Children Take Stimulant Drugs," *New York Times*, June 17, 2008.

9. Leonard Sax, *Boys Adrift*, p. 35.

10. *New York Times*, February 25, 2007.

11. Jane Gross, "Checklist for Camp: Bug Spray, Sunscreen, Pills," *New York Times*, July 9, 2006.

12. *New York Times*, June 6, 2006.

13. My conversation with Glenda Thorne took place at the annual conference of the International Dyslexia Association, Dallas, Texas, November 1, 2007.

14. *New York Times*, February 9, 2007.

15. My conversation with Dr. Robinson took place at the Lindamood-Bell conference in London, England, April 2007.

16. Martha Herbert's remarks appeared in an interview in *Wild Duck Review*, May 29, 2001, p. 1.

17. J. Perrin, S. R. Bloom, and S. L. Gortmaaker, "The Increase of Childhood Chronic Conditions in the United States," *Journal of the American Medical Association* 297 no. 24 (2007): 2755–2759. The conditions of concern to the pediatricians include obesity, asthma, ADHD, autism, and depression.

Chapter 2. What's the Problem?

1. For a thorough and scientifically based reference on executive function disorder, see Lynn Meltzer, ed. *Executive Function in Education*.

2. Martha Bridge Denckla, "Executive Function: Binding Together the Definitions of Attention-Deficit/Hyperactivity Disorder and Learning Disabilities," in Lynn Meltzer, ed., *Executive Function in Education*, p. 11.

3. Since 1994 the fourth version of this manual (*DSM-IV*) has been the textual guru of diagnosis, despite the fact that it is seriously outdated according to current research. Thus the new *DSM-V*, while containing numerous contentious issues, is viewed as a hopeful improvement.

4. Peter S. Jensen et al., *Toward a New Diagnostic System for Child Psychopathology: Moving Beyond the DSM*.

5. Scott Shannon, *Please Don't Label My Child*, p. 2.

6. Ibid.

Chapter 3. What Should We Call This?

1. Dr. Levine, author of important books on learning differences, objects to our tendency to overcategorize children rather than evaluating

and treating each case individually. See his book *A Mind at a Time* for more information.

2. Central Auditory Processing Disorder (CAPD) is a diagnosis that has been accepted by the American Speech-Language-Hearing Association only if the testing is done by an appropriately licensed audiologist. Alternative treatments have received glowing reports from some parents but have not held up in research studies. The ASHA Web site has current information.

3. The Lindamood-Bell Learning Processes have conducted successful pilot studies of programs teaching visual imagery plus verbal training to improve reading comprehension in school districts in Colorado, Alaska, and elsewhere. See, for example, Mark Sadoski and Victor Willson, "Effects of a Theoretically Based Large-Scale Reading Intervention in a Multicultural Urban School District," *AERA Journal* 43 no. 1 (2006): 137–154.

4. Nanci Bell's remarks are paraphrased from a personal conversation that took place on March 13, 2008, in Anaheim, California.

5. Gavin Reid, *Dyslexia: A Complete Guide for Parents*, p. 166.

6. Stephen A. Petrill et al., "Measured Environmental Influences on Early Reading: Evidence from an Adoption Study," *Scientific Studies of Reading* 9 no. 3 (2005): 237–259.

7. Research findings on effective methods of teaching reading are found in Barbara Foorman et al., "Interventions Aimed at Improving Reading Success: An Evidence-Based Approach," *Developmental Neuropsychology* 24 nos. 2 and 3 (2003): 613–639. I also recommend Judith Birsch's book *Multisensory Teaching of Basic Language Skills*.

8. Mark Sadoski, "Effects of a Theoretically Based Large-Scale Reading Intervention in a Multiculture Urban School District."

9. Reid Lyon, *Overview of Reading and Literacy Initiatives* (Report to Committee on Labor and Human Resources, U.S. Senate, 1989), p. 9.

10. My conversation with Dr. Linda Wernikoff took place on May 6, 2008.

11. Helen Tager-Flusberg, "Cognitive Neuroscience of Autism," introduction to symposium, *Journal of the International Neuropsychological Society* 14 (2008): 920.

12. "Evidence for Effectiveness of Treatments for Autism Spectrum Disorders in Children and Adolescents," Health Resources Commission: Office for Oregon Health Policy and Research, October 2008.

13. Comments from Temple Grandin are taken from her presentation at the Courage to Risk Conference held at the Broadmoor Hotel, Colorado Springs, February 10, 2006.

14. "Evidence for Effectiveness," Health Resources Commission.

15. My conversation with Dr. Greenspan took place at his home in Bethesda, Maryland, on December 9, 2005.

16. For the notion that we are allowing "appliances to rear our children," I am indebted to the wise insights of Dr. Lillian Katz, respected early childhood guru.

17. Specific references to this brain area in Siegel's book are on pp. 120 and 201.

18. Joan Almon, director of the Alliance for Childhood, gets credit for the phrase *high-tech, low-touch*, which I also used in my book *Failure to Connect*. There you will find a much fuller discussion of the problems of too much technology in the preschool years.

19. Lucy Jane Miller (www.spdfoundation.net) is heading up the effort to validate both the diagnosis and treatment options.

20. See Bruce Pennington's book *Diagnosing Learning Disorders* for a rundown on current research findings.

21. Structured handwriting practice firms up brain connections for spelling and reading. For extensive information on the neurological benefits of targeted multisensory instruction, consult publications from the International Dyslexia Association (www.interdys.org).

22. The classroom experiment with balance balls appeared on ABC News (TheDenverChannel.com), February 26, 2009.

23. Current information on teaching math may be found through the National Council for Teachers of Mathematics (NCTM): www.nctm .org.

24. A professional program for grades 5–9 is Transitional Mathematics (TransMath) by John Woodward and Mary Stroh, available online from Sopris West: Cambium Learning. A helpful source of information for parents and teachers is the Spring 2008 issue of *Perspectives* 34 no. 2, published by the International Dyslexia Association.

25. Both Rourke's book and a more current book from Joseph Palombo will be found in the Bibliography.

26. Edward M. Hallowell's comment from personal communication, January 9, 2009.

27. James M. Perrin et al., "The Increase of Childhood Chronic Conditions in the United States," *Journal of the American Medical Association*, June 2007: 2755.

28. Alix Spiegel, "Creative Play Makes for Kids in Control," www.NPR.org, February 28, 2008.

29. Michael Posner, "Training Attention in Children and Adults," address presented at annual meeting of the International Neuropsychological Association in Portland, Oregon, on February 7, 2007.

30. Doris A. Trauner, "Neurological Correlates of Cognitive Difficulties in School-Age Children," Seventeenth Annual Nelson Butter's West Coast Neurpsychology Conference, San Diego, March 2007.

Chapter 4. Brain Differences and Learning Differences

1. I know that most of the readers of this book will fall into the "savvy" expectant parent category, but I am very concerned about the growing numbers of young women who bear children in substandard and even toxic environments, without the benefit of either the information or the medical resources to give their youngsters an optimal start on learning. Since all our children will be living in the world together, it is in everyone's best interest to advocate for public health measures to remedy this serious problem.

2. Lise Eliot, *What's Going on in There? How the Brain and Mind Develop in the First Five Years of Life* (New York: Bantam, 2000).

3. Ibid, p. 82.

4. R. de Regnier et al., "Using Event-Related Potentials to Study Perinatal Nutrition and Brain Development in Infants of Diabetic Mothers," *Developmental Neuropsychology* 31 no. 3 (2007): 379–396.

5. Lise Eliot, *What's Going on in There?*, p. 84.

6. Duo Jin et al., "CD38 Is Critical for Social Behaviour by Regulating Oxytocin Secretion," *Nature* 446 (March 1, 2007): 41–45.

7. A very accessible account of this growing problem, including Dr. Monk's quote, is Laurie Tarkan, "Tracking Stress and Depression Back to the Womb," *New York Times Science Times*, December 7, 2004.

8. Erica Noonan, "Giving Birth to a Better Brain," *Boston Globe*, October 31, 2005.

9. Guinevere Eden and Thomas Zeffiro, "Neural Systems Affected in Developmental Dyslexia Revealed by Functional Neuroimaging," *Neuron* 21 (1998): 279–282.

10. Lise Eliot, *What's Going on in There?*, p. 325.

11. Science Daily, October 15, 2008, www.sciencedaily.com/releases/2008/10/081014111156.htm.

12. John Stein, "Wobbles, Warbles, and Fish," presented at the international conference of Lindamood-Bell Learning Systems, London, England, April 27, 2007.

13. An excellent summary of this rapidly advancing area of research, written by R. Douglas Fields, appeared in *Scientific American*, March 2008: 54–61.

14. Marcel Just presented his research about autism and connectivity at the international conference of the Lindamood-Bell Learning Systems, London, April 27, 2007.

15. Lucy L. M. Patson et al., "The Unusual Symmetry of Musicians: Musicians Have Equilateral Interhemispheric Transfer for Visual Information," *Neuropsychologia* 45 no. 9 (2009): 2059–2065.

16. The bizarre story of how Einstein's brain became available to science is told in a fascinating biography, which also provided much of the information in this section: Walter Isaacson, *Einstein: His Life and Universe* (New York: Simon & Schuster, 2007).

17. Sylwester writes an excellent monthly online column for educators for *Brain Connection*, www.brainconnection.com.

18. Thomas S. May, "Terms of Empathy," *BrainWork*, May/June 2006: 4.

19. The study of reduced mirror neurons in autistic brains was conducted by Marco Iacoboni of UCLA and described in *BrainWork*, May/June 2006: 3–4.

20. There are many books on education and differences between boys and girls. For a sampling, see Leonard Sax, *Boys Adrift: The Five Factors Driving the Growing Epidemic of Unmotivated Boys and Underachieving Young Men* and Louann Brizendine, *The Female Brain*. Also con-

sult books by authors Michael Thompson and Michael Gurian, each of whom writes compassionately and knowledgeably about how to support our sons.

Chapter 5. Rewiring Children's Brains

1. See Sally Shaywitz, *Overcoming Dyslexia*, regarding specific information about the remedial methods used to reinforce brain connections for reading.

2. Anahad O'Connor, "Biology of Dyslexia Varies with Culture," *New York Times*, September 7, 2004.

3. A fuller account of how different cultures and different occupations change neural wiring is found in J. M. Healy, *Endangered Minds*.

4. BBC News, World Edition, March 14, 2000.

5. Gerald M. Edelman, *Neural Darwinism* (Oxford: Oxford Books, 1990).

6. Dr. Edelman was quoted in C. G. Coll, E. L. Bearer, and R. M. Lerner, *Nature and Nurture: The Complex Interplay of Genetic and Environmental Influences on Human Behavior and Development* (Mahwah, N.J.: LEA, 2004), p. 209.

7. M. E. Kramer et al., "Long-Term Neural Processing of Attention Following Early Childhood Traumatic Brain Injury," *Journal of the International Neuropsychological Society* 14 (2008): 424–435.

8. Linda Ewing-Cobbs, Marcia Barnes, and Jack M. Fletcher, "Early Brain Injury in Children: Development and Reorganization of Cognitive Function," *Developmental Neuropsychology* 24 nos. 2 and 3 (2003): 669–704.

9. Bruce D. Perry and Maia Szalavitz, *The Boy Who Was Raised as a Dog* (New York: Basic Books, 2007).

10. Bruce Perry's Child Trauma Academy (www.childtrauma.org) aims to help restore the lives of abused and traumatized children. Dr. Perry's remarks excerpted from a talk, "The Nature and Nurture of Brain Development," delivered at University of California, Sacramento, May 7, 2005.

11. H. T. Chugani et al., "Local Brain Functional Activity Following Early Deprivation: A Study of Postinstitutionalized Romanian Orphans," *Neuroimage* 14 no. 6 (2001): 290–301.

12. Fox's study on the Romanian orphans is called the Bucharest Early Intervention Project and includes researchers Nathan Fox, Charles Nelson, Dr. Charles Zeanah, and Dana Johnson.

13. "Study Quantifies Orphanage Link to I.Q." *New York Times*, January 24, 2007.

14. Marcel Just, "Brain Plasticity: Lessons for Learning to Read and Other Skills," symposium presented at International Dyslexia Association Annual Conference, Dallas, Texas, October 31, 2007. For teachers and parents interested not only in the science but also its practical applications, this annual conference is a goldmine of information.

15. Ibid.

16. Sally Shaywitz, *Overcoming Dyslexia: A New and Complete Science-Based Program for Reading Problems at Any Level*.

17. "Brain Plasticity: Lessons for Learning to Read and Other Skills."

18. D. L. Molfese, "Predicting Dyslexia at 8 Years of Age Using Neonatal Brain Response," *Brain and Language* 72 (2000): 238–245.

19. Victoria J. Molfese et al., "The Role of the Environment in the Development of Reading Skills," *Journal of Learning Disabilities* 36 no. 1 (2003): 59–67.

20. P. G. Papanicolaou et al., "Brain Mechanisms for Reading in Children with and Without Dyslexia," *Developmental Neuropsychology* 24 nos. 2 and 3 (2003): 593–612.

21. Jeffrey W. Gilger and Tom M. Talmage, "MRI and Genetic Study of the Gifted Dyslexic," International Dyslexia Association Annual Conference, Dallas, Texas, November 2, 2007.

22. Reported in *Child Development Newswire*, CDWIRE.net, July 1, 2005. The principal investigator was Vincent P. Matthews, Ph.D., of Indiana University.

23. J. P. Murray et al., "Children's Brain Activations While Viewing Televised Violence Revealed by fMRI." *Media Psychology* 8 no. 1 (2006): 25–37.

24. Cautions regarding the limits of imaging technologies were published in *BrainWork*, July/August 2005: 3.

25. "Searching for the Person in the Brain," *New York Times Science Times*, February 5, 2006.

26. Sharon Begley, "How Thinking Can Change the Brain," *Wall Street Journal: Science Journal*, January 19, 2007.

27. Check out the work of Richard Davidson of the University of Wisconsin for some fascinating research on the effects of meditation on the brain, http://psyphz.psych.wisc.edu.

28. C. Creel et al., "Effects of Self-Monitoring on Classroom Prepardness Skills of Middle School Students with ADHD," *Learning Disabilities* 14 no. 2 (2006): 105–113.

29. Michael I. Posner, "Educating the Developing Brain," address delivered at the Annual Convention of the American Psychological Association: Toronto, August 9. 2003. Posner's book is listed in the Bibliography.

Chapter 6. How Your Child's Brain Works

1. Joseph LeDoux's book *Synaptic Self* provides a readable explanation of the science involved in the brain's message transmission systems.

2. Joseph LeDoux, *Synaptic Self*.

3. K. Peter Lesch, "Neuroticism and Serotonin: A Developmental Genetic Perspective" in Plomin et al., eds., *Behavioral Genomics in the Postgenomic Era* (Washington, D.C.: American Psychological Association, 2003).

4. Bruce Perry publishes new findings about children's emotional development at www.childtrauma.org.

5. M.J. Koepp et al., "Evidence for Striatal Dopamine Release During a Video Game," *Nature* 393 (May 21, 1998): 266–268.

6. G. F. Koob and M. LeMoal, *Neurobiology of Addiction* (London: Elsevier, 2006).

7. D. Coch, G. Dawson, and K. W. Fischer, *Human Behavior, Learning, and the Developing Brain: Atypical Development*, p. 241.

8. My information on sales of ADHD medications on college campuses comes from conversations with university students and professionals

who work with them, whose experience has been consistent enough to convince me that such a practice is increasingly common.

9. Good information on this and many other questions is found in Elizabeth J. Roberts, *Should You Medicate Your Child's Mind?*

10. Leonard Sax, *Boys Adrift*, p. 216.

11. Because the elements of brain function are synergistic—that is, they work together and affect each other—it has been suggested that altering one major system may create conditions, such as bipolar illness, that are related to another neurotransmitter group. See Robert Whitaker, "Creating the Bipolar Child: How Our Drug-Based Paradigm of Care Is Fueling an Epidemic of Disabling Mental Illness" in Sharna Olfman, *Bipolar Children*, pp. 46–63.

12. Joseph Chilton Pearce's quote came from a book review of Chris Mercoglianos book *Teaching the Restless: One School's Remarkable No-Ritatin Approach to Helping Children Learn and Succeed* (Boston: Beacon Press, 2004).

13. Daniel Burstyn, "An Invisible Plague: Polypharmacy and the Chemical Colonization of Childhood" in Sharna Olfman, *Bipolar Children*, p. 119.

14. Lisa Popczynski's quote was featured in "Parenting as Therapy for Child's Mental Disorders," *New York Times*, December 22, 2006.

15. Michael E. Ruff, "Attention Deficit Disorder and Stimulant Use: An Epidemic of Modernity," *Clinical Pediatrics*, September 2005: 557–563.

16. L. H. Diller, *Running on Ritalin* (New York: Bantam Books, 1999).

17. Dr. Elaine Walker was quoted in the *APA Monitor*, October 2006, p. 16.

18. Suggestions excerpted from Mel Levine, *A Mind at a Time*, p. 288.

19. The primary source for this "attribution theory" of motivation is the work of Stanford professor Carol Dweck, who describes her research in her book *Mindset: The New Psychology of Success.*

20. I recommend the following sources for helping a child develop intrinsic motivation: Alfie Kohn, *Punished by Rewards*; Richard Lavoie, *The Motivation Breakthrough*; and Mel Levine, *The Myth of Laziness.*

21. I recommend Seligman's books listed in the Bibliography for their thoughtful and practical approach to buffering a child against stress and emotional problems.

22. Martin E. P. Seligman, *Authentic Happiness*, p. 228.

Chapter 7. Genes, Learning, and the Environment

1. From "Wobbles, Warbles, and Fish: The Magnocellular Theory of Developmental Dyslexia," presented at 15th Annual Conference, Lindamood-Bell Learning Processes, London, April 27, 2007.

2. Allan N. Schore is the author of *Affect Regulation and the Origin of the Self*. His comment was based on groundbreaking research described later in Chapter 7. This quote appeared in the *New York Times* on June 29, 2004.

3. Dr. Hewitt's remarks quoted in Etienne S. Benson, "Behavioral Genetics: Meet Molecular Biology," *Monitor on Psychology*, April 2004, p. 42.

4. Bruce Pennington, "Genetics Update: The Genetics of Developmental Disorders," annual meeting, International Neuropsychological Society, Honolulu, February 5, 2003. Bruce F. Pennington is a clinical child neuropsychologist, researcher, and professor at Denver University. I recommend his book *The Development of Psychopathology: Nature and Nurture* as an authoritative reference on the subject.

5. Edmund S. Higgins, "The New Genetics of Mental Illness," *Scientific American Mind*, June/July 2008.

6. Bruce Pennington, "Genetics Update: The Genetics of Developmental Disorders."

7. Barbara Caulfield, *New York Times*, July 1, 2007.

8. SMA Web site, www.fsma.org, May 10, 2006.

9. C. R. Scriver and C. L. Clow, "Phenylketonuria: Epitome of Human Biochemical Genetics," *New England Journal of Medicine* 303 (1980): 1336–1342.

10. Robert Plomin et al., *Behavioral Genetics in the Postgenomic Era*, p. 14.

11. Michael Rutter, *Genes and Behavior: Nature-Nurture Interplay Explained*.

12. Ibid.

13. A. M. Galaburda, "Norman Geshwind and Dyslexia: A Neurobiological Legacy," address presented at International Dyslexia Association Annual Conference Philadelphia, November 5, 2004.

14. Gilbert Gottleib, "Environmental and Behavioral Influences on Gene Activity," in C. G. Coll, E. L. Bearer, and R. M. Lerner, *Nature and Nurture: The Complex Interplay of Genetic and Environmental Influences on Human Behavior and Development*, p. 94.
    Elaine Bearer. "Behavior as Influence and Result of the Genetic Program," in C. G. Coll et al., *Nature and Nurture.*

15. *New York Times Science Times*, December 7, 2004.

16. An informative account of behaviorist views and the arguments against them is given by Steven Pinker in *The Blank Slate: The Modern Denial of Human Nature* (New York: Penguin, 2003). Pinker himself is something of a "nativist," holding out for the idea that many of our important traits are innate and difficult to alter.

17. E. Wanner and L. R. Gleitman, eds., *Language Acquisition: The State of the Art* (New York: Cambridge University Press, 1982), pp. 51–77.

18. My conversation with Warren Rosen took place in his office in Skokie, Illinois, on April 18, 2008.

19. For this useful term I thank Sir Michael Rutter and his book *Genes and Behavior.*

20. Bruce Pennington, *Diagnosing Learning Disorders.*

21. E. Russo, "Researchers Find No Clear Paths on Road to Unraveling Schizophrenia," *The Scientist* 16 no. 2: 30–31.

22. Robert Plomin et al., *Behavioral Genetics in the Postgenomic Era* (Washington, D.C.: American Psychological Association, 2004), pp. 366ff.

23. Ibid.

24. For a thorough discussion of the interaction of different environments with children's genetic propensities, please see Theodore D. Wachs, *Necessary but Not Sufficient.*

25. Steven Suomi, quoted in C. G. Coll et al., *Nature and Nurture*, p. 10. Suomi feels that discovering "structural polymorphisms" (differences)

in these serotonin genes as a function of the animal's rearing environment is the crucial finding that demonstrates an unusually complex "gene-environment interaction."

26. A. Caspi et al., "Influence of Life Stress on Depression: Moderation by a Polymorphism in the 5-HTT Gene," *Science* 301 no. 5631 (2003): 386–389.

27. J. Fraser Mustard, personal communication, April 22, 2005.

28. K. Peter Lesch, "Neuroticism and Serotonin: A Developmental Genetic Perspective" in Robert Plomin et al., *Behavioral Genetics in the Postgenomic Era*.

29. Ian C. G. Weaver, Moshe Szyf, and Michael Meaney, "Epigenetic Programming by Maternal Behavior," *Nature Neuroscience*, June 27, 2004: 1–8.

30. Michael Rutter, *Genes and Behavior*.

31. Ian C. G. Weaver, Moshe Szyf, and Michael Meaney, "Epigenetic Programming by Maternal Behavior."

32. Marvin Zuckerman, "Biosocial Bases of Sensation Seeking" in Turhan Canli, ed., *Biology of Personality and Individual Differences* (New York: Guilford Press, 2006), p. 40.

33. Jerome Kagan, "A Behavioral Science Perspective" in Robert Plomin et al., *Behavioral Genetics in the Postgenomic Era,* p. xix.

Chapter 8. Who's Intelligent?

1. Matt Ridley, *Nature via Nurture: Genes, Experience, and What Makes Us Human.*

2. C. G. Coll, E. L. Bearer, and R. M. Lerner, eds., *Nature and Nurture: The Complex Interplay of Genetic and Environmental Influences on Human Behavior and Development.*

3. E. S. Benson, in *Monitor on Psychology*, April 2004: 44.

4. Dr. Sternberg's books include *Successful Intelligence: How Practical and Creative Intelligence Determine Success in Life* and, as editor, *Why Smart People Can Be So Stupid.*

5. Daniel Goleman, *Emotional Intelligence: Why It Can Matter More than IQ* (New York: Bantam Books, 1992).

6. Robert Sternberg, *Successful Intelligence: How Practical and Creative Intellience Determine Success in Life*.

7. Carla Hannaford, *Smart Moves: Why Learning Is Not All in Your Head, 2nd ed.*

8. P. Shaw et al., "Intellectual Ability and Cortical Development in Children and Adolescents," *Nature* 440 no. 30 (March 2006): 676–679.

9. Robert Sternberg, *Successful Intelligence*, p. 278.

10. Ibid, p. 78.

11. Pat Wolfe, *Brain Matters: Translating Research into Classroom Practice*.

    See also Sally Smith, *Live It, Learn It: The Academic Club Methodology for Students with Learning Disabilities and ADHD* (Baltimore: Paul H. Brookes, 2005).

    Many good sources for teachers are also available from www .ASCD.org.

Chapter 9. Stress

1. Jean M. Twenge, "The Age of Anxiety? Birth Cohort Change in Anxiety and Neuroticism, 1952–1993," *Journal of Personality and Social Psychology* 79 (December 2000).

2. David Elkind was quoted in "The Overscheduled Child?," *The Chronicle of Higher Education*, March 16, 2007.

3. Joseph LeDoux, *The Synaptic Self*, p. 226.

4. Stress survey was conducted by the American Psychological Association in partnership with the National Women's Health Resource Center, *Monitor on Psychology*, April 2006: 28–29.

5. *USA Today*, July 27, 2004.

6. Megan Gunnar and Karina Quevedo, "The Neurobiology of Stress and Development, *Annual Review of Psychology* 58 (January 2007): p. 173.

7. For a fascinating account of the brain's emotional needs in early life, please see Allan N. Schore, *Affect Regulation and the Origin of the Self: The Neurobiology of Emotional Development*.

    See also Sue Gerhardt, *Why Love Matters: How Affection Shapes a Baby's Brain* (New York: Routledge Publishers, 2004).

8. A. C. Dettling et al., "Quality of Care and Temperament Determine Whether Cortisol Levels Rise over the Day for Children in Full-Day Childcare," *Psychoneuroendicrinology* 25 (2000): 819–836.

9. B. Bos and J. Chapman, *Tumbling Over the Edge: A Rant for Children's Play* (Roseville, CA: Turn the Page Press, 2005), p. viii.

10. Mel Levine, *A Mind at a Time*, p. 23.

11. Ibid, p. 23.

12. M. Csikszentmihalyi et al., *Talented Teenagers: The Roots of Success and Failure* (New York: Cambridge University Press, 1993), p. 10.

13. As of this writing, a federal program called Response to Intervention (RTI) is being adopted by many states in the United States, although it is up to each district to determine exactly how it will be implemented. I suggest you consult current, local news sources and school personnel for more information about how this potentially revolutionary concept is working (or not) in your local area.

14. Alice Miller, *The Drama of the Gifted Child: The Search for the True Self* (New York: Basic Books, 1996). (I was amused to note that this subtitle has been changed from that of my original copy, which was *How Narcissistic Parents Form and Deform the Emotional Lives of Their Talented Children.* The publishers no doubt reasoned that making parents feel even guiltier than they already do was probably not a very good way to sell books.)

15. Amy Novotney, "The Price of Affluence," *Monitor on Psychology*, January 2009: 50.

16. David Brooks, "The Organization Kid," *The Atlantic*, April 2001: 40.

17. David McCullough, *John Adams* (New York: Simon & Schuster, 2008), p. 33.

Chapter 10. Brain-Cleaning 101

1. I spoke to Dr. Claire Coles at the Topical Medical Workshop of the Learning Disabilities Association of America (www.ldanatl.org) on March 17, 2004, in Atlanta, Georgia. The LDA has been very active in addressing the relationship between environmental toxins and learn-

ing problems; their annual conferences are excellent sources of information on this and many other topics related to learning disabilities.

2. Two reliable and practical books document the problem and offer constructive suggestions to parents and teachers interested in reducing toxic load in their children: Philip Landrigan, Herbert L. Needleman, and Mary M. Landrigan's *Raising Healthy Children in a Toxic World* and Christopher Gavigan's *Healthy Child Healthy World: Creating a Cleaner, Greener, Safer Home*.

   On the Web, see Learning Disabilities Association Project: www.healthychildrenproject.org; Institute for Children's Environmental Health: www.iceh.org; the Green Guide: www.thegreenguide.com (reviews potentially dangerous chemicals); and Physicians for Social Resposibility: www.psr.org.

3. Philip Landrigan, www.thelancet.com 368 (November 8, 2006).

4. Philip Landrigan et al., *Raising Healthy Children in a Toxic World*, p. 1.

5. Joel T. Nigg, *What Causes ADHD?*, p. 335.

6. Philip Landrigan et al., *Raising Healthy Children in a Toxic World*, p. 2.

7. Doris Rapp, *Is This Your Child?* and *Is This Your Child's World? How You Can Fix the Schools and Homes that Are Making Your Children Sick*.

8. From "Healthy Schools for Healthy Kids," *LDA Newsbriefs*, September/October 2007: 20.

9. This subject is so important that a recent journal featured several articles on the subject. See *Developmental Neuropsychology* 31 no. 3 (2007). The authors do not all agree, which is what keeps science interesting.

10. The international La Leche League (www.llli.org) offers information and resources about breast-feeding.

11. Theo Colborn, MD, personal communication, June 26, 2007.

12. Julie Bick, "Invisible Danger?," *New York Times*, March 12, 2006.

13. More detailed information about managing diet and learning problems is found in Scott Shannon's book *Please Don't Label My Child*.

14. One of many references supporting this linkage is Joel T. Nigg, *What Causes ADHD?*

15. Dr. Rapp spoke at the conference for the Aspen Center for New Medicine, Aspen, Colorado, February 8, 2002.

16. Joel Nigg, *What Causes ADHD?*, p. 278.

17. Dr. Herbert's remarks were quoted on www.ctv.ca/servlet/Article News, September 28, 2007.

18. Martha R. Herbert, "Autism: A Brain Disorder or a Disorder that Affects the Brain?," *Clinical Neurpsychiatry* 2 no. 6 (2006): 354–379.

19. L. M. Powell et al., "Nutritional Content of Television Food Advertisements Seen by Children and Adolescents in the United States," *Pediatrics* 120 (2007): 576–583.

20. "Food for Thought: Television Food Advertising to Children in the United States," Kaiser Family Foundation, March 28, 2007. Another source on increased children's food advertising: "Children's Exposure to TV Advertising in 1977 and 2004," Federal Trade Commission, June 1, 2007.

21. Diet soft drinks have long been suspected to be brain disruptors for susceptible people; Aspertame (NutriSweet, Equal) has been a particular bone of contention. A known brain antagonist for individuals with variants of PKU (see Chapter 7), it has also been reported to cause chronic headaches, seizures, and other symptoms (e.g., depressed mood, insomnia). Initial studies did not show significant brain effects in people without PKU, but more recent research is challenging what some see as a "whitewashing" of evidence. See, for example, P. Humphries et al., "Direct and Indirect Cellular Effects of Aspartame on the Brain," *European Journal of Clinical Nutrition* 62 (2008): 451–462.

22. The Web site of the American Academy of Pediatrics: www.aap.org/healthtopics/nutrition.cfm.

    Doris Rapp's *Is This Your Child?* is especially relevant if you think your child has food allergies.

    Scott Shannon's *Please Don't Label My Child* has a good section on nutrition with practical suggestions.

    Noted health columnist Jane Brody recommends David Ludwig's *Ending the Food Fight* (New York: Houghton Mifflin, 2008).

    M. C. Lapine's *The Sneaky Chef: Simple Strategies for Hiding Healthy Foods in Kids' Favorite Meals* (New York: Running Press, 2007).

    For children 4–8: C. Charney and D. Goldbecky *The ABC's of Fruits and Vegetables and Beyond* (New York: Ceres Press, 2007).

23. "What's the Lowdown on Sweeteners?" *New York Times*, February 12, 2006.

24. Michael Pollan, *In Defense of Food* (New York: Penguin Press, 2008.)

25. *AAP Grand Rounds*, cited in Tara-Parker Pope, "Weighing Nondrug Options for ADHD," *New York Times*, June 17, 2008.

26. *Health*, September 2008: 140–148.

27. Sir Michael Rutter describes this research in *Genes and Behavior: Nature-Nurture Interplay Explained*.

Chapter 11. Brain-Cleaning 102

1. The benefits of sleep are well recognized by scientists studying sleep patterns and sleep deprivation. They were summarized in an article in the *APA Monitor*, January 1, 2006: 56–57.

2. Jean E. Rhodes, "Sleepless in Chicago," *Child Development* 75 no. 1 (2004): 84–95. The follow-up interview appeared in *New York Times Science Times*, February 17, 2004.

3. *New York Times Science Times*, June 13, 2006.

4. Edward Tenner is the author of several books on technology and its consequences, e.g., *Why Things Bite: Technology and the Revenge of Unintended Consequences* (New York: Vintage, 1997).

5. My conversation with Dr. Mendelsohn took place on October 27, 2008.

6. Please see my books *Endangered Minds* and *Failure to Connect* for a thorough discussion of how various types of media affect brain development.

7. A useful book on managing television is Dimitri Christakis's *The Elephant in the Living Room* (Emmaus, PA: Rodale Press, 2006).

8. See, for example, Christakis et al., "Early Television Exposure and Subsequent Attentional Problems in Children," *Pediatrics* 115 no. 4 (2004): 708–713; and Jeffrey G. Johnson, "Television Viewing and the Development of Attention and Learning Difficulties During Adolescence," *Archives of Pediatrics and Adolescent Medicine* 161 (2007): 480–486.

9. Dan Anderson's research on the harmful effects of background TV on young children was published in *Child Development*, July/August 2008.

10. Society for Research in Child Development, press release, July 15, 2008.

11. Maryanne Wolf, *Proust and the Squid: the Story and Science of the Reading Brain*.

12. *Scientific American Mind*, October/November 2008: 44.

13. G. Dawson and R. Bernier, "Development of Social Brain Circuitry in Autism" in D. Coch, G. Dawson, and K. W. Fischer, *Human Behavior, Learning, and the Developing Brain: Atypical Development*, p. 40.

14. *Monitor on Psychology*, October 2008: 52.

15. Daniel Akst, "Raising the Bar: How Parents Can Fix Education," *Wall Street Journal*, August 29, 2008.

16. Dan Anderson's quote is from Tamar Lewin, "See Baby Touch a Screen, But Does Baby Get It?," *New York Times*, December 15, 2005.

17. "Television and the Family," http://aap.org/family/tv1.htm.

18. Selected reference for preventing video game addiction: Terry Waite, *Plugged In: A Clinicians' and Families' Guide to Online Video Game Addiction* (Frederick, MD: PublishAmerica, 2007).

    Olivia Bruner and Kurt Bruner, *Playstation Nation: Protect Your Child From Video Game Addiction* (Brentwood, TN: Center Street, 2006).

    Hilarie Cash and Kim McDaniel, *Video Games & Your Kids*.

19. Marcel Just's study was reported in Stephanie Dunnewind, "Multi-tasking—It's distracting." the *Seattle Times*, May 24, 2003. The study of inefficiency was conducted by Joshua Robinson, David Meyer, and Jeffrey Evans and published in the *Journal of Experimental Psychology: Human Perception and Performance* 27 no. 4 (2001).

Chapter 12.
Successful Environments for Successful Children

1. David Brooks, "Lost in the Crowd," *New York Times*, December 16, 2008.

2. A useful reference is Martha Bronson, *Self-Regulation in Early Child-hood: Nature and Nurture* (New York: Guilford, 2001).

3. Bruce Perry, *The Boy Who Was Raised as a Dog*, p. 134.

4. Dr. Moffitt's letter was published in the *Monitor on Psychology*, July/August 2004: 4.

5. Lise Eliot discusses the development of the auditory system in her book *What's Going on in There?* (Chapter 10).

6. Michael Merzenich was quoted in the online magazine of the University of California San Francisco, December 2004, http://pub.ucsf.edu.

7. Jane Brody, "Personal Health," *New York Times*, December 9, 2008.

8. This study, published in *Lancet*, June 4, 2005, was reported in the *New York Times* on June 14, 2005.

9. M. E. Schmidt et al., "The Effects of Background Television on the Toy Play Behavior of Very Young Children," *Child Development* 79 no. 4 (2008): 874–892.

10. William Bor et al., "The Effects of the Triple P-Positive Parenting Program on Preschool Children with Co-occurring Disruptive Behavior and Attentional/Hyperactive Difficulties," *Journal of Abnormal Child Psychology* 30 no. 6 (2002): 571–587.

11. "Tools of the Mind" are described in a book of the same name, found in the Bibliography. The program can also be referenced at: ies.ed.gov/ncee/wwc/reports/early_ed/tools.

12. Carol Dweck, "The Secret to Raising Smart Kids," *Scientific American Mind*, December 2007/January 2008: 37–41.

13. Ibid, p. 38.

14. Kathy Hopkins's book is called *Teaching How to Learn in a What-to-Learn Culture*.

15. *Monitor on Psychology*, October, 2003: 23.

16. Ibid.

17. For a full explanation of this research see J. Healy, *Endangered Minds: Why Our Children Don't Learn and What We Can Do About It*.

18. Susan H. Landry et al., "The Importance of Parenting During Early

Childhood for School-Age Development," *Developmental Neuropsychology* 24 nos. 2 and 3 (2003): 559–591.

19. Dr. Isquith is a researcher at Dartmouth College and developer of the "BRIEF" (Behavior Rating Inventory of Executive Function). He told this story at the Courage to Risk conference, Colorado Springs, January 25, 2008.

20. *Brain Gym* is trademarked by the Educational Kinesiology Foundation, Ventura, California.

21. Carla Hannaford, *Smart Moves*, p. 235.

22. Antonio Damasio, *Looking for Spinoza: Joy, Sorrow, and the Feeling Brain*, p. 12.

23. James J. Knierem, "The Matrix in Your Head," *Scientific American Mind*, June/July 2007: 44–49.

24. *BrainWorks*, January/February 2006: 4.

25. John Ratey, *SPARK*, p. 53.

26. This study was reported by Dr. Sanjay Gupta on CNN, November 29, 2008.

27. Refer back to Chapter 3, "What Should We Call This?," and to the work of Carol Kranowitz, including *The Out-of-Sync Child*.

28. Sylvia Richardson, "Early Diagnosis of Learning Disabilities," paper presented at the annual conference of the International Dyslexia Association, Dallas, Texas, November 1, 2007.

29. Wright's comments about video game design were quoted in "Game Master," *The New Yorker*, November 6, 2006: 90–99.

30. B. Bos and J. Chapman, *Tumbling Over the Edge: A Rant for Children's Play* (Roseville, CA: Tun the Page Press, 2005), p. xii.

31. See, for example, Tara Parker-Pope. "The 3 R's? A Fourth is Critical, Too: Recess, *New York Times*, February 24, 2009, p. D5.

32. See, for example, Daniel Levitin, *This Is Your Brain on Music: The Science of a Human Obsession* (New York: Dutton, 2006).

33. The term *cafeteria of experience* came to me long ago from Marian Diamond, who is cited in my book *Your Child's Growing Mind*.

34. Research on mindfulness and its effects was summarized in Roger

Walsh and S. L. Shapiro, "The Meeting of Meditative Disciplines and Western Psychology," *American Psychologist*, April 2006: 227–239; and in Michelle Andrews, "How to Beat Stress and Angst Through Meditation," *U.S. News & World Report*, March 2, 2009 (http://health.usnews .com/articles/health/living-well-usn).

35. Eckhard Tolle, *The Power of Now* (New York: New World Library, 2004).

BIBLIOGRAPHY

Attwood, Tony. *The Complete Guide to Asperger's Syndrome*. London: Jessica Kingsley Publishers, 2008.

Bearer, E. L. "Behavior as Influence and Result of the Genetic Program." In C. G. Coll et al. *Nature and Nurture: The Complex Interplay of Genetic and Environmental Influences on Human Behavior and Development*. Mahwah, NJ: LEA, 2004.

Birsh, Judith R. *Multisensory Teaching of Basic Language Skills*, 2nd ed. Baltimore: Paul H. Brookes Publishing Co., 2005.

Bodrova, Elena, and Deborah Leong. *Tools of the Mind: The Vygotskian Approach to Early Childhood Education*, 2nd ed. New York: Prentice Hall, 2006.

Bos, Bev, and Jenny Chapman. *Tumbling Over the Edge—A Rant for Children's Play*. Roseville, CA: Turn the Page Press, Inc., 2005.

Brazelton, T. Berry, and Stanley I. Greenspan. *The Irreducible Needs of Children*. Cambridge, MA: Da Capo Press, 2000.

Caine, Renate N., and Geoffrey Caine. *Making Connections: Teaching and the Human Brain*. New York: Dale Seymour Publications, 1999.

Cash, Hilarie, and Kim McDaniel. *Video Games & Your Kids*. Enumclaw, WA: Idyll Arbor, 2008.

Caspi, A., et al., "Influence of Life Stress on Depression: Moderation by a Polymorphism in the 5-HTT Gene." *Science* 301 no. 5631 (2003): 386–389.

Ceci, Stephen J. "Cast in Six Ponds and You'll Reel in Something: Looking Back on 25 Years of Research." *American Psychologist*, November 2003.

Coch, Donna, Geraldine Dawson, and Kurt W. Fischer. *Human Behavior, Learning, and the Developing Brain: Atypical Development*. New York: Guilford Press, 2007.

————. *Human Behavior, Learning, and the Developing Brain: Typical Development*. New York: Guilford Press, 2007.

Coll, C. G., E. L. Bearer, and R. M. Lerner, eds. *Nature and Nurture: The Complex Interplay of Genetic and Environmental Influences on Human Behavior and Development*. Mahwah, NJ: LEA, 2004.

Damasio, Antonio. *Looking for Spinoza: Joy, Sorrow, and the Feeling Brain*. Orlando: Harcourt, 2003.

Dawson, Peg, and Richard Guare. *Smart but Scattered: The Revolutionary "Executive Skills" Approach to Helping Kids Reach Their Potential*. New York: Guilford Press, 2009.

Dweck, Carol. *Mindset: The New Psychology of Success*. New York: Ballantine Books, 2007.

Edelman, Gerald M. *Bright Air, Brilliant Fire: On the Matter of the Mind*. New York: Basic Books, 1992.

Egan, Amy, et al. *Is It a Big Problem or a Little Problem? When to Worry, When Not to Worry, and What to Do*. New York: St. Martin's, 2007.

Eliot, Lise. *What's Going on in There? How the Brain and Mind Develop in the First Five Years of Life*. New York: Bantam, 2000.

Fletcher, Jack M., et al. *Learning Disabilities: From Identification to Intervention*. New York: Guilford, 2007.

Gardner, Howard. *Frames of Mind: The Theory of Multiple Intelligences*. New York: Basic Books, 1993.

Gavigan, Christopher. *Healthy Child, Healthy World: Creating a Cleaner, Greener, Safer Home*. New York: Dutton, 2008.

Gladwell, Malcolm. *Outliers: The Story of Success*. Boston: Little, Brown & Co., 2008.

Goldberg, Elkhonon. *The Executive Brain: Frontal Lobes and the Civilized Mind*. Oxford: Oxford University Press, 2001.

Grandin, Temple. *The Way I See It: A Personal Look at Autism & Asperger's*. Arlington, TX: Future Horizons, 2008.

Greenough, W., K. Black, and C. Wallace. "Experience and Brain Development." *Child Development* 58 (1987): 539–559.

Greenspan, Stanley I., and Stuart G. Shanker. *The First Idea: How Symbols, Language, and Intelligence Evolved from Our Primate Ancestors to Modern Humans*. Cambridge, MA: Da Capo Press, 2004.

Greenspan, Stanley I., and Serena Wieder. *Engaging Autism: Using the Floortime Approach to Help Children Relate, Communicate, and Think.* Cambridge, MA: Da Capo Lifelong Books, 2009.

Gurian, Michael. *Nurture the Nature: Understanding and Supporting Your Child's Unique Core Personality.* San Francisco: Jossey-Bass, 2007.

Hallowell, Edward M., and John J. Ratey. *Delivered from Distraction.* New York: Ballantine Books, 2006.

Hallowell, Edward M. *CrazyBusy: Overstretched, Overbooked, and About to Snap!* New York: Ballantine Books, 2007.

Hallowell, Edward M., and Peter S. Jensen. *Superparenting for ADD: An Innovative Approach to Raising Your Distracted Child.* New York: Ballantine Books, 2008.

Hannaford, Carla. *Smart Moves: Why Learning Is Not All in Your Head,* 2nd ed. Salt Lake City: Great River Books, 2005.

Healy, Jane M. *Your Child's Growing Mind: Brain Development and Learning from Birth to Adolescence,* 3rd ed. New York: Doubleday, 2004.

———. *Endangered Minds: Why Children Don't Think and What We Can Do About It.* New York: Simon & Schuster, 1999.

———. *Failure to Connect: How Computers Affect Our Children's Minds and What We Can Do About It.* New York: Simon & Schuster, 1998.

Herrnstein, R. J., and C. Murray. *The Bell Curve: Intelligence and Class Structure in American Life.* New York: Free Press, 1994.

Hopkins, Kathleen R. *Teaching How to Learn in a What-to-Learn Culture.* Hoboken, NJ: Jossey-Bass, 2010.

Jensen, Peter S., et al. *Toward a New Diagnostic System for Child Psychopathology: Moving Beyond the DSM.* New York: Guilford Press, 2006.

Johnson, Steven. *Everything Bad Is Good for You: How Today's Popular Culture Is Actually Making Us Smarter.* New York: Riverhead, 2005.

Kagan, Jerome. "A Behavioral Science Perspective." In Plomin, Robert, et al. *Behavioral Genetics in the Postgenomic Era.* Washington, DC: American Psychological Association, 2004.

Klin, Ami, Fred R. Volkmar, and Sara S. Sparrow, eds., *Asperger Syndrome.* New York: Guilford Press, 2000.

Kohn, Alfie. *Punished by Rewards.* New York: Houghton Mifflin, 1993.

Kranowitz, Carol S. *The Out-of-Sync Child: Recognizing and Coping with Sensory Processing Disorder*, 2nd ed. New York: Perigee, 2005.

———, and Joye Newman. *Growing an In-Sync Child*. New York: Perigee, 2010.

Kuhl, P. S., et al. "Linguistic Experience Alters Phonetic Perception in Infants by Six Months of Age." *Science* 255 (1992): 606–608.

Landrigan, Philip, Herbert L. Needleman, and Mary M. Landrigan. *Raising Healthy Children in a Toxic World*. Emmaus, PA: Rodale Press, 2008.

Landry, Susan, ed. "The Biological and Social Determinants of Child Development." *Developmental Neuropsychology: Special Issue* 24 nos. 2 and 3 (2003).

Lavoie, Richard. *The Motivation Breakthrough*. New York: Touchstone, 2007.

———. *It's So Much Work to Be Your Friend*. New York: Touchstone, 2006.

LeDoux, Joseph. *Synaptic Self: How Our Brains Become Who We Are*. New York: Viking, 2002.

Levine, Mel. *The Myth of Laziness*. New York: Simon & Schuster, 2003.

———. *A Mind at a Time*. New York: Simon & Schuster, 2002.

Lesch, K. Peter. "Neuroticism and Serotonin: A Developmental Genetic Perspective." In Plomin, Robert, et al. *Behavioral Genetics in the Postgenomic Era*. Washington, DC: American Psychological Association, 2004.

Louv, Richard. *Last Child in the Woods: Saving Our Children From Nature-Deficit Disorder*. Chapel Hill: Algonquin Books, 2005.

McClelland, James L, and Robert S. Siegler. *Mechanisms of Cognitive Development: Behavioral and Neural Perspectives*. Mahwah, NJ: LEA, 2001.

Meltzer, Lynn. *Executive Function in Education*. New York: Guilford Press, 2007.

Mendelsohn, James. *A Parent's Guide to Tutors and Tutoring*. San Francisco: Jossey-Bass, 2008.

Miller, Edward, and Joan Almon. *Crisis in the Kindergarten: Why Children Need to Play in School*. College Park, MD: Alliance for Childhood, 2009.

Miller, Lucy J., and Doris A. Fuller, *Sensational Kids: Hope and Help for Children with Sensory Processing Disorder*. New York: Perigee, 2007.

Molfese, D. L., V. J. Molfese, S. Key, and A. Modglin. "Reading and Cognitive Abilities: Longitudinal Studies of Brain and Behavior Changes in Young Children." *Annals of Dyslexia* 52, 99–111 (2002).

Molfese, D. L., V. J. Molfese, A. F. Key, and S. D. Kelly. "Influence of Environment on Speech-Sound Discrimination: Findings from a Longitudinal Study." *Developmental Neuropsychology*, 24 nos. 2 and 3 (2003): 541–558.

Monastra, Vincent J. *Parenting Children With ADHD: 10 Lessons That Medicine Cannot Teach*. Washington, DC: American Psychological Association, 2004.

———. *Unlocking the Potential of Patients with ADHD: A Model for Clinical Practice*. Washington, DC: American Psychological Association, 2007.

Nemeroff, Charles B., et al. "Differential Responses to Psychotherapy Versus Pharmacotherapy in Patients with Chronic Forms of Major Depression and Childhood Trauma." *Proceedings of the National Academy of Sciences* 100 no. 24 (November 25, 2003): 14293–14296.

Nigg, Joel T. *What Causes ADHD? Understanding What Goes Wrong and Why*. New York: Guilford Press, 2006.

Olfman, Sharna, ed. *Bipolar Children*. Westport, CT: Praeger, 2007.

———. *No Child Left Different*. Westport, CT: Praeger, 2006.

Owen, Michael J., and Michael C. O'Donovan. "Schizophrenia and Genes." In Plomin, Robert, et al. *Behavioral Genetics in the Postgenomic Era*. Washington, DC: American Psychological Association, 2004.

Ozonoff, Sally, Geraldine Dawson, and James McPartland. *A Parent's Guide to Asperger Syndrome & High-Functioning Autism: How to Meet the Challenges and Help Your Child Thrive*. New York: Guilford Press, 2002.

Palombo, Joseph. *Nonverbal Learning Disabilities: A Clinical Perspective*. New York: W.W. Norton & Co., 2006.

Papanicolaou, A. C., et al. "Brain Mechanisms for Reading in Children With and Without Dyslexia: A Review of Studies of Normal Development and Plasticity." *Developmental Neuropsychology* 24 nos. 2 and 3 (2003): 593–612.

Pearce, Joseph Chilton. *Magical Child*. New York: Plume, 1992.

Pennington, Bruce. *Diagnosing Learning Disorders: A Neuropsychological Framework*, 2nd ed. New York: Guilford Press, 2008.

————. *The Development of Psychopathology: Nature and Nurture*. New York: Guilford Press, 2002.

Perry, Bruce D., and Maia Szalavitz. *The Boy Who Was Raised as a Dog*. New York: Basic Books, 2007.

Pert, Candace B. *Molecules of Emotion: The Science Behind Mind-Body Medicine*. New York: Simon & Schuster, 1999.

Plomin, Robert et al. *Behavioral Genetics in the Postgenomic Era*. Washington, DC: American Psychological Association, 2003.

Ponitz, Claire Cameron, et al. "A structured observation of behavioral self-regulation and its contribution to kindergarten outcomes." *Developmental Psychology 45* no. 3 (May 2009): 605–619.

Posner, Michael I., and Mary K. Rothbart. *Educating the Human Brain*. Washington, DC: American Psychological Association, 2006.

Posner, Michael I. "Educating the Developing Brain." Invited address, American Psychological Association Annual Convention, Toronto, August 9, 2003.

Rapp, Doris. *Is This Your Child's World? How Schools and Homes Are Making Our Children Sick*. New York: Bantam, 1997.

————. *Is This Your Child?* New York: Harper, 1992.

Ratey, John. *SPARK: The Revolutionary New Science of Exercise and the Brain*. Boston: Little, Brown and Co., 2008.

Reid, Gavin. *Dyslexia: A Complete Guide for Parents*. Chichester, England: John Wiley & Sons, 2005.

Ridley, Matt. *Nature via Nurture: Genes, Experience, and What Makes Us Human*. New York: HarperCollins, 2003.

Roberts, Elizabeth J. *Should You Medicate Your Child's Mind?* New York: Marlowe & Co., 2006.

Robinson, Gene E. "The Behavior of Genes." *New York Times*, December 13, 2004.

Rosenzweig, Mark R. "Effects of Differential Experience on the Brain and Behavior." *Developmental Neuropsychology 24* nos. 2 and 3 (2003): 523–540.

Rourke, Byron P. *Syndrome of Nonverbal Learning Disabilities*. New York: Guilford Press, 1989.

Russo, E. "Researchers Find No Clear Paths on Road to Unraveling Schizophrenia." *The Scientist* 16 no. 2: 30–31.

Rutter, Sir Michael. *Genes and Behavior: Nature–Nurture Interplay Explained*. Oxford: Blackwell Publishing, 2006.

Sax, Leonard. *Boys Adrift: The Five Factors Driving the Growing Epidemic of Unmotivated Boys and Underachieving Young Men*. New York: Basic Books, 2009.

Schlaug, Gottfried. "The Brain of Musicians: A Model for Functional and Structural Adaptation." *Annals New York Academy of Sciences* 930 (2001): 281–299.

Schore, Allan. *Affect Regulation and the Origin of the Self: The Neurobiology of Emotional Development*. Mahwah, NJ: LEA, 1999.

Seligman, Martin E. P. *Authentic Happiness*. New York: Simon & Schuster, 2002.

———. *The Optimistic Child: A Proven Program to Safeguard Children Against Depression and Build Lifelong Resilience*. New York: Harper Paperbacks, 1996.

Shannon, Scott M., and Emily Heckman. *Please Don't Label My Child: Break the Doctor-Diagnosis-Drug Cycle and Discover Safe, Effective Choices for Your Child's Emotional Health*. New York: Rodale, 2007.

Shaywitz, Sally. *Overcoming Dyslexia: A New and Complete Science-Based Program for Reading Problems at Any Level*. New York: Knopf, 2003.

Shonkoff, J. P., and D. A. Phillips, eds. *From Neurons to Neighborhoods: The Science of Early Childhood Education*. Washington, DC: National Academy Press, 2000.

Siegel, Bryna. *Getting the Best for Your Child with Autism*. New York: Guilford Press, 2008.

Siegel, Daniel J. *The Developing Mind: How Relationships and the Brain Interact to Shape Who We Are*. New York: Guilford Press, 1999.

Silverman, Stephan M., and Rich Weinfeld. *School Success for Kids With Asperger's Syndrome: A Practical Guide for Parents and Teachers*. Waco, TX: Prufrock Press, 2007.

Solitano, Mary V., Amy F. T. Arnsten, and F. Xavier Castellanos, eds. *Stimulant Drugs and ADHD: Basic and Clinical Neuroscience*. Oxford: Oxford University Press, 2001.

Sternberg, Robert J., and Elena L. Grigorenko. *Our Labeled Children: What Every Parent and Teacher Needs to Know About Learning Disabilities.* Cambridge, MA: Da Capo Press, 2000.

Sternberg, Robert J. *Successful Intelligence: How Practical and Creative Intellience Determine Success in Life.* New York: Plume, 1997.

Sternberg, Robert, ed. *Why Smart People Can Be So Stupid.* New Haven: Yale University Press, 2003.

Suomi, Steven J. "How Gene-Environment Interactions Influence Emotional Development in Rhesus Monkeys." In C. G. Coll, E. L. Bearer, and R. M. Lerner, eds., *Nature and Nurture: The Complex Interplay of Genetic and Environmental Influences on Human Behavior and Development.* Mahwah, NJ: LEA, 2004.

Swanson, H. Lee, Karen R. Harris, and Steve Graham, eds. *Handbook of Learning Disabilities.* New York: Guilford Press, 2003.

Wachs, Theodore D. *Necessary But Not Sufficient: The Respective Roles of Single and Multiple Influences on Individual Development.* Washington, DC: American Psychological Association, 2000.

Watson, John B. *Psychological Care of Infant and Child.* New York: W.W. Norton & Co., 1928 (out of print).

Weaver, Ian C. G., et al. "Epigenetic Programming by Maternal Behavior." *Nature Neuroscience* 7 (June 2004): pp. 849–854.

West, Thomas G. *In the Mind's Eye: Visual Thinkers, Gifted People with Dyslexia and Other Learning Difficulties, Computer Images and the Ironies of Creativity.* New York: Prometheus Books, 2009.

Wilens, Timothy. *Straight Talk about Psychiatric Medications for Kids,* 3rd ed. New York: Guilford Press, 2008.

Wiseman, Nancy. *Could It Be Autism? A Parent's Guide to the First Signs and Next Steps.* New York: Broadway Books, 2007.

Wolf, Maryanne. *Proust and the Squid: The Story and Science of the Reading Brain.* New York: Harper Perennial, 2008.

Wolfe, Patricia. *Brain Matters: Translating Research into Classroom Practice.* Alexandria, VA: ASCD, 2001.

Zull, James E. *The Art of Changing the Brain.* Sterling, VA: Stylus, 2002.

INDEX

Abnormal auditory perception, 51
Absence seizure disorder, 88
Abused and neglected children, 131–33,
    156, 249
Adams, John, 270
Adderall, 17, 26, 49, 146, 151, 155,
    158
Addiction, 157, 185
    to media, 298, 309, 310, 315
Adolescence
    brain chemistry in, 158, 165
    brain development in, 110, 123, 262
    exposure to violence in, 244
    learning styles in, 233
    media use in, 297, 307–8
    parental overemphasis on
        accomplishments in, 269
    sleep habits in, 294, 296
    study skills in, 218
Adoption studies, 62, 203, 211
Adrenal gland, 244
    see also HPA axis
Akst, Daniel, 306
Albert Einstein College of Medicine,
    145
Alcohol, 98, 99, 277
Alexia, 14
Alleles, 183
Allergies, 35, 37, 251, 257, 258
    environmental toxins triggering,
        279
    food, 284–85
Alliance for Childhood, 250, 341, 359
Almon, Joan, 250, 341
Alternative schooling, 242, 264–68
Alzheimer's disease, 183, 274
American Academy of Pediatrics, 307
American Camp Association, 17
American Medical Associaiton, 86
American Psychological Association, 148,
    151, 165, 242–43
American Speech-Language-Hearing
    Association, 359, 363n2
Amphetamine, 158
    see also Adderall
Amygdala, 246, 248
Analytic intelligence, 213

Anderson, Daniel, 300, 307
Angular gyrus, 108, 117
Animal studies
    of brain chemistry, 156–57
    of brain "rewiring," 139
    of diet, 289
    of enculturation, 331, 332
    of gene-environment interaction, 184,
        189–90, 200–203
    of medications, 159
    of oxytocin, 100
    of single-gene disorders, 205
Antidepressants, 151
Antipsychotics, 18
Anxiety, 166, 201, 205
    adolescent, 269
    brain chemistry and, 153, 157
    brain structures mobilized by, 102–3
    parental, 251
    during pregnancy, 99–100
    sleep habits and, 295
    test, 127, 152, 153, 215–18, 246
    treatment of, 146
Applied behavior analysis (ABA), 69–70,
    127
Apraxia, 14
Artificial sweeteners, 288, 377n20
Arts, experiences with, 317, 343–44
Aspartame, 288, 377n20
Asperger's syndrome, 12, 16, 18, 57, 66,
    73–75, 107, 207, 351
    brain development and, 107
    case example of, 23–25
    diagnosis of, 50
    genetic factors in, 68, 193, 196
    hyperlexia in, 24, 64
    media use and, 297–98, 303
    social-emotional learning impairment
        and, 81
    special talents in, 10
    treatment of, 74–75
Association areas, 108–9
Association of Educational Therapists
    (AET), 359
Astrocytes, 113
Atlantic, 269
Attachment, insecure, 71

Attention deficit disorder (ADD), 10, 12, 58, 83, 162, 196, 275, 351, 352
  brain development in, 104
  conditions mimicking, 55
  diagnosis of, 83
  dyslexia and, 60
  environmental toxins and, 275
  media use and, 298–300
  medications prescribed for, 17, 46
  temperament and, 199
Attention deficit/hyperactivity disorder (ADHD), 14, 28, 83–88, 255, 320, 334, 351, 352, 362n17
  brain development in, 104
  case example of, 26–27
  diagnosis of, 17, 37, 83, 84
  diet and, 284, 285, 290
  dyscalculia and, 79
  genetic factors in, 198
  media use and, 301
  motor planning and, 339
  petit mal epilepsy misdiagnosed as, 90
  "pseudo-," 47
  stress and, 243
  treatment of, 17, 84–85, 136, 147, 150, 157–59, 162–65, 167, 323, 369n8
Attention process therapy, 146, 148
Attribution theory, 329–33
Auditory cortex, 139
Auditory processing difficulties, 8, 59, 212, 350
Australia, 328
Authentic Happiness (Seligman), 173
Autism, 12, 14–16, 25, 50, 64, 66–73, 186, 351, 362n17
  brain development in, 97, 104, 114, 120, 132
  diagnosis of, 68–69
  early warning signs of, 43
  environmental factors in, 71–72
  epigenetic changes in, 184
  genetic factors in, 196
  hyperlexia in, 24, 63–64
  "refrigerator mothers" blamed for, 191
  rising rates of, 18–19, 71
  sensory experience in, 324
  treatment of, 69–70, 114, 127
Autism Society of America, 68, 359
Autism Speaks, 359
Autistic spectrum disorders (ASD), 14–15, 67, 69, 74, 275, 298, 351
  brain development in, 119
  definition of, 14–15
  environmental toxins and, 275
  genetic factors in, 68, 72, 74
  hyperlexia in, 63–65
  media use and, 298, 302–3
  prenatal and perinatal influences in, 100
  see also Asperger's syndrome; Autism

Basal ganglia, 104, 110, 157
Behavioral genetics and genomics, 178, 188
Behavioral therapies, 127, 146–49, 162, 191
  medications and, 166–67
  see also specific therapies
Bell, Nanci, 61
Bernier, Raphael, 303
Best Moments, 173
Beta waves, 141
Beth Israel Hospital (Boston), Dyslexia Research Laboratory, 221
Biological functions, brain regions governing, 101
Biological reductionism, 145, 189
Bipolar disorder, 15, 17, 18, 46, 159, 370n11
Birth complications, 35, 76
Blood-brain barrier, 276, 284
Blood sugar, 284, 288
Bonding, 202–3, 282
  lack of, 249, 252
Bos, Bev, 254, 324, 340
Bottle-feeding, 281–82
Boys Adrift (Sax), 17, 159
Boysen, Sally, 331
Boy Who Was Raised as a Dog, The (Perry), 131
Brain, 71–72, 95–123
  cell systems of, 111–14
  chemistry of, *see* Brain chemistry
  connectivity in, 96, 113–19
  gender differences in, 97, 115, 120, 122–23
  genes and, 192–98
  imaging techniques for, 126, 136–38, 140–45
  impact of stress on, 244–51
  injuries to, 124, 130–31, 135
  mapping, 101–11
  prenatal development of, 96–100
  "rewiring," *see* Neuroplasticity

spatial organizers in, 336
see also specific brain structures
Brain chemistry, 151–57
  diet and, 283
  medications and, 150–52, 155–68
  motivation and, 168–76
  stress and, 244, 249–50
  see also Neurotransmitters
Brain-derived neurotrophic factor
    (BDNF), 336, 337
Brain-energizing movement activities,
    217
Brain Gym, 217, 334
Brain Matters (Wolfe), 234
Brainstem, 101
"Brainstorms," 88
Brazelton, Barry, 20
Brazil, 214
Breast-feeding, 281
Brody, Jane, 326
Brooks, David, 269, 318
Brown, Lucy, 145
Brown University, 68
Bullying, 252

Caine, Renata and Geoffrey, 246
Calculation, problems in, 78
California, University of, Los Angeles
    (UCLA), 120
  School of Medicine, 177
Carnegie Mellon University, 114,
    136
  Center for Cognitive Brain Imaging,
    313
Cass Business School, 9
Catecholamines, 200
Caulfield, Barbara, 185
Center for Disease Control, 361n3
Central auditory processing disorder
    (CAPD), 59, 350, 363n
Cerebellum, 104–5, 112, 184
Cerebral cortex, 101, 105–7
Cerebral palsy, 135
Cerebrodiversity, 208, 221–37
  learning style and, 209, 229–36
  talents and, 224–20
Chapman, Jenny, 254, 324, 340
Checklist for Autism in Toddlers (CHAT),
    67
Chemicals, toxic, *see* Toxins
Child Trauma Academy, 157, 367n10
Chimpanzees, 331

Chromosomes, 183
  abnormal, 186
Chugani, Harry, 132
Classroom modifications, 127
Clinical Pediatrics, 164
Clumsy child syndrome, 75
Cocaine, 157
Cod liver oil, 112–13
Cognitive behavioral therapy (CBT), 102,
    127, 146, 247
Cognitive reserve, 272–74
  sleep and, 293
Cognitive style, 231
Coles, Claire, 271
Columbia University, 49, 100
Comorbidity, 12
Compulsive behavior, 247
Computer software, specialized, 127
Computer use, *see* Media use
Concerta, 158
Concordia University, 17
Conduct disorders, 17, 18, 28, 199, 205,
    352
Connectivity, 96, 118–19, 125, 135, 149
  functional, 113–17
  gene expression and, 190
  imaging of, 144
Contingent caregiving, 182
Contingent response, 71
Copernicus, 305
Corpus callosum, 108, 115
Cortisol, 244, 249
*Could It Be Autism: A Parent's Guide to
    the First Signs and Next Steps*
    (Wiseman), 67
Coulter, Dee, 247
CrazyBusy (Hallowell), 314
Creative intelligence, 213
Crisis in the Kindergarten (Alliance for
    Childhood), 341
Cross-cultural studies, 200
Crystallized intelligence, 214, 215
Csikszentmilhalyi, Mihaly, 257
Cystic fibrosis, 186

Damasio, Antonio, 213, 335
Dawson, Geraldine, 303
Dawson, Peg, 328
Decoding, 60
Denckla, Martha, 47
Denmark, 20
Deoxyribonucleic acid (DNA), 182–84, 201

Depression, 166, 190, 343, 362*n*17
  adolescent, 269
  brain chemistry and, 157, 173
  childhood, 15, 17, 198
  epigenetic changes in, 184
  postpartum, 106
  during pregnancy, 99
  temperament and, 198, 201, 337
  treatment of, 127, 146, 156, 161, 247
Determinism, genetic, 191
Developing Mind, The (Siegel), 71
Developmental coordination disorder, 350
Developmental dyspraxia, 75
Developmental language disorder, 59
Developmental milestones, delayed,
  35–36, 43
Developmental readiness, 220, 261–63
Diabetes, 98, 185
*Diagnostic and Statistical Manual of
  Mental Disorders (DSM)* (American
  Psychiatric Association), 49–50,
  362*n*3
Diamond, Adele, 86, 87
Diamond, Marian, 117
Diet, 7, 161, 185, 272, 282–91
  brain development and, 112–13
  neurotransmitters and, 156
  phenylketonuria and, 188
  during pregnancy, 98, 189, 197
  schools and, 280, 287, 289
  test anxiety and, 216
Differential diagnosis, 52–56, 212
Diffusion tensor imaging (DTI), 115, 140,
  144
Dioxins, 277
Discipline techniques, 329
Disinhibition, 199
Divorce, 251
DNA, 182–84, 201
Dopamine, 110, 153, 156–59, 200, 203, 276
Dorsal axis, 111
Down's syndrome, 186
Downshifting, 244–46, 248
Drama of the Gifted Child, The (Miller),
  268
Drug Enforcement Administration (DEA),
  159
Drugs
  abuse of, *see* Substance abuse
  over-the-counter, 278
  psychotropic, *see* Medications
Duke University, 18

Dweck, Carol, 329–30
Dyscalculia, 12–13, 78–80, 350, 321–22
Dysgraphia, 350
Dyslexia, 9, 60–63, 194–96, 210, 221, 222,
  268, 349
  achievement and, 212–13
  brain development in, 112, 142
  case examples of, 21–23, 321–22
  diagnosis of, 37, 53, 58
  dyscalculia and, 79
  environmental factors in, 128
  executive function disorder mimicked
    by, 47
  genetic factors in, 23, 186, 193
  media use and, 297
  prevention of, 62–63
  treatment of, 58, 61–63, 136–40
  visual, 61
Dyslexia: A Complete Guide for Parents
  (Reid), 61

Echolalic speech, 43
Edelman, Gerald, 130
Edinburgh, University of, 61
Educating the Human Brain (Posner), 148
Education, U.S. Department of, 16
Egan, Amy, 48, 354
Einstein, Albert, 116–19, 339
Electroencephalogram (EEG), 89–90, 140,
  141
Electromagnetic radiation, 278, 279
Eli Lilly and Company, 150
Eliot, Lise, 98
Elkind, David, 241
Emory University, 165
  School of Medicine, 271
Emotional abuse and neglect, 131–33
Emotional development, 5
  brain chemistry and, 154–57
  brain structures and, 101, 106–7
Emotional intelligence, 214
Emotional problems, 15, 17
  secondary to learning difficulties, 36,
    63, 139, 194–96, 220, 236–37
  stress and, 242
Enculturation, 331–33
Endangered Minds (Healy), 42
Engaging Autism (Greenspan), 70
Environmental factors, 19–28, 32, 47–48,
  177
  in attention deficit/hyperactivity
    disorder, 83, 85, 164–65

in autistic spectrum disorders, 68,
71–72, 74
in brain chemistry, 152
in brain circuitry, *see* Neuroplasticity
in brain development, 96–98
changes over time in, 178
in dyscalculia, 79
in dyslexia, 139
in executive function disorders, 86, 87
gender differences and, 103, 123
in intelligence, 211
interaction of genetics and, 179–80,
182, 184, 185, 189–92, 197, 203–4,
321, 373n25
in language development, 141, 193
in motivation, 168, 169
in oxytocin secretion, 100
prenatal, 197
in reading disorders, 62, 64, 66
in self-regulation, 318–21
in sensory processing disorder, 76
in temperament, 200–203
toxic, *see* Toxins
see also Lifestyle
Environmental therapies, 127
Epigenetic changes, 180, 184, 197, 289
Epilepsy, 88–91, 130–31
Epinephrine, 244
Equal, 288, 377n20
Essential fatty acids (EFAs), 112–13, 284
Event related potential (ERP), 140
Everything Bad Is Good for You (Johnson),
312
Evidence-based treatment, 58, 61, 69, 80
Evoked response, 141
Ewing-Cobbs, Linda, 131
Executive function disorders, 31, 79,
83–88, 160, 351
brain development and, 107, 110–11
case exaple of, 44–47
dyscalculia and, 79
treatment of, 85, 88
see also Attention deficit disorder;
Attention deficit/hyperactivity
disorder
Exercise, *see* Physical exercise
Expressive language disorder, 47, 59,
199
Extracellular space, 151
Extrinsic motivation, 170
Extroversion, 198, 199
Eye contact, avoidance of, 43

Failure to Connect (Healy), 231, 256, 309
Family history, 35
of language problems, 43, 64
see also Genetic factors
Fearfulness, 198
Federal Trade Commission (FTC), 287
Fight-or-flight response, 153, 244, 248
Finland, 20
First Signs, 359
Flame retardants, 277
Floor Time, 65, 69, 70, 114
Fluid intelligence, 214, 215
Focused prayer, 146
Folic acid, 98
Food, *see* Diet
Food additives, 288–90
Foreign languages, developmental
window for learning, 126
Formaldehyde, 277, 278
Fox, Nathan, 133
Fragile X syndrome, 186
Frames of Mind (Gardner), 213
Frontal cortex, 114
Frontal lobes, 96, 107, 109–11, 248
Functional connectivity, 113–17
Functional magnetic resonance imaging
(fMRI), 138, 140, 143–45
Fusiform face area, 106

"Garden variety" reading disorders,
65–66, 349
Gardner, Howard, 213, 229–31
Gender differences
in brain structure and function, 97, 115,
120, 122–23
enviromental factors and, 103, 123
Gene promotors, 190
Genes and Behavior (Rutter), 189, 321
Genetic factors, 4–5, 26, 32, 177–206
in attention deficit/hyperactivity
disorder, 83
in autistic spectrum disorders, 18, 68,
74
in brain chemistry, 152, 155, 165, 198
in brain development, 97, 112, 117,
192–98
diet and, 285–86, 289–90
in dyscalculia, 79
in dyslexia, 23, 61, 139
in executive function disorders, 86,
87
in intelligence, 211

Genetic factors (*cont.*)
  interaction of environment and, 19–20,
    179–80, 182, 184, 185, 189–92, 197,
    203–4, 291, 321, 373n25
  in language disorders, 59
  in learning styles, 235–36
  medications and, 13, 14
  neuroplasticity and, 125, 128
  in oxytocin secretion, 100
  in sensory processing disorder, 76
  in stress response, 249
  temperament and, 198–204
  toxins and, 276
Gifted and LD, 223
Gilger, Jeffrey, 142
Gladwell, Malcolm, 220
Glia, 113, 117
Goldin-Meadow, Susan, 192
Gonzaga University, 9
Grandin, Temple, 68, 69
Gray matter, 113
Green Guide, The, 360
Greenspan, Stanley, 20, 65, 69, 70, 114
Grid cells, 336
Guare, Richard, 328

Hallowell, Edward M., 85, 314
Handedness, 106
Handwriting, 76, 77, 116, 172, 219, 225, 227,
    234, 235, 285, 293, 311, 312, 339, 364
Hannaford, Carla, 335
Hargreaves, Andy, 29
Harm avoidance, 198, 199
Harvard University, 337
  Medical School, 285–86
Health Magazine, 289
Helplessness, learned, 172–73
Hemispheres, brain, 96, 105–7, 115
  integration of, 108
  multisensory teaching and changes in,
    136–38
  surgical removal of, 130–31
Herbert, Martha, 19, 285–86
Herbicides, 276–77, 279
Heredity, *see* Genetic factors
Hewitt, John, 178
Hippocampus, 135–36, 184, 246, 248, 337
Homeschooling, 237, 265–68
Hopkins, Kathy, 331
Hormones, 100, 103, 153, 154, 244
  diet and, 283
  medications and, 165

HPA axis, 244–46
*Human Behavior, Learning, and the
    Developing Brain* (Dawson and
    Bernier), 303
Hyperlexia, 24, 50, 63–65, 224, 349, 351
Hypervigilance, 248
Hypothalamus, 244
  see also HPA axis

Iacoboni, Marco, 120
Ideation, 305
Identical twins, 180, 196, 203, 211
Illinois, University of, Institute for Health
    Research and Policy, 287
Imaginative play, 86–87
Immune system, 152, 244
Impulsivity, 84, 87, 148, 198–200
In the Mind's Eye (West), 60
Incredible Years Programme, 359
Indoor air quality, 279–80, 360
Infants, 280–81, 322–23
  brain development in, 97, 119–21,
    128–29
  brain scans of, 141
  breast- versus bottle-feeding, 281–82
  media exposure of, 72–73, 297, 307
  movement experiences of, 335–36
  sensory experience of, 323
  stress in, 190–91, 249
Inhibition, 199
Insecure attachment, 71
Institute for Children's Environmental
    Health, 360
Instrinsic motivation, 169–70
Intelligence, 207–38
  attempts to "engineer," 129
  in attribution theory, 329–30
  cerebrodiversity and, 208, 221–37
  connectivity and, 96, 118, 144
  genetic versus environmental factors in,
    178
  of late bloomers, 218–21
  learning style and, 209, 229–36
  overcoming impact of severe
    maltreatment on, 133
  successful, 213–15
  testing, *see* IQ scores
International Dyslexia Association (IDA),
    61, 63, 360
Internet, 267, 355, 358
Intersubjectivity, 67
Introversion, 199

IQ scores, 207–13, 216, 223–25, 317
 attention process therapies and, 148
 brain structures and, 115
 environmental toxins and, 275
 executive function and, 110
 low-average, 51
 parental influence on, 204
Irreducible Needs of Children, The
  (Brazelton and Greenspan), 20
Isaacson, Walter, 116
Is It a Big Problem or a Little Problem?
  (Egan), 48, 354
Isquith, Peter, 333
It's So Much Work to Be Your Friend
  (Lavoie), 82–83
Ivy League universities, 269

Jensen, Peter S., 49
John Adams (McCullough), 270
Johnson, Steven, 312
*Journal of the American Medical
  Association (JAMA)*, 19
Just, Marcel, 114, 136–37, 139, 313

Kagan, Jerome, 204
Kaiser Family Foundation, 287
Kekulé, Friedrich, 303–4
Kilgard, Michael, 139
King's College London, 323
Kranowitz, Carol, 75
Kroupa, Nicole, 9

Labeling, 3, 4, 7, 10, 11, 32, 49–52, 57
Lancet, 275
Landrigan, P. J., 275
Language disorders, 8–9, 31, 59, 166, 350
 case examples of, 38–40, 43, 259
 executive function disorder mimicked
  by, 47
 genetic factors in, 192–93
 homeschooling and, 267
 media use and, 299, 301–2
 red flags for, 43–44
 see also Autism
Language skills, 40–42, 130, 338
 environmental factors in, 141, 193
 in Asperger's syndrome, 73, 74
Last Child in the Woods (Louv), 342–43
Late bloomers, 6, 46, 116, 218–21
Lavoie, Richard, 82–83
LDA Newsbriefs, 278
Learned helplessness, 172–73

Learning disabilities (LD), 11–12, 31, 223,
  224, 349–50
 brain development in, 97, 110, 115
 differences versus, 15
 gender differences in, 122
 movement activities and, 337
 neurodevelopmental, 32
 overdiagnosis of, 49–52
 overlapping, 160
 societal costs of, 16
 unrealistic expectations versus, 8–9
 untreated, stress of, 252
 see also specific disorders
Learning Disabilities Association (LDA),
  162, 271, 274, 278, 360, 375n1
Learning style, 209, 229–36
 arts and, 344
 media use and, 298
 self-regulation and, 328
Levin, Diane, 304
Levine, Mel, 57, 167, 255, 362n1
Lifestyle, 6, 162–65, 272, 282, 291–92
 in attention deficit/hyperactivity
  disorder, 85
 cognitive reserve and, 274
 during pregnancy, 97–98
 stressful, 242
 see also Diet; Sleep habits
Lilly, Cameron, 282
Limbic system, 101, 109, 135
 motivation and, 171
 prefrontal cortex and, 110
 right hemisphere and, 105
 stress and, 246
 test anxiety and, 217
Lindamood-Bell Learning Processes, 360,
  363n
Lipton, Meryl, 81
Logan, Julie, 9
Long-term potentiation, 129
Louv, Richard, 342–43
Low-average IQ, 51
Low birth weight babies, 35, 323
Lyon, Reid, 65

Magical Child (Pearce), 162
Magnetic source imaging (MSI), 141
Magnetoencephalography (MEG), 141
Magnocellular system, 97, 111–13
Making Connections (Caine), 246
March, John, 18
Maryland, University of, 18, 133

Massachusetts, University of, 294, 300
Massachusetts General Hospital, 19
Maternal warmth, 323
Mathematics, problems with, 193–94
  see also Dyscalculia
Mayberg, Helen, 146
McLean Hospital, 19
"Mean world" syndrome, 251
Media use, 7, 43, 55–56, 66, 173, 281,
  296–315
  attention deficit/hyperactivity disorder
    and, 86
  benefits of, 311–13
  brain development and, 120–21,
    130
  in dyscalculia treatment, 80
  dyslexia and, 61, 139, 140
  executive function disorders and, 87
  food advertising and, 287
  in infant care, 72–73, 297, 307
  limiting, 37, 45–46
  multitasking and, 313–14
  neurotransmitters and, 157
  self-regulation impeded by, 318
  setting limits on, 305–6, 315
  sleep habits and, 295
  stress and, 250, 251
  studying versus, 217
  see also Violence, media
Mediation, 331–33
Medications, 5, 7, 13, 14, 46, 255, 330,
  369*n*
  allergies and, 285
  for attention deficit/hyperactivity
    disorder, 83–85
  behavioral treatments versus, 127,
    146
  brain chemistry and, 150–52, 155–68
  diagnostic practices and, 49
  frequency of prescription of, 17, 20
  gender differences in prescription of,
    122, 123
  multiple, 17–18, 161
  nativist justification for, 191
  parental opposition to, 37
  during pregnancy, 98
  treatable issues masked by, 27
  see also specific drugs
Meditation, 146, 344
Memory, 51–53, 314
  brain structures and, 101, 135–36
  language as aid to, 42

sleep and, 216, 293
stress and, 246, 248
Mendelsohn, James, 295
Mental movies, 42, 61
Mental retardation, 129
Merzenich, Michael, 326
Messenger RNA (mRNA), 190
Metals, toxic, 277, 279, 280
Mind pictures, 303–5
Methylin, 158
Methylphenidate, 158
  see also Ritalin
Microglia, 113
Miller, Alice, 268
Miller, Lucy Jane, 75
Miller, Tifany, 77
Mind, theory of, 67
Mindfulness meditation, 146
Mind at a Time, A (Levine), 167
Minimal brain dysfunction, 75
Mirror neurons, 97, 119–22, 244
Mixed receptive/expressive language
  disorder, 51
Moffitt, Terrie E., 323
Molecules of Emotion (Pert), 154
Monk, Catherine, 100
Montessori schools, 265, 340
Mood disorders, 15, 17–18
  see also Bipolar disorder; Depression
Morphology, 133
Motivation, 152, 157, 168–76
  brain structures and, 101
  extrinsic, 170
  impact of stress on, 261
  instrinsic, 169–70
  problems with, 53–54, 352, 159
  self-regulation and, 317, 322–23
  treatments to improve, 127
Motor cortex, 110, 128
Motor planning, 76, 338–39
Motor skills, *see* Perceptual-motor skills
Mount Sinai School of Medicine, Center
  for Children's Health and the
  Environment, 275
Movement disorders, 337–38
Multisensory teaching techniques, 77–78,
  109, 114, 127, 134, 231–34, 237, 364*n*
  physical exercise in, 334
  for reading improvement, 136–40
Multitasking, 217, 313–14
Mustard, J. Fraser, 202
Myelin, 113–16

National Institute of Learning
Development, 331, 360
National Public Radio, 86
National Reading Panel, 65
Nativism, 191, 372n16
Nature, 221
Nature, experiences with, 317, 342–43
lack of, 251
"Nature versus nurture" debate, 177
Netherlands, 20, 203
Neurofeedback, 146, 149
Neurohormones, 154
Neurodevelopmental problems, 32–38
Neuromodulators, 154
Neuroplasticity, 6, 112, 124–49, 291
imaging techniques and, 140–46
individual structural differences and,
133–36
in mirror neurons, 120
self-regulation and, 146–49
serotonin and, 156
teaching and, 136–40, 234
Neurotoxins, *see* Toxins
Neurotransmitters, 110, 153–56, 165, 200,
244, 370n11
diet and, 283, 288
environmental toxins and, 276
exercise and, 337
genes and, 183, 198, 201
long-term effects of medications on, 167
see also Dopamine; Norepinephrine;
Serotonin
Newgrange School, 221
Newsweek, 249
New York City Department of Education,
65
New Yorker magazine, 338
New York Times, the, 205, 282, 326
Nicotine, 277
Nielsen Media Research, 306
Nigg, Joel T., 164, 275, 285
Nobel Prize, 130, 304, 341
Noise pollution, 324–27
Nonverbal learning disorder (NVLD), 50,
80–83, 350, 212
brain development in, 119
genetic factors in, 193
Norepinephrine, 156, 159, 244
Novelty seeking, 198, 199
Numerosity, problems in, 78
NutraSweet, 288, 377n20
Nutrition, *see* Diet

Obesity, 98, 282, 286, 343, 362n17
Object play, 338
Occipital lobe, 108
Occupational therapy, 75–77, 337–38
Ohio State University, 331
Oligodendrocytes, 113
Orbitofrontal cortex, 71
Our Labeled Children (Steinberg), 8
Outliers (Gladwell), 220
Overachievers, 212
Overcoming Dyslexia (Shaywitz), 62, 138
Overscheduling, 251, 295
Oxford University, 112, 177
Oxytocin, 100

Panic, 102–3
Papanicolaou, Andrew C., 141–42
Parent's Guide to Tutors and Tutoring, A
(Mendelsohn), 296
Parietal lobe, 108, 117
Parkinson's disease, 104, 274
Parvocellular system, 97, 112
Pascal, Blaise, 344
Pasternak, Robert, 16
Patience, 339–40
Paxil, 161
Pearce, Joseph Chilton, 162
Pediatric autoimmune neuropsychiatric
disorder associated with strep
infections (PANDAS), 104
Pediatrics, 287
Pennington, Bruce, 182
Peptides, 154
Perceptual-motor development, 6, 31, 350
problems with, 36, 75, 81
Performance anxiety, 47
Perinatal complications, 35, 124
Perry, Bruce, 131–32, 157, 320, 367n10
Personality traits, 198–200
Pert, Candace, 154
Pervasive development disorder (PDD),
see Autistic spectrum disorders
Pesticides, 276–80
Petit mal epilepsy, 88–90
Phenylketonuria (PKU), 187–88, 377n20
Phobias, 153
school, 246–47
Phonemic awareness, 62, 63, 65
Phonological/articulatory disorder, 350
Physical exercise, 127, 272, 317, 333–38
inadequate, 87, 251
Physical therapy, 75, 76, 338

Physicians for Social Responsibility, 360
Pinker, Steven, 372*n*16
Pituitary gland, *see* HPA axis
Plasticity, brain, *see* Neuroplasticity
Plastics, toxic, 278, 279
Play, 6, 7, 300, 317, 340–44
    brain development and, 109, 118
    to buffer stress, 253
    creative, 343–44
    imaginative, 86–87, 304–5
    interactive, 70, 121
    object, 338
    outdoor, 342–43
    symbolic, 64
Plonim, Robert, 188
Pollan, Michael, 288
Polychlorianted biphenyls (PBCs), 277
Popczynski, Lisa, 164
Positive reinforcement, 200
Posner, Michael, 87, 146, 148
Posterior cortex, 107–9
Postpartum depression, 106
Powell, Lisa M., 287
Practical intelligence, 213
Pragmatic language disorder, 350
Prayer, focused, 146
Prefrontal cortex, 96, 110, 136, 247
    in adolescence, 262
    media violence and, 143
    noise pollution and, 327
    in phenylketonuria, 188
Pregnancy, 96–101
Premotor cortex, 143
Prenatal period, 197
    brain development during, 96–98, 133,
        183
    complications during, 35
    noise exposure during, 326
    toxic exposure during, 83, 98, 276
    twins during, 196
Prereading tasks, problems with, 36
Preterm birth, 35, 98
Problem solving, 80, 303–5, 338
Process training, 76
*Proust and Squid: The Story and Science
    of the Reading Brain* (Wolf), 302
Prozac, 146, 155
Pruning, neural, 129
Psychological Care of Infant and Child
    (Watson), 190
Psychotropic drugs, *see* Medications
Pythagorean theory, 338

Quiet time, 344–45
Quindlen, Anna, 249

Raichle, Marcus, 144
Rapp, Doris, 279, 284–85
Ratey, John, 337
Reading disorders, 160
    brain development in, 104–5
    "garden variety," 65–66, 349
    genetic factors in, 192
    See also Dyslexia; Hyperlexia
"Recipe" reports, 51
Receptive language disorder, 59
Reductionism, biological, 145, 189
"Refrigerator mothers," 72, 191
Reid, Gavin, 61
Relaxation techniques, 217, 344
Religious upbringing, 203
Response to Intervention (RTI), 375*n*13
Rett syndrome, 186, 205
Reuptake mechanism, 155
Reward dependence, 198–200
Rhesus monkeys, 200–203
Rhodes, Jean E., 294
Richardson, Sylvia, 236
Rieger, Pearl, 207
Ripke, Judy, 17
Ritalin, 17, 49, 151, 155, 158, 160–61, 255,
        273
Roberts, Elizabeth J., 164
Robinson, Ricki, 18
Romania, orphanages in, 72, 132, 133
Rosen, Warren, 148–49, 195–96
Rourke, Byron, 80–81
Ruff, Michael E., 164–65
Rush Neurobehavioral Center, 81
Rutter, Michael, 189, 321

Safety, need for, 319–21
Sax, Leonard, 17, 159
Scanning techniques, 126, 136–38,
        140–45, 221
Schizophrenia, 184, 191, 196–97
School phobia, 246–47
Schore, Allan N., 177
Scholastic Aptitude Test (SAT), 212, 213,
        215–16
Screen time, *see* Media use
Self-actualization, 317, 346
Self-regulation, 42, 85–87, 147–49,
        316–29, 339
    noise pollution and, 324–27

parenting or caregiving styles for, 327–29
sensory experience and, 323–24
Self-talk, 327
Seligman, Martin, 173, 295
Sensory processing (or integration) disorder (SPD), 12, 31, 50–51, 75–77, 160, 324
  diagnosis of, 37
  treatment of, 37, 75–77, 337–38
  verstibular system and, 104
Sensory stimulation
  brain development and, 108–9, 111–12
  excessive sensitivity to, 69–70
Separable processes, 223–30
Serotonin, 153, 156–57, 161, 200, 201, 203, 276, 373n25
Sesame Street, 64
"Shaken baby" syndrome, 131
Shannon, Scott M., 51
Shaywitz, Sally, 62, 138, 142
Sherman, Gordon, 221–22
Should You Medicate Your Child's Mind? (Roberts), 164
Sickle-cell anemia, 186
Siegel, Daniel, 71
Silver, Larry, 162–63
Single-gene disorders, 186–87, 205
Skill training, 76
Sleep habits, 7, 55, 87, 216, 272, 292–96
  stress and, 251, 257
Smart Moves: Why Learning Is Not All in Your Head (Hannaford), 335
Smart but Scattered (Dawson and Guare), 328
Smell, sense of, 109
Smith, Peg L., 17
Smoking, maternal, 98
Social intelligence, 214
Social skills deficits, 31, 207–8, 228, 351
  attribution theory and, 330–31
  media use and, 302–3
  see also Asperger's syndrome; Autism
Social skills training, 82–83
Social-emotional learning impairment/ disorder (SELI/SELD), 80–83
Solvents, 277, 280
Spain, 20
SPARK (Ratey), 337
Special Education, 15–16
Specific language disability (SLD), 59

Speech disorder, 51
Spinal muscular atrophy (SMA), 187
Splinter skills, 64
Stein, John, 112, 177
Steinberg, Robert, 8, 213
Steroid hormones, 244
Stimulus-bound behavior, 87
Stimulus-response conditioning, 69–70
Strattera, 150, 155, 159
Strep infections, 104
Stress, 7, 87, 129, 241–70, 343
  of academic achievement pressures, 254–64, 268–69
  alternative schooling approaches and, 264–68
  brain chemistry and, 153, 156–57, 172, 242, 244
  brain development impacted by, 135, 249–51
  buffers for, 253, 273–74
  in culture of childhood, 251–52
  emotional toxicity of, 132
  gene expression and, 190, 192, 197, 198
  healthy levels of, 169
  high- and low-level, 247–49
  in infancy, 190–91
  media use and, 120–21, 314
  parental, 20
  performance anxiety and, 47
  during pregnancy, 99–100
  reduction of, 127
  resilience to, 184
  self-regulation impeded by, 318, 319
  sleep habits and, 293, 295
  temperament and, 199, 201
  test anxiety and, 216
Structure, need for, 319–21
Study skills, 217–18
Subcortical areas, 101–2
Substance abuse
  adolescent, 110, 269
  neurotransmitters and, 157, 158
  during pregnancy, 98, 99
Suomi, Steven J., 200, 372n25
Superparenting for ADD (Hallowell), 85
Sweden, 20
Sylwester, Robert, 119
Symbolic play, 64
Synapses, 128, 130, 151, 172, 293
  neurotransmitters in, 155–58, 201
Syndrome, definition of, 14–15

Tactile defensiveness, 36
Tager-Flusberg, Helen, 68
Talents, special, 6, 134, 142, 166
  in autistic spectrum disorders, 67–68, 73
  cerebrodiversity and, 223–30
  handedness and, 106
  play and, 341–42
Tay-Sachs disease, 186
Television viewing, *see* Media use
Temperatment, 198–200
Temporal lobe, 108
Tenner, Edward, 295
Test anxiety, 127, 152, 153, 215–18, 246
Tetris, 80
Texas, University of, 131
  Cortical Plasticity Laboratory, 139
Theory of mind, 67
Theta waves, 141
Thinking
  "big picture," problems with, 181
  brain chemistry and, 154–57
  brain structures and, 101, 105–7, 115
  impact of stress on, 103, 153, 246, 248
  object play and, 338
Thorne, Glenda, 18
"Thought experiments," 117
Thyroid levels, 98
Tics, 68, 104, 161
Tolle, Eckhard, 344
Tools of the Mind, 328
Tourette's syndrome, 68
Toxins, 7, 87, 251, 263, 272, 274–82, 291
  in food, 284
  prenatal exposure to, 83, 98, 197, 276
  in schools, 276–77, 279–80
Transcription factors, 190
Traumatic brain injury (TBI), 131
Traumatic stress disorder, 247
Tumbling Over the Edge: A Rant for Children's Play (Bos and Chapman), 324, 340
Turner's syndrome, 122, 186
"Twice exceptional," 227
Twins, 180, 196, 203, 211

Underachievers, 212
UNICEF, 20
United Kingdom, 20, 323, 326
Unschooling, 265–67

Ventral axis, 111
Vestibular system, 104
Video games, *see* Media use
Violence, exposure to, 120–21, 132, 251
  brain changes and, 143, 244
Visual cortex, 114
Visual deficits, 76
  in dyslexia, 61
Visual-spatial skill deficits, 350

Waldorf schools, 265, 339–40
Walker, Elaine, 165
Wall Street Journal, The, 306
Watson, John B., 190–91
Way I See It, The: A Personal Look at Autism and Asperger's (Grandin), 68
Wernikoff, Linda, 65
West, Tom, 60
What Causes ADHD? (Nigg), 164, 275
What's Going on in There (Eliot), 98
White matter, 96, 113–16
  imaging of, 144
Williams syndrome, 186
Wiseman, Nancy, 67
Wittleson, Sandra, 117
Wolf, Maryanne, 302
Wolfe, Pat, 234
Word retrieval, 44, 60
Wright, Will, 338

Yale University, 62, 138
  Child Study Center, 17
Yoga, 217
Your Child's Growing Mind (Healy), 33, 43, 129, 220, 281, 354

Zito, Julie, 18